ULTIMATE TRUCK & VAN SPOTTER'S GUIDE 1925-1990

Tad Burness

Published by

**krause
publications**

700 E. State Street • Iola, WI 54990-0001
Telephone: 715/445-2214

Please call or write for our free catalog.
Our toll-free number to place an order or obtain a free catalog is 800-258-0929
or please use our regular business telephone 715-445-2214
for editorial comment and further information.

Library of Congress Catalog Number: 00-111280
ISBN: 0-87341-969-3

Printed in the United States of America

Table of Contents

Acknowledgements

Grateful thanks are due to the following individuals and organizations, for certain helpful pictures or bits of information:

Bill Adams
American Motors Sales Corp.
American Truck Historical
  Society
American Trucking
  Associations, Inc.
Jeff Anderson
Larry Auten
Warren J. Baier
Edwill J. Brown
John F. Bunnell
Chevrolet Truck Div. of
  General Motors
John A. Conde

DaimlerChrysler Corp.
Howard De Sart
Dodge Truck Div. of
  DaimlerChrysler Corp.
Jim Evans
Ford Motor Company
Fred K. Fox
Bruce Gilbert
GMC Truck & Bus Div.
  of General Motors
Allan Gutcher
Lawrence C. Holian
International-Navistar Corp.
Elliott Kahn

Lee Kinzer
Daisy Lowenstein
Keith Marvin
Larry Mauck
Pacific Grove Middle School
Walter F. Robinson, Jr.
Jay Sherwin
Bryon Stappler
R. A. Wawrzyniak
White Motor Co. / Volvo
  White
WPC Club

And special thanks to automotive historian Alden C. Jewell, who graciously helped me round up some hard-to-find pictures which were not in my own collection!

INTRODUCTION: WELCOME TO THE WONDER–FILLED WORLD OF OLD TRUCKS, VANS, AND BUSES!

Thousands of different models of old commercial vehicles are still in daily service, or in the appreciative hands of collectors! This book is meant to be a helpful tool to enable you to identify most kinds of trucks, vans and buses you may encounter; and also learn what the rare old ones (which you've never seen) looked like! The large collection of pictures seen here are from original sales catalogs, factory photos, and ads – so they are authentic!

In this new 400-page book you'll find numerous pictures and helpful data not seen elsewhere nor in my previous books in the Spotter's Guide series! Because each year model of truck frequently offered up to dozens of body styles and variations, we tried to select the most typical representatives for each yearly model, from the available pictures. There are some cases where a vehicle remained unchanged for 2 or more years – at least on the outside. This is often the case with many of the minor makes, but in the 1970s and 1980s even some of the major manufactures retained a design longer than usual.

You could roam through an old truck wrecking yard and possibly find several unusual vehicles . . . and photograph them, if allowed to do so. But roaming through the pages of this book is even better: it's much easier, much safer (no junkyard dogs!), you'll see many more rare old vehicles here, and you won't have to climb over a pile of rusted, dirty old wrecks in order to see them!

Moreover, since this book covers a broad range (mid-1920s to 1990) you'll also find many familiar trucks from the years you remember!

Interested in buying an old truck? It could be a lot of fun! Should you see an advertisement for one – without a picture – you can look through this handy volume and see what it looks like, and perhaps learn a few facts about it. Everything is arranged in alphabetical order by make, and each make subdivided in chronological order. If you want to know the difference between a certain year model and the one which either preceded or followed it, check this book. It's a perfect argument-settler!

Okay! I hope you'll enjoy ULTIMATE TRUCK & VAN SPOTTER'S GUIDE for a long time to come, and that you'll have continuous fun in browsing through its contents again and again! A car dealer once advertised "EVERY TIME WE SELL A CAR WE MAKE A FRIEND!" I like to think it's the same way with your purchase of this book!

Sincerely,

Tad Burness
P.O. Box 247
Pacific Grove, CA 93950

A.C.F. BRILL

(1926-1953)

BUSES

AMERICAN CAR and FOUNDRY
CO., PHILADELPHIA, PA.
(IN DETROIT, MICH. UNTIL 1932)
(IN 1925, A.C.F. BOUGHT BOTH
J.G. BRILL CO. OF PHILADELPHIA
and FAGEOL MOTORS CO. of OHIO.)

1928 TO 1932 : "METROPOLITAN"
CITY TRANSIT
(UNDERFLOOR-ENGINED) BUS AVAIL.,
SIMILAR TO "TWIN COACH" BUT
LESS SUCCESSFUL.

↑ 37-PASS.
DUAL MOTOR
ELECTRIC
TROLLEY COACH

('35)

(OLDER-STYLE
TROLLEY COACHES
INTRO. 1930.)

1931 and 1932 ACF
TRUCKS AVAIL., with
HALL-SCOTT ENGS.

PRE-WAR
INTER CITY BUS, with
ITS BULGING FRONT FENDERS
AND FAR-BACK ENTRY DOOR,
HAS THE LOOK OF A PUSHER BUS
THAT COULD HAVE BEEN PLANNED AS A
CONVENT'L.   ('37)

1930s

SILVERSIDES
LATER ADDED,
TO MODERNIZE
PRE-WAR
← TYPE.

CONVENTIONAL
FRONT-ENGINED MODELS
DISCONTINUED AFTER
1932.

('39)

A.C.F. BRILL ~ 1930s

5

A.C.F. BRILL   PREWAR

('41) LOCAL USE TRANSIT BUS

BURLINGTON RAPID TRANSIT COMPANY 260

POSTWAR IC TYPE has CONCEALED FRONT FENDERS, BUT ODD, BULGING HEADLIGHTS AT SIDES

INTERCITY **IC-37**

BUS PRODUCTION SUSPENDED 1942, IN FAVOR OF DEFENSE PROJECTS. RESUMES AFTER WAR.

UNDER-FLOOR 6-CYLINDER HALL-SCOTT ENGINES USED, AS IN PREWAR ERA.

REAR DETAILS

('46-47)

POSTWAR TYPES

NATIONAL TRAILWAYS BUS (BELOW)

IC-41

1940s

new GRILLE, CHANGED FROM VERTICAL TO HORIZONTAL. ('47-48)

Comfort-planned **BUSES**

NATIONAL **TRAILWAYS** BUS SYSTEM

CHICAGO

A LARGE NUMBER OF IC ACF/BRILL BUSES BLT. FOR TRAILWAYS.

1948 FARE SCHEDULE →

BETWEEN AND ↓	CHICAGO	DALLAS	DENVER	ATLANTA	LOS ANGELES	NEW YORK
CHICAGO		$15.50	$18.45	$10.80	$36.85	$13.60
DALLAS	$15.50		13.70	13.15	26.15	22.20
DENVER	18.45	13.70		22.70	20.15	28.50
ATLANTA	10.80	13.15	22.70		37.15	13.10
LOS ANGELES	36.85	26.15	20.15	37.15		45.25
NEW YORK	13.60	22.20	28.50	13.10	45.25	

A.C.F. BRILL ~1940s

A.C.F. BRILL

C-36 and C-44 ARE LARGE CITY TRANSIT POSTWAR MODELS. (HALL-SCOTT ENGS.)

('49)

SMOOTH-SIDED IC TYPES (NARROW GRILLE)

LOWER SIDE VENTS ELIMINATED (1949 AD)

new WIDE GRILLE ON TYPE BELOW

SINCE 47

1948: SMALL C-27 and C-31 CITY BUSES AVAILABLE, with INTERNATIONAL GAS ENGINES and BEARING ONLY THE "BRILL" NAME.

INTERIOR GLIMPSE OF IC (INTERCITY) TYPE.

SILVERSIDES IC

TRAILWAYS' new UPPER BODY PAINT SCHEME IN LATE 1950.

A.C.F. BRILL INTERCITY TYPES CONTINUE TO PLACE FRONT WHEELS AHEAD OF ENTRY DOOR.

(ABOVE) A FEW ALSO SOLD TO Greyhound

TRAILWAYS USED MOSTLY A.C.F. BRILL BUSES TO 1953, THOUGH GMC and OTHER BRANDS SOMETIMES WERE PURCHASED. EAGLE BUSES USED, PRIMARILY, BY TRAILWAYS AFTER 1956.

CITY TRANSIT BUS

SPECIAL

BURLINGTON RAPID TRANSIT COMPANY 570

LOCAL-SERVICE A.C.F. BRILL BUSES NOW BEAR A CLOSER RESEMBLANCE TO GMC AND OTHER POPULAR BRANDS. A.C.F. BRILL ~ 47 ON

ACME MOTOR TRUCK CO., CADILLAC, MI. (1915~1931)

"SEAL OF DEPENDABLE PERFORMANCE"

ACME THE TRUCK OF PROVED UNITS

20 (CONT'D.)

USED AS ACME RADIATOR EMBLEM

SEMI-ENCLOSED CAB

The Pinnacle of Performance

STAKE

New type dump body as built in Acme factory →

21

NEW MODEL "G"

¾ Ton—Worm Drive—$1790 CHASSIS F.O.B. CADILLAC

Speed-TRUCK OPEN CAB

WITH DISC WHEELS 130" W.B. 35 × 5" TIRES

'23 = MODELS ALSO KNOWN BY NUMBERS.

(25-30 PASS. MODEL "K" BUS AVAIL.)

('24)

1924 MODELS :
1 TON 20-L
1½ T 30
2 T 40, 40L
3 T 60, 60L
4½ T 90, 90L
6¼ T 125

24

25 new 6-CYL. MODELS

CLOSED CAB

INTRO. 3-25:
MODEL "21" 4-CYL.
1-TON "FLYER" 5.0 G.R.
130" W.B. "S-4"

CONT. ENG.
(4¼" ×
4½" B+S)
50 HP @
2200 RPM

STAKE (SEMI-ENCLOSED CAB)
MODEL 60 3 TON 152" WB
4 CYL. (4⅛" × 5¼") 4-SP. TRANS.

4 and 6-CYL. MODELS IN '27.
¾ TO 6¼-TON MODELS IN '28.

HEAVY-DUTY CLASS

('29)

28 6-CYL. "56"
2½-TON
167¼" W.B.

29 1-TON TO 7½-TON CHASSIS MODELS

6-CYL. 2-TON MODEL "346" 156" W.B.

DISC WHEELS ACME

(EARLY 1926 MODELS CONTINUATION OF 1925 TYPES.)

ATTERBURY
MOTOR TRUCKS OF MAXIMUM SERVICE

26

"24-R"

new 26-B "SPEEDY 6" (6 CYL.) 1 - 1¼ TON (INTRO. 1926) 132" WB LYCOMING eng.

"24-R" RATING INCREASED TO 2 TONS; OTHER MODELS CONTINUED.

27

30 × 5" TIRES (ON 26-B)

---

new 1½-2 TON "HIGHWAY EXPRESS, JR." MODEL 26-G 145 OR 160" WB 6 CYLS.

2-WHEEL BRAKES

CHASSIS: $1895.

28

OTHER 1928 MODELS:
1¼ TON   26-B-4, 26-B-6
2 TO 2½ TON 27-R-4, 27-R-6
3 TON   22-C-4, 27-C-6
3½ TO 5 TON   22-D-4

ALSO, AT $5650.,
"24-E-4" RATED AT 5 TO 7 TONS

SO-CALLED "SILVER ANNIVERSARY" MODEL

(1-PC. WINDSHIELD)

29 ON

('29) 26-G-6 1½-2 T.
$1895. CHASSIS

2-WH. BRAKES with VACUUM BOOSTER 145 OR 160" WB

6-Cylinder

SPECS. (AS OF 1930; ALL							
A-6	1 TON	132-145" WB	185 CID	LYCOMING eng.	60 HP	@ 3000 RPM	
K	1½	145-160	224	"	61	@ 2750	
G	2	145-160	224	"	"	"	
H	2½	173-199	311	CONTINENTAL eng.	72	@ 2400	
R	3	173-199	340	"	82	@ 2400	
C	4	186-220	381	"	"	"	

(ADDITIONAL NUMBERED MODELS INTRO. 1931.)

LITTLE CHANGE BETWEEN 1931 and FINAL 1935 ATTERBURY TRUCKS, BUT SIMILARITY TO RADIATOR DESIGN OF LARRABEE-DEYO TRUCKS (DISCONTINUED 1932.)

BLT. BY THE ATTERBURY MOTOR CAR CO., BUFFALO, N.Y.

(REPLACED THE 1908~1910 BUFFALO, WHICH REPLACED THE 1904-1908 AUTO-CAR TRUCK *

* NOT AFFILIATED WITH THE BETTER-KNOWN **AUTOCAR** TRUCK of ARDMORE, PA.

Atterbury

1933 MODELS INCLUDE "A," "K," "G," "R," "C," and also "45" (2-2½ TON;) "50" (2½-3 TON;) "60" (3 TON;) "65" (3-3½ TON; "70" (3½-4 TON;) and "100" (5-6 TON) (CONT. and LYC. 6-CYL. engines CONT'D.)

Established 1897

THE AUTOCAR COMPANY, Ardmore, Pa.

Autocar

2-CYL. MODELS AVAIL. 1909 TO 1926.

VARIOUS EARLY CAB-OVER-ENGINE TYPES

2-CYL. **21~UF** (97" WB) AVAIL. 1913~1926
21~UG (120" WB) AVAIL. 1919~1926)

SOME TYPES WITHOUT A WINDSHIELD ↓

AVAILABLE WITH WINDSHIELD (AS BELOW)

Chassis (1½-2 Ton)
$2300, 97-inch Wheelbase
$2400, 120-inch Wheelbase ('19)

('20) 120" W.B.

(ALSO, A FLAT-FRONTED BUS AVAIL.)

The 4-cylinder 5 ton Heavy Duty Autocar

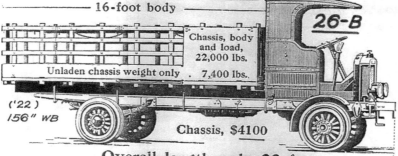

16-foot body

26-B

Chassis, body and load, 22,000 lbs.
Unladen chassis weight only 7,400 lbs.

('22) 156" WB

Chassis, $4100

Overall length only 23 feet

13-26

26-Y and 26-B ARE FIRST 4-CYL. MODELS INTRO. 1920

4-CYL. **ENGINE**

('22-'23)

ELECTRIC "E-5-M" 5-TON MODEL ('25)

SLOGAN: "Wherever there's a road"

27-H (INTRO.'22) SIMILAR TO TRUCK BELOW, BUT W. 114" WB)

('23)

$3075.

27-K 4 CYL. 2-3 TON 138" WB (INTRO. 1922)

MODEL **XXI-F**

1½ TO 2 TON

97" WB

('25)

The engine of all Autocar trucks is placed under the seat

10

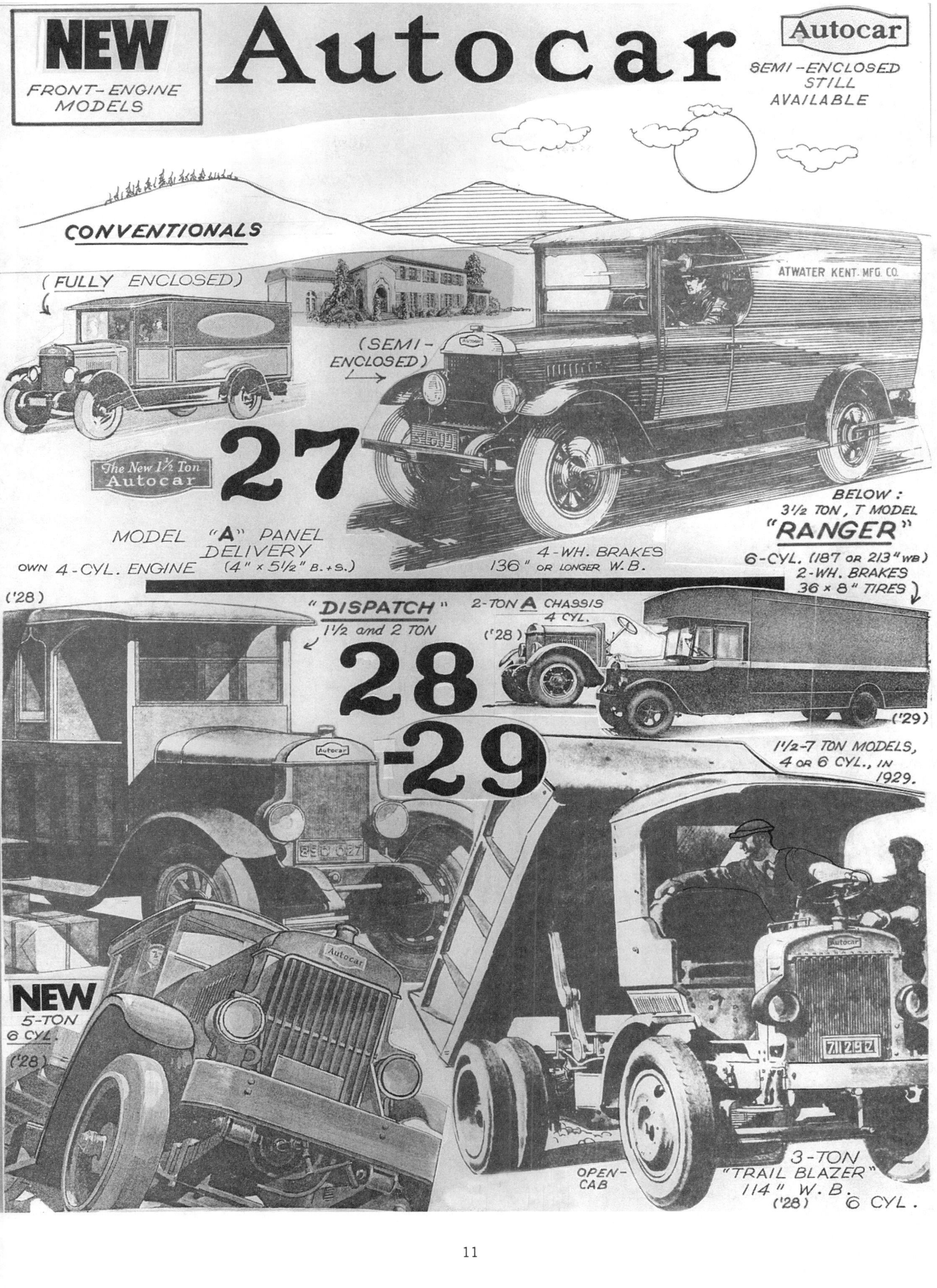

NEW
FRONT-ENGINE MODELS

Autocar

Autocar
SEMI-ENCLOSED
STILL
AVAILABLE

CONVENTIONALS

(FULLY ENCLOSED)

(SEMI-ENCLOSED)

ATWATER KENT MFG CO.

27

The New 1½ Ton Autocar

MODEL "A" PANEL DELIVERY

OWN 4-CYL. ENGINE (4" × 5½" B.+S.)

('28)

4-WH. BRAKES
136" OR LONGER W.B.

BELOW:
3½ TON, T MODEL
"RANGER"
6-CYL. (187 OR 213"WB)
2-WH. BRAKES
36 × 8" TIRES

"DISPATCH"
1½ and 2 TON

2-TON A CHASSIS
4 CYL.
('28)

28 -29

('29)

1½-7 TON MODELS,
4 OR 6 CYL., IN 1929.

NEW
5-TON
6 CYL.
('28)

OPEN-CAB

3-TON
"TRAIL BLAZER"
114" W.B.
('28) 6 CYL.

11

Autocar

(EST. 1897)
TRUCKS SINCE 1907

DIESEL

6-T
220" WB

CALIFORNIA MOTOR EXPRESS LTD.

(4WD OFF-HWY. CHASSIS AVAIL. EARLY 1930s)

C.O.E.s RE-INTRODUCED 1933.

AT RIGHT: **UT** NON-STREAMLINE C.O.E.

WITH STREET FLUSHER BODY

MODEL **S**
DUMP TRUCK

MACASPHALT

6-WHEEL DIESEL TANKER (SHELL)

SHELL

RADIATOR EMBLEM

Autocar (C. '36)

1930s

MODEL ← **C** DIESEL 165" WB

DIESEL **DH**

('37)

HIGHWAY FREIGHT
NEW YORK NEW JERSEY PENNSYLVANIA

('37)

RM, RL FROM $1980.

(1937 LT-DUTY "A" and "B" SERIES CONV. FROM $1095.)

('37)

new 1937 STYLING CONTINUES INTO 1940s

C.O.E.s

INTRO. MAY, 1937

new SHORT WHEELBASE "UA," "UB" (84, 106 OR 124" WB) 6 CYLS. 263 CID (UA) OR 282" (UB) 73 OR 78 HP @ 2300 RPM

HIGHWAY FREIGHT
NEW YORK NEW JERSEY PENNSYLVANIA

AUTOCAR 1930s

12

Autocar

('44)

1940 MODELS :
C-10 THROUGH
C-90 (GAS)
DIESELS ARE DC-10
THROUGH DC-100-D

C.O.E.s ARE U SERIES
4-W-D and 6-WHEELERS ALSO

MILITARY TRUCKS
ALSO BLT., 1940
TO 1945.

1940s A

CONVENTIONALS

ALL 6 CYL.
AUTOCAR,
HERCULES, and
CUMMINS ENGINES
73 TO 150 HP
260 TO 707 CID
1940 CHASSIS PRICE
RANGE :
$1250.
TO $9500.

AIR REDUCTION OXYGEN

AIRCO
AIR REDUCTION
PHILADELPHIA.

('45)

VARITIES WITH EITHER
HORIZONTAL OR VERTICAL
HOOD
LOUVRES

DAVIDSON

('46)

('46)

(1946 PROD.= 5320)

(C.O.E.s ON NEXT PAGE)

AUTOCAR 1940s A

13

HORN CONCEALED.

OTHERWISE, STYLING SIMILAR TO PRE-WAR C.O.E.

LIKE '38 "U" TYPES

with GRILLE VARIATION ('40)

'946 PRODUCTION = 5320

('44)

TANKER (LEFT SIDE)

ALL WITH 6-CYL. GAS OR DIESEL ENGINES (377 TO 672 CID) ('46)

1940 S B

(6-WHEELER DC10064; DC100643 w. CUMMINS DIESEL ENG.

('45)

1946 MODELS	CID	HP @ RPM
C~50; C~50T; U-50; U~50T;	377	119 @ 2800
C~70; C~70T; U~70 U~70T;	447	133 @ 2500
C~70 S; C~70TS; U~70 S; U~70TS; C-90 C-90D; C~90T; U~90 U~90T		145 @ 2500
DC~100; DC~100T DC~100D (ALL 3 w. CUMMINS DIESEL ENGS.)	672	150 @ 1800

(C.O.E.)

(MILITARY)

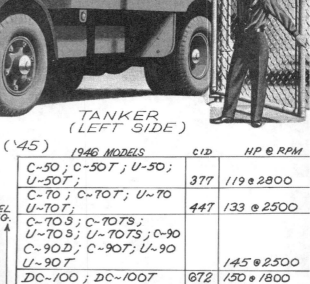

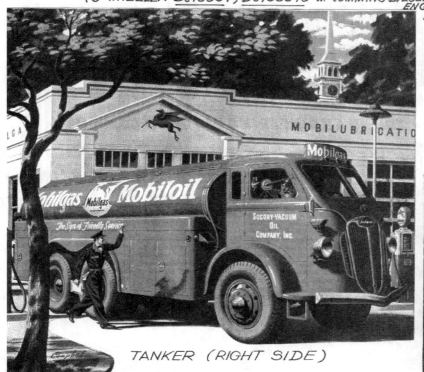

TANKER (RIGHT SIDE)

T DESIGNATION DENOTES TRAILER HAULING
TRACTOR TRUCK

AUTOCAR ~ 1940s

14

Autocar

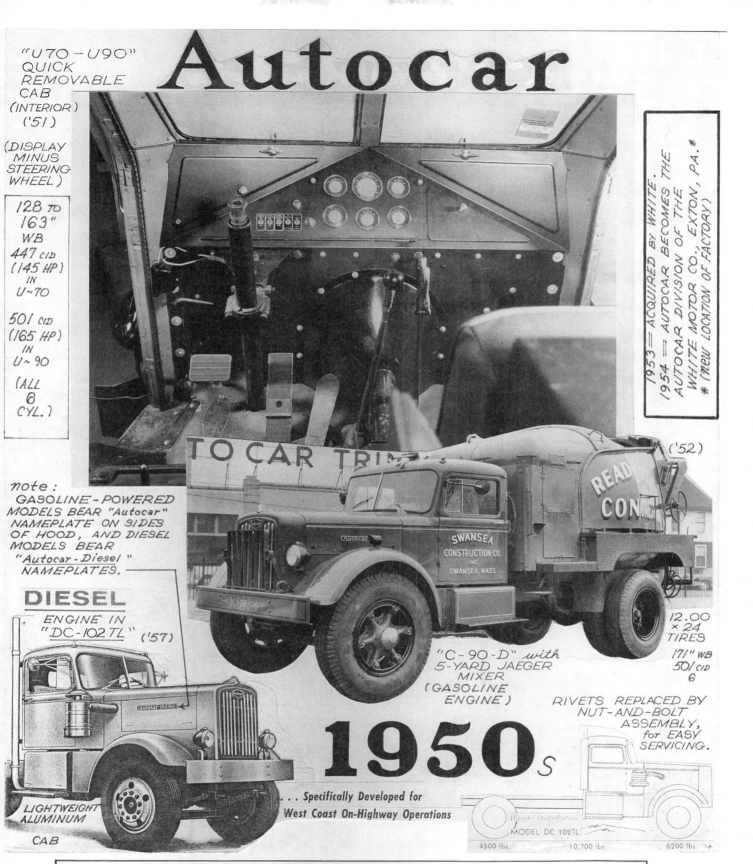

"U70 – U90"
QUICK
REMOVABLE
CAB
(INTERIOR)
('51)

(DISPLAY
MINUS
STEERING
WHEEL)

128 TO
163"
WB
447 CID
(145 HP)
IN
U~70

501 CID
(165 HP)
IN
U~90

(ALL
6
CYL.)

1953 = ACQUIRED BY WHITE.
1954 = AUTOCAR BECOMES THE
AUTOCAR DIVISION OF THE
WHITE MOTOR CO., EXTON, PA. *
* (NEW LOCATION OF FACTORY)

('52)

note:
GASOLINE-POWERED
MODELS BEAR "Autocar"
NAMEPLATE ON SIDES
OF HOOD, AND DIESEL
MODELS BEAR
"Autocar-Diesel"
NAMEPLATES.

SWANSEA
CONSTRUCTION CO.
INC.
SWANSEA, MASS.

READ
CON

DIESEL
ENGINE IN
"DC-102TL" ('57)

"C-90-D" with
5-YARD JAEGER
MIXER
(GASOLINE
ENGINE)

12.00
× 24
TIRES

171" WB
501 CID
6

RIVETS REPLACED BY
NUT-AND-BOLT
ASSEMBLY,
for EASY
SERVICING.

1950s

... Specifically Developed for
West Coast On-Highway Operations

LIGHTWEIGHT
ALUMINUM
CAB

Weight Distribution
MODEL DC 102TL

4500 lbs.   10,700 lbs.   6200 lbs.

MANY MODELS AND SPECS. SIMILAR TO THOSE IN 1946 LIST
ON PRECEDING PAGE, BUT 844 CID ENG. (180 HP @ 1800 RPM) IN
DCB~100T (165 to 180" WB) and 935 CID " (268 HP @ 2000 RPM) IN
C~100T, AS OF 1951 SPECS.

AUTOCAR ~ 1950s

Autocar 60-61

DC-9564 ('60)

WITH CEMENT MIXER

62

CUMMINS OR CATERPILLAR DIESEL ENGINES IN MOST AUTOCAR TRUCKS OF THE 1960s.

MODEL "A-75-T" OR   MODEL "DCV72-64 TL"

6-CYL. DIESEL 220 H.P.   →   V-8 DIESEL 265 H.P.

WITH FIBER-GLASS HOOD

OTHER MODELS, RESEMBLING EXAMPLE BELOW : "D6V72-64TL" WITH 6-CYL. DIESEL "A-102-T" (6 CYL. DIESEL, 220 HP, 4-SP. MAIN, 3-SP. AUX. TRANS. "A-7564-T" (6-CYL. DIESEL, 220 HP, WT. 12,750 lbs.

12,850 pounds

(235 HP DIESEL V8s OPT. FOR 6-CYL.)

MUCH ALUMINUM USED IN "A" TYPES **63**

IO SPEED TRANSMISSION, UNLESS NOTED OTHERWISE.

AT RIGHT : MODEL "A-10264" →

6-CYL. DIESEL 220 H.P. 4-SPEED MAIN 3-SPEED AUX. TRANSMISSIONS

POPULAR IN THE WEST

12,675 pounds

AUTOCAR 60~63

Autocar

DIVISION OF
THE WHITE MOTOR COMPANY
EXTON, Pennsylvania

64

AU-7064-T
TRACTOR *with*
TANK TRAILER

DC-7654-T
(ABOVE)

TANDEM AXLE MIXER TRUCK

Autocar

65

DC-9964-OHNES

66-67

('67)

('67) *with*
SAND
TANKER

QUADRUPLE
HEADLIGHTS
NOT
TYPICALLY
SEEN.

Autocar

MIXER

68-69

with 218-H.P. DETROIT DIESEL ENGINE and FULLER RT00-913 "ROADRANGER" TRANS.

(AUTOCAR PRODUCTION FIGURES INCLUDED IN **WHITE**'s TOTAL.)

MODELS ('72)
A42-B; A64-B; A42-F; A64-F;
ALSO NUMEROUS DC SERIES VARIATIONS,
and CK64B; CK64F HALF-CABS.

HALF-CAB MIXER

('70)

CONVENTIONAL MIXER

('70)

TANKER/TRLR. COMBINATION

TRACTORS

('71)

CONVENTIONALS

70-72

CAB ('72)

MODEL A64F
(3-AXLE)
('70 TO
('72)

434 HP V12 DETROIT DIESEL ENG. AVAIL.

IMPROVED ALL-ALUMINUM FRAME

325-HP DIESEL ENG. STD.
and 13-SPEED TRANSMISSION*
(* FULLER "ROADRANGER")

AUTOCAR 68-72

18

Autocar

THE BIG 4
AUTOCAR. ...
FREIGHTLINER.
WESTERN STAR.
WHITE.
WHITE MOTOR CORPORATION

VARIOUS MODELS

('73½)

better-buy-Autocar

TILT HOOD MADE OF FIBERGLASS

CONVENTIONAL

73 ON

IN 1974, AUTOCAR MOVED ITS PRODUCTION FACILITIES TO A MORE MODERN FACTORY IN OGDEN, UTAH.

AUG., 1981 WHITE (and AUTOCAR) BOUGHT BY VOLVO TRUCK, CREATING VOLVO WHITE TRUCK CORP.

air conditioning

1975 = new "CONTRACTOR" WITH OFFSET CAB and SHORT WHEELBASE

radiators

Our specially designed radiator is available in 975-, 1300-, and 1440-square-inch frontal areas. Our engineers will recommend the size most suited for the job your Autocar will be doing. They are all nut-and-bolt construction with superior de-aeration characteristics. To eliminate any possibility of damage from frame twisting and racking motions, they're mounted to the frame at three points. Its all-aluminum construction eliminates the need for a sheet-metal radiator shell.

new 1977 MODEL DC-7386-DC HAS TANDEM AXLES BOTH FRONT and REAR. (NOT ILLUSTR.)

('74)

A, DC, KK, and HALF-CAB CK SERIES IN 1975 144-295" WB

S and A SERIES (B and F MODELS); C and DC SERIES (INCL. U MODELS) IN 1978

INTERIOR

"CONSTRUCKTOR 2" CONVENTIONAL REPLACES WHITE "CONSTRUCKTOR, 1978.

19

Autocar

('84)

CONVENTIONAL

INSTRUMENT PANEL

84 ON

> "CONSTRUCKTOR" SERIES DISCONTINUED IN 1985.
>
> "THE NEW FAMILY" OF VOLVO-WHITE-AUTOCAR INCREASED SALES FROM 4.9% TO OVER 10% OF THE HEAVY TRUCK MARKET IN 1986.

> THE POPULAR AT64 SERIES STILL AVAIL. IN THE MID-1980s.

SINCE LATE 1980s, CAB DESIGN SIMILAR TO VOLVO-WHITE.

> FIRST "HIGH HAT CAB" AUTOCAR TRUCK (WITH new HIGH WINDSHIELD) BLT. AT OGDEN, UTAH FACTORY, SPRING, 1981. (2" MORE HEADROOM THAN PREVIOUS TYPES.)

TRADITIONAL RADIATOR EMBLEM

BY-PASS FILTER AND POWER STEERING RESERVOIR

> JAN., 1988: VOLVO-WHITE and GMC HEAVY TRUCK OPERATIONS MERGE INTO VOLVO GM HEAVY TRUCK CORP.
> 1994: ONLY AVAIL. MODEL IS "WHITE GMC AUTOCAR ACL" CONVENTIONAL.
> 1995: AUTOCAR RE-NAMED "VOLVO AUTOCAR."

1997: 5 BASIC MODELS, USING VOLVO DIESEL ENGINES.

AUTOCAR 84 ON

(1912 ~ 1977) **BROCKWAY**

4 CYL. CONTINENTAL ENGINES ON __ALL__, (THROUGH 1921)

ORIGIN: WM. N. BROCKWAY'S BROCKWAY CARRIAGE FACTORY, IN HOMER, N.Y. FROM 1851 TO 1912.

2½ TON K-5   ('21)   152" WB

1-TON MODEL "E" (1922-1923) USES 4-CYL. BUDA ENGINE.

4-CYLINDER WISCONSIN ENGINES ON "E" and "S" (STARTING '24)

6-CYL. WISCONSIN ENGINE INTRO. ON 1¼-TON "E-7" ('26)

4-CYL. BUDA ENGINE RETURNS IN 1927, IN __new__ 7½-TON "BT"

5-TON "T" (1924)
36 × 5 FRONT (SOLID
40 × 14 REAR   TIRES)
4 CYL., 4¾" × 6" CONT'L. ENG.

1920s

BROCKWAY ACQUIRES INDIANA TRUCK CORP., OF MARION, INDIANA, IN 1928.

('28)

BROCKWAY = 1920s

1929 MODELS	
JUNIOR	1¼ TON
JF, CJBF	1¼, 1½
CJB	1½
E, S	1½, 2
EM	1½
EYW, SY	2 TON
K	3
KW	3
KR, R	3, 4
RT, T	4, 5
T-18	5 TON
BT	5½

BROCKWAY

(1912 ~ 1977)

(MFD. BY BROCKWAY MOTOR TRUCK CO., CORTLAND, N.Y.)

NUMERICAL MODEL DESIGNATIONS ADDED IN 1930.

MODEL E ('29-'30)

1930 MODELS:

1-TON	60, 65
1¼	JUNIOR, 75
1½	E-45, 90
2	S-31, 120
2-2½	140
2½	170
3	KW, 190
3-3½	195
3½-4	220
4	R, RT
5	T, 250
7½ TON	290

('30)

DASH

BROCKWAY-INDIANA 290 (116 HP 6) ('31) HEAVY-DUTY

(4 and 6 CYL. CONT'L. and WISC. ENGS., 38 TO 116 HP)

HORIZONTAL HOOD LOUVRES ON MANY MODELS

1930s

WHITE PURCHASES INDIANA TRUCK ('32)

BROCKWAY ELECTRIC ALSO AVAIL., 1933 TO 1938, IN TRUCK LINE.

('37)

FACTORY SCENE (MID~'30s)

1939 MODELS:

1½-2 TON	78; 83(1½-2½;) 88 (1½-3)
2-2½	87 92 (1½-4;) 94 (1½-5)
2½-3	90X, 96, 120
3 TON	110, 112, 125X; 140 (3-3½ TON)
3½-4	128, 130, 141, 145
4	150X4, 150X5; 130 PS (4-4½)
4-5	160X, 170X
5-7	165X
5-7½	175X, 195X
6-7½	240X
7½-10	220X
10	260X, 260S

ALL '39s with 6-CYL. CONT'L. ENGS., EXCEPT=
* 15-TON V-1200 (V-12 AM. LA FRANCE ENG.)

THIS BROCKWAY STYLING CONT'D. THROUGH 1940s and to EARLY '50s, WITH ADDITION OF GRILLE GUARD. (SEE FOLLOWING PAGE)

* V-1200 INTRO. 1934   BROCKWAY~1930s

BROCKWAY

DURING THE 1940s, A FRONT GUARD CONCEALS GRILLE OF MID - '30s STYLE

260 HEAVY-DUTY TYPE

BELOW : TANKER WITH SLEEPER CAB ('46)

154 WH MODEL (ABOVE)
(6-CYL. CONT.
46B ENG.)

MILITARY
(W.W. II)

1940s

PRODUCTION, EXCLUSIVELY, OF
6 - WHEEL - DRIVE (6 × 6)
MILITARY TRUCK CHASSES

(BETWEEN
4-1-42
and
3-19-44.)

MILITARY TRUCK
(W.W. 2)

VARIOUS OTHER
1946 MODELS : 78, 83, 88, 92, 94,
112, 128, 146, 147 (T,) 152, 153 (T,) 154 (T,)
156 (T,) 162, 166, 170X, 175X, 195X, 220X,
240X, 260X, 260S
6 CYL. CONTINENTAL ENGINES
(210 TO 501 CID, 71 TO 144 HP)
138 " TO 219 " WHEELBASES

BROCKWAY ~ 1940s

BROCKWAY

1951 MODELS :
88WH, 128W, 146W, 148W, 152W, 260XWL, 154W (T,) 154WH (T,) 260XW (T)
6 CYL.
290 TO 572 CID, 100 TO 203 HP
138" TO 221" WB

PANORAMIC WINDSHIELD

with GRILLE GUARD

DAIRYLEA MILK

WITH

EATON EATON MANUFACTURING COMPANY, CLEVELAND, OHIO
MORE THAN 2 MILLION EATON AXLES IN TRUCKS TODAY

2-SPEED *Truck* AXLE
AVAILABLE
(SINCE 1940s)

1950s

1954 MODELS: 260XL, 260XWL,
88WH, 128W, 146W, 148W, 151W, 152W, 153W ; TRUCK TRACTORS : 154W 154WH,
154WHS, 154WHL, 260XW
(SPECS. AS IN '51.)

SINCE EARLY 1950s,
VARIOUS MODELS USE
6-CYLINDER BROCKWAY-CONTINENTAL
ENGINES

BROCKWAY BECOMES AN AUTONOMOUS (SELF-GOVERNING) DIVISION OF MACK TRUCKS, INC., AS OF OCTOBER 1, 1956.

('57)

1957 MODELS :
128WX, 147WL, 148WD, 153WD, 260LD, 260WLD,
TRUCK-TRACTORS : 147W, 155W, 254W, 255W, 256W, 258W, 260WD
330 TO 572 CID
125 TO 230 HP
135" TO 221" WB
5-SPEED FULLER TRANS.

new "HUSKIE" LINE INTRODUCED 1958.

4.77 TO 7.80 GEAR RATIOS

INSIGNIA ('57)

BROCKWAY SALES =
959 ('58)
1196 ('59)

BROCKWAY

(FITS JUST ABOVE V-SHAPED GRILLE)

BROCKWAY ~ 1950s

BROCKWAY

CHROMED "HUSKIE" DOG SYMBOLIC RADIATOR MASCOT (ABOVE) CHANGED TO GOLD IN 1962, TO COMMEMORATE BROCKWAY'S GOLDEN ANNIVERSARY OF MOTOR TRUCK PRODUCTION.

"HUSKIE" LINE and STYLING EXTENDED INTO LIGHTER MODELS, 1961.
new "44BD" ENGINE has O.H.V., 6 CYL., 478 CID, 200 HP @ 3000 RPM.

NEW C.O.E. MODELS INTRO. 1963.

1960s

new 300-SERIES CONVENTIONALS BEGIN IN MID-1960s.

TANKER

ORIGINAL HUSKIDRIVE
OTHERS WILL IMITATE BUT NONE CAN DUPLICATE THE TRUE HUSKIDRIVE THAT COMES FROM BROCKWAY

TWIN GOLDEN HUSKIE DOG RADIATOR MASCOTS ON "HUSKIDRIVE" MODEL.

This is the little switch destined to revolutionize heavy-duty trucking, because it's an integral part of a new diesel power concept currently available only from Brockway.
With Huskidrive, you multiply a constant flow of high torque to start or back any legal load through a five-speed box. With Huskidrive, you merely flip a dash-mounted switch to attain cruising speed and increase engine horsepower while simultaneously improving fuel economy and extending truck life. Engineered and introduced by Brockway, Huskidrive is a great new power train combination that provides all the advantages of a high torque rise engine with a five-speed transmission. It utilizes the highly-acclaimed Cummins NHCT Custom Torque Diesel to provide constant horse-power through the operating range of 1500 to 2100 r.p.m. Dana 1700 joints and shafts transmit this power from the Fuller five-speed twin countershaft transmission to a single or tandem Eaton Multiplier Rear Axle. You're assured of top performance and economy when you "switch" to Huskidrive.
Huskidrive permits you to cruise in the ideal operating range of 1800 r.p.m., where the engine develops 248 h.p. Huskidrive utilizes all of the advantages offered by this outstanding engine to maintain the highest legal highway speeds, so there's little need for downshifting.
You get maximum starting ability, also. Huskidrive in low multiplies torque at the rear wheels and not forward in the power train where excessive torque can cause transmission, drive shaft or bearing failure. You get flexibility, too. There's no firm pattern—shift through five, and switch to Huskidrive, anytime. This gives greater acceleration plus fuel savings and longer life for the entire power train. You easily reduce over-the-road time and driver fatigue.

('70)

"HUSKIDRIVE" INTRODUCED 1968.

CUMMINS, CATERPILLAR, and DETROIT DIESEL ENGINES AVAILABLE, 1963 ON

CONTINENTAL GASOLINE ENGINES PHASED OUT BY BROCKWAY DURING THE LATE 1960s.

C.O.E. INTERIOR

C.O.E.

CONVENTIONAL

('69

(REPLACED BY WRAP-AROUND DASH IN MID-1971.)

11-MONTH SALES: 1967 = 1117 1968 = 1095

BROCKWAY~1960s

('70)

SERIES 358LL TANDEM AXLE

BROCKWAY

TANDEM AXLE SERIES 359LL

1970s A

169" OR 182" WB

182" STD. WB

('70)

IMPROVED COOLING SYSTEM

CAB

MODEL NUMBERS have LETTER PREFIXES INDICATING ENGINE TYPES
6 CYL.= C, E, F, N PREFIXES
V8 = K, T, V
V12 = U

BACK-MOUNTED RAD. SHUTTERS

DUMP TRUCK ('70)

358 T

ITHACA DELIVERY INC
ITHACA, N.Y.
P.S.C. 3398
ICC-MC 55817

('71)

('70)

SERIES 361T SINGLE AXLE TRACTOR

148" STD. WB

CAB

BROCKWAY TRUCKS POPULAR on EAST COAST OF U.S.A. and IN PUERTO RICO. EXPORTED TO 65 FOREIGN COUNTRIES!

359 TL

('71)

(CONT'D. NEXT PAGE)

BROCKWAY ~ 1970s A

26

"HUSKITEER 527"
C.O.E.
new
('72)

BROCKWAY

WITH AVAIL.
CUMMINS OR DETROIT
DIESEL ENGINE
(185 TO 270 HP)
10.00 × 20
TIRES

WITH
OVERHANG.
HIGH DUMP
BODY

('71)

MIXER

230 HP DIESEL
6.14 G.R.
11.00 × 22
TIRES
(10.00 × 20
TIRES ON
MOST
OTHER
MODELS.)

160" WB

360 TL (TANDEM - AXLE MODELS)

360 TYPES have FORWARD-SET
FRONT AXLE. 361s with
SET-BACK FRONT AXLE

1970s
(CONT'D.) B

SERIES 361TL

IN 1976, 9 FACTORY-OWNED SALES/SERVICE
OUTLETS, and 91 INDEPENDENT DEALERS
(MOSTLY IN EASTERN STATES
OF U.S.A.)

359 TYPE
RADIATOR
DETAIL

(1976
C.O.E.
WITH SINGLE HORIZ.
PC. ACROSS RAD., AS
ON CONVT'L.,
ABOVE.)

400 Series Cabover   ('71)

new
700 SERIES CONV.
(1974-77) has 1-PC. CURVED
WINDSHIELD. SOME LATE -
MODEL CONVENTIONALS ALSO
AVAIL. WITH 2-PC. WINDSHIELD
(TYPE SEEN IN C.O.E. AT
RIGHT.)

700 has
new
SUPERIOR-
BLT. CAB,
LIKE MACK
R and U
SERIES
CONVENTIONAL.

EARLY 1977: UNAUTHORIZED
STRIKE CRIPPLES PRODUCTION.

PRODUCTION
ENDS 1977 *

*AS OF JUNE 8.
BROCKWAY ~ 1970s B

CHEVROLET

CARS SINCE 1912
TRUCKS SINCE 1918

4-CYLINDER OVERHEAD-VALVE ENGINES (THROUGH 1928)

MFD. BY CHEVROLET DIV. OF GENERAL MOTORS

for Economical Transportation

CHEVROLET

CHEVROLET'S TRADITIONAL "BOW-TIE" EMBLEM

UTILITY EXPRESS

('24)

('23)

"SUPERIOR" MODELS

23-24
(CONT'D.)

"SUPERIOR" NAME CONTINUES

103" WB ON ½ TON CHASSIS
124" " " 1-TON REPLACES 120" ('26.)

EARLY '25 IS MODEL "M." $550. (UTILITY EXP. CHASSIS)

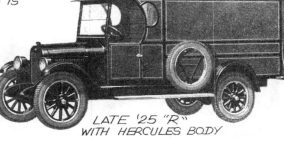

LATE '25 "R" WITH HERCULES BODY

STAKE

25-26

('27)

LATE '26 MODEL "X" has NEW CHEVROLET-BUILT, FULLY ENCLOSED BODY.

"LM" HAS 1 TON CAP., 124" W.B., 30×5 TIRES ALL AROUND, AS DOES 1926 MODEL "X."

DELUXE 1-TON PANEL $755.

STAKE $680.

OPEN EXPRESS

9-562

DASH

27
"CAPITOL" MODEL NAME
(YEAR-MODEL NAMES USED UNTIL 1933.)

new RADIATOR HAS DIP AT CENTER OF UPPER PAN.

28

CHEVROLET

FINAL 4-CYL. CHEVROLET
CARS and COMMERCIAL
VEHICLES
(UNTIL THE 1960s)

ROOF-VISOR
(LT. MODEL)

Pickup

UTILITY TRUCK with 4-SPEED
TRANSMISSION and 4-WH. BRAKES
(8-28)

1927-1928
TRUCKS DO NOT
HAVE STEERING
COLUMN LOCK
(AS USED ON
'27-'28 CHEVROLET
CARS.)

IN 1-TON, 124"-W.B. MODELS, EARLY '28 IS "LO," LATER '28 IS "LP."

28

"NATIONAL"

new RADIATOR
SHELL DESIGN
ON 1/2 - TON
LT. DUTY
(107" WB)

4-WHEEL BRAKES on
LT. DUTY MODELS

JENESEN
FANCY GROCERIES
TELEPHONE MAIN 8100

*Illustrating the Light Delivery Chassis
equipped with Panel Body*

29 × 4.40 TIRES (30 × 5 REAR on 1-TON)

COUPES WITH PICKUP BOXES
AVAIL. 1928 TO 1942.

CHEVROLET = 28

CHEVROLET

SEDAN DELIVERY STYLING MORE LIKE THAT OF A CHEVROLET CAR.

← NEW

NEW 6-CYL. ENGINE IN 1929

194 CID (THROUGH '32)

CANOPY ('29)

Instrument Panel →
(1929 CAR, LT. DUTY)

Includes choke, gas and spark controls, ignition switch, water temperature indicator, speedometer, oil gauge, ammeter and electro lock.

The Utility 1½ Ton Chassis with Chevrolet cab, equipped with power dump body built of reinforced steel to withstand concentrated weight. Popular among coal dealers, contractors, road builders, etc.

STARTING 1930, SOME CANADIAN MODELS BEAR THE "MAPLE LEAF" NAME.

INTERNATIONAL SERIES (1929)

29-30

118,253 SOLD ('30)

UNIVERSAL SERIES (1930)

'29 : AC (½ TON) 107" WB (THROUGH '30)
LQ (1½ TON) 131" WB

ALL MODELS HAVE 4-WH. BRAKES IN 1930.

1930 MODEL HAS *new* DASH with SMALL CIRCULAR GAUGES (INCLUDING ELECTRIC FUEL GA.) ILLUSTRATED

('30)

FUEL GAUGE ADDED 1930

Gasoline

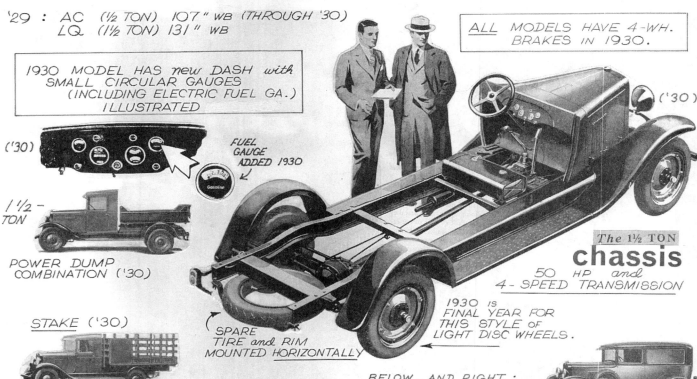

('30)

The 1½ TON **chassis**
50 HP and 4-SPEED TRANSMISSION

1½-TON

POWER DUMP COMBINATION ('30)

STAKE ('30)

SPARE TIRE and RIM MOUNTED HORIZONTALLY

1930 IS FINAL YEAR FOR THIS STYLE OF LIGHT DISC WHEELS.

BELOW, AND RIGHT : DELIVERY MODELS OF 1930

SEDAN DELIVERY

'30 : AD (½ TON)
LR (1½ TON) (LATER BECOMES "LS") 131" WB
1½-TON CANOPY EXPRESS

PANEL DELIVERY

CHEVROLET ACQUIRES MARTIN-PARRY BODY CO. IN 1930.

(ROADSTER PICKUP ALSO AVAIL.)

SIMILAR CANADIAN-BUILT "MAPLE LEAF" TRUCKS AVAIL. FROM 1930 THROUGH THE LATE 1940s.

LIGHT DELIVERY

CHEVROLET ≡ 29~30

CHEVROLET

31A

"INDEPENDENCE"
SERIES

IND. COM.	½ TON	109" WB
Y UTILITY	1½	131
UL DUAL	1½	157

(ALSO KNOWN AS AE (½ T.)
LT, MA, MB, MC, MD
(1½ T.) MODELS)

50 HP @
2600 RPM.
CARTER CARB.

4.75 × 19 TIRES
ON ½-TON.
(ALSO EARLY '32)

new
LONGER GROUP
OF MORE
HOOD LOUVRES,
SET *in* SURROUNDING
PANEL.

SEDAN DELIVERY
(EARLY MODEL *with* TWO-BLADE
BUMPERS)

LATER MODEL *with*
SINGLE BLADE BUMPER

DISC WHEELS
STILL AVAILABLE,
BUT WIRE WHEELS
TYPICAL AFTER 1930.

Open Cab Pick-up—Pick-up box 66 inches long, 45 inches wide and 13 inches deep. Body sides are so designed that they meet floor at right angles, permitting compact loading and generous capacity. Roadster-type cab. Disc wheels. Price of complete unit $440.

1½-TON
OPEN EXPRESS
(HEAVY PICKUP)
with 157" WB,
30 × 5
TIRES

BRITISH-BUILT VERSIONS OF CHEVROLET TRUCKS PHASED OUT
IN 1931, TO BE REPLACED BY _BEDFORD_ TRUCKS (BLT. BY
VAUXHALL AT LUTON.)

(CONT'D. NEXT PAGE)

CHEVROLET = 31-A

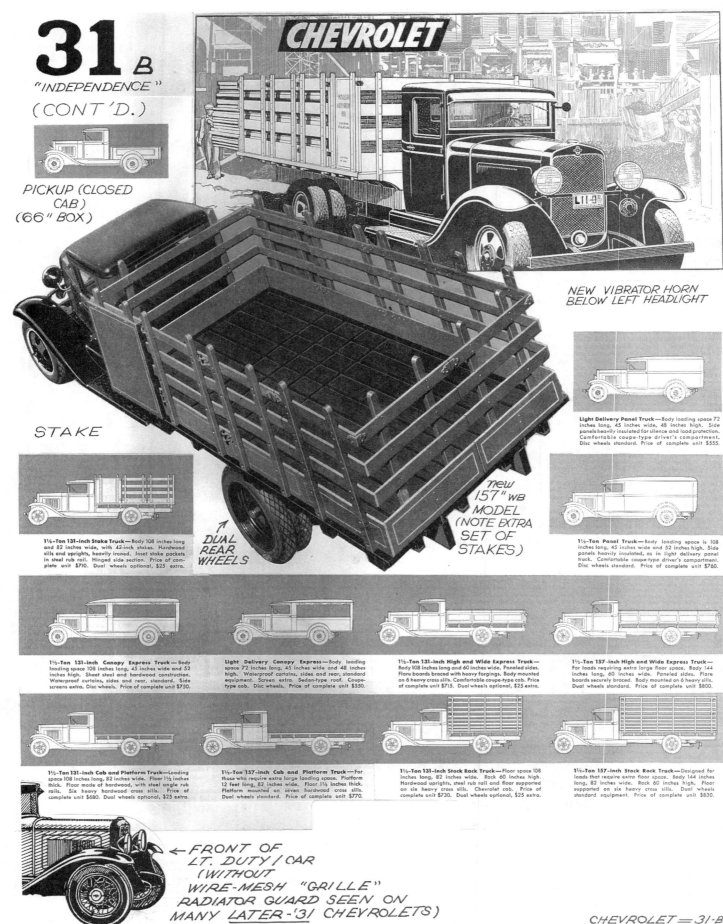

31 B

"INDEPENDENCE"

(CONT'D.)

PICKUP (CLOSED
CAB)
(66" BOX)

CHEVROLET

NEW VIBRATOR HORN
BELOW LEFT HEADLIGHT

STAKE

new
157" WB
MODEL
(NOTE EXTRA
SET OF
STAKES)

↑ DUAL
REAR
WHEELS

Light Delivery Panel Truck—Body loading space 72 inches long, 45 inches wide, 48 inches high. Side panels heavily insulated for silence and load protection. Comfortable coupe-type driver's compartment. Disc wheels standard. Price of complete unit $555.

1½-Ton Panel Truck—Body loading space is 108 inches long, 45 inches wide and 52 inches high. Side panels heavily insulated, as in light delivery panel truck. Comfortable coupe-type driver's compartment. Disc wheels standard. Price of complete unit $760.

1½-Ton 131-inch Stake Truck—Body 108 inches long and 82 inches wide, with 42-inch stakes. Hardwood sills and uprights, heavily ironed. Inset stake pockets in steel rub rail. Hinged side section. Price of complete unit $710. Dual wheels optional, $25 extra.

1½-Ton 131-inch Canopy Express Truck—Body loading space 108 inches long, 45 inches wide and 52 inches high. Sheet steel and hardwood construction. Waterproof curtains, sides and rear, standard. Side screens extra. Disc wheels. Price of complete unit $750.

Light Delivery Canopy Express—Body loading space 72 inches long, 45 inches wide and 48 inches high. Waterproof curtains, sides and rear, standard equipment. Screen extra. Sedan-type roof. Coupe-type cab. Disc wheels. Price of complete unit $550.

1½-Ton 131-inch High and Wide Express Truck—Body 108 inches long and 60 inches wide. Paneled sides. Flare boards braced with heavy forgings. Body mounted on 6 heavy cross sills. Comfortable coupe-type cab. Price of complete unit $715. Dual wheels optional, $25 extra.

1½-Ton 157-inch High and Wide Express Truck—For loads requiring extra large floor space. Body 144 inches long, 60 inches wide. Paneled sides. Flare boards securely braced. Body mounted on 6 heavy sills. Dual wheels standard. Price of complete unit $800.

1½-Ton 131-inch Cab and Platform Truck—Loading space 108 inches long, 82 inches wide. Floor 1½ inches thick. Floor made of hardwood, with steel angle rub rails. Six heavy hardwood cross sills. Price of complete unit $680. Dual wheels optional, $25 extra.

1½-Ton 157-inch Cab and Platform Truck—For those who require extra large loading space. Platform 12 feet long, 82 inches wide. Floor 1½ inches thick. Platform mounted on seven hardwood cross sills. Dual wheels standard. Price of complete unit $770.

1½-Ton 131-inch Stock Rack Truck—Floor space 108 inches long, 82 inches wide. Rack 60 inches high. Hardwood uprights, steel rub rail and floor supported on six heavy cross sills. Chevrolet cab. Price of complete unit $730. Dual wheels optional, $25 extra.

1½-Ton 157-inch Stock Rack Truck—Designed for loads that require extra floor space. Body 144 inches long, 82 inches wide. Rack 60 inches high. Floor supported on six heavy cross sills. Dual wheels standard equipment. Price of complete unit $830.

← FRONT OF
LT. DUTY / CAR
(WITHOUT
WIRE-MESH "GRILLE"
RADIATOR GUARD SEEN ON
MANY LATER-'31 CHEVROLETS)

CHEVROLET = 31-B

32

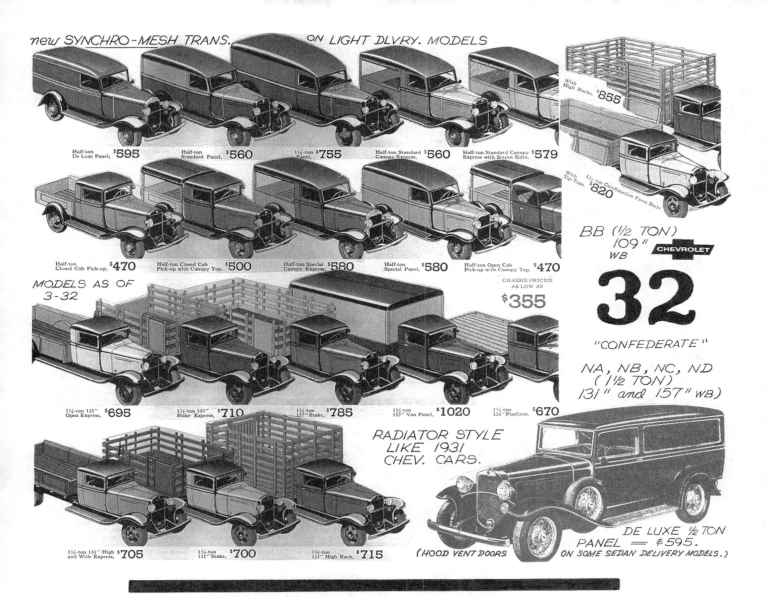

new SYNCHRO-MESH TRANS. ON LIGHT DLVRY. MODELS

Half-ton De Luxe Panel, $595

Half-ton Standard Panel, $560

1½-ton Panel, $755

Half-ton Standard Canopy Express, $560

Half-ton Standard Canopy Express with Screen Sides, $579

With High Racks, $855

1½-ton Combination Farm Body With Tip-Tops, $820

Half-ton Closed Cab Pick-up, $470

Half-ton Closed Cab Pick-up with Canopy Top, $500

Half-ton Special Canopy Express, $580

Half-ton Special Panel, $580

Half-ton Open Cab Pick-up with Canopy Top, $470

BB (½ TON) 109" WB CHEVROLET

32

"CONFEDERATE"

NA, NB, NC, ND (1½ TON) 131" and 157" WB

MODELS AS OF 3-32

CHASSIS PRICED AS LOW AS $355

1½-ton 131" Open Express, $695

1½-ton 131" Stake Express, $710

1½-ton 157" Stake, $785

1½-ton 157" Van Panel, $1020

1½-ton 131" Platform, $670

RADIATOR STYLE LIKE 1931 CHEV. CARS.

1½-ton 131" High and Wide Express, $705

1½-ton 131" Stake, $700

1½-ton 131" High Rack, $715

DE LUXE ½ TON PANEL = $595.

(HOOD VENT DOORS ON SOME SEDAN DELIVERY MODELS.)

33 "EAGLE" and "MASTER" MODELS

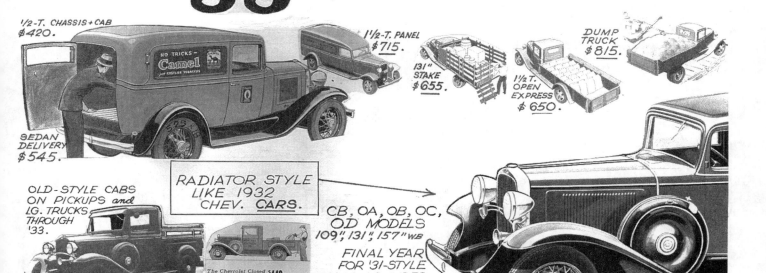

½-T. CHASSIS + CAB $420.

NO TRICKS — Camel just costlier tobaccos

1½-T. PANEL $715.

131" STAKE $655.

1½ T. OPEN EXPRESS $650.

DUMP TRUCK $815.

SEDAN DELIVERY $545.

OLD-STYLE CABS ON PICKUPS and LG. TRUCKS THROUGH '33.

RADIATOR STYLE LIKE 1932 CHEV. CARS.

The Chevrolet Closed Cab Pick-Up....... $440

new 206 CID (THROUGH '36)

CB, OA, OB, OC, OD MODELS 109", 131", 157" WB

FINAL YEAR FOR '31-STYLE HOOD LOUVRES

½-TON PANEL $530.

33

CHEVROLET
FULL LINE

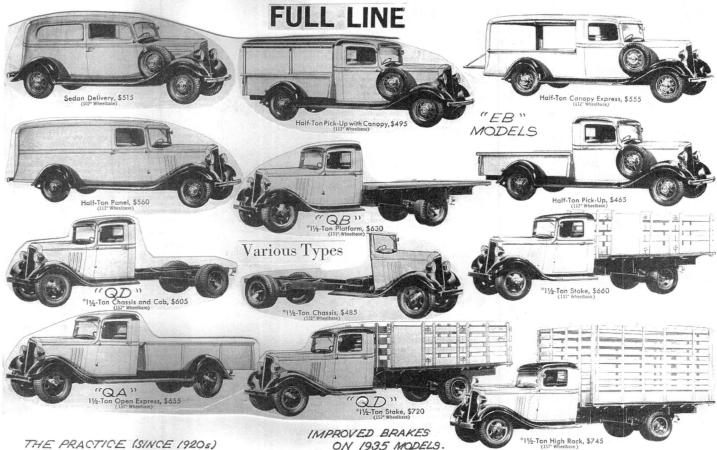

Sedan Delivery, $515
(107" Wheelbase)

Half-Ton Pick-Up with Canopy, $495
(112" Wheelbase)

Half-Ton Canopy Express, $555
(112" Wheelbase)

"EB" MODELS

Half-Ton Panel, $560
(112" Wheelbase)

"QB"
*1½-Ton Platform, $630
(131" Wheelbase)

Various Types

Half-Ton Pick-Up, $465
(112" Wheelbase)

"QD"
*1½-Ton Chassis and Cab, $605
(157" Wheelbase)

*1½-Ton Chassis, $485
(131" Wheelbase)

*1½-Ton Stake, $660
(131" Wheelbase)

"QA"
1½-Ton Open Express, $655
(131" Wheelbase)

"QD"
*1½-Ton Stake, $720
(157" Wheelbase)

IMPROVED BRAKES
ON 1935 MODELS.

*1½-Ton High Rack, $745
(157" Wheelbase)

34-35

THE PRACTICE (SINCE 1920s)
OF USING CODE NAMES
FOR YEARLY MODELS
IS DISCONTINUED
ON POST-1933
CHEVROLETS.

1935 PRICES SHOWN.
MOST PRICES SAME AS
IN 1934.

'34 MODELS: DB,
PA, PB, PC, PD
FROM $445. (½-T. CH.+CAB)

'35 MODELS: EB,
QA, QB, QC, QD

COMMERCIAL	W.B.	GEAR RATIO
½ TON	112" (new) (107" ALSO)	4.11
UTILITY		
1½ TON	131" (157" ALSO)	5.43

TIRE SIZES

5.50 × 17   (½ TON)
30 × 5 (FRONT) 32 × 6 (REAR)
(6.00 × 20)   (1½ TON)

207 CID "BLUE FLAME" ENG. (70 HP @ 3200 RPM)
CARTER CARB.

CLOSER VIEW
OF
CANOPY EXPRESS
('34)

8-PASS. SUBURBAN CARRYALL WAGON
(ON TRUCK CHASSIS) INTRO. 1935.
(WITH STEEL BODY)

CHEVROLET = 34~35

CHEVROLET

LOWEST-PRICED
½ TON CHASSIS CAB =
$450.

36

new HORIZONTAL
HOOD LOUVRES

$475.

FB
LIGHT-DUTY ½-TON
PICKUP

SEDAN DELIVERY HAS GRILLE
LIKE 1936 CHEVROLET *CAR*.

PANEL
DELIVERY = $565.

VISORLESS
LATER '36
CAB
STYLE

LATE '36 1½-TON PICKUP
has STEEL ARTILLERY WHEELS.

½ TON : "FB" MODEL (112" WB)
1½ TON MODELS :
  RA (131" WB) $590.
  RB (131" WB, DUAL
    REAR WHEELS)
  RC (157" WB) $615.
  RD (157" WB,
    DUAL REAR
    WHEELS)

10,110 POUNDS PAY LOAD
CERTIFIED WEIGHT
SAFE DRIVING ROAD TEST
CHEVROLET MOTOR CO. DETROIT, MICH.

1½-TON

SHALLOW OUTER
VISOR ON
EARLY '36
STYLE
CAB

new INSTRUMENT
PANEL SIMILAR
TO THAT IN
1936
CHEV.
"MASTER"
SERIES
CAR
(THROUGH
'39.)

GEAR RATIOS

4.11 (½ TON)
5.43~6.17
(1½ TON)

HYDRAULIC BRAKES
ON ALL BUT EARLY
1½-TON "R."

FINE FOOD
PRODUCTS

SCREENSIDE
CANOPY TRUCK

CHEVROLET = 36

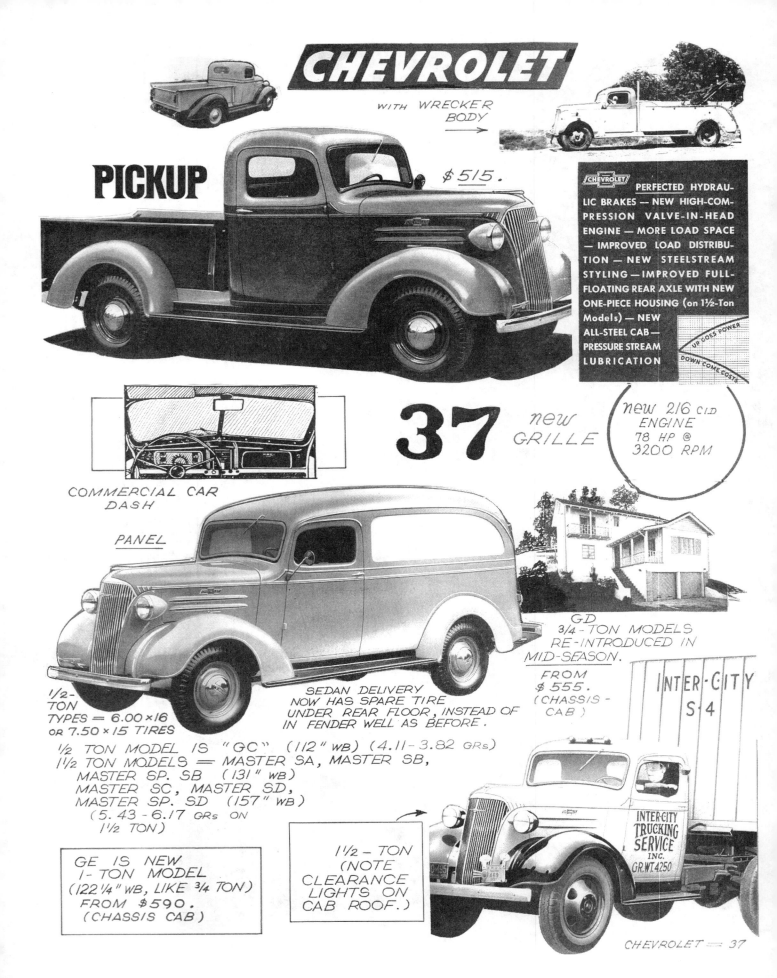

CHEVROLET

WITH WRECKER BODY →

PICKUP

$515.

PERFECTED HYDRAULIC BRAKES — NEW HIGH-COMPRESSION VALVE-IN-HEAD ENGINE — MORE LOAD SPACE — IMPROVED LOAD DISTRIBUTION — NEW STEELSTREAM STYLING — IMPROVED FULL-FLOATING REAR AXLE WITH NEW ONE-PIECE HOUSING (on 1½-Ton Models) — NEW ALL-STEEL CAB — PRESSURE STREAM LUBRICATION

UP GOES POWER
DOWN COME COSTS

COMMERCIAL CAR DASH

37 new GRILLE

new 216 C.I.D. ENGINE 78 HP @ 3200 RPM

PANEL

GD
¾-TON MODELS RE-INTRODUCED IN MID-SEASON.

FROM $555. (CHASSIS - CAB)

½-TON TYPES = 6.00 × 16 OR 7.50 × 15 TIRES

SEDAN DELIVERY NOW HAS SPARE TIRE UNDER REAR FLOOR, INSTEAD OF IN FENDER WELL AS BEFORE.

INTER-CITY S-4

INTER-CITY TRUCKING SERVICE INC. GR. WT. 4250

½ TON MODEL IS "GC" (112" WB) (4.11-3.82 GRs)
1½ TON MODELS = MASTER SA, MASTER SB, MASTER SP. SB (131" WB) MASTER SC, MASTER SD, MASTER SP. SD (157" WB) (5.43 - 6.17 GRs ON 1½ TON)

GE IS NEW 1-TON MODEL (122¼" WB, LIKE ¾ TON) FROM $590. (CHASSIS CAB)

1½ - TON (NOTE CLEARANCE LIGHTS ON CAB ROOF.)

CHEVROLET = 37

LARGER, IMPROVED DIAPHRAGM-
SPRING CLUTCH,
VOLTAGE -
REGULATOR
GENERATOR

OVERHEAD RACK is OPTIONAL.

CHEVROLET

C.O.E.
(RARE)

½-TON
PICKUP
$**560.**

WT. =
2805
lbs.

38

new GRILLE with
HORIZONTAL POS.

IMPROVED HAND BRAKE

HC,
HD,
HE,
TA, TB,
TC, TD
MODELS

CAB
INTERIOR
(ABOVE)

IMPROVED
SEATS

1½-TON
STAKE
FROM $750.

┌─────────────────────────────┐
│ 45 MODELS, 8 WHEELBASES   │
│   IN 1939   │
└─────────────────────────────┘

new TRUCK GRILLE *with* HEAVIER
HORIZONTAL
MEMBERS

JC (½ TON ;)
JD (¾ TON ;)
JE (1 TON ;)
VA, VB, VC, VD (1½ TON ;)
VE, VF, VG, VH, VM,
VN (1½ TON C.O.E.)

39

78 HP @ 3200 RPM
new 113½" WB *and up*
½-T. PICKUP = $545.
¾-T. PICKUP = 630.
½-T. PANEL   = 630.
1½-T. STAKE = FROM 730.

New Chevrolet-Built
CAB-OVER-ENGINE
MODELS

new V-WINDSHIELD
ON *ALL* 1939 MODELS.

$645.

UNLIKE
PANEL TRUCK,
SEDAN
DELIVERY
IS STYLED LIKE
CHEVROLET
CAR.

CHEVROLET = 38~39

CHEVROLET

40

SEDAN DELIVERY
(STYLED LIKE CHEVROLET
CAR)

new — SEALED-BEAM HEADLIGHTS, and PARKING LIGHTS ON FENDERS.

TOP PIECE OF GRILLE IS VERT. WIDENED

new HYPOID REAR AXLE
FULL-FLOATING REAR AXLE ON HEAVY-DUTY MODELS with VACUUM-POWER BRAKES and 2-SPEED REAR AXLE OPTIONS.

new 4.55 GR ON ¾ TON and 1-TON

MODELS: KC (½ TON;) KD, KE (¾ TON;) KF (1 TON)

KP (½-TON PARCEL DELIV.;)*
WA, WB (1½ TON;)
WD, WE,
WF (1½ TON C.O.E.)

* = SPRING INTRODUCTION

C.O.E.
(LOGGER)
C.O.E STAKES $845.
(107"WB)
$900.
(131"WB)

(1940 CHEVROLET CAR-TYPE INSTRUMENT PANEL REPLACES 1936 TYPE (EXCEPT IN SCHOOLBUS AND FLAT-FACE COWL TYPE.)

BEFORE WORLD WAR II, ALL GM-BUILT TRUCKS OVER 1½-TON CAP'Y. SOLD UNDER GMC NAME.

"WC" IS 1½-TON SCHOOL BUS CHASSIS.

6 CYL., 216 CID
78 OR 80 HP

PRICED FROM
$541. f.o.b.
(½-TON, 113" WB CAB/CHASSIS)

HEAVY DUTY DUMP TRUCK

MILITARY ('43)

CHEVROLET

60 bigger models IN '41

nine longer wheelbases

massive new truck styling

DUMP TRUCK

THIS SHIELD EMBLEM
IS MISSING FROM 1943 TO 1945
WARTIME MODELS

192 FOOT POUNDS TORQUE

(new '41) 235 CID
**93-HORSEPOWER
HEAVY DUTY
"LOAD-MASTER"
ENGINE**

(Optional at extra cost on Heavy Duty trucks)

174 FOOT POUNDS TORQUE

**90-HORSEPOWER
STANDARD
ENGINE**

216 CID

TANKER (C.O.E.)

1941 MODELS: AK, AJ (115" WB;)
AL (125";) AN, YR (134";) YS (160".)
1942 LETTERS START WITH B or M
  (1943 – EARLY 1945 WARTIME, SAME.)
1946 LETTERS START WITH C or O
1947   "   "   "   D or P

41-47

WARTIME
MODELS
HAVE
LESS CHROME
and
NO
FLOOR MAT.

2-TON
MODELS AVAIL. IN 1946.

ENTIRE LINE EXPANDED TO 99 MODELS IN 1946.
1946-47 PRICES FROM $884., f.o.b. (1/2-TON)

STEP-VANS INTRODUCED 1951.
4-CYL., 90-HP
DETROIT
DIESEL ENG.
AVAIL. 1952,
BUT RARE.

Chevrolet

TRACTOR-
TRLR.

90 OR 93 HP IN 1948.
1948
1½-T. STAKE
$1256.
UP

STAKE
CONVENTIONALS
(ABOVE and RIGHT)

HOG
TRANSPORT
WITH
RAMP
(OTHER
APPLICATIONS
ALSO,
CUSTOM-
MADE)

48-53

New
Advance-Design
(TOTALLY RESTYLED)
INTRO. SUMMER, 1947

I.D. TIPS:
EARLY '48 HALF-TON has
GAS FILLER NECK on BOX SIDE,
INSTEAD OF in CAB SIDE.
1952 has NEW PUSH-BUTTON
DOOR HANDLES.
1953 has NEW 60-LB. OIL PRESSURE GA.
(92, 102, 105 HP INCREASES
IN 1950; 92, 107, 108 HP
IN 1953.)

('49)
PICKUP

DUAL REAR-
WHEELED
STAKE
C.O.E.

PANEL

('48)

('49)

HVY. PANEL

Claudia FLORIST

YEAR DETERMINED
BY FIRST LETTER IN
MODEL DESIGNATION:

E, Q	=	1948
G, S	=	1949
H, T	=	1950
J, U	=	1951
K, V	=	1952

WIDE VARIETY of ALPHABETICAL
SINGLE LETTER 1953 MODEL
DESIGNATIONS.
1953 SERIAL # STARTS WITH
53-001 001, FOLLOWING
LETTER PREFIX.

('51)

DUMP TRUCK

CHEVROLET

"ADVANCE-DESIGN" NAME CONT'D.

EARLY 54-55

STAKE

FIRST STYLING CHANGE SINCE EARLY '48 MODELS.

FINAL CANOPY EXPRESS (1-TON) IN 1954, AT $2012.

1/2 TON SERIAL # 1154~00/001 UP

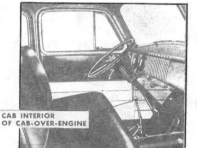

DRIVER'S COMPARTMENT OF PANEL TRUCK

CAB INTERIOR OF CAB-OVER-ENGINE

CABS.

New

GRILLE and 1 PIECE WINDSHIELD
'54 FROM : $1419.
EARLY '55 : 1494.

New Comfortmaster Cab: Offers new comfort, safety and convenience. New one-piece curved windshield provides extra visibility.

New Chassis Ruggedness: Heavier axle shafts in 2-ton models . . . newly designed clutches, and more rigid frames in *all* models.

New Ride Control Seat: Seat cushion and back move as a unit to eliminate back-rubbing. It "floats" you over rough roads with ease.

New Automatic Transmission: Proved truck Hydra-Matic transmission is offered on ½-, ¾- and 1-ton models.

New, Bigger Load Space: New pickup bodies have deeper sides. New stake and platform bodies are wider, longer and roomier.

THREE 6-CYL. ENGINES : "THRIFTMASTER 235," "LOADMASTER 235", "JOBMASTER 261"

new SHORTER 114" W.B.

(THE EARLIEST 1955 CHEVROLET TRUCKS RESEMBLE THE 1954 MODELS) (6-CYL. TYPES ONLY)

55

TOTALLY RESTYLED EARLY IN 1955.

New Overdrive or Hydra-Matic Your choice of Synchro-Mesh or, as extra-cost options, new Overdrive (½-ton models) or Hydra-Matic (½-, ¾- and 1-ton).

New Power Brakes, Tubeless Tires Power Brakes are standard equipment on all 2-ton models, optional at extra cost on others. Tubeless tires on all ½-ton models.

STAKE

PANEL FROM $1776.

$1956.

CAMEO
NEW

New styling in trucks

CHEVROLET

1½-TON STAKE, $2310.

(2-TON AVAIL. IN 14' OR 16' BED LENGTHS.)

NEW CHEVROLET Task·Force TRUCKS

new V8 ENGINES AVAIL.

new 12-VOLT IGNITION

NEW

LIGHT DUTY SERIAL NO. STARTS AT H-255-00/001

"WRAP-AROUND" PANORAMIC WINDSHIELD

SERIAL NO. STARTS AT 3A 56-001001

1/2 TON PICKUP $1670. MODEL 3104

MODEL 1508 SEDAN DELIVERY STYLED LIKE CHEVROLET CAR.

$1811.

115" WB

1956 HOOD EMBLEM *has* LOWER SIDE WINGS THAN '55 EMBLEM.

56

1956 RESEMBLES 1955, EXCEPT THAT '56 SIDE NAMEPLATE IS MOVED UP, ABOVE FENDER CREASE

DUAL REAR WHEELS

1 1/2 TON CAB-FORWARD STAKE

$3118. WITH 12' BED (MODEL 5409~S)

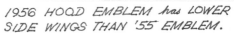

GRILLE of CAR/SEDAN DELIVERY

DUMP TRUCK (BELOW)

HVY. TRACTOR

DELUXE-STYLE "CAMEO" (WIDE BED w. FIBERGLASS OUTER SIDES) AVAIL. '55-57

Pickups

STD. 1/2-TON "3104" PICKUP = $1626. (6-CYL.)

LONG-WHEELBASE MODEL "3204" (123" WB)

V8 = $113. EXTRA

SHOWN ON ALCAN HIGHWAY (CANADA-ALASKA)

57 **new**

GRILLE (LT. DUTY) SERIAL NO. STARTS AT 3A 57-100001

NEW TASK·FORCE 57 CHEVROLET TRUCKS

NEW

TOTAL PRODUCTION: 278,632

6'-BED PICKUPS FROM
$1884.
114" WB

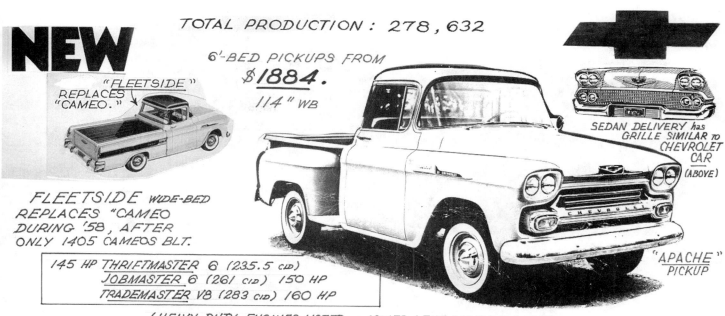

"FLEETSIDE" REPLACES "CAMEO."

SEDAN DELIVERY has GRILLE SIMILAR TO CHEVROLET CAR (ABOVE)

"APACHE" PICKUP

FLEETSIDE WIDE-BED REPLACES "CAMEO" DURING '58, AFTER ONLY 1405 CAMEOS BLT.

145 HP THRIFTMASTER 6 (235.5 CID)
JOBMASTER 6 (261 CID) 150 HP
TRADEMASTER V8 (283 CID) 160 HP

(HEAVY-DUTY ENGINES LISTED AT LOWER LEFT SIDE OF PAGE)

(BELOW) SERIES 100 TANKER WITH "WORKMASTER" V8

58
FRONT END RESTYLED. new 4 HEADLTS.

VARIOUS VANS (SOME WITH BODIES BY OTHER MFRS.)

1958 CHEVROLET HEAVY-DUTY Spartan MODELS

With the industry's newest and finest V8's, these modern heavy-weights are ready to handle heavy-duty hauling jobs more economically and dependably than ever!

C.O.E. TRACTOR

V8 1½-TON C.O.E. STAKE 136" WB
$3494.
MODEL 5409-S

STEP-VAN →
Complete unit . . . body and chassis . . . from Chevrolet

HD TASKMASTER 283 CID V8 (160 HP; "SUPER" 175 HP)
LOADMASTER 322 CID V8 (190 HP)

CHEVROLET ≡ 58

SERIES 50-H
and 60-H
MIDDLEWEIGHTS

114" WB WITH
6' BED
$1948.

FLEETSIDE

CHEVROLET 1959

123" WB WITH 8' BED
$1986.

SERIAL NO.
3A59-
100001
UP

59
new
HOOD-VENT
FRONT
EMBLEM

TOTAL PRODUCTION:
326,102

Inside.

('59)
1959 DASH AND INT.
SIMILAR TO 1958.

Task·Force 59
Trucks

new
EL CAMINO
PICKUP IS
STYLED LIKE 1959
CHEVROLET CAR
(119" WB)
$2352. WITH
135 HP 6
OR
$2470. WITH
185 HP V8

(EL CAMINO INTRO.
10-16-58)

HEAVY-DUTY
COMPACT L.C.F.
TRACTOR (V8 ENG.)

THIS WAY TO THE
ELEPHANTS
RHINOS
HIPPOS

L2714

CHEVROLET 59

1960 CHEVROLET

$2028.

"FLEETSIDE" PICKUP

235 C.I.D. 6 CYL. ENG.

(V8s ALSO)

CARRYALL

$2361. FOR FINAL SEDAN DELIVERY

$2690.

EL CAMINOS FROM $2352.

EL CAMINO (FINAL EL CAMINO UNTIL SERIES RESUMES IN new 1964 CHEVELLE LINE)

60

new GRILLE, RESTYLED FRONT END

AIR-COOLED CORVAIR CAR INTRODUCED. CORVAIR, CORVAN and GREENBRIER VANS and TRUCKS FOLLOW.

Chevrolet **New** "TILT-CAB" C.O.E.

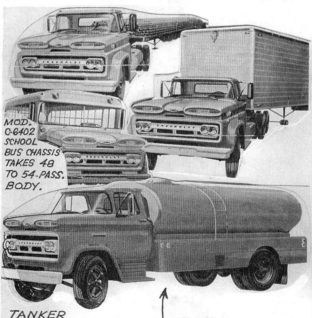

MOD. C-6402 SCHOOL BUS CHASSIS TAKES 48 TO 54-PASS. BODY.

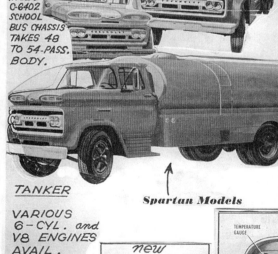

TANKER

Spartan Models

VARIOUS 6-CYL. and V8 ENGINES AVAIL.

new "K" SERIES 4-W-D AVAIL. (CHASSIS-CAB, PICKUP, PANEL, CARRYALL)

STURDI-BILT TRUCKS
Rotary Valve Power Steering
AVAIL. ON 60, 70 and 80 SER.

INSTR. PANEL (IN TRUCKS TO 2-TON CAP'Y.)

TEMPERATURE GAUGE — GENERATOR TEL-TALE INDICATOR — HIGH BEAM INDICATOR — OIL PRESSURE INDICATOR — GASOLINE GAUGE

L.H. DIRECTION SIGNAL INDICATOR — ODOMETER — SPEEDOMETER — R.H. DIRECTION SIGNAL INDICATOR

INSTRUMENT CLUSTER

TOTAL 1960 PRODUCTION 394,017

CHEVROLET = 60

45

Chevrolet

70 SERIES

I.D. # STARTS AT
1C/40 (A)
10000/

60 SERIES
(Middleweight)

61

new GRILLE

PRODUCTION:
342,659

$2350.

MODEL C3604 STEPSIDE PICKUP
(w. 133" WB, 9' BOX)

115" WB
PICKUPS
FROM $1991.

LIGHT DUTY

FLEETSIDE

REAR

LT. DUTY
FRONT END

I.D. # STARTS
AT
2C/40 (A)
10000/

60 SERIES

62 FRONT ENDS
RESTYLED,
WITH OVAL
HOOD PODS
ELIMINATED
and A RETURN
TO ONLY TWO
HEADLIGHTS.

PROD.: 396,940

JOBMASTER

46

FOR BETTER VISIBILITY, DISTANCE (WIDTH) ACROSS FENDERS UP TO 7" NARROWER ON CONVENTIONAL MEDIUM and HEAVY-DUTY MODELS, WHICH HAVE STD. SOLID FRONT AXLE and VARIABLE-RATE SPRINGS.

new GRILLE

63

new GRILLE ON LT.-DUTY

STEPSIDE PICKUP

C-1404 PICKUP (6½' BED) $**2009.**

new LADDER-TYPE FRAMES IN LIGHT-DUTY MODELS.

Conventional

new HIGH-TORQUE 230 C.I.D. and 292 C.I.D. 6-CYL. ENGS.

1½-TON STAKE 157" WB $2896.

CAR GRILLE SIMILAR TO COMMERCIAL OR FLEET SEDAN.

C SERIES ON 115, 127, 133 and 157" WB

C SERIES I.D. # 3C140(A) 100001 UP

DUMP TRUCK

L SERIES C.O.E. (2-TON) 145"-WB TYPE PRICED AT $3245. (L-5309)

1963 PRODUCTION: 483,158

the "New Reliables"

47

STEP-VAN MODELS

7' BODY

8', 10' OR 12' BODY

STEPSIDE WITH 9' BED 1-TON 6½' AND 8' ALSO AVAIL. $2370.

STEP-VAN KING

REAR

10', 10½', 12' OR 12½' BODY CARRYALL (4-W-D AVAIL.)

SERIES 80 DIESEL TANDEM WITH 6 CUBIC YD. CONCRETE MIXER

(C-50 IS CHASSIS-CAB CONVENTIONAL)

STEPSIDE DETAIL (ABOVE) $2629.

T SERIES 80 DIESEL TILT-CAB (C.O.E.) TRACTOR WITH 40' SEMI-TRAILER

$2324.

½-TON PANEL (1-TON also)

Conventional

SERIES 80 TANDEM 10-CU.-YARD DUMP TRUCK (409 CID V8 ENGINE)

C, 80 SERIES I.D. # 4C140 (A) 100001 UP (COMPACT CHEVY-VAN INTRODUCED)

WITH 292 CID 6-CYL. ENG.

SERIES 60 TRAILING-AXLE TANDEM WITH 15' PLATFORM BODY.

STD. CAB

64 new GRILLE

G-1205 CHEVY VAN 6 CYL. 90" WB $2105.

new

(FRONT DETAIL OF SIMILAR '65 CHEVY VAN NEXT PAGE)

C-10 (½ TON)
C-20 (¾ TON)
C-30 (1-TON)
4-W-D MODELS ALSO

$2044.

CHEVROLET FLEETSIDE—best for all-around use. Full-width body has double-wall construction.

CHOICE OF 18 LIGHT-DUTY, 258 MEDIUM and HEAVY-DUTY MODELS IN 1965! FROM $2023.

HEAVY-DUTY STYLING UNCHANGED

STAKE FROM $2284.

CHEVROLET

PICKUP 115" 127" OR 133" WHEEL BASE

'65

PROD.: 619,690

THE LONG STRONG LINE FOR '65

C SERIES SERIAL # FROM C1445 (-) 100001 UP

EL CAMINO

(EL CAMINO PART OF CHEVELLE SERIES SINCE '64)

$2523. ($2642. IN WEST)

EL CAMINO WITH HI THRU! 194 CID 6, TURBO-FIRE 283 CID V8, OR V8s UP TO 327 CID

VARIOUS OTHER 1965 TYPES ILLUSTRATED BELOW

AVAIL. 4 CYL., 6 OR V8 GAS ENGINES (also FOUR DIESEL ENGINES)

$2324.

$2518.

2105.

SEEN FROM FRONT TO REAR:

CHEVY-VAN, STEP-VAN 7, 60 SERIES TRUCK with VAN BODY, 80 SERIES DIESEL TRACTOR C.O.E.

($2324. 1/2-TON PANEL ACROSS THE STREET.)

INSTRUMENTS

TEMP. GAUGE
FUEL GAUGE
HI BEAM INDICATOR

TEMPERATURE
DIRECTION SIGNAL INDICATOR
DIRECTION SIGNAL INDICATOR
GENERATOR TELL-TALE INDICATOR
HIGH BEAM INDICATOR
OIL PRESSURE TELL-TALE INDICATOR
GASOLINE GAUGE

PROD. 621,354

PICKUPS FROM $2066.

OIL PRESSURE GAUGE
SPEEDOMETER
ODO

AMM

O.: 54

new LT.-DUTY 250 CID 6. TO 327 CID V8 IN 1/2-TON.

SIDE EMBLEM RETURNED TO A LOWER POSITION ON COWL.

66

SERIES 60 MEDIUM-DUTY
I.D. # FROM C-1446 (–) 100001 (C SERIES LT. DUTY)

new SERIES 70000 and 80000 LARGE TRUCKS with new V6 GAS ENGINES TO 478 CID, also V6 and V8 DIESELS TO 637 CID.

UP TO 48,000 LBS. GVW

new CONVENTIONAL MIDDLEWEIGHT TRUCK WITH new 96" SHORT CAB

HEAVY-DUTY TRUCK

TANDEM DUMP TRUCK (GAS OR DIESEL)

New 4-WAY HAZARD FLASHER SYSTEM, REDUCED-GLARE INSTRUMENT PANEL, IMPROVED DOOR LOCKS.

CAMPER

new 250 CID 6 is STD.; 327 CID V8 OPT.

LT. DUTY

FLEETSIDE

DASH

11-MONTH SALES = 505,570

MED. DUTY and PICKUP
67
TOTALLY RESTYLED
I.D. # STARTS AT CE147 (–) 100001.
PICKUPS FR. $2152.

("CST" PLATE ON WINDOW SILL DENOTES A new "CUSTOM SPORT TRUCK" MODEL.)

DESIGN IS
NEW

50

CHEVROLET '68 *Job Tamer* TRUCKS

PICKUPS FROM $2371.

PROD.: 680,931
I.D.# STARTS AT CE148(-)10001

note HUBCAP CHOICES (LT. DUTY)

NEW
SIDE SAFETY LTS. AT EITHER END.
11-MONTH SALES = 558,400

68

250 CID 6 (155 HP) STD.
292 CID 6 (170 HP) AVAIL.
new 307 CID V8 (200 HP)
327 CID V8 OR 396 CID V8
(310 HP) ALSO

MORE BRIGHTWORK AT FRONT

464 DIFF. MODELS FOR 1968.
TOTAL REDUCED, FOR SIMPLICITY, TO 272 FOR 1969.

PICKUPS with new ALUMINUM GRILLE with CHEVROLET NAME ACROSS CENTER PIECE

69

I.D.# STARTS AT CE149(-)10001

PRODUCTION: 684,748

WITH CAMPER BODY (ABOVE)

6 CYL. OR V8 $2412. UP (90" OR 108" WB)

'69 Chevy-Van

new SEAT BACKS

MED. DUTY

(ABOVE) CAMPER SHELL OPTIONAL

FLEETSIDE CST

new 350 CID V8 AVAIL. (200 OR 250 HP)

PICKUPS FROM $2435. (BLAZER is new)

4 new LP-GAS ENGINES ALSO AVAIL.

CHEVROLET = 68~69

TOTAL 1970 PRODUCTION:
492,601

70, 80, and 90 HVY.-DUTY SERIES

CHEVROLET
BLAZER (S.U.V.)
INTRO. DURING
SPRING, 1969
$**2852.** UP

LT. DUTY FROM 115" WB
$2654. UP

250 CID (115 HP) 6
OR 307 CID (200 HP) V8
ALSO 292 CID 6,
350 CID V8,
OR 400 CID
V8
AVAIL.

new
LONG
CONVENTIONAL CAB
HVY. DUTY DIESEL
TANDEM TRACTOR
90 SERIES
(ABOVE) 2-CYCLE
DETROIT DIESELS and
4-CYCLE CUMMINS DIESELS
TO 855 CID
(218 TO
335
HP)

new
LT. DUTY
GRILLE
WITH 12 SETS
OF SMALL
HORIZONTAL
RIBS →

3
OR
4-SP.
MANUAL
TRANS.
OR 2-SP.
POWERGLIDE
OR 3-SP. Turbo
Hydramatic AVAIL.
(LT. DUTY)

I.D. #
CE 140 (−)
100001

70
New
←

Titan 90
HEAVY
DUTY
WITH
SLEEPER
CAB
(ALUMINUM)
(PREVIOUS STYLE
STEEL TILT-CAB
ALSO CONT'D.)
CHEVROLET ═ 70

<u>C.O.E.</u> 110"
TO 76,800 LBS. G.V.W. TO
235"
WB

(OPT.
V-12
DIESEL ENG.
has 390, 434 OR 475 HP)

1971 Chevrolet

DASH

ENGINES: 250 SIX (145 HP); 292 SIX (165 HP); 307 V8 (200 or 215 HP); 350 V8 (250 HP); 400 V8 (300 HP)

hallmark

71 A

new GRILLE ON LT. DUTY TRUCKS and CHEVY VAN/ SPORTVAN

FLEETSIDE VARIETIES

new Cheyenne

CUSTOM (and CUSTOM DELUXE)

(STEPSIDE SHOWN ON NEXT PAGE.)

8' FLEETSIDES $2977. UP

SHOWN WITH "OPEN ROAD" RAISED TOP CONVERSION

STEP-VAN KING

(INTRO. MID-1970) new W.B. 110" OR 125" RESTYLED and ENLARGED

(PARSONS CONVERSION)

Chevy Van/Sportvan

(1971 MODELS CONT'D. NEXT PAGE)

Conventionals
Short
Long

Series 70·80·90

C.O.E.

Water and oil-fill access doors speed maintenance checks.

CHEVROLET

Titan 90
Aluminum Tilt

VEGA (new)
PANEL EXPRESS

MODEL 1410.5 140 CID 4 90 HP

97" WB
$2372.

VEGA AVAIL. UNTIL 1977. (PANEL EXP. UNTIL 1975.)

71^B

1 TON CH.-CAB = $3376.
1½ T. = $4037.
2 T. = 4352.

There will always be a place for Stepside's unique cargo box advantages.
The convenient side step makes loading the cab end of the box a simple matter.
And the smooth interior walls take cargo neatly up to 50" wide.
The standard wood floor has steel skid strips to help things slide in easy like.

Famous Stepside utility.

1-TON STEPSIDE $3265. →

CHASSIS-CAB STAKE

I.D. NO.
CE 141 (-)
100001 UP

Chevy conventionals may be adapted to an almost unlimited range of applications with available power-plants. Gasoline models are powered by a standard 401-cubic-inch V6 or optional 478 V6. Both have established outstanding durability records on the job.
Diesel models offer a wide selection of Detroit Diesel and Cummins engines. 2-cycle Detroit Diesels available are: 6V-53N, 6-71N and 8V-71N. Four-cycle Cummins diesels available are: NH-230, NHC-250, NHCT-270 and NTC-335.

CHEVROLET

9' BOX 133" WB

LT. DUTY = FRONT DISC BRAKES

Sure-stopping long-lasting disc brakes now standard.

Functional, easy-to-read main instrument cluster.

Steel Tilt

Steel Tilt Cab

54

Chevrolet

SERIES 60 TANDEM TRACTOR

SERIES 50 CONV.

SERIES 70

Steel tilt cabs: only 72" from bumper to back of cab.

Conventional cab **72**

LITTLE CHANGE FROM 1971, BUT SOME H.P. DECREASES

PICKUPS FROM **$2796.**

OPTIONAL

Special instrumentation

Ammeter, oil pressure and temperature needle gauges replace the standard warning light system. Available with or without tachometer.

Tilt cab interior
SERIES 70

(SERIES 90 TITAN TILT CAB *has* WRAPAROUND INSTRUMENT PANEL.)

interiors

CHEYENNE

LT. DUTY I.D. #
CE 142 (-)
100001 UP

new
Cheyenne Super

has WOODGRAIN EFFECTS ON GLOVEBOX DOOR.

CHEVROLET = 72

Totally tougher to last longer. **CHEVROLET**

$3092. UP ('74)

Special window combinations

110" WB **CHEVY VAN** 125" WB AVAIL.

Chevrolet

Step-Van $3453. UP ('73)

HEAVY and MEDIUM-DUTY TRUCKS IMPROVED FOR 1974

TILT-CAB TANKER

NEW 454 CID V8 AVAIL.

Refrigerated Transport (TITAN-STYLE)

TANDEM 90

1973 MODELS ILLUSTR., UNLESS OTHERWISE INDICATED.
6½' PICKUPS FROM
$2887. ('73)
3207. ('74)

NEW STYLING FOR 1973 LT. and MEDIUM-DUTY MODELS.

Chevrolet's medium-duty models feature all-new styling for '73.

73-74

LT. DUTY '73 I.D. # CC (X or Y) 143 (F) 100001 UP

LT. DUTY '74 I.D.# CC (V) 144 (F) 100001 UP

Detroit Diesel options include the 6-71, 8V-71 and 12V-71. The Cummins NH 230, NHC 250, NTC 290, NTC 335, NTC 350, and V903 are also available.

DUAL REAR WHEEL PAIRS AVAIL. ON CAMPER PICKUP

GCW's up to 76,800 lbs., GVW's up to 50,500 lbs.

DIESEL TANDEM 90 290 HP

('74)

Chevrolet heavies

56

133" WB

125" WB 10' ¾ TON $5172. ('75)

12' 1-TON $5536. ('75)

Step-Vans

$4532. ('75)

½ TON

102" WB

Step-Van 7: in steel (7 or 8 ft.) or aluminum (8-ft. bodies).

LASTING CHEVY VALUE

3+3 CREW CAB $5002. ('75)

3/4 TON

Suburban
FROM $4707. ('75)

DASH (CONV. 50,60,65)

LT. DUTY 1975
I.D. # FROM
CC(Q)145(F)
100001

75 -76

LT. DUTY 1976
I.D. # FROM
CC(V)146(F)
100001

Chevy Suburban seats up to nine facing forward.

CHEVROLET

513 GB

Custom Deluxe Interior

STEPSIDE (6½ BED)

FLEETSIDE FROM
$3652. ('75)
3908. ('76)

CHEVROLET

5168 EB

4-wheel drive avail. on V8 pickups

SLIDE-OUT SPARE →

New catalytic converter
Hot exhaust gases flow through stainless steel exhaust pipe to the converter, where a catalyst changes hydrocarbons and carbon monoxide to water vapor and carbon dioxide. With primary emissions control moved outside the engines, they're tuned for improved fuel economy.

CE65 with farm body

CE-65

(1975 EXAMPLES ILLUSTRATED)

57

Chevrolet
4-WH

FOUR ON THE FLOOR
DRIVE

SOME SPT. MODELS *have* PARTIALLY BLACKED-OUT GRILLE.

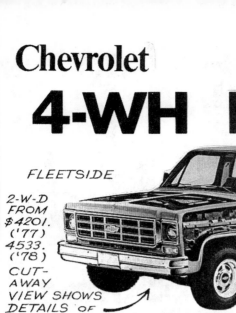

FLEETSIDE

2-W-D FROM $4201. ('77) 4533. ('78) CUT-AWAY VIEW SHOWS DETAILS of BODY CONSTR.

('77)

STEPSIDE

LIGHT TRUCK SALES
1,078,692 ('77)
1,233,932 ('78)

CHEVY 4-WHEELERS ARE THE MOST POPULAR IN AMERICA.

In the first 10 months of 1977, R. L. Polk & Co. registrations of Chevrolet 4-wheel-drive Blazers, Suburbans and Pickups were 25% ahead of the nearest sales competitor.

VROLET

BLAZER (REAR, 10-76)

95.7% OF ALL CHEVY TRUCKS, IN THE TEN MOST RECENT MODEL YEARS RECORDED, WERE STILL ON THE JOB:

SUBURBAN

FROM $5458. ('77) $5800. ('78)
$7299 IN WEST $7968 IN WEST

SEATS 9

CHEVY TRUCKS
BUILT TO STAY TOUGH.

85.1% '67
86.9% '68
93.0% '69
94.4% '70
95.3% '71
98.3% '72
98.3% '73
98.9% '74
OVER 99.9% '75
OVER 99.9% '76

(2-W-D STILL STD., BUT MUCH ADVERTISING of 4-W-D MODELS.)

new GRILLE (1977)

CAN SEAT, HOLD, TOW, DO MORE THAN ORDINARY WAGONS.

SUBURBAN I.D. # CC (L) 167 (F) 100001 UP ('77) CC (L) 168 (−) 100001 UP ('78)

77-
79 A

CHEVY-VAN I.D. NOS. START AT CG (D) 157 (F) 100001 ('77) CG (D) 158 (−) 100001 ('78) PRICED FR. $4166. ('77) $4533. ('78)

PICKUP PRICES START FROM
$4201. $4533. $5765.
('77)   ('78)   ('79)(FLTSD.)

(CONT'D. NEXT PAGE)

PICKUP I.D. NOS. START AT
CC (V) 147 (F) 100001 ('77)
CC (−) 148 (−) 100001 ('78)
CC (L) 149 (−) 100001 ('79)

CHEVROLET 77-79-A

Chevrolet

DASH ('79)

ENGINES WITH LIGHT-MEDIUM-DUTY						ENGINES WITH HEAVY-DUTY EMISSIONS FOR MODELS OF 8501-LB. GVWR AND ABOVE			
EMISSIONS FOR MODELS OF 8,500-LB. GVWR AND BELOW FOR CALIFORNIA									
4.1L (250) L6	5.7L (350) V8	6.0L (400) V8	7.4L (454) V8	5.7L (350) V8 DIESEL	DISPLACEMENT—LITRE (CU. IN.)	4.8 (292) L6	5.7 (350) V8	6.0 (400) V8	7.4 (454) V8
LE3(B)	LS9(C)	LF4(B)	LF8(E)	LF9(D)	ENGINE ORDERING CODE	L25(B)	LS9(C)	LF4(B)	LF8(E)
3.9 x 3.5	4.0 x 3.5	4.1 x 3.8	4.3 x 4.0	4.06 x 3.38	BORE & STROKE (IN.)	3.9 x 4.1	4.0 x 3.5	4.1 x 3.8	4.3 x 4.0
8.3 to 1	8.2 to 1	8.2 to 1	8.0 to 1¼	22.5 to 1	COMPRESSION RATIO	7.8 to 1	8.3 to 1	8.3 to 1	7.9 to 1
130 @ 4000**	155 @ 3600	170 @ 3600	205 @ 3600	120 @ 3600	SAE NET HORSEPOWER @ RPM	115 @ 3400	165 @ 3800	180 @ 3600	210 @ 3600
205 @ 2000**	260 @ 2000	305 @ 1600	335 @ 2800	220 @ 1600	SAE NET TORQUE (LB.-FT.) @ RPM	215 @ 1600	255 @ 2800	310 @ 2400	340 @ 2800

('79)

Chevy K30 Chassis Cab Big Dooley

WITH WRECKER BODY

SOME 1979 LT. DUTY MODELS WITH BLACK VERTICAL PCS. IN GRILLE.

MEDIUM-DUTY

DUAL REAR WHEELS

77-79 (CONT'D.) B

Series 90 long and short conventional diesels.

SERIES 90

HEAVY-DUTY TRUCKS

BISON

new FOR 1977

New FOR 1978: BRUIN

TITAN 90 C.O.E. has new LARGE GRILLE (1979 ON.)

('79)

59

Chevrolet

STEPSIDE →

Gasoline and diesel engine specifications.

ENGINES WITH LIGHT-DUTY EMISSIONS FOR MODELS OF 8500-LB. GVWR AND BELOW.

DISPLACEMENT—LITRE (CU. IN.)	4.1L (250) L6	5.0L (305) V8	5.7L (350) V8*	6.0L (400) V8	7.4L (454) V8	5.7L (350) V8 DIESEL
ENGINE ORDERING CODE	LE3(B)	LG9(C)	LS9(C)	LF4(B)	LF8(E)	LF9(D)
BORE & STROKE (IN.)	3.9 x 3.5	3.74 x 3.48	4.0 x 3.5	4.1 x 3.8	4.3 x 4.0	4.06 x 3.38
COMPRESSION RATIO	8.3 to 1	8.4 to 1	8.2 to 1	8.2 to 1	8.0 to 1‡	22.5 to 1
SAE NET HORSEPOWER @ RPM	130 @ 4000	140 @ 4000	165 @ 3600	185 @ 3600	205 @ 3600	120 @ 3600
SAE NET TORQUE (LB.-FT.) @ RPM	210 @ 2000	240 @ 2000	270 @ 2000	300 @ 2400	335 @ 2800	220 @ 1600

ALL STATES EXCEPT CALIFORNIA

Chevenne trim.   (Available Silverado trim - Chevy's finest.)   Stepside Sport.

BUILT TO STAY TOUGH

DIESEL

Tough V8 diesel half-ton pickup.
Introduced just last year, the 5.7 Litre V8 diesel pickup may be ordered as either a C10 Fleetside or Stepside with either 6½-ft. or 8-ft. box.

(DIESEL **Available** SINCE 1978)

(DIESEL V8 FROM OLDS. DIV. OF GM)

CHEVROLET

PICKUPS FROM $5308.

I.D. # CC (L) 149 (-) 100001 UP

Fleetside

FLTSD. REAR DETAILS

SPT. GRILLE

VAN DASH

OPT. WH. CVR.

Custom Deluxe trim - it's standard.
Available Scottsdale trim.

LT. TRUCK SALES 1,832,454 **79**

VANS FROM $5210.

SLOTTED AREA BELOW PICKUP GRILLE IS NOW OF BRIGHT METAL.

Caravan.

G SERIES CHEVY-VAN

Option

AVAIL WH. COVERS. (STD. VAN WHEELS LIKE THOSE ON FLEETSIDE P.U. ILLUSTR. NR. TOP RT.)

VAN I.D. # CG (D) 159 (-) 100001 UP SPT. VAN: CG (-)169 (-) ETC.

60

CHEVROLET PICKUPS PRICED FROM $5738.

note → ROUND HDLTS. ON THIS MODEL.

CHEVY VAN FROM $5671.

G-SERIES

STEPSIDE 2-WHEEL DRIVE
A step between the door and extended rear fender helps you get at cargo. The 6½-ft. (C10) or 8-ft. box has a sealed wood floor with seven flush steel skid strips.

C10 DIESEL PICKUP
Chevy's C10 half-ton diesel pickup comes in Fleetside or Stepside styling. Its tough 5.7 Liter V8 diesel engine eliminates ordinary tune-ups. See page 11 for the wide range of standard equipment.

EPA EST. MPG **17** | EST. HWY **24**
TOUGH MILEAGE TO BEAT.

CHEVY VAN I.D. # CG (D) 16A (-) 100001 UP

135 HP @ 4200

STYLED | RALLY | CAST ALUMINUM

130 HP @ 4000

4.1 LITER SIX (250 CUBIC INCH)

4.8 LITER SIX (292 CUBIC INCH)

5.0 LITER V8 (305 CUBIC INCH)

5.7 LITER V8 (350 CUBIC INCH)

165~175 HP

115 HP @ 3400

PICKUP I.D. # CC (L) 14A (-) 100001 UP

80 A new GRILLE

ENGINES

6.6 LITER V8 (400 CUBIC INCH)

7.4 LITER V8 (454 CUBIC INCH)

5.7 LITER V8 DIESEL

180 HP @ 3600 | 210 HP @ 3800 | 125 HP @ 3600

BIG-10
Chevy BIG-10 is a heavy-duty half-tonner equipped to haul over a ton of payload, including driver, passengers, fuel and cargo. Heavy-duty suspension, brake system and tires help give it available GVWRs of 6050 to 6200 lbs.

CHEVY TRUCKS
BUILT TO STAY TOUGH

INTERIOR (SILVERADO)

CREW CAB/BONUS CAB 4-WHEEL DRIVE
Crew Cab 4x4 gets up to six workers to off-road jobs. Bonus Cab 4x4 carries up to three with extra cab cargo room for their gear. GVWRs for both: 8600 to 10,000 lbs. Big Dooley available.

CREW/BONUS CAB I.D. # CC (L) 23A (-) 100001 UP

164" WB

FR. $8047. (CR. CAB)

15 MPG (EPA) CITY

LT. TK. SALES 1,114,847

PICKUPS with 117, 131, 135, 149, 159 or 164" WB

Silverado instrument panel

DASH

(CONT'D. NEXT PAGE)

61

SUBURBAN C~20
FROM $7787.*
(I.D. # CC(L)16A(-)10000/ UP)

12 MPG (EPA) CITY
(w. 350 cid V8, A/T)

$6195. – $12,683.
1/2 – 3/4 – 1 – 2 TON PRICE RANGE

3-TON TILT CAB STILL AVAIL.
FROM $15,176.
BISON, BRUIN, TITAN AVAIL.

17 Main Transmissions. Take your choice of standard 4-speed or available synchromesh automatic and manual transmissions. There's even a Fuller 13-speed transmission available.

15 Wheelbases. Our wheelbases range from 125" to 254" with GVWRs from 13,800 to 50,000 lbs., and GCWRs from 32,000 to 60,000 lbs. And (in most states) our short cabs let you pull longer trailers with bigger payloads.

*
MIN. PRICE INCR. TO $8265. DURING 1980.)

CHEVY SUBURBAN.

SEATS UP TO 9.

new GRILLE (LT. DUTY/ SUBURBAN MODELS)

80 B
(CONT'D.)

4870 WAYS TO SPEC ONE TOUGH TRUCK
Above all, 1980 Chevy Mediums offer you choice. There's such an incredibly wide range of dependable components that you're bound to find the combination you need for your job.
25 Rear Axles. Choose from single, tag and tandem axles with capacities from 11,000 to 38,000 lbs.

NEW KODIAK
FIBERGLASS
TILT- HOOD
CAB WITH WIDE
GRILLE IS A REQUIRED
OPTION WITH THE ORDER OF A
CATERPILLAR OR CUMMINS
ENGINE.

Chevrolet's commitment to Medium-Duty trucks is demonstrated by our broad range of power and components for 1980.

BIG NEWS FOR 1980!

3 DIESEL CHOICES FOR TOUGH CHEVY MEDIUMS.

THE CATERPILLAR 3208
The "Cat" has built its reputation on high performance (up to 199 net HP in 49 states, 189 net HP in California). (Available after March 1, 1980.)

THE CUMMINS VT-225
This Cummins diesel features a heavy-duty design and it delivers 212 net horsepower at 3000 RPM. (Delivery later in 1980.) Not available in California.

THE DETROIT DIESEL ALLISON "FUEL PINCHER"
Direct from a leading diesel maker comes a brand-new 8.2 Liter V8 engine that's suited for the '80s. "The Fuel Pincher." (Available after March 1, 1980.)

DIESEL ENGINES ILLUSTRATED

CHEVROLET = 80-B

New Silverado instrument panel.

Chevrolet PICKUP

DASH NO LONGER *has* VERT. PCS. BY GAUGES.

STD. 2 HEADLTS. #1GCCC14 G(-)B(-) 10000I UP

new GRILLE ON PICKUP and SUBURBAN

4 HEADLTS. OPTIONAL

new PARK. LIGHTS MOVED TO BUMPER.

FROM $6392. (PICKUPS) $6639. (VANS)

CHEVROLET

STEPSIDE

STEP VANS FROM $10064.

VANS

Chevy Van Sport

CHEVY VAN ½ TON, 110" WB = $6750.*
3/4 TON, 110" WB = $7072.*
1 TON, 125" WB = $8415.
*$184. EXTRA FOR 125" WB

81

Step-Van.

G SERIES CHEVY-VAN
#1GCCG15D(-)B(-)10000I UP

18 MPG CITY, 25 HWY (250 CID 6)
17 CITY, 22 HWY. (new 305 CID V8)

CHEVROLET = 81

63

MEDIUM/HVY. 1981 MODELS AS BEFORE *

FRONT OF LT. DUTY MODELS TOTALLY **RESTYLED.** 2 HEADLIGHTS OR 4.

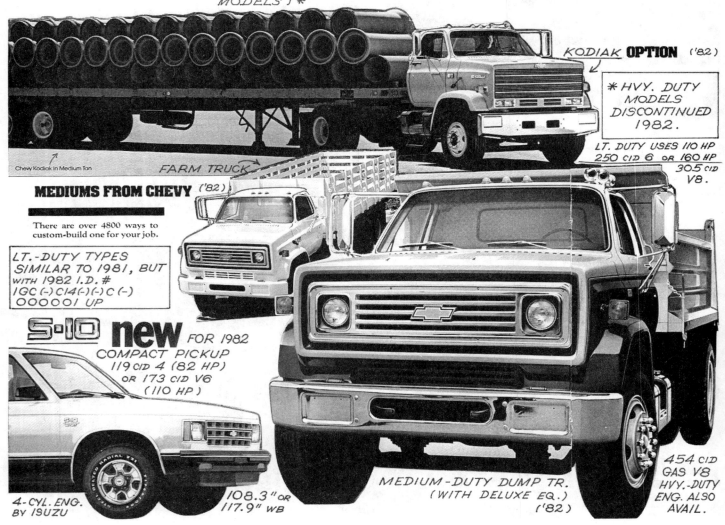

Chevrolet

DIESEL ENGINES.
6 HP VARIATIONS

DISPLACEMENT AND TYPE	8.2L V8 DIESEL	8.2L VBT DIESEL
BORE & STROKE (IN.)	4.25 x 4.41	4.25 x 4.41
COMPRESSION RATIO	18.3:1	16.9:1
SAE GROSS HORSEPOWER @ RPM	165 @ 3000	205 @ 3700
SAE NET HORSEPOWER @ RPM	153 @ 3000	193 @ 3000
SAE GROSS TORQUE (LBS. FT.) @ RPM	350 @ 1200	431 @ 1700
SAE NET TORQUE (LBS FT) @ RPM	337 @ 1200	414 @ 1700
DISPLACEMENT AND TYPE	3208 V8 DIESEL*	3208 V8 DIESEL*
BORE & STROKE (IN.)	4.5 x 5.0	4.5 x 5.0
COMPRESSION RATIO	18.2:1	18.2:1
SAE GROSS HORSEPOWER @ RPM	160 @ 2800	166 @ 2800
SAE NET HORSEPOWER @ RPM	149 @ 2800	154 @ 2600
SAE GROSS TORQUE (LBS FT) @ RPM	366 @ 1400	348 @ 1300
SAE NET TORQUE (LBS FT) @ RPM	362 @ 1400	343 @ 1300
DISPLACEMENT AND TYPE	3208 V8 DIESEL	3208 V8 DIESEL
BORE & STROKE (IN.)	4.5 x 5.0	4.5 x 5.0
COMPRESSION RATIO	16.5:1	16.5:1
SAE GROSS HORSEPOWER @ RPM	175 @ 2800	185 @ 2600
SAE NET HORSEPOWER @ RPM	164 @ 2800	175 @ 2600
SAE GROSS TORQUE (LBS FT) @ RPM	(2)405 @ 1400	452 @ 1400
SAE NET TORQUE (LBS FT) @ RPM	(2)390 @ 1400	425 @ 1400
DISPLACEMENT AND TYPE	3208 V8 DIESEL	3208 V8 DIESEL
BORE & STROKE (IN.)	4.5 x 5.0	4.5 x 5.0
COMPRESSION RATIO	16.4:1	6.4:1
SAE GROSS HORSEPOWER @ RPM	200 @ 2800	210 @ 2800
SAE NET HORSEPOWER @ RPM	189 @ 2800	199 @ 2800
SAE GROSS TORQUE (LBS FT) @ RPM	490 @ 1400	500 @ 1400
SAE NET TORQUE (LBS FT) @ RPM	473 @ 1400	473 @ 1400

*Not Available in Calif. **For use in Calif. only
(c) Federal ratings 425 @ 1400 Net in California
(d) Federal rating 413 @ 1400 Net in California

292 CID 6; 350, 366 OR 427 CID V8s (USED IN MED. DUTY).

$6679.-$9197. ('81)

1/2 - 3/4 - 1 TON PRICE RANGE

$7297.-$10,572. ('82)

('81)

81-82

GAS ENGINES. 4 DIFFERENT MODELS (125-210 HP)

(FINAL 1½ and 2-TON HEAVY-DUTY MODELS) *

KODIAK **OPTION** ('82)

* HVY. DUTY MODELS DISCONTINUED 1982.

LT. DUTY USES 110 HP 250 CID 6 OR 160 HP 305 CID V8.

Chevy Kodiak in Medium Tan

FARM TRUCK

MEDIUMS FROM CHEVY ('82)

There are over 4800 ways to custom-build one for your job.

LT.-DUTY TYPES SIMILAR TO 1981, BUT WITH 1982 I.D. # 1GC (-) C14(-)(-) C (-) 000001 UP

S-10 new FOR 1982 COMPACT PICKUP 119 CID 4 (82 HP) OR 173 CID V6 (110 HP)

4-CYL. ENG. BY ISUZU

108.3" OR 117.9" WB

MEDIUM-DUTY DUMP TR. (WITH DELUXE EQ.) ('82)

454 CID GAS V8 HVY.-DUTY ENG. ALSO AVAIL.

Chevrolet

NEW 6.2 DIESEL V8 379.4 CID (130 HP @ 3600 RPM) (AVAIL. AT EXTRA COST)

STEPSIDE

SCOTTSDALE

CREW CAB (ABOVE)

CUSTOM DE LUXE IS STILL THE STD. LOW-PRICED SERIES, WITH LESS TRIM, NO WINDSHIELD BRIGHTWORK.

new 4-SP. AUTO./ OVERDRIVE TRANSMISSION AVAILABLE

82 GAS ENGINES: 250 CID 6 (110 HP) 292 CID 6 (115 HP) * 305 CID V8 (160 HP) ★; 350 CID V8 (165 HP) 454 CID V8 (210 HP @ 3800 RPM)

★ = MADE IN CANADA
* = MADE IN MEXICO

SILVERADO (note ORNAMENT ON HOOD)

SILVERADO DASH

← OPTIONS →

SEE ALSO: GMC truck

CHEVY IS THE POWER IN TRUCKS.

1/2 TON, 6 1/2' BED	117" WB	=	$7297.
1/2 " 8' "	131" WB	=	7447.
3/4 " 8' "	131" WB	=	8656.
1 " 8' "	131" WB	=	9273.

CHEVROLET = 82

1 TON CAB-CHASSIS MODELS HAVE 135" WB = $9359. OR 159" WB = $9438. (1 1/2 and 2-TON CAB CHASSIS MODELS ALSO)

Chevrolet

CREW / BONUS CAB

MEDIUM DUTY

KODIAK

C-60, C-70

83 *new* GRILLE ON LT.-DUTY MODELS

VEHICLE I.D. #
IG (C or T) -
(W809) -D-#

VAN PRICES = $7738. TO $13,837.

6.2 LITER
(379 cid)
DIESEL V8
IS NOW OPTIONAL
IN
CHEVY VANS and
SPORTVANS
(GAS V8 or 6 STD.

4-W-D STEPSIDE →

$7551.-$10,797.
CONVENTIONAL
1/2 -3/4 -1 TON
PRICE RANGE

pickups

CAB (MED. DUTY)

CHASSIS-CAB

CHEVROLET

DIESEL 6.2 L

21M058

CHEVROLET 83

66

$7038. CHASSIS-CAB

108", 117" or 122" WB S-10 COMPACT MODELS

MAXI-CAB (T-10 4WD MODELS ALSO)

Chevrolet

S-10 4X4 BLAZER

(ABOVE) 125" WB
SPORTVAN.
PRICED FROM $11,653.

(110" WB G-SERIES VAN $8114. UP)

PICKUP GRILLE IS SIMILAR (LIKE '83)

84

S-10 100" WB BLAZER (ABOVE)

KODIAK

brand new

C.O.E. TILTMASTER

TURBO-DIESEL
STEEL TILT CAB

165 NET HP @ 3000 RPM (155 HP IN CALIF.)

142" 165", 181" OR 197" WB

MEDIUM-DUTY GRILLE

VEHICLE I.D. #
1G (C OR T)-
(W809)-E-#

CONVENTIONAL PICKUPS = $7918. UP
1 TON CAB-CHASSIS (135 OR 159" WB = $9672. UP
BONUS CAB = $10,597. UP
CREW CAB = 10,927. UP

CHEVROLET = 84

67

C20 Crew Cab Scottsdale in Doeskin Tan.

C-30

$11,395. and up CREW CAB

C20 Stepside Custom Deluxe with long box

C30 Chassis-Cab Custom Deluxe in Frost White with stake body provided by an independent supplier.

$10,824. 1 TON CHASSIS-CAB w. 164" WB

Electronic speed control and intermittent wiper shown on standard multi-function switch

PUSH
CRUISE WIPER OFF ON
OFF ON R/A DELAY LO

85

new 4.3 L "VORTEC" 262 CID V6 (155 HP)

ALSO 305, 350 or 454 CID (GAS) V8s OR 379 CID DIESEL V8 AVAIL.

LT. DUTY HAS new GRILLE w. FEWER HORIZ. PCS., new HEADLIGHT PLACEMENT. →

MODEL DESIGNATIONS:
C = 2WD
K = 4WD

10 = ½ T.
20 = ¾ T.
30 = 1 TON

CHEVROLET TFW202

(MED.-DUTY ON NEXT PAGE)

WHEEL STYLES

Cast aluminum wheels

Styled sport wheels

Rally Wheels

Wheel covers

SCOTTSDALE ↓

REAR STEP BUMPER IS OPTIONAL, AS IS SLIDING REAR WINDOW AND THE CARGO LIGHT ABOVE IT.

VEHICLE I.D. #
1G (C or T) – (W80Z) – F – #

CONVENTIONAL 117" WB ½-TON @ ½' FLT. BED PICKUP $8297.

117", 125", 131", 135", 159", and 164" WHEELBASES ON CONVENTIONAL MODELS.

INSTRUMENT PANEL (SILVERADO)

CHEVROLET

VARIATION IN LTS. (SCOTTSDALE)

Shown C10 Fleetside Silverado Custom Two-Tone in Silver and Midnight Black.

Chevrolet

TILTMASTER
WITH 5.7 LITER
TURBOCHARGED DIESEL ENG.
165 HP @ 3000 RPM
(155 HP IN
CALIFORNIA)

C-70 KODIAK
(KODIAK CAB OPTION
REQUIRED WITH THE
CATERPILLAR 3208
DIESEL ENG.)

(ABOVE)
TILTMASTER C.O.E.
DIESEL (137-209" WB)

85 B
(CONT'D.)
(16 AVAILABLE WHEELBASES, AS
WELL AS A CHOICE OF 4 GAS
AND 15 DIESEL ENGINES.)

MEDIUM-DUTY
CONVENTIONAL
DUMP
TRUCK

INSTRUMENT
PANEL (ABOVE)

C-50
(GAS)
125-167"
WB

C-60
(GAS, DSL.)
125-218"
WB

C-70
(GAS)
(DIESEL OPT.)
125-254"
WB

Grab
handles

CLOSER
DETAILS OF
REAR QUARTER
SECTION (CONV.
MED. CAB)

TRANSMISSIONS MFD. BY =
ALLISON
NEW PROCESS
CLARK
FULLER OR
SPICER

MEDIUM-DUTY AVAILABLE ENGINES:
GASOLINE = 5.7 L 350 CID V8 ; 6L 366 CID V8 ; 7L 427 CID V8 ;
OR 292 CID 6 (125 HP)
DIESEL = 8.2 L V8 DETROIT DIESEL OR CATERPILLAR 3208 (160 TO 250 HP)

CHEVROLET = 85-B

CHEVY TRUCK

COMPACT SIZED
S-10 BLAZER
FROM $12858.('86) $13635.('87)
101" WB

BLAZER V8 V.I.N. K18H ('86) V18H ('87)
("C" SUFFIX
IF A
DIESEL
V8)

(FINAL EL CAMINO
CAR/PICKUP IN 1987)

BLAZER

S-10 PICKUPS FROM
$6456. ('86) (EL)
$6690. ('87)

$14146. ('86)
$15229. ('87)
107" WB

S-10
108,118 or
123" WB
4 CYL.
OR
V6

V.I.N.
S14E
(4WD
"T"
SUFFIX)

('87)
S-10

FULL SIZED 117" WB
PICKUPS FROM
$10444. ('86)
$11266. ('87)
117" or 131"
WHEELBASE
V6, V8 or V8 DIESEL

DASH
(S-10)

T18E   S10 BLAZER
'87)

Pickups

GRILLE
OF FULL-SIZED
VAN is SIMILAR

GRILLE
(FULL SIZED
PICKUPS)

SIDE
TRIM

1986

86-87

1986 EXAMPLES, UNLESS
OTHERWISE INDICATED

ASTRO
MINI VANS

4 CYL. M15E ('86)

M15Z ('87) V6

FROM $11038. ('86)

FROM $12043.
('87)

Van

ASTRO
INTRODUCED 1985
111" WB 4 CYL. or
V6

ASTRO
CARGO
VAN
$8633.
('86)
$9384.
('87)

LARGER
VANS
ON
FOLLOWING
PAGES

CHEVROLET TRUCKS and VANS   86~87

CHEVROLET = 86~87

COMPACT
S-10 PICKUPS FROM $7198.
FULL-SIZED
EXTENDED CAB PICKUPS C-1500
(156" WB LONG BED) $13824.

CHEVROLET

R-2500 FULL-SIZED
BONUS CAB PICKUPS (165" WB)
$15673. UP
CREW CAB
$16109. UP (165" WB)

THE *Heartbeat* OF AMERICA
TODAY'S CHEVY TRUCK $6990.
(EL)
S-10

S-10 BLAZER $14897.
$14987.

REGULAR CAB

S-10

S-10
MAXI CAB
$9357.

T18R

CHEVROLET

new GRILLE

S-10
4 CYL. OR V6 (V.I.N. S14E)

CHEVROLET

117" OR 131" WB
C-1500 PICKUPS (½ TON)
$12427. and up V.I.N. C14H

C-2500 (¾ TON)
$13454. and up
V6, V8 OR
V8 DIESEL

REAR
(FULL-SIZED
PICKUP)

88

C 3500 CHASSIS CAB 131" WB

CHEYENNE
FULL SIZED
PICKUPS

SILVERADO

C-3500 (1 TON)
$13853.
and up
V.I.N. C34K

SPORTVAN
$13315.
and
up
V.I.N.
G15F.

G-SERIES
Chevy Cargo and
Passenger Vans.

$12586.
and up
(CARGO
VANS)
V6, V8 OR V8
DIESEL
G15Z

CHEVROLET TRUCKS and VANS   88

71

CHEVROLET TRUCKS

EACH YEAR, REFERRED TO AS EITHER "CHEVY" OR CHEVROLET TRUCKS

S10 BLAZER ('89)

$15221. ('89)

STD. CAB (LONG BOX)

S-10

MAXI-CAB

OLDER STYLE S10 GRILLE ('89)

EXTENDED CAB DETAIL (AS ON SILVERADO)

C/K SPORTSIDE

(4WD S-10 "EL" has BLACK GRILLE w. 3 VERT. PCS. and CENTER HORIZ. PC. BEARING EMBLEM.)

STEP VAN ←

(454 SS has BLACKED OUT GRILLE)

C3500 HD CHASSIS CAB

MEDIUM DUTY / HVY. TRUCKS AVAILABLE EACH YEAR.

K3500 CHASSIS CAB w. LANDSCAPER'S BODY FROM INDEPENDENT SUPPLIER

↙ ASTRO VAN ↘

111" WB

4 OR V6

ASTRO FROM $13746. ('89) TO $16726. ('92)

89-92

1992 EXAMPLES UNLESS OTHERWISE INDICATED

(ASTRO CARGO VANS ALSO AVAIL.)

LUMINA APV (SINCE 1990)

↙ SPORTVAN ↘ EXTENDED BODY 12 ~ 15 PASS.

V6 110" WB

WITH FIBERGLAS BODY

(compare WITH GMC RALLY WAGON)

LUMINA APV
1990 = $15300.
1991 = 16045.
1992 = 17255.

(APV CARGO VANS ALSO AVAIL.)

1989	SPORTVAN $15393. UP	CARGO VAN	$13084. UP
1990	17056.		14506.
1991	18518.		15496.
1992	19266.		16246.

CHEVROLET = 89~92

Corbitt

* NO TRUCKS 1953 TO 1956

LEELAND HOTEL

RICHARD J. CORBITT, FOUNDER

('21) 3½-TON "A" $4650.

CORBITT BUSES ALSO, STARTING 1915

('23) 1-TON SPEED TRUCK

MODELS (1927)
(CONTINENTAL ENGS.)

20-21	1 TON	6 CYL.
25	1½	4
40, C	2	"
B	2½	"
3-4 TON		"
70	5	"

Truck

ALL 4-CYL. UNTIL 1926

('24) 2½ TON B $2970.
152" WB

NOTE OVAL QUARTER WINDOWS IN CAB.

NEW 56 2½-TON TANKER
('28)
4 CYL., 152" WB

CONTINENTAL ENGINES
BUDA ENG. IN SOME 5-TON MODELS.

('29) 1¼ TON "620"
$1400. 6 CYL.
(CHASSIS) 137" WB
HYDRAULIC BRAKES

1920s-1930s

SCHOOL BUS

1934 AUBURN CAR → (NOTE SIMILARITY)

(C. '36)

LIGHTWEIGHT SER. SAME FRONT END AS A 1934 AUBURN CAR.

1935-1936 MODELS, USING 1934 BODY DIES BOUGHT FROM AUBURN

AVAIL. TO 1938 w. LYCOMING ENG.

COCA COLA BOTTLER'S TRUCK ('34) ↓

CAB / CHASSIS ('35)

CORBITT ~ TO 1930s

(CONT'D. NEXT PAGE)

Corbitt Trucks

('37) note OLD-STYLE CAB W. ARCH WINDOWS.

CORBITT ('34) BUSES

1930s (CONT'D.)

HVY. TRACTOR

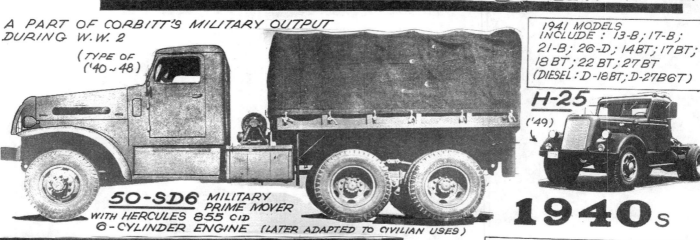

A PART OF CORBITT'S MILITARY OUTPUT DURING W.W. 2

(TYPE OF ('40~48)

50-SD6 MILITARY PRIME MOVER WITH HERCULES 855 CID 6-CYLINDER ENGINE (LATER ADAPTED TO CIVILIAN USES)

1941 MODELS INCLUDE: 13-B; 17-B; 21-B; 26-D; 14BT; 17BT; 18BT; 22BT; 27BT (DIESEL: D-18BT; D-27B6T)

H-25 ('49)

1940s

CONTINENTAL, HERCULES, and CUMMINS ENGINES

$1500. TO $7750., 1941 CHASSIS PRICE RANGE

Corbitt HENDERSON, N.C.

CORBITT RADIATOR INSIGNIA

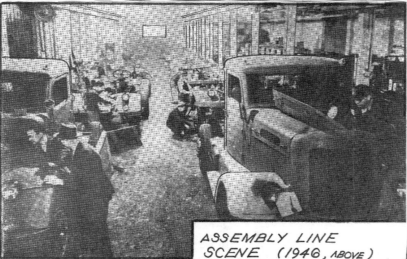

ASSEMBLY LINE SCENE (1946, ABOVE)

(600 SOLD IN 1946)

DIESEL

FRONT END RESTYLED

1950s

NEW GRILLE with HORIZONTAL PCS.

CUMMINS "HRBB" 175 HP DIESEL ENGINE IN 1951 MODEL →

('52) WITH NEW 1-PC. WINDSHIELD

(FINAL CORBITTS SIMILAR TO ABOVE ILLUSTRATION)

CORBITT ~ 70 1950s

Diamond Reo

(1967 - 1975) (1977 ON)

EMBLEM

DIAMOND REO TRUCKS
A Division of White Motor Corporation / Lansing, Michigan 48920

(FORMED 1967 THROUGH A MERGING
OF *DIAMOND T* and *REO*.)

(MAY 1, 1967 IS OFFICIAL
DATE OF CONSOLIDATION.)

68-69

CF-59 COMPACT (BELOW)

FORWARD TILT HOOD SECTIONS
(ON C-90-D, C-114,
OPTIONAL ON C-101)

(SHORT 90" BBC)

"CF-68 TREND" with (GASOLINE OR DIESEL ENGINES)

←TILT CAB OF PLASTIC-LIKE "Royalex."

C-90-D →

"GOLD COMET" 6 CYL. and V-8 GASOLINE ENGINES (130 H.P. TO 235 H.P.)

C-101

ALSO, A SELECTION OF 27 DIESELS (CUMMINS, DETROIT, CATERPILLAR.)

"CF-83"
(with FORWARD-TILT CAB = FIBERGLASS OPTIONAL.)

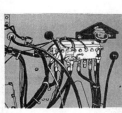

LOW-MAINTENANCE ELECTRICAL SYSTEM

CO-78

(SHORT W.B., GAS OR DIESEL)

(with 84" SLEEPER BUNK, 190 TO 335 H.P. DIESEL ENGINES

C-114

(CHOICE OF STEEL OR ALUMINUM COMPONENTS, FRONT AXLE FORWARD OR SET BACK.)

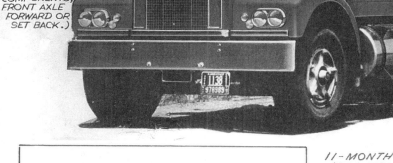

ABOVE:

CAB OF MODELS C-90-D, C-114, and DC-101

DIESEL ENGINES AVAILABLE
(TO 335 H.P.)

11-MONTH SALES, 1967
(MAY INCLUDE DIAMOND T and REO) = 3643
1968 = 3245

DIAMOND REO 68-69

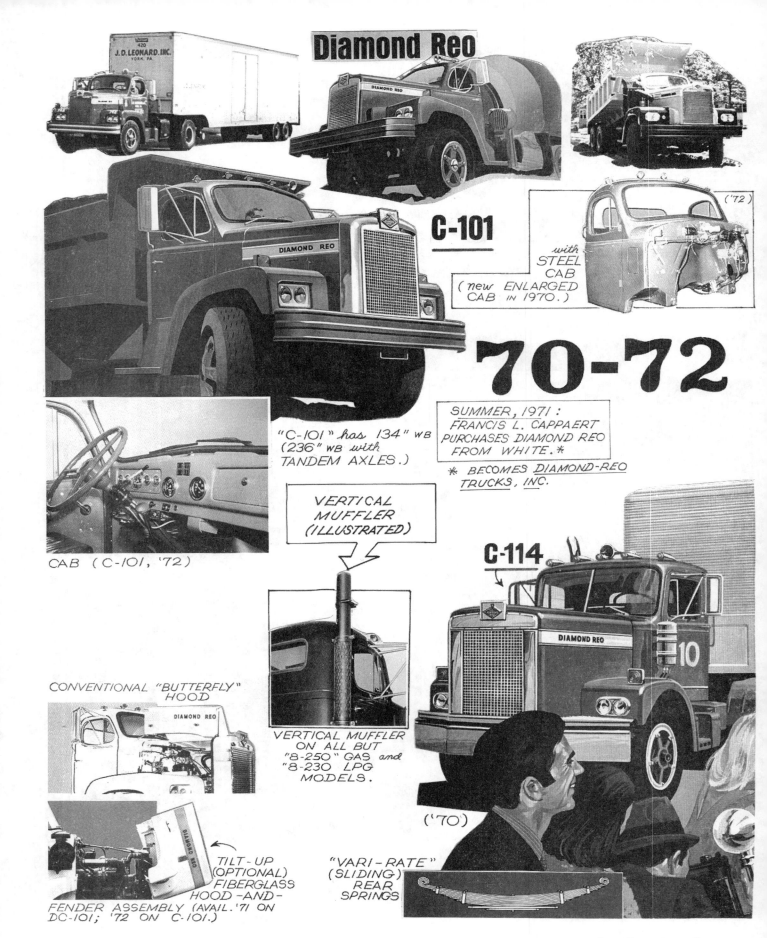

Diamond Reo

C-101

('72)
with STEEL CAB
(new ENLARGED CAB IN 1970.)

70-72

SUMMER, 1971: FRANCIS L. CAPPAERT PURCHASES DIAMOND REO FROM WHITE.*

* BECOMES DIAMOND-REO TRUCKS, INC.

"C-101" has 134" WB (236" WB with TANDEM AXLES.)

CAB (C-101, '72)

VERTICAL MUFFLER (ILLUSTRATED)

VERTICAL MUFFLER ON ALL BUT "8-250" GAS and "8-230" LPG MODELS.

C-114

DIAMOND REO

10

('70)

CONVENTIONAL "BUTTERFLY" HOOD

TILT-UP (OPTIONAL) FIBERGLASS HOOD -AND- FENDER ASSEMBLY (AVAIL.'71 ON DC-101; '72 ON C-101.)

"VARI-RATE" (SLIDING) REAR SPRINGS

DIAMOND REO 70~72

DOUBLE TOP TANK REMOVES TRAPPED AIR FROM RADIATOR.

Diamond Reo

DC-101

CityTime Service
VI.9-2222

50 - GALLON FUEL TANK STANDARD (40, 43, 62 OR 65 - GAL. TYPES ALSO AVAIL.)

NO. 61

gasoline, LPG and diesel

("ROYALE" C.O.E. INTRO. FALL, 1972. 6, V8 OR V-12 DETROIT DIESEL ENGS. USED)

"GOLD COMET" GAS ENGINES from 170 TO 250 HP.

"CLEAN-AIRE" LPG ENGINES from 190 OR 230 HP.

72 ON

CUMMINS DIESEL

CUMMINS OR DETROIT DIESEL ENGINES

DC-101

CAB ('72)

"C-92-D" new FOR '72.

CONVENTIONALS RENAMED "APOLLO," WITH 6 CYL. OR V8 CUMMINS, DETROIT OR CATERPILLAR ENG.

('72)

(SPRING, 1974 new "RAIDER" C-119 CONVENTIONAL has COLUMN OF 7 DIAMONDS ON LARGE GRILLE.)

POWER HYDRAULIC STEERING OPTIONAL

DIAMOND REO TAKEN OVER NOV. 3, 1975, BY CONSOLIDATED INDUSTRIES, COLUMBUS, OHIO.

DIAMOND REO MILITARY TRUCKS' PRODUCTION RESUMED 1972, FOR THE FIRST TIME SINCE 1968.

PRODUCTION OF 6 AVAIL. MODELS SUSPENDED SEPT., 1975. RESUMES 1977 WITH ONE MODEL, BY OSTERLUND, INC., HARRISBURG, PA.

OSTERLUND SELLS ITS DIAMOND-REO GIANT CO. TO NEW DIAMOND T CO. IN 1993.

DIAMOND REO "GIANT" AVAIL. SINCE 1978.

MODEL C-11664-DB

DIAMOND-REO TRUCKS AVAILABLE IN MID-1990s.

DIAMOND REO 72 ON

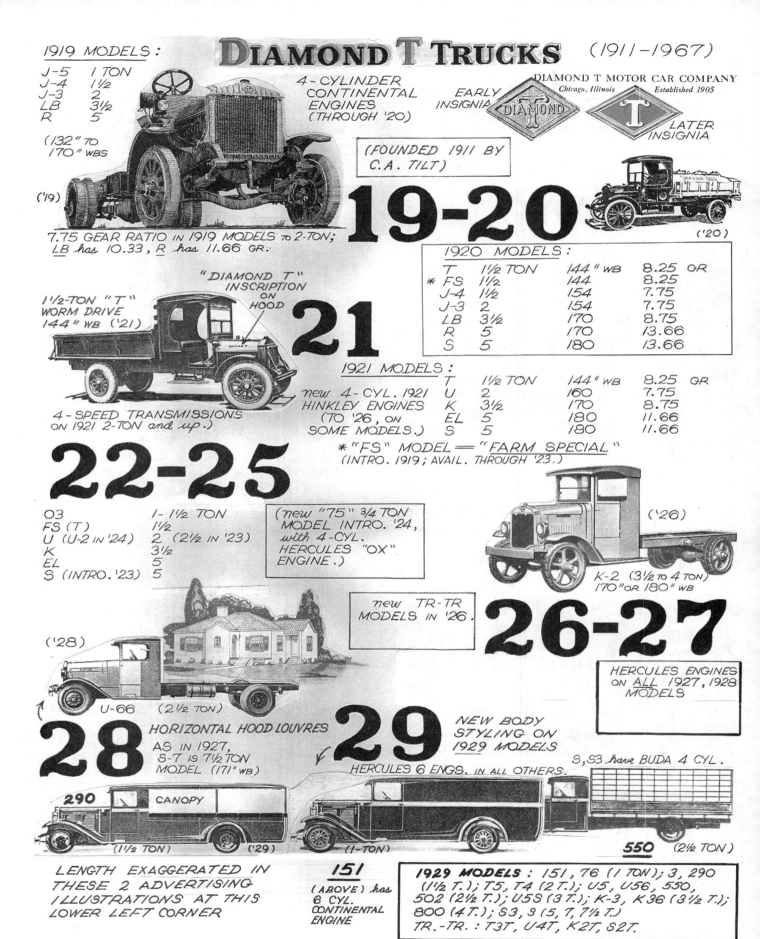

DIAMOND T TRUCKS (1911–1967)

DIAMOND T MOTOR CAR COMPANY
Chicago, Illinois — Established 1905

EARLY INSIGNIA — DIAMOND / T — LATER INSIGNIA

1919 MODELS:

J-5	1 TON
J-4	1½
J-3	2
LB	3½
R	5

(132" TO 170" WBS

('19)

4-CYLINDER CONTINENTAL ENGINES (THROUGH '20)

(FOUNDED 1911 BY C.A. TILT)

19-20

('20)

7.75 GEAR RATIO IN 1919 MODELS TO 2-TON; LB has 10.33, R has 11.66 GR.

1½-TON "T" WORM DRIVE 144" WB ('21)

"DIAMOND T" INSCRIPTION ON HOOD

21

4-SPEED TRANSMISSIONS ON 1921 2-TON and up.)

1920 MODELS:

T	1½ TON	144" WB	8.25	GR
* FS	1½	144	8.25	
J-4	1½	154	7.75	
J-3	2	154	7.75	
LB	3½	170	8.75	
R	5	170	13.66	
S	5	180	13.66	

1921 MODELS:

new 4-CYL. 1921 HINKLEY ENGINES (TO '26, ON SOME MODELS.)

T	1½ TON	144" WB	8.25	GR
U	2	160	7.75	
K	3½	170	8.75	
EL	5	180	11.66	
S	5	180	11.66	

* "FS" MODEL = "FARM SPECIAL" (INTRO. 1919; AVAIL. THROUGH '23.)

22-25

O3	1-1½ TON
FS (T)	1½
U (U-2 IN '24)	2 (2½ IN '23)
K	3½
EL	5
S (INTRO. '23)	5

(new "75" ¾ TON MODEL INTRO. '24, with 4-CYL. HERCULES "OX" ENGINE.)

('26)

K-2 (3½ TO 4 TON) 170" OR 180" WB

new TR-TR MODELS IN '26.

26-27

HERCULES ENGINES ON ALL 1927, 1928 MODELS

('28)

U-66 (2½ TON)

28

HORIZONTAL HOOD LOUVRES AS IN 1927, S-7 IS 7½ TON MODEL (171" WB)

29

NEW BODY STYLING ON 1929 MODELS

HERCULES 6 ENGS. IN ALL OTHERS.

S, S3 have BUDA 4 CYL.

290 CANOPY (1½ TON) ('29)

(1-TON)

550 (2½ TON)

LENGTH EXAGGERATED IN THESE 2 ADVERTISING ILLUSTRATIONS AT THIS LOWER LEFT CORNER

151 (ABOVE) has 6 CYL. CONTINENTAL ENGINE

1929 MODELS: 151, 76 (1 TON); 3, 290 (1½ T.); T5, T4 (2 T.); U5, U56, 550, 502 (2½ T.); U5S (3 T.); K-3, K36 (3½ T.); 800 (4 T.); S3, 9 (5, T, 7½ T.)
TR.-TR.: T3T, U4T, K2T, S2T.

DIAMOND T = 19~29

DIAMOND T TRUCKS

DIAMOND T MOTOR CAR CO., CHICAGO

30

MODELS: 200, 151 (1 TON;)
290 (1½ T;) 303 (2 T;)
551, 503, 506 (2½ T;)
602, 606 (3 T;) 700 (3½ T;)
1000 (5 TON;)
    TR.-TR.: 303 (2 T;)
    503, 551 (2½ T;)
    602 (3 TON)

31

HOOD VENT DOORS AS ON '33 (BELOW)

4-CYL., 57 HP BUDA ENG. IN "200."
6-CYL., 61 HP BUDA ENG.
IN new "215" (1-TON, 135" WB.)
"503" DISCONTINUED.

32

new 8-TON "1603" 6-WHEELER
has 6-CYL., 127-HP WAUKESHA
ENGINE. 6-CYL. HERC. ENGS.
(56 TO 124 HP) CONT'D. IN OTHERS.

$545 STANDARD CHASSIS

1933 MODELS: 210 SF, 210 FF (1½ TON;)
240A (1¾ T;) 310 (2 T;)
350 (2½ T;) 410A, 410B,
504A, 506A (3 T;)
603, 606B (3-4 T;)
510 (4 T;) 750 (4-5 T;)
6-WHEELERS: 801 (4 T;)
1201 (6 T;)
1602, 1603 (8 TON)

4 and 5-SP. TRANSMISSIONS
135" WB and up

('33)
MODEL 210
228 CID
80 HP

1½ ton, six-cylinder

('33½)

$595

new 1½ TON DELUXE "211," with
new GRILLE and V-WINDSHIELD
(INTRO. SUMMER, 1933)
228 CID **$595**.

33-34

$575. = "210 SF" 1½ TON CH.

1934 MODELS:
211 SF, 211 FF, 226.
(1½ TON;) 241 (1¾ T;)
311, 261 (2 T;)
351, 326B, 326 DR (2½ T;) 410A,
376 (3 T;) 510, 425 (4 T;) 603A,
525 (5 T;) 740 (5-6 T;) 750,
750H (5-7 T;) 1515 (7½ T)
(SAME 6-WHEELERS
AS IN 1933.)

SERIAL # FROM	
54353	('33)
56758	('34)
77001	('35)

(LATE '33)
140"-WB SUPER-STREAMLINED
1500-GALLON TANKER with
6-CYL. (4½" × 5¼")
REAR ENGINE

35

211A (1½ T;) 220, 227, 243 (1½-2 T;)
311C (2 T;) 312 (2-2½ T;) 351C (2½ T;)
352 (2½-3 T;) 412B (3 T;) 512B, 412 DR,
(4 T;) 512 DR (5 TON)

63 TO 118 HP

STREAMLINED 1935 BODY AND
new HORIZ. VENT TRIM

('35)

(LENGTH EXAGGERATED)

PANEL STAKE

$575

135" WHEELBASE
1935 1½-TON CHASSIS
211-A
$555.

DIAMOND T = 30 ~ 35

DIAMOND T TRUCKS

301 CHASSIS

301
1-1½ TON STARTS JUNE, 1937.

¾ TON 80 →

new GRILLE and LOUVRES

36-37

$525.*

*= CHASSIS PRICE

PANEL

PICKUP

80 (¾ TON) is new FOR 1937, with 205 CID ENG. (61 HP @ 3300 RPM) and 119" WB (4.5-5.1 GR) D-20, D-30 DIESELS also new. 412 B and 228 S   4.5 TO 7.27 GRS DISC.
'37 SER. # FROM 302003 (¾ TON); 3010001 (1 TON); 209276 (1½ TON)

1936 MODELS:
212 AS (1½-2 TON;) 212 BS (1½-2½ T;) 221 S, 228 S (1½-3 T;) 244 S (2-3 T;) 313, 320 (2-4 T;) 353, 360 (2½-4 T;) 412 B (3-4 T;) 512 B, 412 DR (4-5 T;) 512 DR (5-6½ TON)
1936 SERIAL #s START AT 204001 (1 TON, 1½ TON) 300001 (¾ TON)   63 TO 118 HP, 228-404 CID ALL HERC. 6 ENGINES, AS BEFORE.

'38 = 304324 (¾ TON); 3010427 (1 T.); 213077 (1½ T.)

38

INTRO. OCT., '37. new C.O.E. MODELS →

VAN BODY

new GRILLE ('38)

80 (¾ TON;) 301, 304 (1-1½ T;) 401 (1½-2 T C.O.E.;) 402 (1½-2½ T C.O.E.;) 404, 212 AS (1½-2½ T;) 212 BS, 221 S, 405, 406 (1½-3 T;) 507 (2-3 T C.O.E.;) D-20 (2-3½ TON DIESEL;) 244 S, 509 (2-3½ T;) 607 (2-4 T C.O.E.;) 313, 320, 611, 612 (2-4 T;) 609 (2½-4½ T C.O.E.;) 353, 613 (2½-4½ T;) 360, 614 (2½-5 T;) D-30 (2½-4½ TON DIESEL;) 512 B, 412 DR (4-5½ T;) 512 DR (5-6½ T)

GRILLE JOINED with LOUVRES ON 1938 CONVENTIONALS.

PANEL STAKE

78 TO 118 HP ('38)
4.5 TO 7.37 GEAR RATIOS

('38)

1939 SERIAL #s FROM 2010368 (1 TON) 3060183 (1½ TON)

61 TO 118 HP
4.5 TO 8.4 GEAR RATIOS

39

new HEAVIER GRILLE, STRAIGHT BUMPERS

new HEADLIGHT MOUNTS

201 (1 TON;) 305 (1-1½ T;) 306 (1½ T;) 401 (1½-2 T C.O.E.;) 402 (1½-2½ T C.O.E.;) 404 (1½-2½ T;) 405, 406 (1½-3 T;) 507 (2-3 T C.O.E.;) 513 (2-3½ TON DIESEL;) 509 (2-3½ T;) also, MANY OTHER MODELS, from #231 to 804, up to 5-6½ TON "512-DR."

(new DOOR-TO-DOOR DELIVERY UNITS: MODELS 231, 332, 333)

DIAMOND T = 36~39

DIAMOND T

('40)

1940 PRICE RANGE :
$575. (MODEL 201)
TO
$5600. (MODELS
807 OR 808
DIESELS)

C.F. and C.O.E.
TYPES AVAIL.

STARTING
1940,
CUMMINS
ENGINES
AVAIL. IN
SOME DIESEL
MODELS.
(100 OR 150 HP)

"PaK-Age-Car" DELIVERY
UNITS INCLUDED IN
LINE (1940-1942)
(PURCHASED IN
SPRING, 1939 BY
DIAMOND T, has
133 CID, 4-CYL.
LYCOMING ENGINE
with 32 HP @ 2400 RPM.)
FROM $1095. ('40)

AS BEFORE, 6-CYL.
HERCULES GAS and
DIESEL ENGINES IN
OTHER MODELS.
UP TO 132 HP (1940)

heavy-duty

1940 MODEL
LINE UP =
201, 306, 404, 404-H,
406, 509, 509-H,
612, 612-H, 614,
614-DR, 614-H, 614-HDR, 805, 806,
513*, 615*, 807*, 808*, 900, 306-SC (C.F.), 404-SC (C.F.),
404-SCH (C.F.)   C.O.E.s: 201-C, 404-C, 509-C, 612-C, 614-C,
805-C, 806-C, 513-C*, 615-C*   (ALSO MODELS
(* = WITH DIESEL ENGINE)   91 and 117
PAK-AGE-CARS)

EARLY-1940s

1940 SERIAL
NOS. FROM
2011012 (201-S, D)
306/259 (306-S)
4045002 (404-S
LT. MODELS)

VARIOUS
PRE-WAR and WARTIME
MODELS ON THIS PAGE.

('42)

LT.

HVY.
(note HEADLIGHT and
BUMPER DIFFERENCE
BETW. LT., HVY.)

ARMORED
"HALF TRACK"
(ABOVE)

('42)

MILITARY VEHICLES
(W.W. 2 YEARS)

('43)

REAR
SECTION OF
THIS TYPE USUALLY
COVERED BY CANVAS IN
COLD OR RAINY WEATHER.

MILITARY
6 × 6 "PRIME MOVER"

1941 LT. CIVILIAN SERIAL NOS.
FROM 2011639 (201-L, 201-S
or 201-D)
FROM 4046817 (404-S)

DIAMOND T = EARLY 40s

DIAMOND T
LATER
1940s

GAS ENGINES = HERCULES
DIESEL   "   = CUMMINS
77 to 150 HP

HEAVY-HAULING TRACTOR/TRAILER

('45) GRILLE and TRIM PAINTED IN BODY COLOR.

FEWER POSTWAR MODELS FOR 1946: 404HH, 509, 509 SC, 614H, 702, 806H, 900; 910 DIESEL

6 WHEELERS:
900 SD300PA;
910 SW3002PA DIESEL,
910 SD462W DIESEL

STANDARD OF CALIFORNIA

ROY E. SMITH

('47) CAB-FORWARD TANKER

MORE MODELS IN 1947:

201, 306, 306H, 404HH, 404 SC, 404 SCH, 509, 509H, 509 SC, 614H, 703, 809, 901;

910 DIESEL

ALSO, 5 6-WHEELERS

CONTINENTAL ENGINES IN 703, 809, 901 MODELS (START. 1947.)

AIR BRAKES

DIAMOND T TRUCKS

MODEL 201 ('49)

PICKUP

DIESEL "910"
TRACTOR/TRAILER RIG   ('47)
172" TRACTOR WB
672 CID CUMMINS "HB~600"
ENGINE 150 HP @ 1800 RPM

7.08 and other GEAR RATIOS

Diamond T Model 910 handles 68,000 pounds gross weight with Diamond T reliability. Golden Gate Bridge in background.

Big Rig

DIAMOND T=LATER '40s

82

DIAMOND T TRUCKS

NO LT. DUTY MODELS AFTER 1951.

1950s and LATER

1953 MODELS:
323, 422, 522, 622, 660, 720, 722, 920;
DIESELS: 723, 921, 921BR, 921FN, 950RS, 951S
6-WHEELERS ALSO

(SOME O.H.V. ENGINES)

HEAVY-DUTY

Models 422—112 Horsepower . . . . for 3-5 ton loads
Models 522—123 Horsepower . . . for 3½-6 ton loads
Models 622—141 Horsepower . . . . for 4-7 ton loads

with Diamond T Valve-in-head Engines

CONTINENTAL, HERCULES, OWN, CUMMINS and BUDA 6-CYL. ENGINES ('53) (112 TO 300 HP)

('52)

MODEL "660"
162 HP (164 HP @ 2700 in '53.)

new TILT-CAB C.O.E. (SPRING, 1953 INTRO.)

ACQUIRED 1958 BY WHITE MOTOR CO.

NEW MODEL 353 1½ TON

with 6-CYL. OHV 252.6 CID ENG. 113 HP @ 3500 RPM

T-662 ('59) (AVAIL. THROUGH 1950s)

1960: PROD. MOVED TO REO FACTORY

C.O.E. DESIGN LATER SOLD TO INTERNATIONAL.

DIESEL ('61)

GAS-POWERED ('62)

C.O.E.
('59)

DIESEL
OWN, CUMMINS and HALL-SCOTT 6 CYL. ENGINES (153-262 HP)

DURING 1967, BECOMES **Diamond Reo**

DIAMOND REO

('67)

C.O.E. (1960s)

DIAMOND T = 50 ON

DODGE
Dodge Brothers Trucks

DODGE BROS., DETROIT (1917~1928) DODGE DIVISION OF CHRYSLER CORP. (SINCE JUNE, 1928)

17-21
4 CYL. (TO '28)

(ALSO CARS SINCE LATE 1914)

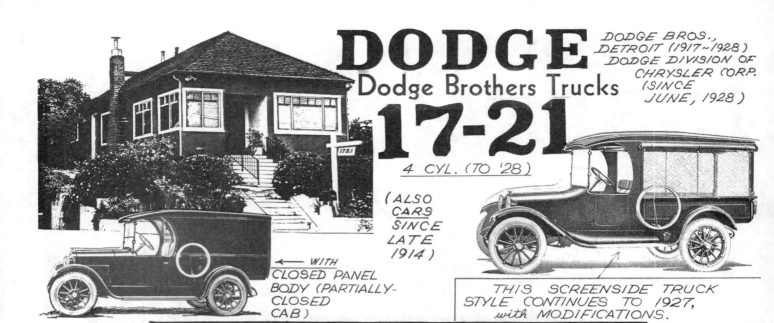

← WITH CLOSED PANEL BODY (PARTIALLY-CLOSED CAB)

THIS SCREENSIDE TRUCK STYLE CONTINUES TO 1927, with MODIFICATIONS.

(ABOVE) ('25) (ONE OF THOSE SOLD UNDER "DODGE BROS." NAME)

22-28

DURING THESE YEARS, MOST DODGE BROS. TRUCKS SOLD UNDER "GRAHAM BROS." NAME. SEE "GRAHAM BROS." (GRAHAM BROS. '22 TO EARLY '27 TRUCKS ESSENTIALLY DODGE BROS.)

"DODGE BROS." NAME RETURNS ON TRUCKS, JANUARY, 1929.

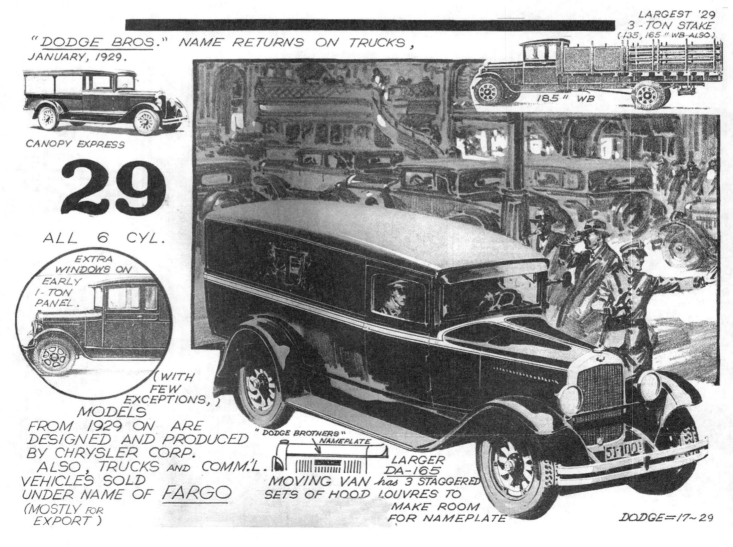

LARGEST '29 3-TON STAKE (135, 165" WB ALSO) 185" WB

CANOPY EXPRESS

29

ALL 6 CYL.

EXTRA WINDOWS ON EARLY 1-TON PANEL.

(WITH FEW EXCEPTIONS,) MODELS FROM 1929 ON ARE DESIGNED AND PRODUCED BY CHRYSLER CORP. ALSO, TRUCKS AND COMM'L. VEHICLES SOLD UNDER NAME OF FARGO (MOSTLY FOR EXPORT)

"DODGE BROTHERS" NAMEPLATE

LARGER DA-165 MOVING VAN has 3 STAGGERED SETS OF HOOD LOUVRES TO MAKE ROOM FOR NAMEPLATE

DODGE = 17~29

DODGE
Profitable Truck Engines
30

CANOPY TRUCK

SOME CANOPY and STAKE TRUCKS (UP TO 3 TON) AVAIL. WITH SAME FRONTAL STYLING AS 1927½–1928 GRAHAM BROS. (AS ABOVE)

(10', 1½, 2 OR 3 TON)

6 CYL., L-HEAD

HALE AND SON HAULING

No 24

BASIC MODELS:

½ TON	109" WB	4 CYL.	45 HP
1 TON	140	6	
1½ TON	150, ETC.	6	63
2 TON	" "	6	
3 TON	135-185	6	78

¾ AND 1-TON AVAIL. SUMMER, 1930, with 4 OR 6 CYL. ENGINE, AFTER 4-CYL. RETURNS. (40 MODELS WITH 12 WHEELBASES)

PANEL TRUCK 8', 1 TON 4 OR 6 CYL.

LATER IN YEAR, 1½ TON PRICES BEGIN AS LOW AS $595.

NOTE THE DIFFERENCES IN THE RADIATOR DESIGNS

189.8 CID 6 CYL. (60 HP @ 3400 RPM) TOURING CAR CAR ('30½) (LT. COMMERCIAL SPECS. SIMILAR)

109" WB

1930½ DODGE 6 CAR and LIGHT COMMERCIAL INTERIOR

DODGE = 30

85

DODGE

QUARTER WINDOWS CONT'D.
IN SOME HEAVY DUTY MODELS.

3 TON F-60, 61, 62 W.
96 HP 6

31

2-TON
6-CYL.
F-40
and
F-41 WITH
96 HP @
3000
RPM

UNUSUAL "DB" SPIDER
RADIATOR GUARD

STAGGERED LOUVRES ON HVY. DUTY

F-41 165" WB
TRACTOR TRAILER (SEMI)
WITH SLEEPER CAB

(F TYPES CONTINUE)
ALSO, 2 TON **CHASSIS**
73 HP   136" OR 165" WB
5-SPEED TRANSMISSION

7.00
X 20
DUAL REAR
WHEELS W.
HELPER SPRINGS

32

(A)

HEAVY-DUTY MODELS UP TO
7½ TONS GROSS CAPACITY.

(B)

4 CYL. MODELS
STILL AVAILABLE
UNTIL
1933.

ABOVE : A = FLATBED STAKE
B = PANEL DELIVERY
TRUCK

DODGE = 31~32

86

DODGE

('35)

33-35

Walter P. Chrysler

STRAIGHT-8
G-80 (4/7½ TON)
AVAIL. 1933 to 1935
(CHRYSLER CUST. IMPRL. ENG.)

"AIRFLOW" TRUCKS
AVAILABLE 1935
UNTIL 1940
(TOTAL OF 265 BLT.)

$595.
COMMERCIAL PANEL

$595.
('35)

"AIRFLOW" K52
TANKER
(2 VIEWS)
190 or 200"
WB

6 CYL. 309.6 CID
95 HP

('33)

"DODGE
BROTHERS" NAME
STILL ON SIDE of HOOD.

EXTERNAL VISOR
ELIMINATED

AS OF 8-35, LOWER
WINDSHIELD CORNERS
CURVED, and NAME
ON SIDE OF HOOD IS
SHORTENED TO
"DODGE."

$535.
COMMERCIAL PANEL 116" WB

new GRILLE ON
SOME TYPES;
OTHERS
CONTINUE
1935
GRILLE
AS
SHOWN
BELOW.

70 TO 96 HP,
201 TO 309 CID
6-CYL. ENGINES.
(STRAIGHT-8,
385 CID, 115 HP
ENG. IN G-80.)

(VERTICAL FRONT EDGE OF DOOR
STARTS AUGUST, 1935.)

36

LC, LD and
LE SERIES

MODELS:
LC (COMMERCIAL)
LE-15 (3/4 TON)
LE-20; LF-28; LH-29 (1 TON)
LE-30; LHD-30; LF-35 (1½-2 TON)
LD-35; LS-35 (1½-3 TON)
LG-40 (1½-4 TON)
LT-35; LH-45 (2-4 TON)
K-50 (2-5½ TON)
K-60 (3-5½ TON)
G-80 (4-8 TON)

96 HP

3-TON
$1695. (CH.)

1937 SALES = ALMOST 65,000

DODGE TRUCKS

STAKE

STYLING OF DODGE PICKUPS IS SIMILAR TO THESE TRUCKS.

('38)

37-38

"AIRFLOW" TANKER (AVAIL. TO '40)

new GRILLE WITH HORIZONTAL PCS.

SERIES MC, MD, ME (1937); RC, RD, RE (1938)

TC, TD and TE SERIES

(new DIESEL ENGINE AVAIL = 6 CYL. 95 HP)

Swift's Premium Swift
SWIFT & COMPANY · PURVEYORS OF FINE FOODS
HAM · BACON · SAUSAGE

CHASSIS-CAB

"DODGE" NAME ON BOTH SIDES, ABOVE GRILLE

C.O.E.

CAB

39

TOTALLY RESTYLED

VC, VD and VF SERIES

9 ft. Platform body . . 133" wheelbase
12 ft. Platform body . . 160" wheelbase

9 ft. Stake body . . 136" wheelbase
12 ft. Stake body . . 160" wheelbase

2-TON

ON 17 WHEELBASES

40

"DODGE" NAME MOVED DOWN TO CENTER OF GRILLE

9 ft. Express body
133" wheelbase

CHASSIS with FLAT FACE COWL
3-TON to ½-TON

In wheelbase lengths ranging from 220" to 116"

CHASSIS with WINDSHIELD COWL—3-TON to ½-TON

In wheelbase lengths ranging from 220" to 105" including C.O.E. models

CHASSIS with CAB—3-TON to ½-TON

In wheelbase lengths ranging from 220" to 105" including C.O.E. models

1½-TON C.O.E.

9 ft. Platform body—C.O.E. . . 105" wheelbase
12 ft. Platform body—C.O.E. . . 129" wheelbase

Job-Rated MEANS: A Truck That Fits YOUR Job! Here's Why!

	DODGE	TRUCK 2	TRUCK 3
ENGINES	6	1	3
WHEELBASES	17	9	6
GEAR RATIOS	16	6	9
CAPACITIES (Ton Rating)	6	3	4
STD. CHASSIS and BODY MODELS	96	56	42
PRICES Begin At	$465	$450	$474¹⁸

88

DODGE

82½, 85, 92, 99, 106 HP GAS ENGINES

C.O.E. 112 BODY and CHASSIS TYPES ON 18 DIFF. WBs. 100-HP (DIESEL AVAIL. IN 3-TON TYPE.)

41

PRICED WITH THE LOWEST

Chassis .. $500 (WITH COWL)	Pick-Ups $630	
Chassis .. $595 (WITH CAB)	Panels .. $730	
	Stakes .. $740	

WC, WD and WF SERIES

CENTER of GRILLE RE-DESIGNED, and new HORIZ. CHROME STRIPS (DLX. CONV.)

ICE CREAM DELIVERY TRUCK WITH STREAMLINED REFRIG. BODY

42-45

WHETHER YOU NEED ½ TO 3-TON GAS OR HEAVY-DUTY DIESEL ... YOU CAN **DEPEND ON DODGE**

OVER 75,000 DODGE MILITARY TRUCKS BUILT BY JANUARY, 1942.

REMEMBER THE DODGE POWER WAGONS OF WWII? Dodge has been building four-wheel-drive Power Wagons for military and civilian use. In World War II, Dodge supplied over 20 variations of these hard-working vehicles to our armed forces.

"BLACK-OUT" MODELS HAVE LESS CHROME TRIM.

1942~1945 PRICES SAME

WC ½ TON PICKUP (116" WB) $651.
WD-15 ¾ TON " (120" ") $705.
WD-20 1 TON " " " $787.
(ALSO PANEL and STAKE TYPES)

CIVILIAN TRUCK PRODUCTION RESUMES 1944.

CAB-OVER ENGINE 1½ TON STAKE
WFM-35 (105" WB) $971.
WFM-37 (129" WB) $1015.
WGM-40 (105" WB) $1352.; WGM-42 (129" WB) $1437.

DODGE = 41~45

89

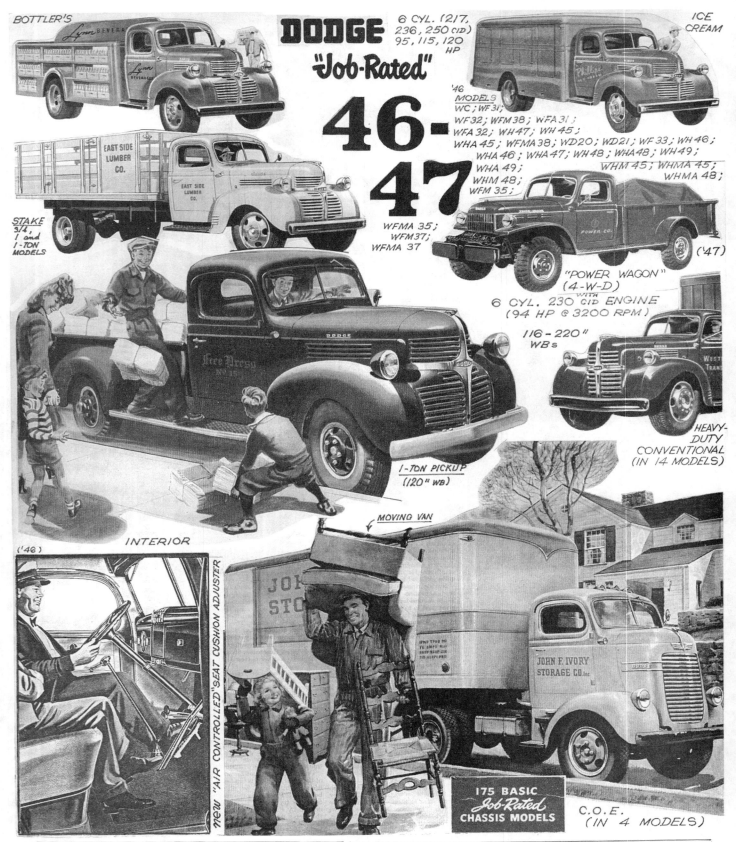

BOTTLER'S

Lynn BEVERAGE

ICE CREAM

DODGE
"Job-Rated"
6 CYL. (217, 236, 250 CID) 95, 115, 120 HP

46-47

'46 MODELS
WC; WF31; WF32; WFM38; WFA31; WFA32; WH47; WH45; WHA45; WFMA38; WD20; WD21; WF33; WH46; WHA46; WHA47; WH48; WHA48; WH49; WHA49; WHM45; WHMA45; WHM48; WHMA48; WFM35;

WFMA35; WFM37; WFMA37

EAST SIDE LUMBER CO.

STAKE 3/4, 1 and 1-TON MODELS

"POWER WAGON" (4-W-D) ('47)

6 CYL. 230 CID ENGINE with (94 HP @ 3200 RPM)

116-220" WBs

HEAVY-DUTY CONVENTIONAL (IN 14 MODELS)

Free Press

1-TON PICKUP (120" WB)

INTERIOR

('46)

NEW "AIR CONTROLLED" SEAT CUSHION ADJUSTER

MOVING VAN

JOHN F. IVORY STORAGE CO. Inc.

175 BASIC *Job-Rated* CHASSIS MODELS

C.O.E. (IN 4 MODELS)

1/2-TON PICKUPS PRICED FROM
$934.

3/4-TON: $1021.

1-TON: $1092.

LAWS TODAY WOULD PROHIBIT A CHILD FROM ASSISTING A MOVER!

1/2-TON "WC" PICKUP/PANEL SERIAL #s
1946-47 DETROIT: 81172529 UP
LOS ANGELES: 9221570 UP

1948 DETR.: 82A44001 UP

L.A.: 9227001 UP

DODGE = 46-47

important NEW features

SER. #s START AT 82A44001 (DETROIT) OR 9227001 (L.A.)

SHORTER new 108" WB ON 1/2-TON MODELS

PANEL $1278. UP

↑ DETAILS OF "BUTTERFLY" SWING-UP HOOD PANELS

TOTALLY **NEW** STYLING!

1 1/2-TON STAKE $1560. UP

48-49

B-1-B SERIES

1/2 TON PICKUPS FROM $1113. ('48) $1263. ('49)

FLUID DRIVE AVAIL. **new** STEERING-COLUMN GEARSHIFT and SYNCHRO-SHIFT TRANS.

2 1/2 TON

"B-2" SERIES

50

RESEMBLES 1948-49, BUT 3 VERTICAL BUMPER GUARDS ARE ELIMINATED (AS OF LATE '49.)

6 CYL. "Powered by NEW 377 cu.in. Heavy-duty Engine!" 154 H.P.

"NEW Twin Carburetion for High Power, with Economy!"

"NEW 5-speed, Helical Constant-mesh Transmission!"

"Rugged 10 1/8" Frame... 7 Big Cross-members!"

"Extra-heavy 18,000-lb. Capacity Rear Axle!"

WHARTON PRODUCE CO.

BIG New 4-TON Heavy-Duty

"Y" SERIES (ABOVE)

ROUTE VANS have 102" WB; OTHER MODELS have SAME WB RANGE AS BEFORE.

PRODUCTION NOW IN DETROIT or IN SAN LEANDRO, CALIF.

DODGE = 48~50

91

DODGE

MIXER

DUMP

C.O.E.

LIGHT PICKUP
with REAR
QUARTER WINDOWS

51-53

"B-3" SERIES *
new GRILLE

(*=1953 is "B-4" SERIES.)

MEDIUM-DUTY
STAKE TRUCK

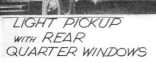

½ TON SERIAL NUMBERS
START
AT 82215001 (DETROIT, 1951)
85308001 (SAN LEANDRO, 1951)
82257601 (DETROIT, 1952)
85313701 (SAN LEANDRO, 1952)
82302001 (DETROIT, 1953)
85322001 (SAN LEANDRO, 1953)

½-TON PICKUPS PRICED FROM
$1293. ('51)
$1420. ('52) $1480. ('53)

DODGE ══ 51~53

DODGE

LT. DUTY FROM $1331. 100 TO 172 HP 6 STD., BUT 241 OR 331 CID V8 AVAIL.

"C-1" SERIES **54** RESTYLED new GRILLE, 1-PC. WINDSHIELD

GREAT LAKES SHIPPING

SER.# FROM 82338001 (DETROIT) 85328001 (SAN LEANDRO) (1/2-TON)

4WD

POWER WAGON

School Bus

STOP LITTLEVILLE SCHOOL DISTRICT

C.O.E. OIL TANKER

CENTRAL OIL CO.

(MODEL G SIMILAR) **1 1/2** TON MOD. **F** (ALSO BELOW)

55 -56

new

C-3 SERIES

LT. DUTY FROM $1501. ('55)* $1530. ('56)

*SALE PRICE $1368.

(1955 EXAMPLES ILLUSTR.)

CARINE FEED CO.

GRILLE CENTER TRIM MODIFIED

"WRAP AROUND" WINDSHIELD

J&L AUTO PARTS

1956 MODELS START 10-7-55.

DODGE = 54~56

DODGE

(1957 MODELS START 10-15-56.)

1/2, 3/4, 1 or 1 1/2 T. STAKE

FROM $1764.

Stake models

132" WB
C-500 C.O.E. 1 1/2-T.
FROM $3045.

4-wheel-drive models up to 18,000 lbs. G.V.W.

Tandem models up to 46,000 lbs. G.V.W.

Tractor models up to 65,000 lbs. G.C.W.

Cab-over-engine models

$1906.

Cab and chassis models

Panel models

57

FRONT RESTYLED

1/2-TON FROM $1653.

120 TO 232 HP

1957 DASH →

new
MODEL (SUFFIX) NUMBERS:
D-100 (1/2 TON;) D-200
(3/4 TON;) D-300 (1 TON;)
D-400 (1 1/2 TON;)
ALSO UP TO D-800,
PLUS C (C.O.E.) and
P (CAB-FORWARD)

MODEL PREFIX OF K-6 OR K-8
(6 CYL.)   (V-8)

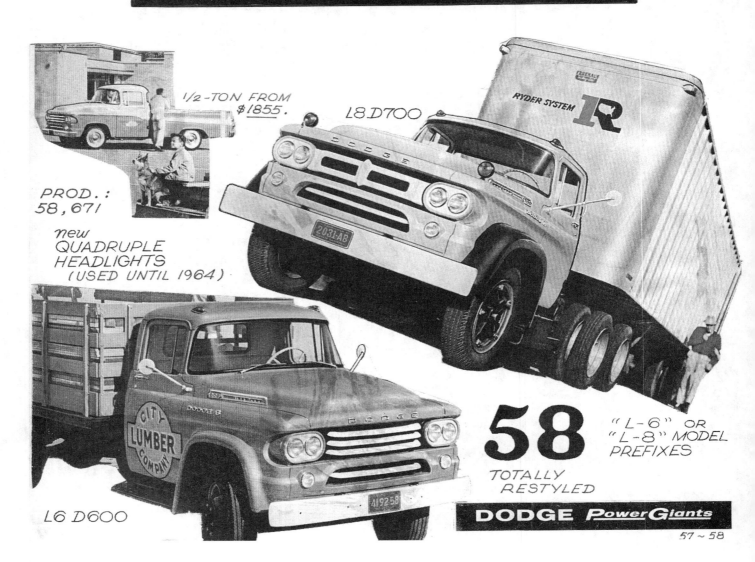

1/2-TON FROM $1855.

L8 D700

RYDER SYSTEM R

PROD.: 58,671

new QUADRUPLE HEADLIGHTS (USED UNTIL 1964)

L6 D600

58
TOTALLY RESTYLED

"L-6" OR "L-8" MODEL PREFIXES

DODGE *Power Giants*

57 ~ 58

94

DODGE

59

new GRILLE

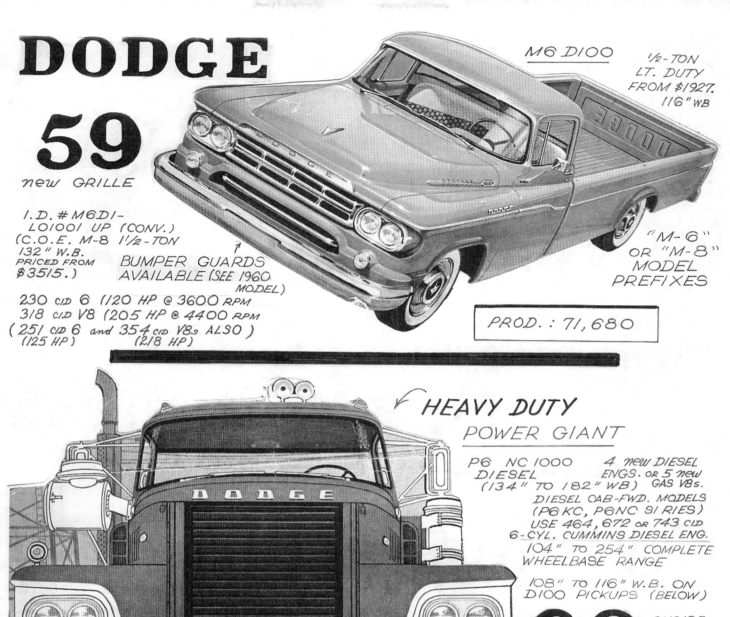

M6 D100   ½-TON LT. DUTY FROM $1927. 116" WB

I.D. # M6D1-L01001 UP (CONV.) (C.O.E. M-8 1½-TON 132" W.B. PRICED FROM $3515.)

BUMPER GUARDS AVAILABLE (SEE 1960 MODEL)

"M-6" OR "M-8" MODEL PREFIXES

230 CID 6 (120 HP @ 3600 RPM
318 CID V8 (205 HP @ 4400 RPM
(251 CID 6 and 354 CID V8s ALSO)
(125 HP)   (218 HP)

PROD.: 71,680

HEAVY DUTY

POWER GIANT

P6 NC 1000 DIESEL (134" TO 182" WB)

4 new DIESEL ENGS. or 5 new GAS V8s.

DIESEL CAB-FWD. MODELS (P6 KC, P6NC SERIES) USE 464, 672 or 743 CID 6-CYL. CUMMINS DIESEL ENG.

104" TO 254" COMPLETE WHEELBASE RANGE

108" TO 116" W.B. ON D100 PICKUPS (BELOW)

60

CHOICE OF 140 MODELS!

"P-6" AND "P-8" SERIES

SWEPTLINE

BIG-220

AS IN SOME ADS, LENGTH EXAGGERATED

new GRILLE (ALUMINUM) STD. FROM 1958.

120 TO 228 HP (V8 PICKUP TO 200 HP)

SWEPTLINE OFFERS OPTIONAL "LOAD-FLITE" PUSHBUTTON AUTO. TRANS.

6-CYL. P-6 I.D. # STARTS AT 1160-100001

PROD.: 70,305

95

DODGE

new GRILLE

Adventurer

D-100 PRICED FROM $2196. ('67)
$2390. ('68)
$2442. ('69)

PRODUCTION :
141,685 ('67)
173,769 ('68)
165,133 ('69)

DASH (ADV.)

"C-700"

67-69

CN-900 has CHOICE OF 3 OPT. CUMMINS DIESEL ENGS., 13½ TO 26½ TON GVW ('68)

Dodge Builds Tough Trucks   DODGE DIV

MED. DUTY (ABOVE)

HVY. DUTY (RT.)

('69)

✓ ILLUSTRATED 1969 LT. DUTY HAS *new* SIDE SAFETY LTS. (ROUND) NEAR FR. END, and RESTYLED HOOD.

CHRYSLER CORPORATION

ADVENTURER

6~CYL. VANS		
A100 (½ TON, 90" WB)	FROM	$2290.
A108 (¾ TON, 108" WB)		2445.
P200 (¾ TON, 104" WB)		1846.
P300 (1 TON, 125" WB)		1953.
P400 (1½ TON, 137" WB)		2296.

(1967 PRICES)

new L-600 2-TON TILT-CAB V8 12' BED STAKE TRUCK IN 1967. 105" WB
$4677. $4543. ('68) $4756. ('69)

DODGE = 67~69

97

DODGE

WITH G78-15B TIRES

D-100 CUSTOM SWEPTLINE

CUMMINS 6 or DETR. DIESEL 6 or V8 IN SLEEPER-CAB HEAVY-DUTY TILT → (4 MODELS AVAIL.) ('70)

('71)

(GAS LOW CAB FWD. AVAIL. WITH V8s TO 549 CID) DIESELS AVAIL. ALSO

LNT-1000 DIESEL TILT-CAB (CUMMINS NH-230 ENGINE)

SIMILAR LN-1000 TYPE AVAIL. SINCE MID-'60s

SHORT (or 2 SIZES SLEEPER CABS)

SCHOOL BUS

70-71

new GRILLE (LT. and MED.)

BELOW: **B-300** 127" WB (EXTENDED) SEATS UP TO 14 CHILDREN. OPTIONAL AIR COND., POWER STEER., POWER FRONT DISC BRAKES, AUTO. TRANS. (SMALLER 109" WB 5, 8, or 12-PASS. BUS ALSO)

('71)

('71)

S600 DODGE SCHOOL BUS CHASSIS

1972 SCH. BUS SAME AS ABOVE

SCHOOL BUS ENGINES

318-3 HEAVY-DUTY PREMIUM V8 (STANDARD)
Lightweight, powerful, high in torque, this Dodge 318-cubic-inch V8 is great for economy. Its premium features include these: hardened and shot-peened forged crankshaft; trimetal main and connecting rod bearings; Stellite-faced exhaust valves with Roto-Caps; stainless steel head gaskets. Standard V8 for all Dodge school bus chassis, this engine uses regular fuel.

361 HEAVY-DUTY PREMIUM V8
Biggest, most powerful Dodge school bus engine. Optional in all models. With a displacement of 361 cubic inches and with such premium features as: induction-hardened crankshaft journals; trimetal main and connecting rod bearings; hydraulic valve lifters; sodium-filled exhaust valves with Roto-Caps; and a chrome-alloy cast-iron cylinder block. Uses regular fuel.

U.S. SERVICE CENTERS

PICKUPS

A-100 ½TON $2454.	D-100 ½TON (6½' BED) $2667.	D-100 ½TON (8' BED) $2703.
D-200 ¾TON (8' BED) $2915.	D-200 ¾TON CREW CAB (6½' or 8' BED) $3663. UP	
D-300 1-TON 9' UTIL. PICKUP $2995.		

DODGE ══ 70~71

DODGE

$4134.   8' BED

CREW CAB PICKUP.   105" WB

WHEEL COVER VARIATION

Go camping with Dodge. The only all-new pickup for 1972.

LIGHT-DUTY TOTALLY RESTYLED

72

A

SWEPTLINE D100 (6½' BOX, 115" WB) $2871.

DODGE D100 UTILINE PICKUP.

LIGHT-DUTY STAKE.

D-100 STAKE = $3059. D-200 = $3322.

THIS STYLE OF DODGE VAN STARTS '71.

STAKES: D-400 (1½ TON) D-500 (2 TON)

DODGE FOUR-WHEEL-DRIVE POWER WAGON.

12½' BED

CONVENTIONAL STAKE. MEDIUM-DUTY

MEDIUM-DUTY LCF (GASOLINE).

B SERIES VANS $2795. UP

DODGE TRADESMAN VAN.

DODGE FORWARD CONTROL VAN.

B-100 ½ TON B-200 ¾ TON; B-300 1 TON
DODGE TRADESMAN MAXIVAN...AMERICA'S BIGGEST COMPACT VAN.

DODGE TRADESMAN VISION VAN.

Dodge. Depend on it.   *(CONT'D. NEXT PAGE)*

Dodge. Depend on it.

BODIES BY THESE BUILDERS ARE AVAIL. (SCHOOL BUS)
SUPERIOR, BLUE BIRD, WAYNE, WARD, THOMAS, CARPENTER

72^B (CONT'D.)

TYPICAL SERVICE STATION OF 1972, WITH HIGH CANOPY (TO ACCOM. LARGE TRUCKS, RVs, ETC.)

The easy-to-service Dodge LCF now has four new engines to choose from.

new CN-900 SER.

Heavy Duty Low Cab Diesels from Dodge

DODGE HEAVY-DUTY CONVENTIONAL.

DODGE HEAVY-DUTY LCF TANDEM (GASOLINE).

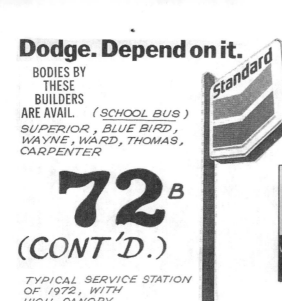

HEAVY-DUTY LCF TANDEM (DIESEL).

"PRACTICAL" IS THE WORD for Dodge Truck's new CN 900 series. For starters, eye those swing-out fenders, providing walk-in accessibility to powerful and economical engines. Single axle wheelbases range from 134" to 182". Tandem wheelbase lengths range from 146" to 200", with a BBC of less than 90 degrees for both models. This means easier manueuverability in close quarters. GVW ranges from 28,000 to 52,000 lbs.; top GCW for both single and tandem axle models is 76,800

DODGE HEAVY-DUTY LCF (GASOLINE).

LS-1000

DODGE HEAVY-DUTY TILT CAB (DIESEL).

DODGE HEAVY-DUTY LCF (DIESEL).

LCF's

CN-900, CNT-900 WITH CUMMINS V-903 OR DETROIT 8V-71 DIESEL ENG. new CUMMINS V-555 OR V8-210 AVAIL. IN C-800, CT-800.

ABOVE = CAB-CHASSIS TRUCK TRACTORS, BUILT TO HAUL SINGLE, DOUBLE and TRIPLE FREIGHT TRAILERS AS SEEN AT LOWER RIGHT.

DODGE = 72-B

DODGE

Camper

LT. DUTY

BI-TORQUE GAUGES. Except for the speedometer and the tachometer, every gauge in the Bighorn is an expensive Stewart-Warner waterproof bi-torque gauge.

new Club Cab 73

1972 TYPES

CONTINUE

BIGHORN

all-new heavy-duty truck.

INTRO. SPRING, 1973

(BELOW, AND RIGHT)

MODEL CN-950 (LONG CONV.)

Extra care in engineering makes a difference in Dodge...depend on it.

INTERIOR

(new BIGHORN)

½ TON PICKUP (D-100) 6½' BED, 115" WB. FROM $**3046.**

D-100 CLUB CABS (133" WB) FROM $**3292.**

D-200 CREW CABS FROM $**4077.** 6½ BED, (149" WB)

WITH CUMMINS NTC-350 OR CATERPILLAR 1100 DIESEL ENGINE (OR OTHERS AS AVAIL. (INCL. GAS) DURING THE 1973 SHORTAGE OF HEAVY-DUTY TRUCK ENGINES.

new MEDIUM-DUTY "KARY-VAN" CONV. ALSO INTRODUCED EARLY 1973. SEE 1974~1976 PAGE FOR ILLUSTRATION.

BIGHORN HOOD MASCOT ↗

DODGE ══ 73

DODGE

new
↖LT.
new
D-700
MEDIUM
"KARY-VAN"
900

DODGE SPORTSMAN WAGONS (tow up to 8,000 lbs.)

SPTSMN. I.D. #
B12, 22 OR 32
A (B) 4 (V)
000001 UP

B-100 (109"WB)
SPTSMN. PRICES
START AT
$4279.

225 CID 6 CUT
TO 105 HP

Sportsman wagon...

SEATING

VANS PRICED
FROM
$3265.

NEW **ROYAL SPORTSMAN SE.**

Tradesman Van

74 new GRILLE

SWING-OUT
CARGO DOORS
(SLIDING DOORS
AVAIL. ALSO)
(VAN I.D. # B11
(A) (B) 4 (S)
000001 UP)

new GRILLES
FOR VANS,
ALSO

STD. PICKUPS
PRICED FROM
$3368.

CLUB CABS →
FROM
$3621.

PICKUP I.D. #
D13 (A) (E)
4 (S) 000001 UP

**DODGE TRUCKS.
DEPEND ON 'EM.**

258,563
LT. TK. SALES

133" OR
149" WB
CLUB
CABS
(SINCE '73)

PICKUP.
Club Cab

For extra people

SIDE-FACING REAR SEATS

DODGE

THE 1975 DODGE DYNA-TRAC DUAL REAR WHEEL OPTION.

Dodge offers dual rear wheels on the conventional cab and the Club Cab.

The Dodge pickup, with Dyna-Trac dual rear wheels, has a number of strong advantages—especially for those of you who use your pickup to carry a slide-on camper unit. Dodge has become the recognized *leader* in recreational vehicles. A Camper Special pickup—in conventional cab or Club Cab with Dyna-Trac dual rear wheels—can be just what you're looking for in your next pickup camper rig.

DODGE HEAVY TRUCKS NOT AVAIL. AFTER 1975.

CREW CAB FROM $4879. ('75) $4901. ('76) MODEL # D~22

DASH

New Dodge pickup instrument panel.

DYNA-TRAC CLUB CAB ('75)

NOTE new DUAL REAR WHEELS AVAIL.

RAM-CHARGER REAR DETAILS ('76)

Dodge Ramcharger

52 MODELS

75-76

A

new DASH and SIDE TRIM

EASY-OFF TAILGATE... CONVENIENT!
All Dodge Sweptline models have an easy-off tailgate that can be removed easily and simply (including the straps) without tools.

RAMCHARGER
(INTRO. 1974)
PLYMOUTH "TRAIL DUSTER" SIMILAR
(REAR DETAILS AT FAR LEFT)

$4640. UP
4WD ('76)
106" WB
6 OR 3/8 CID V8

PICKUP REAR DETAILS

NOTE VARIATIONS IN MIRRORS, BOX RAILS, WHEELS, TOP COLOR AVAIL.

3336 EB

STD. FR. $3779. ('75) $3777 ('76)

52 MODELS IN ALL

BUMPER GUARDS STILL AVAIL.

STANDARD EQUIPMENT
• 225 Slant Six or 318 V8 engine
• Front disc brakes
• Power brakes (optional on D100)
• 3-speed synchro-shift transmission

FROM CLUB CAB $4078.('75) 4073.('76)

AVAIL. 4WD

OPTIONAL - FOR 1975, DODGE HAS FULL-TIME FOUR-WHEEL DRIVE. With full-time four-wheel drive, there's no need to shift the front wheels in and out of "drive" or to be bothered getting out to lock (or unlock) the front wheel hubs. (Our Dodge Ramcharger sport/utility models offer full-time four-wheel drive as well.) Chrysler-built New Process gear boxes have such a solid reputation Ford and Chevy buy them for their trucks, too.

LT. TK. SALES: 250,453 ('75) 333,201 ('76)

PICKUP I.D. # D13 (-)(-)5 (-) 000001 UP ('75) or D13 (-)(-) 6 (-) 000001 UP ('76)

(VANS ON NEXT PAGE)

DODGE

REAR

102.0"
79.6"

KARI-VAN →
127" or 145" WB
I.D. # STARTS WITH C-30

DODGE SPORTSMAN WAGON
Extra care in engineering makes a difference.

VAN REAR

FULL-WIDTH REAR DOOR
This is a brand-new option for 1975.

TRADESMAN

75-76
B

B SERIES

VAN I.D. #
B11(-)(-)5(-)
000001 UP ('75)

B11(-)(-)6
(-)000001 UP ('76)

No wonder we're number one.

DASH

OPTIONAL

TRADESMAN VAN...

CARGO AREA SHOWN
AT UPPER RIGHT
OF PAGE.

DCR-193

DODGE — 75~76-B

| VANS PRICED FROM |
| $3699. ('75) $3876. ('76) |

DODGE

ADVENTURER SE

THE ADULT TOYS FROM DODGE.

new OPT.

77

#D14 (-)(E)7(-) 100001 UP

NEW GRILLE and LIGHTS. "DODGE" NAME ON TOP GRILLE BORDER.

PICKUPS PRICED FROM 4587.

VANS SIMILAR TO '76,

385,125 LIGHT TRUCK SALES

(D-150 MODELS ADDED TO ½-TON LINE, JOINING D-100.)

(W MODELS ARE F-W-D)

OPT. 6 CYL., 243.3 CID (103 HP @ 3700 RPM)

VANS PRICED FROM $4268.

I.D. # B11 (A)(B) 7 (-) 000001 UP

396,268 LIGHT TRUCK SALES

THE LOWEST PRICED PICKUP BUILT IN AMERICA.

(SPECIAL SPRING, 1978 PRICE)

$4147.00

($87. EXTRA FOR W.S.W. TIRES, WH. CVRS.)

D-100 pickup

$6687. RAMCHARGER 4×4 →

CREW CAB POWER WAGON

UTILINE POWER WAGON

SNO-COMMANDER

4×4

CLUB CAR POWER WAGON

MACHO POWER WAGON

new 243 CID 6 MITSUBISHI DIESEL ENG. AVAIL. IN W-150 OR W-200 SERIES PICKUPS.

PICKUP I.D. # D14 (A)(E) 8 (-) 000001 UP

4-WHEEL-DRIVE

(ON 6 MODELS SHOWN ABOVE)

B-100 $4997.

VANS

I.D. # B-11 (A)(B) 8 (-) 00000/ UP

new WRAP-AROUND (VANS) WINDOWS

ALL-NEW INSTRUMENT PANEL

STEERING LOCKS WHEN IGN. OFF

NEW DODGE VANS

78

B-200 $5137.

MAXIVAN $5921. ↑

VANS RE-STYLED, PRICED FROM $4572.

B-300 5311.

new SUN ROOF AVAIL.

23MPG HWY/ 17MPG CITY.

ALL-NEW SEATS...

DODGE

PROSPECTOR SPECIAL

I.D. #D14 (A)(E)9(–) 100001 UP

CLUB CAB FR. $5874. #D17

STD. PICKUPS FROM $5169.

DODGE IS INTO TRUCKIN' LIKE AMERICAS INTO JEANS.

4-W-D

1979 DODGE

400,945 LT. TRUCK SALES

✗ PROSPECTOR

Rail-Track Pickups RD-200

RD200 models are really something different in pickups. They're built to run as functionally and effectively on rails as they do on the road.

VAN PRICES (109" WB)

B-100 1/2 TON	B-200 3/4 TON	B-300 1 TON
$5750.	$6150.	$6389.

($5320. SPECIAL PRICE)

79 new GRILLES

(4 CYL. D-50 MITSUBISHI-BLT. PICKUPS ALSO, STARTING '79)

KARY VAN I.D. # C30 (B)(T) 9(–)100001 UP

VANS

VAN I.D. #B11 (A)(B) 9 (–)100001 UP

FROM $7721.

$6933. UP

MAXI VAN WITH 127½" W.B. (SPORTSMAN PKG. EXTRA)

B-100

Kary Van

2. REAR DOOR CHOICES

SLIDE-UP   SWING

ROYAL VAN

SPORTS-MAN

SPTSMN. #B1,2, or 3 (2)(A)(E)9(–)100001 UP

FROM $7632. TO 10,789.

THE COMFORT. Plaid pattern vinyl as shown here is the standard van upholstery. Deluxe single-tone vinyl is optional. Standard driver's seat is a thickly padded low-back bucket mounted to improve both seating position and headroom. There are also optional high-back Command bucket seats with striped cloth-and-vinyl side facings. And with the Royal Van only, reclining high-back Command bucket seats in textured velour with vinyl side facings. Both high-back Command seats are also available with optional swivel bases.

1/2-TON D150 FROM $6155.
3/4-TON D200 FROM 6976.
1-TON D300 STAKE FROM 7661.
1-TON D300 CAB-CHASSIS FROM 8247.
CLUB CABS $7131. TO $8943.
CREW CABS $8220. TO $9158.

RAM TOUGH Dodge Trucks

THE NEW CHRYSLER CORPORATION
QUALITY ENGINEERED TO BE THE BEST

I.D. #
EXPLANATION:
EXAMPLE : D14(A)(B)9(S)012345
D=2WD PICKUP ; 1 = 1/2-TON CLASS ;
4 = CONV. CAB SWEPTLINE ; A = TO 6000 lbs. GVW;
B=ENGINE TYPE ; 9 = MODEL YEAR ; S = CITY
WHERE ASSEMBLED ; 012345 = UNIT NO.

347,138 LIGHT TRUCK SALES

ADVENTURER SE

D-150 NOW THE LOWEST- PRICED SERIES.

With 26 Ram Tough models in all.

D-150

I.D.#D14(-)EA(-)10001 UP

PICKUPS PRICED FR. $5668.

17 MPG (EPA) CITY (6-CYL.)

80

new PICKUP GRILLES NOW BLACKED OUT IN CRISS- CROSS DUAL INSETS.

ADV. SE PICKUP

Engines for Domestic Pickups[1]

No. Cyl.	Displacement	BHP @ rpm	Torque (lb-ft) @ rpm
Slant Six	3.7-liter (225 CID)	95 hp @ 3,600 rpm	170 lb-ft @ 1,600 rpm
V-8	5.2-liter (318 CID)	135 hp @ 4,000 rpm[2]	240 lb-ft @ 2,000 rpm[2]
V-8	5.9-liter (360 CID)	170 hp @ 4,000 rpm	270 lb-ft @ 2,000 rpm

1-LIGHT-DUTY EMISSION CYCLE, FEDERAL
2-140 HP @ 4000 RPM and 240 lb. ft.
@2400 RPM with AUTO. TRANS.

VANS SIMILAR TO 1979, PRICED FROM $5567.

VAN DASH

Double SIDE DOORS are standard. They provide a 49.26-inch wide opening and are available with optional windows, fixed or vented.

SLIDING SIDE DOOR for unloading in tight quarters is available as an option, with or without an optional window.

Double REAR DOORS are standard and provide a 49.26-inch wide opening. Door windows are available.

Dodge's EXCLUSIVE SINGLE REAR DOOR option features a big fixed rear window. A rear vented window is also optional with this door.

Attractive, functional instrument panel.
Features large glove box, and handy fuse box located beneath glove box door. Instrumentation includes ammeter, temperature gauge, fuel gauge, oil pressure indicator light and speedometer/odometer.

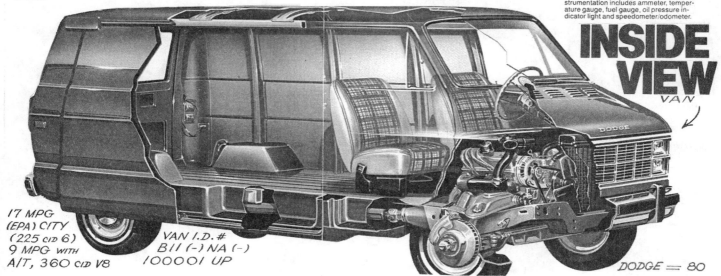

INSIDE VIEW VAN

17 MPG (EPA) CITY (225 CID 6) 9 MPG with A/T, 360 CID V8

VAN I.D. # B11 (-) NA (-) 10001 UP

DODGE = 80

DODGE
DODGE TRUCKS ARE RAM TOUGH

CREW CAB

$8716. UP

1981 I.D.# 1B7E(-)(-)4E(-) B(-)100001

ROYAL S.E. PICKUP DASH ('81)

new HOOD ORNAMENT AVAIL.

STD. '81 FROM $6292.

SLIDING WINDOW OPTION

STEERING WHEEL HUB IS TOTALLY
New FOR 1982 → (VANS ALSO)

('82)

D-150 RAM ROYAL

81-82

new GRILLE and LIGHTS (PICKUP)

CLUB CAB FROM $7527.

(VAN) WAGON 1981 DASH

new MINI-RAM PASS. VAN HAS 109.6" W.B.
$8137.('81)

250 (95 HP)

Dodge Wagon instrument panels are smartly styled and convenient. Note the large glove box with a handy fuse box located beneath glove box door within easy reach. Standard instrumentation includes ammeter, temperature gauge, fuel gauge, oil pressure indicator light, and speedometer/odometer calibrated in miles per hour (primary scale) and kilometers per hour (secondary scale). Gauges are easy to read. Controls are easy to reach. Royal instrument panel shown.

"RAM" NAME ON VAN DOORS

1981 VAN I.D.#
187FP(-)3E(-)
B(-)100001 UP
1981 RAM WAGON
I.D.# 1B4HB
(-)1E or 1P(-)
B(-)100001 UP

WHEELS

ROYAL S.E. WITH OPT. GRAINED PANEL FROM $10,909.

127.0" W.B.

D-350 $9787. ('82)
STAKE
131" WB

149" W.B. (1-TON) D-350 CAB-CHASSIS $9971. UP ('82)

D-350 DUMP

"KARY VAN"

(CONVENTIONAL)

RAM TOUGH
Dodge Trucks

THE NEW CHRYSLER CORPORATION
QUALITY ENGINEERED TO BE THE BEST

TURBOCHARGED DIESEL ENGINE

83

UP TO 45 MPG IN RAM 50. 34 EPA MPG IN POWER RAM 50

4 CYL. (2.3L) AVAIL. IN RAM 50 OR POWER RAM 50

POWER RAM 50 4WD

RAM 50 2WD

27 EPA MPG

ABOVE (FROM TOP, CLOCKWISE:)
RAM VAN; RAMCHARGER; RAMPAGE; RAM PICKUP; RAM WAGON VAN

RAM 50: REAR DETAILS

(RAM 50 MADE IN JAPAN BY MITSUBISHI. SIMILAR PICKUPS ALSO IMPORTED WITH MITSUBISHI NAME, 1983 ON)

$5665* (* REG. $6198.)
DODGE RAM 50

V.I.N. = (1 OR J) B (4 OR 7) - (Z44C) - D - #

TWO STEEL WALLS

19/25 MPG

DODGE MINI RAM
PASSENGER VAN
FULL SIZE, 109" WB
9587. and up
225 CID SLANT 6 ENGINE (95 HP @ 3600 RPM)

SLANT 6 ENGINE IN RAM MISER also

21/30 MPG

7 STEEL CROSSMEMBERS IN THE FRAME

RAM MISER: STANDARD FULL SIZE PICKUP. $5999.*

D-350 CAB/CHAS. WITH 135" OR 159" WB

D-150 PICKUP (6½' BED) (115" WB) $7581.; (WITH 8' BED, 131" WB $7735.)

¾ TON D-250 PICKUP (8' BED, 131" WB) $8482.; 1-TON D-350 PICKUP (8' BED, 131" WB) $9493.

1-TON D-350 (CREW CAB, 6½' BED, 149" OR 165" WB) $10647. OR $11417.

DODGE 83

109

Dodge Truck

EST MPG 25 EST HWY 40

RAM 50

$5,684.

CUSTOM PICKUP REG. $6128. (ROYAL, $6734.) (SPORT, $7360.)

POWER RAM 50 (4WD) FROM $8433.

EPA EST MPG 26 EST HWY 32

EST MPG 30 EST HWY 39
2.3L TURBO DIESEL FOUR-WHEEL DRIVE

POWER RAM 50

FINAL YEAR FOR
RAMPAGE
Z44C = 7599.
Z64C 2.2 = $8128.
4 CYL. 104" WB

# 84 A
V.I.N. = (1 or J) B (4 or 7) - (Z44C) - E - #

AVAIL. 2.3L TURBO DIESEL 4 (80 HP @ 4200 RPM)
2.L and 2.6L GAS ENGINES ALSO.

VANS

225 CID SLANT-6 or 318 or 360 CID V8s IN VANS.
109" or 127" WB

FROM $8299. CARGO VAN

REAR COMPARTM'T. (CARGO VAN)

Choice of hinged or optional sliding side doors.

Industry's longest cargo area: B250 Maxi Van

Widest standard side door opening in class: 49.3" x 47.2" high.

All-welded integral body-frame design.

3 Wheelbase-Body Lengths: 109.6"/178.9" 127.6"/186.9" 127.6"/222.9"

EPA EST MPG 19 EST HWY 26

LONG RANGE RAM VAN

RAM TOUGH

Dodge Trucks

PASSENGER VAN

RAM VALUE WAGON

$11794. and up

D-100 and D-150 ARE EACH 1/2 TON PICKUPS.
D-250 3/4 T. " PRICED AT $8950.
D-350 1-T. MODELS $9670. UP

new CARAVAN PASSENGER MINI VAN AND CORRESPONDING SMALL MINI RAM FREIGHT MINI VAN ON NEXT PAGE

DODGE 84-A

110

DODGE

FROM $ 10252. (ILLUSTR.)

all new "MINI VAN"

K13C

INTRODUCING DODGE CARAVAN.

SEATS 7

NOT AS LONG AS A FULL-SIZE STATION WAGON, YET IT HOLDS 40% MORE CARGO. AND IT'S ABOUT THE SAME HEIGHT AS THE AVERAGE AMERICAN WOMAN. IT HAS FRONT-WHEEL DRIVE, GETS INCREDIBLE MILEAGE, AND IS BACKED BY 5/50 PROTECTION.

(new PLYMOUTH "VOYAGER" is SIMILAR, BUT WITH ALL-HORIZONTAL GRILLE PIECES.)

37 MPG HWY
24 MPG EPA
112" WB
4 CYLS.

ALSO SE $ 10489. LE $ 11077.

NEW 84 B

SIZE COMPARISON BETWEEN FULL-SIZED DODGE VAN and new MINI RAM

K13C SERIES INCLUDES THE MINI RAM, CARAVAN, and PLYMOUTH VOYAGER.

NEW "MINI RAM" has 104" WB.

CARGO VERSION of new CARAVAN **$7,627, as shown.**

front wheel drive DODGE MINI RAM VAN.

25 est. mpg.*

DODGE = 84~B

111

FULL-SIZED DODGE PICKUPS PRICED FROM $9306.
CREW CABS FROM
$11217.

D-250 PICKUP
(8' BED, 131" WB) $9410.

1-TON D-350
PICKUP and
CAB/CHASSIS
$10013. UP

POWER RAM 50
(4WD)
CUSTOM
$8610.

ROYAL
$9117.

N14K

Ram 50's

RAM 50 CUSTOM

N14K

$6222.

DO4T
FULL-SIZE PICKUP
D100 D150
D250 or
D350

4WD
POWER
RAM

V.I.N.=
(I or J)
B or P (4 or 7)–(WIIT)–F

85

B250 MAXI VAN

6 or V8

127"
WB   B250 Maxi Van   Long Range Ram Van

LONG
RANGE
RAM VAN

$10516.
and up

AVAIL. with GRAINED SIDES
(ABOVE)

CARAVAN
$10875.
SE 11121.
LE 11733.

CARAVAN
DRIVER'S SEAT

MINI
RAM
VAN
$8555.
and up

DODGE=85

DODGE

New Ram 50 Sport. $5995*
(* REG. $7090.)

SPORT HAS HORIZONTAL BANDS OF STRIPES ALONG SIDES.

RAM 50
FROM $5788.*
(* REG. $6214.)

(new RAIDER 4WD SPORTS/UTILITY $10721.)

FROM $8907. $11287. UP
↓ MINI RAM / CARAVAN

Dodge makes history with America's only 5 year/50,000 mile warranty for trucks.

POWER RAM 4WD

V.I.N. ==
(I or J) B or P
(4 or 7) —
(WIIT) — G — #

86

B 350 15-PASS. MAXIWAGON
$14090. and up

(8, 12 and 15-PASS. SEATING AVAILABLE)

B 150   **FULL SIZE**
$13361. UP   Dodge Ram Vans and Wagons

$11189. and up

B 250 $13949.
←

CARAVAN SE $11566.
"   LE $12309.

3/4 TON D-250 CAB/CHASSIS AVAILABLE (131" WB)
AT $11600.

DODGE-86

113

DODGE

new RAIDER 4-CYL., 93" WB S.U.V. = $10721.

(REG. $6747.)
('87½)

RAM 50
AVAIL. WITH CHROME BUMPER

SPECIAL VALUE DODGE RAM 50. $6661.

6½' "S" SWB 119" WB $7080.
" PICKUP 112" WB $8019.
8'   124" WB $8254.
4WD " 6½' 112" $10729.
" 8' 124" WB $10963. ↙

DODGE DAKOTA
THE FIRST TRUE MID-SIZED PICKUP EVER MADE.

4 CYL.
OR
V6
111.9"
OR
123.9"
WB
(6½' OR 8' BED)

V.I.N. =
(1 OR J) B (4 OR 7)
─ (J43E) ─ H ─ #

NEW

DAKOTA CAB →

N14C
V6 OPT. IN 2WD
" STD. " 4WD

RAM PICKUP

REAR (DAKOTA)
$7080. UP

87

new 3.9L V6 ENG. AVAIL.
(MITSUBISHI 3.0 L V6 IN MINIVANS (OPTIONAL))

FROM $14484.
TO 16651.
PLUS OPTIONS

VAN
RAM WAGON (8-PASS. VAN) ↓

('87½)
$8818. UP (D-100)

DODGE RAM

(B-150 CARGO VANS $10624. and up)

DODGE RAM WAGON

CARAVAN = $12263. UP

DURING 1987 SEASON, new 119" WB, V-6 "GRAND CARAVAN" ALSO AVAILABLE (4 CYL. OR V-6 IN 112" WB MODELS)

Dodge Mini Ram Van
ALSO GETS 119" WB and V6 OPTIONS.

$9824. UP

new CARAVAN GRILLE and HEADLIGHT TREATMENT

DODGE = 87

DODGE

K13C MINI RAM
112" WB   119" WB
$10197. $10879.

K13C CARAVANS PRICED AT: $12783. $13483. (SE) $14491. (LE)
GRAND CARAVAN and V6 OPT.:
$15031. (SE)
$15989. (LE)

6½' BED

4WD   2WD

88

Dakota Interior

DAKOTA

Dodge Power Ram 50 Express. The Japanese 4x4 that turns the standards up. And discounts the price by $600.

RAM 50 FROM $7321.

3/36 LIMITED WARR. ON IMPORT TRUCK (50 SER.)

DAKOTA SE w. 8' BED

RAM WAGON   FROM 15395.

2.2 L 4 OR 3.9 L V6 (V8 ALSO AVAIL.)

YOUR CHOICE OF THREE DIFFERENT BODY SIZES, STANDARD V-6 AND V-8 ELECTRONIC FUEL INJECTION, OPTIONAL FRONT AND REAR AIR CONDITIONING AND SOUND SYSTEMS, ROOM FOR UP TO 15 OF YOUR MOST VALUABLE PLAYERS AND THE BEST WAGON WARRANTY IN ANY LEAGUE, THEN SIGN UP THIS ALL-STAR!...IT'S GOTTA BE A DODGE RAM WAGON. **7/70**

IF YOU'RE LOOKING FOR THE BEST FULL-SIZE PICKUP VALUE ANYWHERE,* WITH OVER 20 STANDARD FEATURES INCLUDING NEW ELECTRONIC FUEL INJECTION, BIG 15" WHEELS AND TIRES, A 1,410 LB. PAYLOAD, AMERICA'S BEST TRUCK WARRANTY,** A LOW $8,853 PRICE†

DODGE RAM 100

7/70 LIMITED WARRANTY

CHRYSLER MOTORS

V.I.N.= (1 OR J) B OR P (4,5 OR 7)–(J43E)–J

IT'S GOTTA BE A DODGE.

FROM $11340.

DODGE=88

115

RAM 50 DASH

THE TOUGH NEW SPIRIT OF DODGE
THE PERFORMANCE DIVISION OF CHRYSLER MOTORS

REAR DETAILS

B

RAIDER (4 CYL.)
$14316.
V6 AVAIL.
J43E
IMPORTED DODGE RAIDER

RAM 50 CUSTOM
(7' 4.3" BED)
$9024.
$10662.
6' BED

RAM 50 SPORT
(w. 5-WINDOW SPORTS CAB)

DAKOTA
4WD
(new DAKOTA CAB-CHASSIS ALSO AVAIL.)

RAM PICKUP
$11352. UP

"DODGE" NAME and RAM MASCOT ON HOOD

DODGE 89

RAM 50
(GRILLE COLOR MATCHES BODY COLOR or AVAIL. in BLACK)

NO NOTEWORTHY STYLING CHANGES ON CARAVAN MINIVANS BETWEEN THE 1987 and 1990 MODELS.

"RAM WAGON" PASSENGER VANS = FROM $15639.

V.I.N. = (I or J) B or P
(4 or 7) —
(J43E) —

89

360 cid V8 AVAIL.

B-150 CARGO VANS FROM 13241.

RAM VAN

B250

B 150

116

DODGE

$8700. RAM 50 UP

POWER RAM 50 $13673.

DAKOTA SPORT CONVERTIBLE PICKUP

DAKOTA

new CLUB CAB →

Import Trucks.

(DAKOTA "S" PICKUP $8410.)

4 CYL. OR V6 DAKOTAS

160 HP TURBO DIESEL (5.9 L CUMMINS) AVAIL. on D and W 250 and 350 PICKUPS and CHASSIS CABS.

POWER RAM 4WD

D150 (115" OR 131" WB)

POWER RAM

D 350 DUAL REAR-WHEEL CHASSIS CAB 135" WB

90

V.I.N.= (1 OR J) B OR P (4 OR 7) - M18Y-L

new CHRYSLER "TOWN and COUNTRY" MINIVANS SIMILAR TO "CARAVAN" and "VOYAGER" (CONTINUING SER.)

RAM

VANS

B350 MAXIVAN

B250 $17339.

V6 OR V8 RAM WAGONS

6 OR V8   109.6" OR 127.6" WB

COMMUNITY CABLE VISION CCV

B150 $16739.

B350 $17897. UP

new REAR WHEEL ANTI-LOCK BRAKES.

CARAVAN CV

(CARGO VAN)

$11640. 4 CYL.

CARAVAN = $13957.

SE $14637.; LE $17222.

ES/LX TURBO 4-CYL. $18320.

GRAND CARAVAN SE $16775. LE 18840. (119" WB)

112" WB 2.5 L TURBO 4 OR 3.0 L V6 OPTIONAL (119" WB CV WITH V6: $13965.)

DOVER

(1929-1930)

MFD. BY THE HUDSON MOTOR CAR CO., DETROIT

(MECHANICALLY SIMILAR TO HUDSON'S LOW-PRICED 1929 ESSEX CAR.)

3/4 TON

New **29**

110½ WB
6-CYL.
160 C/D
L-HEAD ENG.
55 HP @ 3600 RPM

SIGN ON SIDE RESEMBLES RADIATOR EMBLEM.

DOVER
THE COMMERCIAL SUPER SIX
Built by HUDSON

DOVER *Built by* HUDSON MOTOR CAR CO.

See the ESSEX RELIABILITY CAR.

(2,130 SOLD)

MANY BOUGHT BY U.S. POST OFFICE FOR MAIL DELIVERY SERVICE.

(1,066 SOLD)

30

1929 SPECIFICATIONS CONTINUE

new LOWER ROOFLINE *and* BODY LAMPS ON PANEL DELIVERY.

FLYING HORSE RADIATOR EMBLEM MISSING FROM SCREEN-SIDE EXPRESS (AT UPPER LEFT)

(SEE ALSO: *TERRAPLANE*)

DIRECTLY ABOVE: PANEL DELIVERY TRUCK

(1908 ~ 1961)

DUPLEX

Duplex Truck Company
Lansing · Michigan

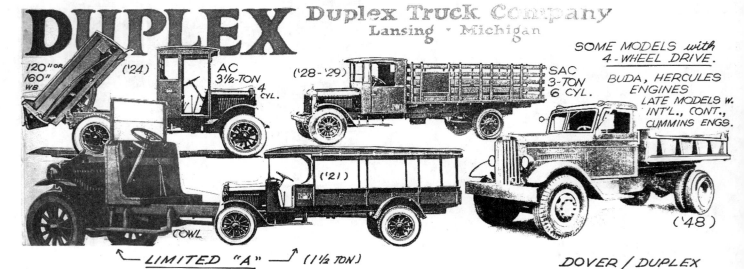

120" OR 160" WB

('24)

AC 3½-TON 4 CYL.

('28-'29)

SAC 3-TON 6 CYL.

SOME MODELS *with* 4-WHEEL DRIVE.

BUDA, HERCULES ENGINES
LATE MODELS W. INT'L., CONT., CUMMINS ENGS.

('21)

DUPLEX

('48)

COWL

← LIMITED "A" → (1½ TON)

DOVER / DUPLEX

T/A MODEL
460 CID FORD V8 ENG.
176" WB

ElDorado Falcon

EMC
ElDorado Motor Corporation
Minneapolis, KS 64767

INTERIOR (T/A)

460 CID FORD OR 350 CID CHEV. ENG.

capacity range of 12 to 25

22 Passenger

Base Floor Plans

23 Passenger

"Tee" Type Passenger Windows have emergency egress capability and a 31% tint. Upper portion slides open for ventilation.

MST

EXIT

HANDICAPPED BUS

MST

31 Passenger **MST**

Paratransit

MST

REAR

NEW $65,000.

1984 EXAMPLES ILLUSTR. V8 8.2 L. DETR. DIESEL ENG. IN MST (165 H.P.)

Falcon MST

30" Double Opening Entry Door is driver-controlled and air operated. Stainless steel grab rail, padded stanchions, modesty panel and automatically lighted step well are standard features. Optional clear opening widths, wheelchair access doors and power lifts also available.

INTERIOR, LOOKING REARWARD (CLERESTORY ROOF)

EL DORADO FALCON

FAGEOL

(1916 – 1954)

2½, 3½, 5 TON MODELS

4 CYL. WAU. ENGS. ('20)

144" OR 172" WB ('20)

FAGEOL MOTORS, OAKLAND, CALIF. (THROUGH '38)

CONVENTIONAL FAGEOLS OF 1920s and 1930s have UNIQUE, CHARACTERISTIC "SAWTOOTHED" RIDGE RUNNING ALONG TOP CENTER OF HOOD.

SOME WITH "7 SPEEDS" PAINTED ON RADIATOR CORE.

and TwinCoach CORPORATION

(EST. 1927 AFFILIATED WITH FAGEOL

KENT, OHIO

FAGEOL SAFETY COACH ('22)

A TYPICAL FAGEOL TRUCK OF 1920s. (1930 VIEW) ('27)

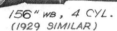

TRUCKS 1920s

MODEL 130 "FLYER" 1½ TON ('28)

CHASSIS: $1900.

156" WB, 4 CYL. (1929 SIMILAR)

1½ TO 10-TON MODELS AVAILABLE. "GOLDEN BEAR" TRUCK ('29) BELOW

TANDEM TRACTOR (ALUMINUM CAB)

('29)

New

TWIN COACH TRANSIT BUSES INTRO. 1927

44-PASS. (EARLY 1927)

FLAT-FRONT TYPE WITH WIDER ENTRY

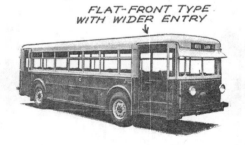

(LATE 1928)

EARLY FLAT-FRONT "PUSHER-TYPE" BUSES of LATE 1920s WERE SOMETIMES REFERRED TO AS "STREETCAR-TYPE" COACHES BECAUSE OF ABSENCE OF A CONVENTIONAL EXTENDED HOOD IN FRONT.

FAGEOL and TWIN COACH = 1920s

FAGEOL and TWIN COACH

RIGHT SIDE VIEW

TWIN COACH

LEFT SIDE

BUY BREAD AT YOUR DOOR

19 QUINBY'S

('30) TRUCK
FAGEOL HEAVY DUTY

Frank R. Fageol
President

CITY DELIVERY

THESE QUAINT, BOXY LITTLE DOOR-TO-DOOR ROUTE DELIVERY VANS WERE MFD. FROM 1929 TO 1936, WHEN OPERATION ABSORBED BY DIVCO.

STILL IN USE IN THE 1950s

TYPE BELOW BLT. OCT. '31 TO MAY '35
MODEL 15
Twin Coach
MINI BUS (17 PASS.)

1930s

"AS IS" UNRESTORED 1936 FAGEOL TRUCKS. NOTE 2 DIFFERENT CAB TYPES.

DRIVER OPENS SIDE-DOOR MECHANICALLY BY OVERHEAD RODS.

INTERIOR VIEW

FRONT RT. SEAT FACES BACKWARD

132" WB

('32)
WITH 73 HP 6-CYL. HERCULES 282 cid L-HEAD ENGINE

REAR END OF LATER '30s BUS IS STREAMLINED.

New ('37-38)

TWIN COACH
2 VIEWS

1½ TO 10-TON MODELS (1938): 106 BK 135 BK 250 BK MK RA 300HP, ETC. 6-CYL. WAU. OR CUMMINS ENGINES, 82 TO 150 H.P.

50-VISITACION

25

SMALL TRANSIT BUS WITH REAR ENGINE

FAGEOL

('37) NOTE 2 DIFFERENT FRONT END STYLES

('38)

FAGEOL

FREIGHTWAYS

C.O.E. OAKLAND PRODUCTION ENDS JAN. 1, 1939 =STERLING TEMPORARILY ACQUIRES ASSETS.

FAGEOL and TWIN COACH

TRANSIT BUS

THIS 6-PC. WINDSH. STYLE LATER ON FLXIBLE.

INTERCITY TYPE

Propane-power

OPTION ON BUSES

(note: NO FAGEOL TRUCKS DURING 1940s.)

Fageol Twin Coach

(POSTWAR, WITH MULTI-PIECE WINDSHIELD)

40-53

(90 TO 250 H.P.)
1952 ENGINES ILLUSTR.

FAGEOL GASOLINE ENGINES

HORIZONTAL

PROPANE ENGINES RESEMBLE THESE 2, BUT LABELED "PROPANE"

VERTICAL

as used by the Flxible Co.

FAGEOL LEYLAND DIESEL ENGINES

HORIZONTAL

VERTICAL

VERTICAL

CITY TRANSIT BUS

FAGEOL TRUCKS RESUME 1950, BY **TWIN COACH CO.**

(RE-ORGANIZED)

new SERIES STARTS 1950.

Twin Coach of 1950. Operating on 125 octane Propane, it saves an average of up to 2 cents per mile on fuel costs alone.

Super Freighter

(New)

50

Designed with Fruehauf Model SS (GT55) Stainless Steel Van

TWIN COACH COMPANY
KENT, OHIO

In Canada: Twin Coach of Canada, Ltd.
Toronto 5, Ontario

FAGEOL GAS/PROPANE ENGINES IN CONVERTED FRUEHAUF TRAILERS ('50) 6 CYL., 162 TO 250 HP

Fageol Super Freighter KENT OHIO

DESIGNED BY

L. J. FAGEOL

POWER STEER. AVAIL.

FRONT VIEW

CAB

FAGEOL=40~50

FAGEOL VANS

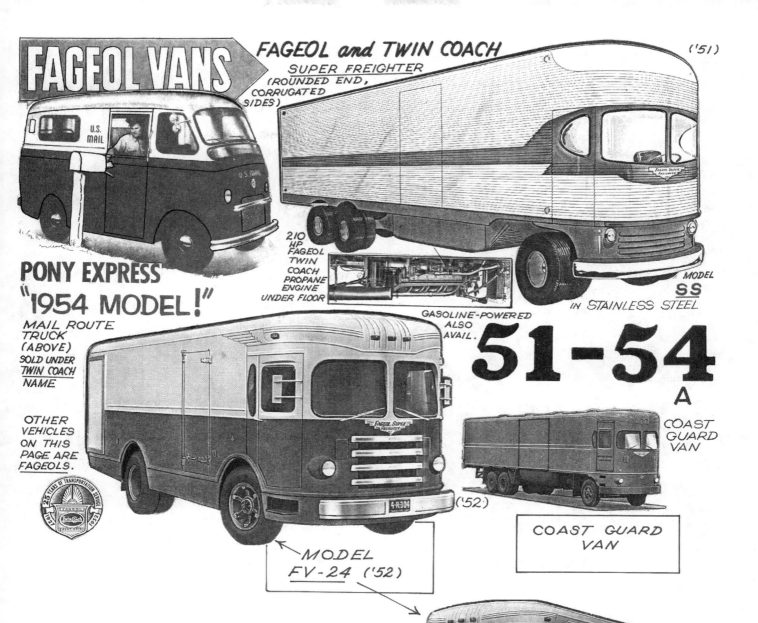

FAGEOL and TWIN COACH ('51)

SUPER FREIGHTER (ROUNDED END, CORRUGATED SIDES)

PONY EXPRESS "1954 MODEL!"

MAIL ROUTE TRUCK (ABOVE) SOLD UNDER TWIN COACH NAME

OTHER VEHICLES ON THIS PAGE ARE FAGEOLS.

210 HP FAGEOL TWIN COACH PROPANE ENGINE UNDER FLOOR

GASOLINE-POWERED ALSO AVAIL.

MODEL SS IN STAINLESS STEEL

51-54 A

COAST GUARD VAN

COAST GUARD VAN

MODEL FV-24 ('52)

('52)

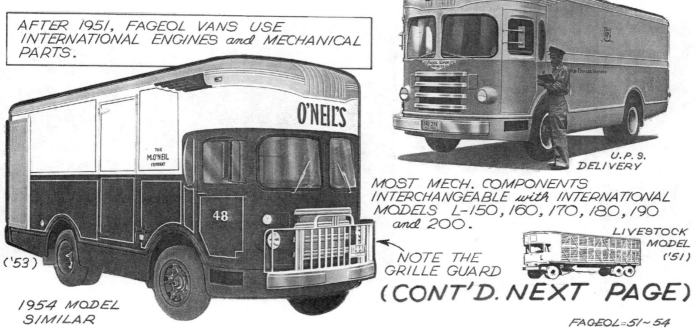

AFTER 1951, FAGEOL VANS USE INTERNATIONAL ENGINES and MECHANICAL PARTS.

O'NEIL'S

THE M. O'NEIL COMPANY

48

('53)

1954 MODEL SIMILAR

U.P.S. DELIVERY

MOST MECH. COMPONENTS INTERCHANGEABLE with INTERNATIONAL MODELS L-150, 160, 170, 180, 190 and 200.

NOTE THE GRILLE GUARD

LIVESTOCK MODEL ('51)

(CONT'D. NEXT PAGE)

FAGEOL = 51~54

123

THE FAGEOL
Twin Coach "CONVERTIBLE"

DESIGNED BY L.J. FAGEOL ('51½)

SEATS CAN BE REMOVED, SO FREIGHT CAN BE HAULED

CIVILIAN TYPE 35' LONG

With seats in place, "Convertible" is light, airy, comfortable, deluxe bus.

Seats telescope into compact pile to permit use as cargo truck carrying 5-ton payload, or seats can be removed completely).

REAR OF MILITARY TYPE

Rear view. Locking hasp protects cargo. Emergency release inside vehicle permits opening of rear doors even if doors are locked by outside hasp. Rear step is retractable.

INTERIOR (CIVILIAN)

MILITARY TYPE, RT., HOLDS A JEEP, AND ALSO 24 SEATED PASSENGERS. →

51- 54 (CONT'D.)

BRAND NEW

for Military Service

(IN 1953, (FLXIBLE BUYS TWIN COACH BUS PROD.)

ONE OF 1509 CONVERTIBLE BUSES BLT. FOR U.S. ARMY

The "Convertible" fills the long existent military need for a high speed vehicle which can be used separately or simultaneously as a personnel-carrying bus, high capacity cargo truck or field ambulance. Each vehicle can be divided into separate sections for combination use of any desired type.

WITH CHRYSLER V8 ENG. ('68)

TWIN COACH NAME RETURNS 1968, ON SMALL BUSES BLT. AT KENT, OHIO, BY HIGHWAY PRODUCTS CO.

The University of California at Santa Cruz is presently running a propane-powered Twin Coach Model TC-29.

68 ON

25 OR 33-PASS. AVAIL. W. CHRYSLER HT-413 LP GAS POWER (ABOVE) ('71)

RADIO-DISPATCHED "DIAL-A-RIDE" BUS ('72)

FAGEOL / TWIN COACH

FEDERAL (1910–1959)

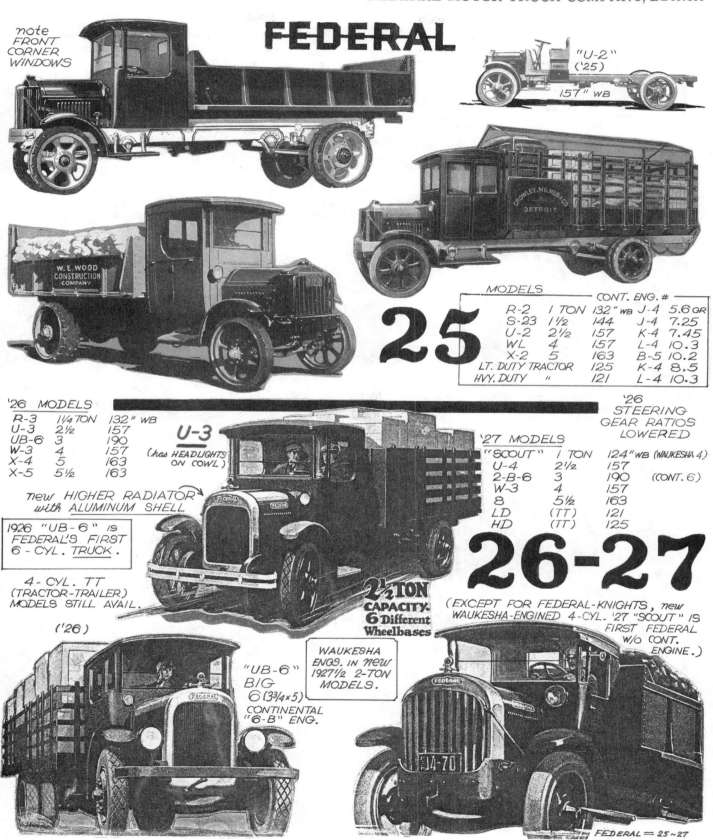

FEDERAL MOTOR TRUCK COMPANY, Detroit

FEDERAL

note FRONT CORNER WINDOWS

"U-2" ('25)
157" WB

W. E. WOOD CONSTRUCTION COMPANY

CROWLEY-MILNER CO. DETROIT

25

MODELS			CONT. ENG. #	
R-2	1 TON	132" WB	J-4	5.6 GR
S-23	1½	144	J-4	7.25
U-2	2½	157	K-4	7.45
WL	4	157	L-4	10.3
X-2	5	163	B-5	10.2
LT. DUTY TRACTOR		125	K-4	8.5
HVY. DUTY "		121	L-4	10.3

'26 MODELS

R-3	1¼ TON	132" WB
U-3	2½	157
UB-6	3	190
W-3	4	157
X-4	5	163
X-5	5½	163

U-3
(has HEADLIGHTS ON COWL)

new HIGHER RADIATOR with ALUMINUM SHELL

1926 "UB-6" IS FEDERAL'S FIRST 6-CYL. TRUCK.

4-CYL. TT (TRACTOR-TRAILER) MODELS STILL AVAIL.

('26)

'26 STEERING GEAR RATIOS LOWERED

'27 MODELS

"SCOUT"	1 TON	124" WB	(WAUKESHA 4)
U-4	2½	157	
2-B-6	3	190	(CONT. 6)
W-3	4	157	
8	5½	163	
LD	(TT)	121	
HD	(TT)	125	

26-27

2½ TON CAPACITY 6 Different Wheelbases

WAUKESHA ENGS. IN new 1927½ 2-TON MODELS.

(EXCEPT FOR FEDERAL-KNIGHTS, new WAUKESHA-ENGINED 4-CYL. '27 "SCOUT" IS FIRST FEDERAL w/o CONT. ENGINE.)

"UB-6" BIG 6 (3¾ x 5) CONTINENTAL "6-B" ENG.

34-70

FEDERAL ≡ 25~27

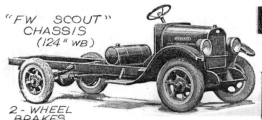

"FW SCOUT" CHASSIS (124" WB)

2-WHEEL BRAKES

FEDERAL 28

CONTINENTAL and WAUKESHA 4 and 6-CYL. ENGINES

2 TON : T-20, T-2B, T2W, T6B, T6W
2½ TON : U-5   3 TON : 2B6
4 TON : W-4   7½ TON : X-8
TRACTOR TR. : LD, HD

"F-6" IS NEW 1-TON 124" WB MODEL WITH 6-CYL. CONTINENTAL ENGINE.

NO MORE KNIGHT-ENGINED FEDERALS
SEE : **FEDERAL-KNIGHT**

WORM DRIVE and BEVEL GEAR DRIVE MODELS

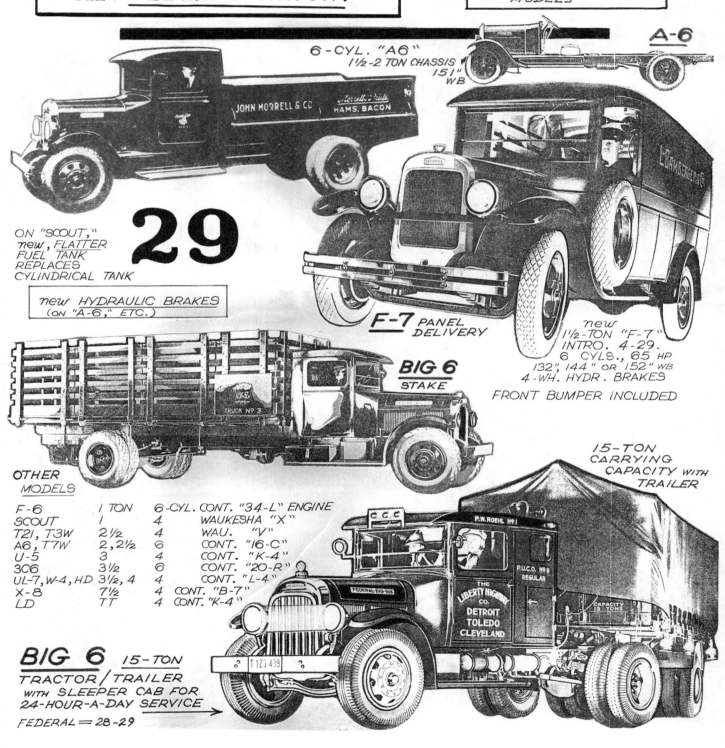

6-CYL. "A6" 1½-2 TON CHASSIS 151" WB

A-6

JOHN MORRELL & CO   *Morrell's Pride* HAMS, BACON

29

ON "SCOUT," *new*, *FLATTER FUEL TANK* REPLACES CYLINDRICAL TANK

new HYDRAULIC BRAKES (ON "A-6," ETC.)

F-7 PANEL DELIVERY

new 1½-TON "F-7" INTRO. 4-29. 6 CYLS., 65 HP 132", 144" OR 152" WB 4-WH. HYDR. BRAKES

FRONT BUMPER INCLUDED

BIG 6 STAKE

15-TON CARRYING CAPACITY WITH TRAILER

OTHER MODELS

F-6	1 TON	6-CYL.	CONT. "34-L" ENGINE
SCOUT	1	4	WAUKESHA "X"
T21, T3W	2½	4	WAU. "V"
A6, T7W	2, 2½	6	CONT. "16-C"
U-5	3	4	CONT. "K-4"
3C6	3½	6	CONT. "20-R"
UL-7, W-4, HD	3½, 4	4	CONT. "L-4"
X-8	7½	4	CONT. "B-7"
LD	TT	4	CONT. "K-4"

BIG 6 15-TON
TRACTOR / TRAILER
WITH SLEEPER CAB FOR
24-HOUR-A-DAY SERVICE

FEDERAL = 28~29 →

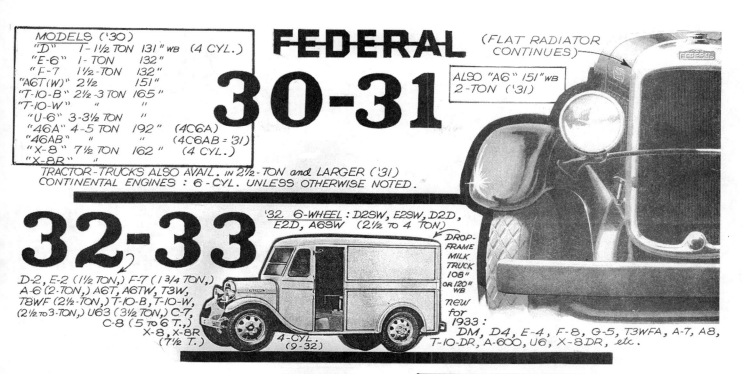

FEDERAL 30-31

MODELS ('30)				
"D"	1-1½ TON	131" WB	(4 CYL.)	
"E-6"	1- TON	132"		
"F-7"	1½-TON	132"		
"A6T(W)"	2½	151"		
"T-10-B"	2½-3 TON	165.5"		
"T-10-W"	"	"		
"U-6"	3-3½ TON	"		
"46A"	4-5 TON	192"	(4C6A)	
"46AB"	"	"	(4C6AB = '31)	
"X-8"	7½ TON	162"	(4 CYL.)	
"X-8R"	"	"		

(FLAT RADIATOR CONTINUES)

ALSO "A6" 151" WB 2-TON ('31)

TRACTOR-TRUCKS ALSO AVAIL. IN 2½-TON and LARGER ('31)
CONTINENTAL ENGINES : 6-CYL. UNLESS OTHERWISE NOTED.

32-33

'32 6-WHEEL: D2SW, E2SW, D2D, E2D, A6SW (2½ TO 4 TON)

DROP-FRAME MILK TRUCK 108" OR 120" WB

D-2, E-2 (1½ TON,) F-7 (1¾ TON,)
A-6 (2-TON,) A6T, A6TW, T3W,
T8WF (2½-TON,) T-10-B, T-10-W,
(2½ TO 3-TON,) U63 (3½ TON,) C-7,
C-8 (5 TO 6 T.,)
X-8, X-8R
(7½ T.)

4-CYL.
(9-32)

new for 1933:
DM, D4, E-4, F-8, G-5, T3WFA, A-7, A8,
T-10-DR, A-600, U6, X-8DR, etc.

('34)

$645
and up
with hydraulic brakes and full-floating axle

V-GRILLE

34

new 6-CYL. HERCULES ENGINES (IN "15," "20," "25.")

new FOR 1934 :
MODELS 15, 20,
25, 30, 40, 40-DR, etc.

MODELS "DM"		MAKE of ENGINE CONTINENTAL "W-10"	50 HP
		HERCULES	61 HP
15, 15-X	1½ TON		
18-X	2	"	
20	2	"	
25	2½	"	
30	2½ TO 3	WAUK.	
40, 40-DR	3½ TO 4	"	
T-10 (VARIATIONS)	"	CONT.	
50	4½ TO 5	WAU.	
C-7, C-7W	6	"	
C-8, C-8W	6	"	
X-8, X8DR	7½	CONT.	
X-8RDR, X8R	7½	WAU.	

new HORIZONTAL HOOD LOUVRE TRIM

DM IS ONLY 4-CYL. MODEL; OTHERS 6-CYL.

35 (RESTYLED)
$745.
(1½ TON CHASSIS)

UP TO 110 HP
(IN 517 CID WAUKESHA "6-SRK" ENGINE)

IN 1935 =
"25TH ANNIVERSARY" MODELS
FEDERAL = 30~35

FEDERAL

36

CONTINENTAL 4 and 6,
HERCULES 6, and
WAUKESHA 4 and 6-CYL. ENGINES
199 TO 517 CID
50 TO 110 HP

The New ¾-1 TON FEDERAL

MODELS DM, 10, 15, 18, 20,
25, 28, 29, 30, 40, 40DR,
T-10B, T-10W, 50, C7, C7W,
C8, C8W, X-8, X8DR,
X8R, X8RDR

5.14 TO 11.14 GEAR RATIOS

CAPACITIES TO 7½ TONS

¾ TON
4-CYL.
CHASSIS
FROM
$645.
(THROUGH
'39)

MODEL 28 NO
LONGER AVAIL.

FINAL YEAR
FOR 7½ TON
"X"
MODELS

37

new MODEL "9" REPLACES "DM," with 4-CYL. "C-400"
CONT. 143 CID ENGINE (33 HP @ 2500 RPM) (for MILK ROUTES)
105" WB, ¾ TO 1-TON CAP'Y.,
MODEL 11 ALSO new
GR: 5.14-5.83

new LOWER
RUNNING-
BOARDS

SLEEPER-CAB TYPE
(AVAIL. '38,
WITH V-WINDSHIELD
ON DE LUXE CAB)

(CAB-OVER-ENGINE TYPES:
new 75, 80, 85, 89 MODELS INTRODUCED.)

new GRILLE with
RADIATOR FILLER
UNDER HOOD.
V-WINDSHIELD ON
DE LUXE CAB

STANDARD CAB

38

5.14 TO 11.2
GEAR RATIOS

104"
TO
249"
WB

new STYLING
BY
HENRY DREYFUSS

MODELS 9, 10, 11, 11-H, 15, 15-H, 18, 18-H,
20, 20-H, 25, 25-H, 29, 29-H,
40, 40-DR, 50, 50-H, C-7, C-7W,
C8, C-8W, C-8H (¾ TO 7½ TONS)
C.O.E.s: 75, 75-H, 80, 80-H, 85,
85-H, 89, 89-H. (1½ TO 5 TONS)
(43 MODEL VARIATIONS)

6 CYLS., EXCEPT 4-CYL. "9"
(CONTINENTAL ENGINE) and
4-CYL. "10" (HERCULES ENGINE)
50 TO 115 HP

39

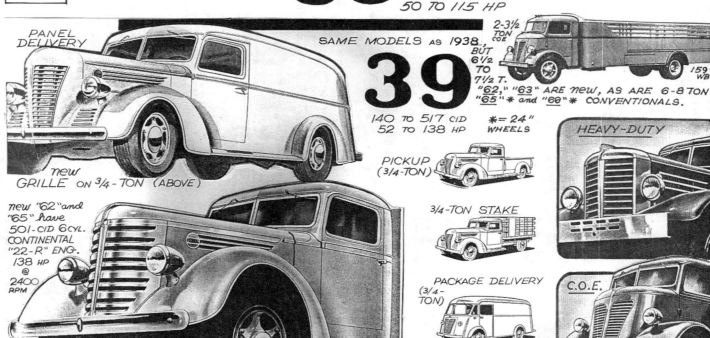

PANEL
DELIVERY

SAME MODELS AS 1938,
BUT 6½ TO 7½ T.

2-3½
TON
COE

159"
WB

"62," "63" ARE new, AS ARE 6-8 TON
"65"* and "68"* CONVENTIONALS.

140 TO 517 CID
52 TO 138 HP

*= 24"
WHEELS

new
GRILLE ON ¾-TON (ABOVE)

new "62" and
"65" have
501-CID 6CYL.
CONTINENTAL
"22-R" ENG.
138 HP
@
2400
RPM

PICKUP
(¾-TON)

¾-TON STAKE

PACKAGE DELIVERY
(¾-
TON)

new "202" TO "892"
6-WHEELERS

HEAVY-DUTY

C.O.E.

20" WHEELS,
MOST MODELS

FEDERAL = 36-39

52 TO 139 HP (1940)

40-45 FEDERAL

'40 MODELS : 7, 8, 11, 12, 14, 15, 18, 20, 25, 29, 29-H, 40, 50, 50-H, 62, 63, 65, 66

C.O.E.s : 75, 80, 85, 89, 89-H

FINAL WAUKESHA ENGINES IN '41 "63" and "66."

Plant facilities covering over half a million square feet of floor space produce the famous series of Federal Trucks.

Federal was cited four times for its excellence in war production—building trucks of all types for the Armed Services.

↑ WARTIME MODEL ('43) WITH LOWER SECTION OF GRILLE COVERED

MODELS 11-15, 40, 50, 75 NOT LISTED IN '41. 16, 17, 35, 45, 55, 55-H and C.O.E.s 76, 77, and 90 SERIES new IN '41. 7, 29-H, 63-66 NOT LISTED IN '42.

1941 ENGINES:						MODELS USING :
CONTINENTAL	F-4140	4 CYL.	140 CID	52 HP @ 2500 RPM		7
HERCULES	QXB3F	6	205	66 @ 3500		8
"	JXFF	6	232	75 @ 3000		16
"	JXGF	6	245	79 @ 3000		17
"	JXBF	6	263	82 @ 3000		18, 20

OTHER HERCULES 6 ENGINES ALSO, OF 282, 320, 383, 404 CID (85 TO 125 HP.) ALSO WAUKESHA and CONTINENTAL 6 ENGINES (TO 501 CID, 150 HP.)

(FINAL 4-CYL. MODEL IN 1941)

HERCULES or CONT. ENGINES (6 CYL., 263 TO 501 CID)

93 TO 148 HP

THESE BOTTLE-RACK TRUCKS POPULAR IN THE 1940s.

46-48

18M, 18M2, 29M, 29M2, 29MA, 45M, 45M2, 55M, 55MA, 60MA, 60M2, MODELS ('46)

20" WHEELS

5-SPEED CLARK TRANS.

SEPT., 1947 = 2 SERIES (5 MODELS) INTRODUCED : "25" SERIES (25M, 25M2, 2½ TO 3½ TON FOR TRUCK-TRAILER COMBINATIONS with HERCULES JXC(F) GAS ENGINE.) "29ML" SERIES SIMILAR TO EXISTING "29M" SERIES, has HERCULES JXLD(F) GAS ENGINE.

all MODELS with LOCKHEED FRONT BRAKES and TIMKEN (REAR.)

BENDIX Hydrovac ON all.

FEDERAL = 40-48

FEDERAL

49-50

6 CYL.

15M, 16M, 16M2, 18M, 18M2, 25M, 25M2, 29M, 29M2, 29MA, 29ML, 29ML2, 29MLA, 35M, 35M2, 45M, 45M2, 55M2, 55MA, 60MA, 60M2, 65M2, 65MA. MODELS ('49) HERC. ENG BELOW "35M;" CONT. ENGINES IN OTHERS.

22-24" WHEELS ("45M" and up)   6.50 × 20 TIRES

15-M UTILITY EXPRESS
3/4 TO 2 TON TYPES
6 CYL.
HERCULES ENG.
93 HP @ 3400
5.67 or 6.67 G.R.

INTRO. 4-49

---

51 (INTRO. LATE SUMMER, 1950)

RESTYLED
new CURVED WINDSHIELD

5.56 to 8.53 GEAR RATIOS

new SWING-UP FENDER SECTIONS

9 DIFFERENT 6-CYL. ENGINES, 236 TO 602 CID 90 TO 205 HP   136" TO 250" WB
28 MODELS : 1501-T, 1601-T, 1602-T, 1801-T, 1802-T, 2501-T, 2502-T, 2901-T, 2902-T, 2904-T, 3001-T, 3002-T, 3004-T, 3401-T, 3402-T, 3404-T, 45-M, 45-MA, 45M2, 55-M, 55-MA, 55M2, 60-M, 60-MA, 60M2, 65-M, 65-MA, 65M2

52

new CONTINENTAL "POWER CHIEF" OVERHEAD-VALVE 6-CYL. 371 CID ENGINE 145 HP @ 3000 RPM

Federal Announces New Style Liner Models and Improved Engine Design

3401, 3402, 3404 MODELS

('52)

WITH new O.H.V. 6-CYL., 371 CID "POWER CHIEF" ENG. (145 HP @ 3000 RPM) 136 TO 250" WB

1956 MODELS   (133" TO 216" WB)
400 PREFIX : R-1 THROUGH R-8 (427 CID)
500 PREFIX : R-1 THROUGH R-5 (501 CID)
600 PREFIX : R-1 and R-2 (602 CID)
4-W-D : T-400R-1; T-500R-1; T-600R-1; T600R-4
ALL WITH 6-CYL. CONT. ENGINES (170 HP @ 3000 RPM, 182 HP OR 212 HP @ 2800 RPM) (ALL WITH 5-SPEED TRANS.)

59

145" TO 193" WB ('59)

MODELS :
200 R1 ; 200 R2 ; 300 R1, 300 R2 ; 400 R1, 400 R2, 500 R1, 500 R2, 600 R1, 600 R2, "D" PREFIX ON ABOVE MODELS INDICATES CUMMINS DIESEL ENG. D700R1, D700R2 and NUMEROUS ADDITIONAL MODELS WHICH END IN R53 OR R54 SUFFIX.
R44 SUFFIX INDICATES 4-WHEEL DRIVE.
R66   "   "   6-WHEELER.

HERCULES, CONTINENTAL, CUMMINS, TD ENGINES 116 TO 232 HP

NAPCO

IN LATER '50s, NAPCO INDUSTRIES OWNED FEDERAL, and MOVED OPERATIONS TO MINNEAPOLIS.

FEDERAL TRUCKS

49~59

FEDERAL-KNIGHT (1924 TO 1927)

24-26

THE FEDERAL MOTOR TRUCK COMPANY

INITIALLY INTRODUCED 1924 AS FEDERAL'S LOWEST-PRICED LINE CHASSIS =

$1095.

1½-TON "9-25-6" and 2-TON "9-27" (BOTH WITH 144" WB) ALSO AVAIL. AFTER '25. KNOWN AS "S-25" and "S-1" IN 1927.

('24)

1-TON FEDERAL-KNIGHT with 4-CYL. KNIGHT SLEEVE-VALVE ENGINE

3 5/8" × 4½" BORE and STROKE (TO '27)

Willys-Knight engine

OIL TANKER TRUCK (SPRING, '25)

(SPRING, '25) OPEN CAB

FULLER DELIVERY SERVICE / FULLER BRUSHES / THE FULLER BRUSH CO. / N° 5007 / CAP. 1750 LT.WT. 3250 R.P.N. 90 M.

124" WB

SEMI-ENCLOSED CAB

L. BAMBERGER & C°

NEWARK N.J.

BLUE RIBBON MAYONNAISE. C.C.SKAFGAARD DISTRIBUTOR

CLOSED CAB (SUMMER, '25)

$1095.

(FALL, '25)

1½ TO 2 TON (FALL, '25)

(STILL AVAIL. IN 1927)

FULLY-CLOSED CAB ('26)

1924
Prices of other Federal Models

Fast Express	·	$1675
1½-Ton	·	2150
2½-Ton	·	3200
3½ to 4	·	4200
5-6 Ton	·	4750
7-Ton	·	5000
Light Duty Tractor	·	3200
Heavy Duty Tractor	·	4235

The only Knight Engined Truck on the market *

* AS OF THE MID-1920s

SEE ALSO: *FEDERAL*

FEDERAL-KNIGHT

FLXIBLE

THE FLXIBLE CO., LOUDONVILLE, O. (EST. 1924)

(FIRST TYPES = CONVERTED BUICKS, WITH LONG WHEELBASES.)

—1938, CONVERTED TO PRIVATE COACH

Bowling Green Hopkinsville Bus Co.

VERMONT TRANSIT 233

new CLIPPER SERIES (STARTS '37) (BUICK OR CHEVROLET ENGS.)

(C. '40)

('37) NOTE THAT FR. DOOR IS BACK OF FR. AXLE (20-PASS.) (REAR-ENGINED "CLIPPER 25" STARTS '38)

30s-40s

SOME EARLY CLIPPERS have 3-TIERED BUMPERS.

1935 = 16-PASS. "AIRWAY"
1936 = 19-24 PASS. "

MICHAUD BUS LINES INC. SALEM, MASS.
Scenic Special

('48)

(SLANTED SIDE WINDOWS SINCE '41)

VISICOACH ONE OF THE FINAL "CLIPPER" TYPES, with LONGER WINDOWS.

AIR SCOOP COOLS REAR ENGINE

('48)

CHARTERED 673 1251

('55)

673

50s

UNIQUE STYLING

new **VL100 FLXIBLE** ('56) "VISTA-LINER"

(INTRO. 1956)

BIG BUS

FLXIBLE CONTINUES TWIN COACH CITY BUS TYPES.

('81)

FLXETTE BUS

70s

(ABOVE TYPE STARTS 1961.) (17-55 PASS. TYPES IN 1972.)

GRUMMAN

BUYS FLXIBLE FR. ROHR INDUSTRIES 1977.

80s ('80)

H MAIN AND PEARL

GRUMMAN 205 CONNECTICUT TRANSIT
STATE 2-757 CONNECTICUT

GRUMMAN-FLXIBLE "870" (SINCE '78)

FLXIBLE

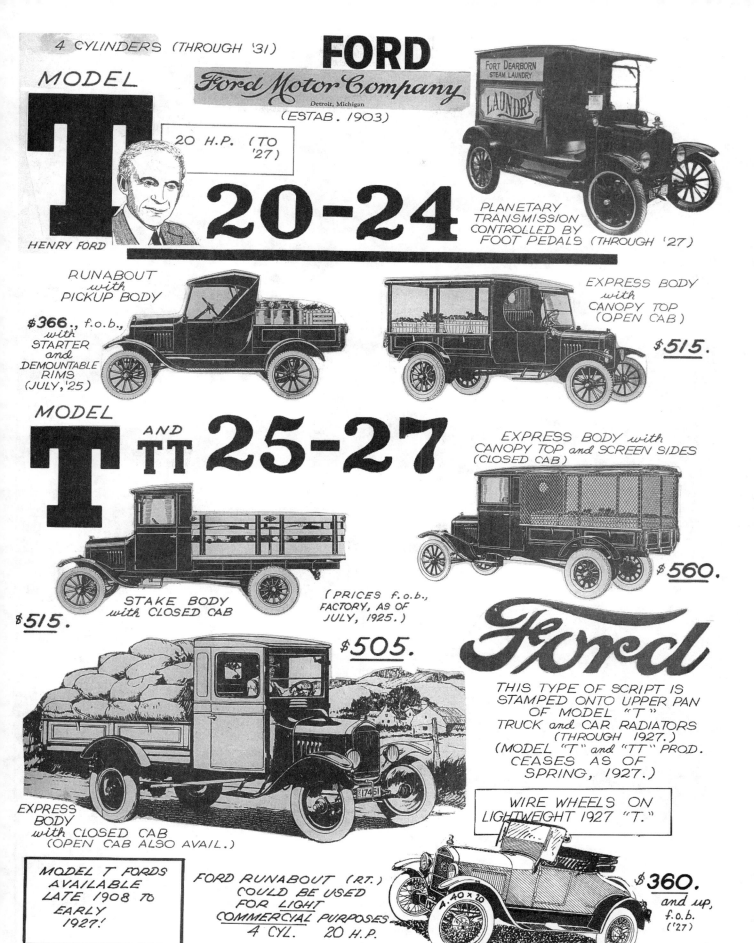

4 CYLINDERS (THROUGH '31)

FORD

Ford Motor Company

Detroit, Michigan

(ESTAB. 1903)

MODEL T

HENRY FORD

20 H.P. (TO '27)

20-24

PLANETARY TRANSMISSION CONTROLLED BY FOOT PEDALS (THROUGH '27)

RUNABOUT *with* PICKUP BODY

$366., f.o.b., *with* STARTER *and* DEMOUNTABLE RIMS (JULY, '25)

EXPRESS BODY *with* CANOPY TOP (OPEN CAB)

$515.

MODEL T AND TT 25-27

EXPRESS BODY *with* CANOPY TOP *and* SCREEN SIDES (CLOSED CAB)

$560.

STAKE BODY *with* CLOSED CAB

$515.

(PRICES f.o.b., FACTORY, AS OF JULY, 1925.)

$505.

Ford

THIS TYPE OF SCRIPT IS STAMPED ONTO UPPER PAN OF MODEL "T" TRUCK *and* CAR RADIATORS (THROUGH 1927.) (MODEL "T" *and* "TT" PROD. CEASES AS OF SPRING, 1927.)

EXPRESS BODY *with* CLOSED CAB (OPEN CAB ALSO AVAIL.)

WIRE WHEELS ON LIGHTWEIGHT 1927 "T."

MODEL T FORDS AVAILABLE LATE 1908 *To* EARLY 1927!

FORD RUNABOUT (RT.) COULD BE USED FOR LIGHT COMMERCIAL PURPOSES 4 CYL. 20 H.P.

$360. *and up,* f.o.b. ('27)

FORD = '20~27

133

new MODEL "A"
(COMPLETELY RE-DESIGNED)

FORD

ROADSTER
PICKUP

new
OVAL EMBLEM
new CONVENTIONAL-STYLE
SLIDING-GEAR TRANSMISSION

MODEL **A**
New **28-29**

pickup

New Power

4-CYLINDER
ENGINE IMPROVED
(new 40 HP @
2300 RPM)
200.5 CID

1929
INTERIOR

CAB

1½ TON
STAKE
Truck
(ABOVE)

HEAVY DUTY
WHEELS

MORE DETAILED
INTERIOR VIEW (1928) →

RED
IN
1928

EARLY MODELS (1928)
HAVE EMERGENCY BRAKE LEVER
AT FAR LEFT SIDE

FORD = 28~29

134

NEW FORD

SPIRAL-BEVEL GEAR REAR AXLE →

Loads that bulk large can be hauled at small cost

1½-TON PANEL DELIVERY

TAIL-LIGHT ↙

LARGER and HIGHER RADIATOR THAN IN 1929.

REAR CHASSIS DETAIL

30 (RESTYLED) **MODEL -32A** and **AA**

SOME 1931½-32 LT. DLVRY., CARS HAVE THIS FRONT END STYLE. ↗

4-SPEED TRANS. IS STD. EQUIP. ON "AA" TRUCKS SINCE AUTUMN OF 1929.

FORD CAR RADIATOR DESIGN (MODEL A)

HVY. FORD TRUCK RADIATOR SHELL DOES NOT HAVE A HEART-SHAPE DIP AT THE CENTER OF UPPER PAN.

SHIFT PATTERN (BELOW) 4-SPEED TRANSMISSION

('30)

('30)

1½-TON STAKE (131½" OR 157" WHEELBASE) 200.5 CID 4 CYL. ENG.

new HORIZONTAL GROOVES ADDED TO CENTER INSTRUMENT PANEL IN 1931.

Ford

ROADSTER PICKUP **$536.**

FORD = 30 ~ 32 (A)

FORD

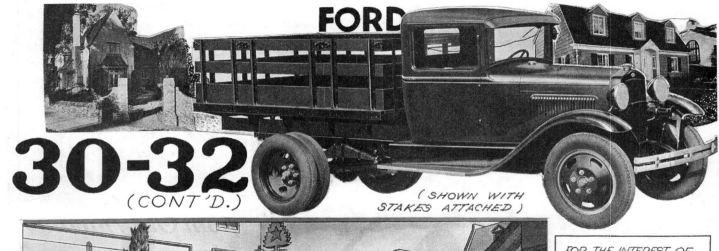

30-32 (CONT'D.)

(SHOWN WITH STAKES ATTACHED)

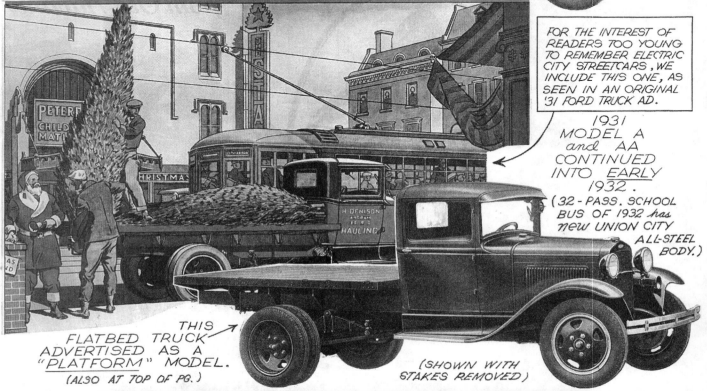

FOR THE INTEREST OF READERS TOO YOUNG TO REMEMBER ELECTRIC CITY STREETCARS, WE INCLUDE THIS ONE, AS SEEN IN AN ORIGINAL '31 FORD TRUCK AD.

1931 MODEL A and AA CONTINUED INTO EARLY 1932. (32-PASS. SCHOOL BUS OF 1932 has new UNION CITY ALL-STEEL BODY.)

THIS FLATBED TRUCK ADVERTISED AS A "PLATFORM" MODEL. (ALSO AT TOP OF PG.)

(SHOWN WITH STAKES REMOVED)

new MODEL B (4-CYL.) (ALSO "BB")

new SMALLER WHEELS

DELIVERY

(PANEL)

GAS TANK NO LONGER IN COWL, AS WAS ON MODEL A, AA

32 (LATER SERIES)

new GRILLE AND BODY TYPIFIES THE "TRUE 1932" FORDS.
(ALSO, new OVAL INSTRUMENT PANEL)

NEW

(INTRO. SPRING, 1932)

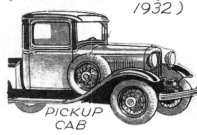

PICKUP CAB

MODEL B 5-WINDOW COUPE → $440. UP

new V8 ALSO AVAIL., APRIL 1932 ON

FORD = 30~32 (B)

136

FORD
TRACTOR-TRAILER

BOXY, 1930 CAB STYLING ON **HEAVY-DUTY**

← SERIAL # FROM 18-203127 ('33) 18-457478 ('34)

1/2 TON CHASSIS PRICE FROM $370. ('33) OR $360. ('34)

('33)

SEDAN DELIVERY STYLED LIKE A FORD CAR. → **$565.**

33-34
OVAL INST. PANEL CONTINUES IN MOST TRUCKS

('34) **$550.**

↑ PANEL

DUMP

CAB

112", 131" OR 157" WHEELBASES (THROUGH '37)

NOTE V EMBLEMS ON 1934 V8 MODELS.

4-CYL. ALSO AVAIL. (THROUGH '34)*

1/2-TON OR 1 1/2-TON MODELS

2ND-HAND TRUCK ILLUSTRATED HERE ↓

('34)

AC 218

21F·532
L·50·885

* (THROUGH '33, IN CARS.)

ON ABOVE TRUCK, VERTICAL BUMPER GUARD and FOG LIGHT ARE NOT ORIGINAL EQUIPMENT

FORD =33~34

MFD. BY **FORD DIVISION** DEARBORN, MI.
FORD MOTOR COMPANY

FORD

(ESTABLISHED 1903)

WARREN TRANSFER CO.
CHARLOTTE N.C.

TRACTOR-TRAILER

(ABOVE)
1½ TON PANEL $760.
DELIVERY (131" WB)

1½ TON STAKE TRUCK
131" WB $675.
157" WB $735.

MODELS:
48 = COMMERCIAL
50 = ½ TON
51 = 1½ TON

Checker Express Co.
PARCEL DELIVERY AND TRUCK RENTAL

35
(RESTYLED)
V8 ENGINES ONLY
(THROUGH '39)

CUSTOM-BLT. C.O.E.'s AVAIL. 1935 TO 1938 (FACTORY-BLT. C.O.E. STARTS MAY, 1938.)

SEDAN DLVRY.
STYLED LIKE FORD CARS OF SAME YEAR

48 SERIES

221 CID
L HEAD V8
(90 HP)

(WIRE WHEELS ON LT. FORD TRUCKS)

½ TON PANEL DELIVERY $565.*
112" WB

(½ TON PICKUP STYLING SIMILAR, 112" WB ALSO $480.)*

SERIAL # 18-1234857 UP

*(SAME PRICE IN 1936)

TYPICAL 1936-STYLE HOUSE

1½ TON STAKE $670.
(131" WB)

($730. w. 157" WB)

CAR CARRIER (WITH RACK of NEW 1936 FORD AUTOMOBILES)

FORD EMBLEM MOVED FORWARD ON SIDE OF HOOD

36

MODELS:
68 = COMMERCIAL
67 = ½ TON
51 = 1½ TON

CITY TRANSIT BUS CHASSIS AVAIL. SINCE 1934, FIRST FLEETS SOLD TO CITY OF DETROIT. 25-PASS. FORD TRANSIT BUS INTRODUCED OCT., 1936. "70" SERIES

NEW STEEL ARTILLERY WHEELS
(A FEW SEEN WITH WIRE WHEELS)

pickup

PLATFORM TRUCK

FORD

NEW STYLING

OPTIONAL GEAR RATIOS AVAILABLE

FORD "70-A" and "70-B" (2' LONGER) CITY TRANSIT BUSES AVAIL. (TO 1939.)

new **37** RESTYLED

new CHOICE OF 60 OR 85 HORSEPOWER V8 ENGINES, 3 WHEELBASES (PICKUPS FROM $516.)

60 HP MODELS :
74 (COMM'L.;)
73 (½ TON;) 75 (1½ TON)

85 HP MODELS :
78 (COMM'L.;)
77 (½ TON;)
79 (1½ TON)

THIS SEDAN DELIVERY "COMMERCIAL CAR" STYLED LIKE 1937 FORD AUTOMOBILES.

"74" (60 HP) $639.
"78" (85 HP) $649.

new V-WINDSHIELD

new HOOD LOUVRES with V8 EMBLEM

new GRILLE

STAKE TRUCK $526. - 683.

TRACTOR with VAN TRAILER

FORD V·8 TRUCKS

60 HP			60 HP		
SERIAL # 54-6602 UP		112" HP	SERIAL # BB-54-39101 UP		
MODEL # 74	SED. DLVRY. —	$639. UP	73	½ T STAKE —	$548. UP
73	½ T PICKUP —	516. UP	75	1½ T PANEL —	778. UP
73	½ T PANEL —	618. UP	75	1½ T STAKE —	683. UP
85 HP SERIAL # 18-8331857 UP			85 HP SERIAL # BB18-835247 UP		FORD = 37

1938 has ⚡ (V-8) ← GRILLE MEDALLION

VERTICAL BUMPER GUARDS ON MANY 1938 MODELS.

CHASSIS DETAIL

FORD

60-HP MODELS 82-C (COMM'L. and ½ TON;) 82-Y (1 TON) ½ TON FROM $580.

38

NEW ROUNDED GRILLE and new LOUVRES (THROUGH '39)

CAB

NEW 1-TON MODELS WITH 122" WB $660. UP

MORE STYLE is found in the new treatment of radiator grille and the massive fenders which harmonize with the new hood and body lines.

New This Year! THE FORD V·8 ONE-TONNER! A unit that fills the gap between Ford Commercial Cars and the Big Ford Trucks

85-HP MODELS : 81-C (COMM'L. and ½-TON ;) 81-Y (1-TON ;) 81-T, 817-T (1½ T ;) 81-W, 811-W (1½ TON C.O.E.)

FINAL YEAR FOR FORD's MECHANICAL BRAKES

1938 SERIAL # FROM — 54358335 (60 HP) 18-4186447 (85 HP)

1939 SERIAL # FROM BB54-506300 (60 HP) 18-466/001 (85 HP) new "91-D" ¾ TON MODELS ADDED, FROM $595.

new 25'-9", 27-PASS. TRANSIT BUS WITH 95-HP V8 (TRANSVERSE AT REAR)

60-HP MODELS : 922-C (½ TON) 922-D (¾ TON) 92-Y (1 TON)

39

NO GRILLE MEDALLION IN 1939

$630. UP

THE "ONE-TONNER"

1 TON PICKUP

$935. UP SEE THE FORD V-8 CAB-OVER-ENGINE TRUCK! Another great truck in the Great Ford Line!

new HYDRAULIC BRAKES ON 1939 MODELS.

85-HP MODELS : 91-C (½ TON ;) 91-D (¾ TON ;) 91-Y (1 TON ;) 91-T, 917-T (1½ TON) 911-W, 91-W (1½ TON C.O.E.)

FORD 38~39

FORD

SERFAL NUMBERS :
(60 HP) = BB 54 - 506501 UP
(85 HP) = 18 - 5210701 UP

SEDAN DELIVERY and COMMERCIAL
LINE has FORD AUTOMOBILE STYLING.

NEARLY ALL 42 OF THE
1940 TYPES WERE PRICED
UNDER $1000., f.o.b., EXCEPT
FOR THE 134" WB C.O.E. 1½ TON
STAKE @ $1010.

60-HP MODELS :
O22-A (COMM'L.;) O2-C (½ TON ;)
O2-D (¾ TON;) O2-Y (1 TON)

OTHER MODELS : O1-A (COMM'L.;) O1-C (½ T.;)
O1-D (¾ TON)
O1-Y (1 TON)
O1-T, O18-T
(1½ TON)
O11-W, O1-W
(1½ TON C.O.E.)

40

$705.

new LONGITUDINAL FRONT SPRINGS ON TRUCK CHASSIS (NO TORQUE TUBE)

OTHER FORD TRUCK MODELS with OWN GRILLE, HOOD LOUVRES, HEADLIGHTS SEPARATE FROM FENDERS

V/8 EMBLEM PLACED AHEAD OF HOOD LOUVRES.

$775.

158" WB TYPE PLATFORM TRUCK (ABOVE)

CAB VIEW FROM ACTUAL PHOTO →

STAKE CAB

85 and 95-HP V8 ENGINES (FINAL YEAR FOR V8-60) 4 CYL. ALSO AVAIL.

ALSO SEE MARMON-HERRINGTON

CHASSIS/CAB
122" (¾ T.)
$630.
122" (1 TON
$665.

134" $680.
158" 705.
(ALSO C.O.E.
CHASSIS/CABS AVAIL.)

FORD = 40

SEDAN DELIVERY HAS GRILLE LIKE 1941 FORD CAR.

← $745.(V8)

FORD

41

1/4 TON PICKUP $620.

PICKUP'S FRONTAL STYLING MUCH LIKE THAT OF 1940 FORD CAR (STD.)

6-CYL. FORD CARS INTRO. DURING '41.

SOME 6-CYL. FORD TRUCKS REPORTED

ALSO CHOICE OF 85-90 HP V8 OR new 30 HP 4-CYLINDER ENGINE

4-CYL. MODELS :
INC (1/2 TON)
IND (3/4 TON)
INY (1 TON)

V8 MODELS :
11-C (1/2 TON)
11-D (3/4 TON)
11-Y (1 TON)
11-T, 118-T, 198-T, 114-T (11/2 TON ;)
111-W, 11-W, 118-W (11/2 TON C.O.E.)

STAKE

SERIAL #s :
6-CYL. (ALL)
87H UP

V8 1/2 TON
18-5898295 UP
V8 3/4 and 1 TON
18-5896295Y UP
V8 11/2 TON
BB18-5896295 UP

FORD=41

FORD

FORD 1942-44 CAB-FORWARD MODELS ILLUSTRATED IN MARMON-HERRINGTON SECTION.

1942-1945 MODELS:
21-A (SED. DLVRY.)
21-C (½ TON)
21-D (¾ TON) *
21-Y (1 TON)
21-T, 218-T, 214-T
(1½ TON ;)
211-W, 21-W, 218-W
(1½ TON C.O.E.)

1946 MODELS:
69-C, 69-Y,
69-T, 698-T,
691-W, 69-W, 698-W

1947 MODELS:
79-C, 79-Y, 79-T,
798-T, 791-W, 79-W,
798-W

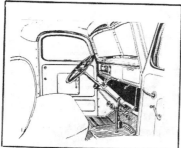

INTERIOR (1944-1947)
V8 OR
new 6-CYL.
90 H.P. and up

new STYLING IN 1942

42 -47

114, 122, 134, 158 or 194" WHEELBASES (101, 134 OR 158" ON C.O.E.s)

FLATBED ('45)

STAKE ('46)

6 CHASSIS TYPES IN 1945.

SLOGAN: "FORD TRUCKS LAST LONGER."

TRANSIT BUS ('46)

THESE BUSES BLT. BY MARMON-HERRINGTON AFTER 4-50.

TRUE TRUCK ENGINEERING

Powerful truck engines—Six chassis types—for 95% of all hauling jobs.

'42-45 21-A SEDAN DLVRY. STYLED LIKE FORD CAR. →

* = ¾-TON TRUCKS DROPPED AFTER 1944.

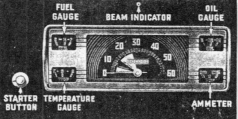

FUEL GAUGE   BEAM INDICATOR   OIL GAUGE

STARTER BUTTON   TEMPERATURE GAUGE   AMMETER

PICKUP INSTRUMENT PANEL ('42)

FORD='42~47

CLOSE-UP OF
INSTRUMENT PANEL

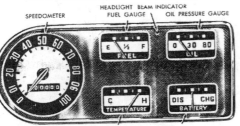

SPEEDOMETER | HEADLIGHT BEAM INDICATOR / FUEL GAUGE | OIL PRESSURE GAUGE
TEMPERATURE GAUGE | BATTERY GAUGE

FORD

F-4 STAKE

('49)

ROUGE 226 CID 6 (95 HP) OR
ROUGE 239 CID V8 (100 HP)

NEW 1-PIECE
WINDSHIELD
new GRILLE

F-3

Model F-3; 6,800 lbs. G.V.W.
Express or Stake

F-4

Model F-4; 10,000 lbs. G.V.W.
with Duals

Model F-5; 14,000 lbs. G.V.W.
Wheelbases; 134, 158 and 176 in.

F-5

48-50

RESTYLED 1948
3/4-TON MODELS
RETURN '48.

OVER 175 DIFFERENT
MODELS IN 1950.

PARTS NUMBERS INCLUDED

Model F-5 Cab-Over-Engine
14,000 lbs. G.V.W.

F-5

Model F-5 School Bus Chassis
Wheelbases; 158 and 194 in.

F-6

Model F-6 Cab-Over-Engine
16,000 lbs. G.V.W.

Model F-6; 15,500 lbs. G.V.W.
Wheelbases; 134, 158 and 176 in.

F-7

F-8

Model F-7; 19,000 lbs. G.V.W.
35,000 lbs. G.T.W.

Model F-8; 21,500 lbs. G.V.W.
39,000 lbs. G.T.W.

WITH
VAN
BODY

('50)

C.O.E.s

CAB-AND-
CHASSIS

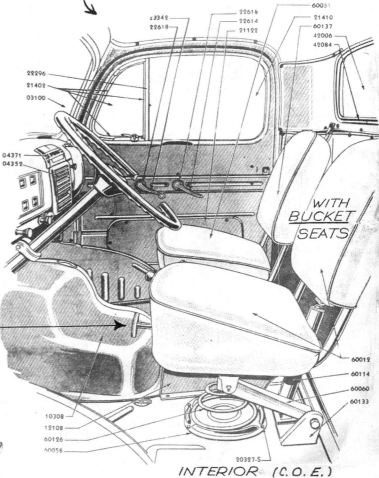

SEAT
ADJUSTMENT
KNOB

WITH
BUCKET
SEATS

INTERIOR (C.O.E.)

FORD V8 PICKUP $**1337.** ('48)
" " " $**1220.** ('49 and '50)
(114" WB)

F-4 1 TON (134" WB)
F-5 1½ TON (134 or 158" WB)
F-6 2 TON (134 or 158" WB)

LIGHT TRUCKS WITH
6-CYL. OR 100 HP V8

1948 SERIAL # STARTS WITH
88 —

FORD=48-50

144

$1280. UP
(F-1 PICKUP)

FORD
New
GRILLE

226 OR 254 CID 6,
239 OR 337 CID V8

51

F-1 (½-TON)
F-2, F-3 (¾ ")
F-4 (1-TON)
F-5 (1½ ")
F-6, F-7, F-8
and C.O.E.
MODELS
ALSO AVAIL.

95 HP @ 3300 (6)
100 HP @ 3800 (V8)
110 HP @ 3400 (BIG 6)
145 HP @ 3600 RPM
(BIG V8)

OVER 180
MODELS
IN
ALL

1½ TON F-5 = **$1722.** UP

6 (note DIFFERENT HOOD TRIM ALONG SIDES)

52

V8
HAS SMALL
8
EMBLEM
ON
HOOD

new LARGER, LOWER-PLACED "FORD" LETTERING ABOVE GRILLE and new TRIM ON FRONT and SIDES OF HOOD.

H.P. INCREASED
101, 112 HP (6)
106, 145, 155 HP (V8)

FINAL YEAR WITH THIS INTERIOR

new O.H.V. ENGINES AVAILABLE

F-900
HEAVY-DUTY

RESTYLED
53
A

(C.O.E.)
C-800

110 OR 134 " WB

$2188. UP

6
/7/7.

V8
/75/.

"COURIER" SEDAN DELIVERY CONTINUES TO BE STYLED LIKE A FORD CAR. 115" WB

½ TON PICKUP F-100 —— $1586.
½ TON PANEL " —— 1748.
¾ TON PICKUP F-250 —— 1655.
¾ TON STAKE F-250 —— 1728.
1 TON EXPRESS F-350 – 1824.
1 TON STAKE —— " 1916.
(PICKUP ON NEXT PAGE)

F-500 IS 1½ TON SERIES **$2012.** UP

FORD=51~53

new F-100, F-250, F-350, F-500 SERIES

OVER 190 INDIVIDUAL MODELS

NEW "DRIVERIZED" CABS cut driver fatigue!
New one-piece curved windshield. 55% bigger! Wider seat, with new *shock absorber.* Larger door opening, pushbutton handles.

new INTERIOR *and* DASH

FORD

F-100 ½ TON PICKUP $1586. (V8)

($1494., 6 CYL.)

CONT'D. **53** B

new GRILLE *and* PUSHBUTTON DOOR HANDLES

new MODELS INTRODUCED 3-13-53

new SYNCHRO-SILENT TRANS. STD. EQUIPMENT (O.D. OR FORD-O-MATIC OPT. ON F-100)

▬PICKUP▬

F-100 *has* NEW 223 CID "COST CLIPPER" 6 (115 HP) OR *new* 239 CID "POWER KING" V8 (130 HP)

VACUUM BOOSTED POWER BRAKES *newly-available* ON ½ TON F-100 (OPT.)

new 6½' PICKUP BOX

4' WIDE REAR WINDOW (444 SQ. IN. OF GLASS)

F-100 PICKUP $1318. (6) 1389. (V8)

new GRILLE

54 A

SERIAL # F10 D4A 100001 UP

new UPHOLSTERY (VINYL)

('54)

CABS

(1955 CAB SIMILAR)

(CONT'D. NEXT PAGE)

Half-Ton Panel

110" WB

HEAVY STEEL DOORS

NEW F-100 8-ft. PANEL Payload (equipment, etc.) up to 1385 lbs.

6 $1528.
V8 $1599.

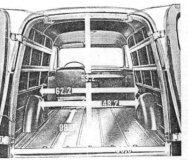

BIG, 155.8 CU. FT. CAPACITY
FORD ═ 53-B, 54-A

SERIES F-900
Max. G.V.W. 27,000 lbs.
Max. G.C.W. 55,000 lbs.

CONCRETE MIXER
156- and 175-in. wbs.

LOGGER
156-, 175- and 192-in. wbs.

FORD

CONVENTIONALS

NEW F-900 **BIG JOB TRACTOR**
Max. G.C.W.—55,000 lbs.
Wheelbases: 132 and 114 in.

HENRY FORD II

VAN (CHASSIS and CAB FRONT FORD-BLT.)

(CONT'D.)

(CONT'D.) **54** B

PARCEL DELIVERY CHASSIS
P-350: Max. G.V.W. 7,800 lbs.
P-500: Max. G.V.W. 14,000 lbs.

SAFETY REAR STAKE LOCK

"CAB-FORWARD" (C.O.E.) 1½ TON STAKE $**2001.** UP

POWER STEERING ON T-800, AVAIL. ON MOST "BIG JOB" HEAVY TRUCKS.

CAB FORWARD
6 New Series
C-500, C-600
C-700, C-750
C-800, C-900

TANKER

1954 CAB

239 or 256 CID **POWER KING** V8
130 or 138 HP

Refrigerator Van

Coal Dump

Furniture Van

Gasoline (Oil, Milk) Tank

Garbage Body

279 or 317 CID **CARGO KING** V8
152 or 170 HP

('53 CAB SIMILAR)

FORD - 54 - B

6-CYL. FROM $1346.
V8 FROM $1462.

HOLLAND MOTOR EXPRESS Inc.

"You Can't Beat the Big Dutch Fleet"

FORD

I.D. #F10D5A 100001 UP

PICKUPS have SHORT-STROKE ENGS. (6-118 HP; V8-132 HP)

new GRILLE (V8 has V and 8 IN CENTER OF TOP PIECE)

MASTER-GUIDE POWER STEERING

IMPROVED FORD-O-MATIC AUTOMATIC TRANS.

55

P-350
P-500

SEDAN DELIVERY $1598. UP

DELIVERY CHASSIS

C-600 (3 V8s AVAIL.)

C-750 UTILITY C.O.E.s

C-800

Globe

To 25 TONS G.C.W.

F-350 WRECKER

175 OR 186 HP V8s

POWER STEERING and AIR BRAKES AVAIL. ON F-800 (TO 200 HP) AVAIL. ON SOME OTHER MODELS.

T-800

C-900

F-500 1½ TON

CONVENTIONAL

F-600 2-TON

6 OR V8

F-750 with TACHOMETER

F-800

12-TON G.V.W.

to 200 HP V8

FLAMMABLE   FLAMMABLE

F-700 "BIG JOB" TYPE

56

SERIAL #F10-D6A-100001 UP

CHECK INSIGNIA ON SIDE OF HOOD.

new GRILLE $1346. UP

LT. DUTY 110 OR 118" WB

new 133 HP 6 OR 167 HP V8 ("Y-8")

FORD

FORD=55~56

148

FORD PANEL 2057. UP

6 or 272 V8 (AS IN RANCHERO) BUT WITH 139 or 170 HP

RANCHERO PICKUP-CAR 116" WB

$2149 "CUSTOM" SERIES

NEW

223 cid 6 (144 HP)
272 cid V8 (190 HP)
or 292 cid V8 (212 HP)

(BELOW) F-900 "BIG JOB" WITH NEW HEAVY-DUTY 5-SPEED TRANS.

HEAVY TRUCKS.

60,000 lbs. GCW

New TILT-CAB C.O.E. (2 VIEWS)

TRACTOR / TRAILER

T-800 TANDEM DUMP

212 HP H.D. V8 WITH new HYDRAULIC CLUTCH and POWER STEERING (65,000 lbs. GCW)

LARGE CONVENTIONALS WITH 3 HOLES IN LOWER FRONT SHEET METAL. (LT. DUTY WITH SMALL VERTICAL SLOTS (AS IN ILLUSTRATION BELOW, LEFT)

TOTALLY RESTYLED FOR 1957

57

STANDARD "FLARESIDE" PICKUP

NEW

pickup

new PARALLEL GROOVES ALONG HOOD ↓

F-350 1-TON has SIMILAR FRONT STYLING.

← WIDE-BED F-100 STYLESIDE CUSTOM CAB 6½' OR 8' BED LENGTH (NARROW-BED AVAIL. ALSO)

FORD = 57

CONVENTIONAL INSTRUMENT PANEL AND CONTROLS

PARCEL DELIVERY INSTRUMENT PANEL AND CONTROLS

FORD

$1874. 1/2 TON PICKUP (6 1/2' BED, 110" WB)

$1913. (8' BED, 118" WB)

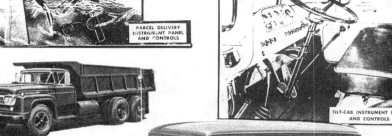

TILT-CAB INSTRUMENT PANEL AND CONTROLS

VEHICLE I.D. #
F10J8A
10001 UP

TANDEM DUMP

TILT CAB (IN 6 SER.)

PRODUCTION:
242,890
AVAIL.
6 1/2' OR 8' FLARESIDE, BUT SMOOTH *STYLESIDE* BED STD. EQUIPMENT IN LT. DUTY,

3 new "SUPER DUTY"
V8 ENGINES =
401 CID, 226 HP;
477 CID, 260 HP;
534 CID, 277 HP

VARIED IN 6 1/2', 8' and 9' LENGTHS IN 1958.

OVER 300 MODELS!

STAKE

58 NEW 4 →

HEADLTS., new GRILLE ON CONVENTIONAL

VEHICLE I.D. # F10J9A 10001 UP
PRODUCTION : 331,348

PICKUPS =
$1932.

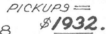

DASH

59

new ALL-HORIZONTAL GRILLE MEMBERS new "FORD" LETTERING ABOVE GRILLE REPLACES BADGE EMBLEM.

CUSTOM CAB

ALSO AVAIL.:
new 4-W-D P.U.

PRODUCTION: 337,468

FORD

FORD TRUCKS COST LESS
LESS TO OWN...LESS TO RUN...BUILT TO LAST LONGER, TOO!

STYLESIDE
(BELOW)

1½-TON STAKE
$2680. UP

WITH

Certified Economy

F-600 STAKE (ABOVE)
6 OR V8

60

TILT CAB
$3753. UP

new GRILLE.
BADGE EMBLEM
RETURNS

VAN

PICKUPS
PRICED
FROM
$1955.

DASH

CONVENTIONAL INSTRUMENT PANEL
AND CONTROLS

PRESSURE GAUGE ON HVY. TRUCKS
WITH AIR BRAKES

FINAL FORD COURIER
DELIVERY WAGON 119" WB
$2456.

FORD = 60

151

FORD

FORD TRUCKS COST LESS

I.D. #
F10J (A)
100001
UP

F-100 PICKUP FROM $1940.

135 HP 6 OR 160 HP V8

NOW ONLY 1 HDLT. ON EACH SIDE

"FORD" NAME IN CENTER OF new GRILLE

new "CENTER-SWEEP" WIPERS

REAR DETAILS

64.5

28% MORE GLASS AREA IN new PICKUP BACKLIGHT

F-100 **NEW** 114" WB

64.5" WIDE "GRAIN TITE" TAILGATE with "SNAP-LOCK" LATCHES

61 A

PICKUPS TOTALLY RESTYLED

SEDAN DELIVERY NOW IN COMPACT 109" FALCON SERIES. WB $2089.

Econoline

New $2092.

E-113

FORD Econoline STATION BUS

ECONOLINE compact CARGO VAN

E-123 CUSTOM STATION BUS PRICED AT $2247.

$1956. E-103

E-103 $1956.

FLAT FLOOR (VAN)

New

ECONOLINE MODELS (90" WB) USE 6-CYL., 144 CID FALCON ENGINE. (85 HP @ 4200 RPM)
ECONOLINE I.D. # E10S (A) 100001 UP

Chiquita

FORD

E-103 ECONOLINE PICKUP

$1833.

(CONT'D. NEXT PAGE)

FORD

5 Cummins Diesels or 5 Ford "Big V" gas engines in these new highway tractors. Service is coast to coast!

Space-saving sleeper increases cab length by only one inch. Short 28-inch axle setting, GCW's up to 76,800 pounds, permit top legal loads.

984 pounds more payload is big advantage of new, lightweight "pusher type" tandem axles. Over 500 engine-axle-transmission combinations, all told!

Most popular Tilt Cabs on the American road! Four series—up to 65,000 pounds GCW—with new chassis strength, new weight-saving options for bigger loads.

New compact sleeper adds only 2½ inches to cab length, lets you haul 40-foot trailers in 50-foot states. Wide range of optional tractor equipment available on all models.

Tandem-axle models are also available in the C-Series. As with conventional tandems, aluminum walking beams, wheels and fuel tanks are offered to cut weight, boost payload.

C-550 TILT CAB 1½ T. STAKE (111" WB) PRICED AT $3616.

61 *A RETURN TO ONLY 2 HEADLTS.*
B *(CONT'D.)*

115 NEW HIGH-STRENGTH CONVENTIONAL CAB MODELS

New huskier tractors feature lighter, stronger frames of high-tensile steel . . . heavier gauge metal and stress-isolating mounting for cabs. New 28-in. BA for extra payload!

New tougher tandems offer new strength in chassis, cab sheet metal . . . new shock-swallowing front suspension. Powered by rugged "Big V" engines, Ford tandems range up to 51,000 lbs. GVW, 75,000 GCW.

SUPER DUTY

(CONT'D. NEXT PAGE)

FORD=61-B

153

SERIAL #
F-10J-100001 UP
(F SERIES)

FORD

COLORS: *MONTE CARLO RED, GOLDENROD YELLOW, RAVEN BLACK, MINT GREEN, HOLLY GREEN, CARIBBEAN TURQUOISE, ACADEMY BLUE, STARLIGHT BLUE, CORINTHIAN WHITE, (and 2-TONES ON STYLESIDE PICKUPS)*

New "Big Six" engine for more power!

F SERIES

2-TON MEDIUM DUTY

all-new 262 CID "BIG SIX" ENGINE AVAIL. IN 2-TON

NEW TOUGHER HEAVIES
New, stronger hi-tensile frames! Huskier axles! Wider power-train choice! Short, 28-in. front axle setting! New high-durability cabs and sheet metal!

T *SERIES*

NEW LOW-COST TILTS
New sleeper cabs! New weight-saving options for greater payloads! Money-saving ease of servicing!

61 C
(CONT'D.)

619 new models! It's the biggest change-over in Ford history with more trucks to match more jobs, more savings on any job! New "Big Six" power for two-tonners! New Super Duty Diesel Tilts with the nation's most popular diesel engines! Suspensions that give up to twice the tire life of other types! New Econoline models that pack more load in three feet less truck length! New engines that deliver up to 40% more gas mileage! And all this at prices that give you a flying start to long-term savings! So for super-economy pickups all the way up to super-duty diesels, see your Ford Dealer . . . economy never came in such a choice!

new GAS-ENGINED "H" TILT-CAB MODELS ALSO AVAIL.

HEAVY DUTY DIESEL C.O.E.

H *SERIES* ➡

NEW!

CHOICE OF 5 CUMMINS DIESEL ENGINES OR 5 FORD "BIG V" GAS ENGINES

OVER 500 ENGINE-AXLE-TRANSMISSION COMBINATIONS IN "H" SERIES ALONE!

NOW! ONLY FROM FORD
100,000-MILE WARRANTY
ON ALL SUPER DUTY ENGINES

401, 477 OR 534 CID V8s

1961 PRODUCTION : 333,985

FORD = 61-C

154

ECONOLINE I.D. #
E103 (A) 20500 UP

FORD

E-100
ECONOLINE PICKUP   1856. (7')
VAN   2045. (7½')

SERIAL #
F-10J (A) 205000 UP
(1962 F SER.)

F-250 3/4 TON
FLARESIDE
62
new GRILLE ON LIGHT *and* MEDIUM-DUTY F SERIES

H SERIES

TON		WB	PRICE
½	F 100	114	$1962
¾	F 250	122	2117
1	F 350	132	2305
1½	F 500	156	2810
2	F 600	156	3225
1½	C 550	111	3913
2	C 600	111	4046

VARIOUS OTHER SERIES ALSO, INCLUDING SCHOOLBUS CHAS.

LOWEST-PRICED MODELS IN EACH SERIES OF F and C LISTED ABOVE.

1½ TON C550 STAKE
$**3615.**

TILT CAB

C-750
SUPER DUTY TILT CAB TRACTOR AND TRAILER

MEDIUM DUTY
F SERIES *(new BIG 6 ENGINE AVAIL.)*

FORD TRUCKS COST LESS
SAVE NOW.. SAVE FROM NOW ON!

ECONOLINE STATION BUS $2574.
(CUSTOM MODEL BECOMES CLUB WAGON, AT $2723. UP)

I.D. # E11S (—) 20500 UP

FORD—62

F-100

NEW! Low gear synchronized for easier downshifting!

LARGER F SERIES AVAIL. WITH CUMMINS V6 DIESEL OR FORD "SUPER DUTY" GAS V8.

DIESEL

AVAILABLE
CUMMINS V6 DIESEL ENGINE (588 cid, 200 HP)
CUMMINS V8 DIESEL (785 cid, 265 HP)

FORD

NEW 89" BBC LINE CUTS LENGTH, ADDS MANEUVERABILITY!

SERIAL #
F-10J (A)
325000 UP
STARTS
10-1-62
F-100
FROM
$1962.

63

new FRONT STYLING

N SERIES
IS

NEW

VAN

ECONOLINE DASH   SERIES and ENGINE #

64

luxury interior

F-250	128"		2163.
F-350	132"		2337.
F-500	156"		2889.
F-600	156"		3247.

new GRILLE

F-100 PICKUPS FROM $2004. (114" WB)

WARRANTY NUMBER
F25 RB 445000

W.B.	COLOR	MODEL	BODY	TRANS	AXLE
128	SM	F250	E81	A	26

MAX G.V.W. LBS.	CERT. NET H.P.	R.P.M.	D.S.O.
7500	132	3600	72

IDENTIFICATION PLATE (ABOVE)

DISTRICT CODE SPECIAL ORDER #

(new 330, 361 and 391 cid V8s FOR HVY. DUTY MODELS)

SERIAL # F-10J 445000 UP
STARTS 10-1-63

SERIAL #
F-10 (J) (—)
580000 UP
STARTS 10-1-64

THREE ALL-NEW ENGINES! Now standard in Ford pickups: brand-new 240 cubic inch economy Six! Optional: new 300 cubic inch Big Six, powerful new 352 cubic inch V-8!

new GRILLE

65

new 115" WB ON F-100

F SERIES
$1970. UP

WITH

TWIN I BEAM

INDEPENDENT SUSPENSION

156

FORD

SLOGAN:
YOU'RE AHEAD
IN A FORD
ALL THE WAY

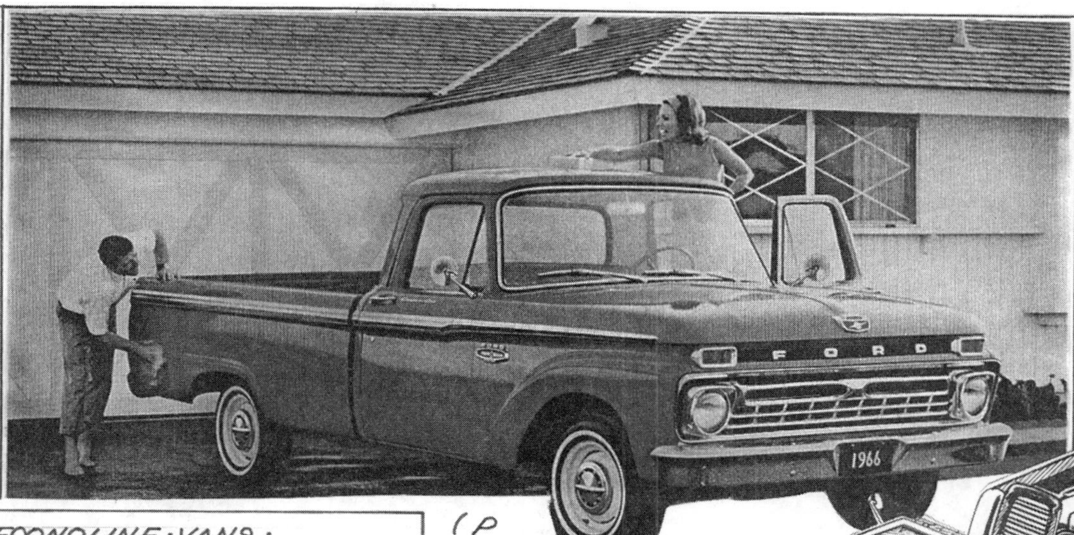

F-100
$2125.
AND UP

90" WB ECONOLINE VANS:
E100 (PICKUP) ——— $1922.
E140 VAN ——— 2219.
E150 PANEL VAN ——— 2164.
E160 SUPER VAN ——— 2340.
E170 SUPER PANEL VAN— 2285.

2 SANGAMO TACHOGRAPHS (OPT.)

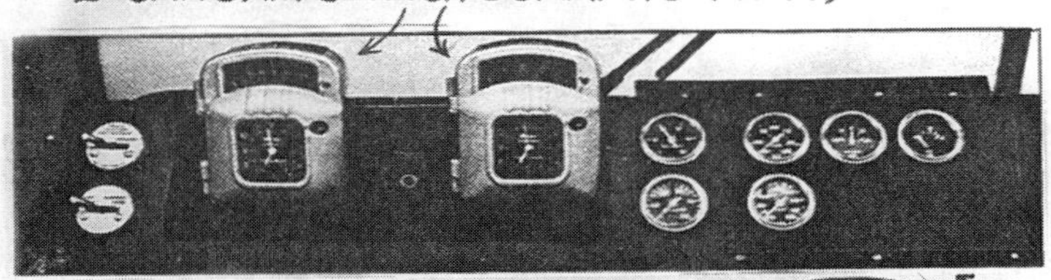

(P SERIES PARCEL DELIV. CHASSIS
FROM ½ TON P-100
TO 1½ TON P-500
$1365.—2063.)

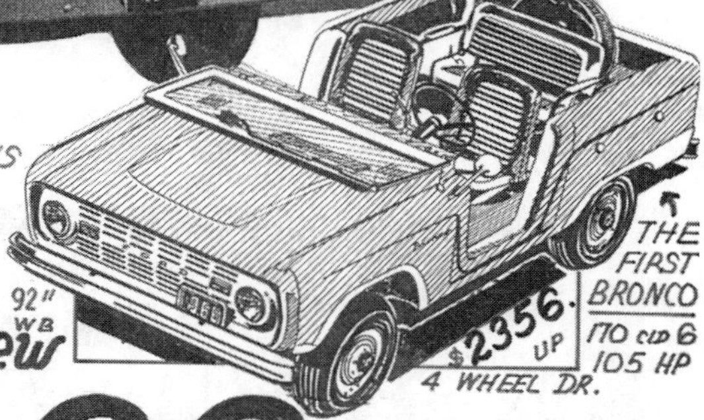

92" WB
new

$2356. UP
4 WHEEL DR.

THE FIRST BRONCO
170 CID 6
105 HP

66
new GRILLE ON F SERIES

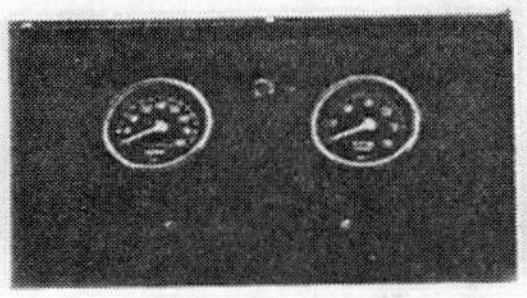

STEWART-WR.
GAUGES STD.

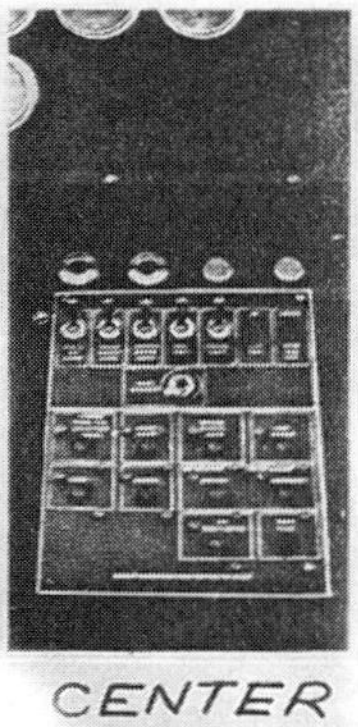

W SERIES DASH

W SERIES (new)
STARTS SPRING, 1966

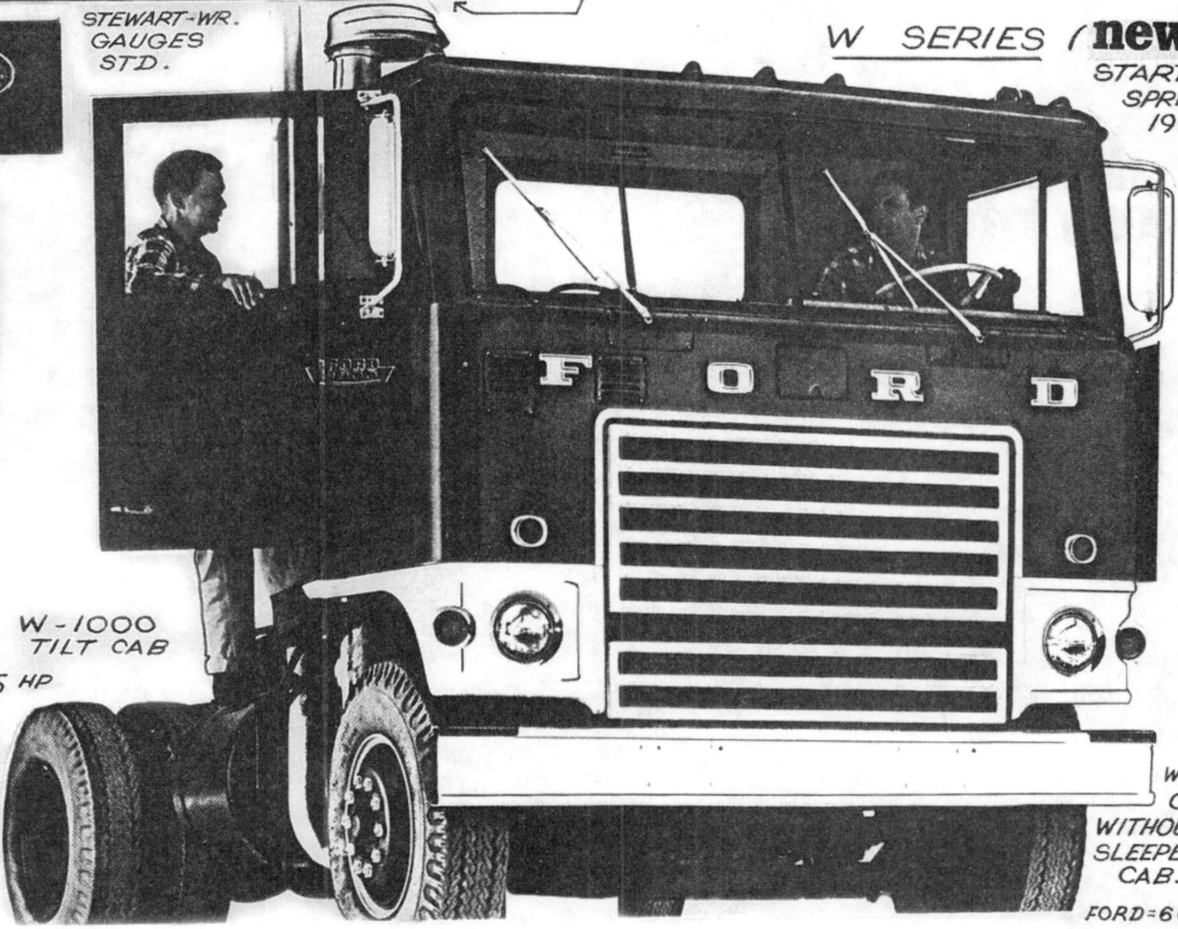

CENTER CONSOLE

W-1000 TILT CAB

WITH 195 TO 335 HP
DIESEL ENGS.
BY CUMMINS,
DETROIT
DIESEL, OR
CATERPILLAR.

F O R D

WITH OR WITHOUT SLEEPER CAB.

FORD=66

157

F-100

FORD

NEW 89" BBC LINE CUTS LENGTH, ADDS MANEUVERABILITY!

NEW! Low gear synchronized for easier downshifting!

LARGER F SERIES AVAIL. WITH CUMMINS V6 DIESEL OR FORD "SUPER DUTY" GAS V8.

SERIAL #
F-10J (A)
325000 UP
STARTS
10-1-62
F-100
FROM
$1962.

63

new FRONT STYLING

N SERIES IS

NEW

DIESEL

AVAILABLE
CUMMINS V6 DIESEL ENGINE (588 CID, 200 HP)
CUMMINS V8 DIESEL (785 CID, 265 HP)

ECONOLINE DASH   SERIES and ENGINE #

VAN

WARRANTY NUMBER
F25 RB 445000
NOT FOR TITLE OR REGISTRATION PURPOSES

W.B.	COLOR	MODEL	BODY	TRANS	AXLE
128	SM	F250	E81	A	26

MAX G.V.W. LBS.	CERT. NET H.P.	R.P.M.	D.S.O.
7500	132	3600	72

64

IDENTIFICATION
PLATE
(ABOVE)

DISTRICT CODE SPECIAL ORDER #

luxury interior

F-250	128"	2163.
F-350	132"	2337.
F-500	156"	2889.
F-600	156"	3247.

new GRILLE

F-100 PICKUPS FROM
$2004. (114" WB)

SERIAL # F-10J 445000 UP
STARTS 10-1-63

(new 330, 361 and 391 CID V8s FOR HVY. DUTY MODELS)

SERIAL #
F-10 (J) (–)
580000 UP
STARTS 10-1-64

THREE ALL-NEW ENGINES! Now standard in Ford pickups: brand-new 240 cubic inch economy Six! Optional: new 300 cubic inch Big Six, powerful new 352 cubic inch V-8!

new GRILLE

F SERIES $1970. UP

65

new 115" WB ON F-100

WITH

TWIN I BEAM

INDEPENDENT SUSPENSION

158

FORD

11-MONTH
SALES FIGURE =
462,545

95 Short-Haul Tractors (N-750's)
N-750

N-SERIES SHORT CONVENTIONAL CAB:
N-500, 600, 700, 750, 850, 950,
1000, N-6000, 7000, 8000,
1000-D, NT-8000 *, 850, 950,
850-D, 950-D

DIESEL OR
V8 GAS.

N-850-D

Ryder
Truck Lines modernizes fleet; invests
over \$5 million in Ford Trucks

C-700

67 B
(CONT'D.)

C-850

1½ TON
C-550 STAKE $ **4188.**
C-600 STAKE **4570.**
2 TON

C - SERIES
TILT CAB :
C-550, 600, 700,
750, 800, 850,
950, 1000,
C-6000, 7000,
8000, CT-750,
800, 850, 950,
8000 *

* = AVAILABLE ON
SPECIAL ORDER.

W - SERIES INTERIOR

DIESEL W-1000-D CR WT-1000-D

FORD=67-B

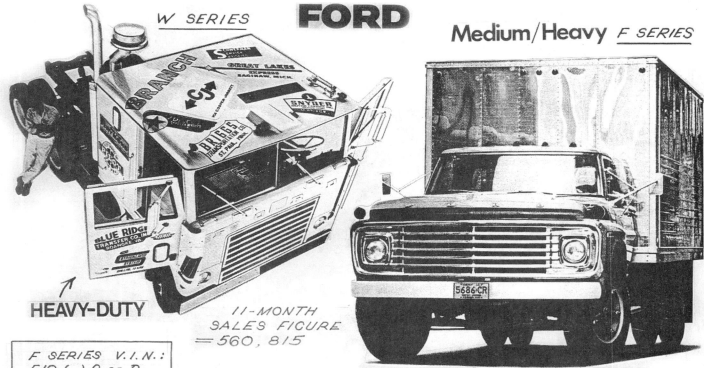

W SERIES

FORD

Medium/Heavy F SERIES

BRANCH

HEAVY-DUTY

11-MONTH SALES FIGURE = 560,815

F SERIES V.I.N.:
F10 (—) C or D
00001 UP

F100 ½ T. PICKUP 115" WB, 6½' STYL. BED		**$2397.**
" " " 131" WB, 8' STYL. BED		**2433.**
F250 ¾ T. " " " " " "		**2619.**
F350 1 TON " 135" WB 9' BED		**2715.**
SEVERAL OTHER MODELS IN F SERIES.		

RANGER NAME NEAR REAR

68 new GRILLE

EXCEPT FOR MINISCULE CHANGES IN ASH TRAY DOOR, 1967, 1968, 1969 F SERIES INSTR. PANEL UNCHANGED (SEE 1967 EXAMPLE) FOR MORE DETAIL.)

F-100 "RANGER"

F SERIES INTERIOR

WITH RANGER TRIM (ABOVE)

WITH CAMPER

GRILLE DETAILS (RANGER)

WORKS LIKE A TRUCK RIDES LIKE A CAR

Ford = 68

CLUB WAGON SERIES

E110 TO E330

240 cid 6 (150 HP) or

CLUB WAGON, CUSTOM, and CHATEAU MODELS 105½" or 123½" WB

$2900. UP (I.D. # E11 (-)(-) C70000 UP)

"The switch is on... to Ford"

PRODUCTION: 658,534

FINAL YR. FOR N, F-800 UP, and T-800 UP.

69

new GRILLE (LIGHT F SERIES)

FORD HEAVY-DUTY TRUCK

W SERIES

He covers 9% more ground than the rest of the fleet.

ECONOLINE I.D. # E14F (--) C70000 UP (105" or 123½" WB

F SERIES I.D. # F10 (-) D82000 UP 115", 131," 135" OR LONGER WB

"CAT DIESEL POWER" FILLER DOOR EMBLEM (ABOVE) INDICATES CATERPILLAR DIESEL ENG.

6 CYL. OR V8 P SERIES PARCEL DELIVERY VAN I.D. # P35 (--) D82000 UP 104," 122," OR 137" WB

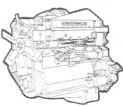

CATERPILLAR "1674" DIESEL ENGINE

Works like a truck. Rides like a car.

F-100

pickup.

$2433. UP

4 DR. PICKUPS ALSO AVAIL. (F350)

Medium/Heavies

F-750 (BELOW)

C SERIES

TILT CAB I.D. # C55 (--) D82000 UP

FORD=69

161

FORD

UP TO 335 HP *with* DIESEL.

LN (MEDIUM) SHORT CONVENTIONAL (93.3" BBC)

L SERIES

LOUISVILLE LINE

BLT. AT FORD'S *new* LOUISVILLE, KY. BRANCH FACTORY. (INTRO. 12-69)

NEW

70

4 DIGITS IN MODEL NUMBER DENOTES A DIESEL ENG. (LS = SHORT W.B., WITH FRONT AXLE SET BACK)

HEAVY-DUTY TRUCKS

DUAL-CIRCUIT AIR BRAKES (new)

TANDEM-AXLE LT DUMP

STD. CAB →

LINEHAUL PANEL (IN CUSTOM CAB)

AIR CLEANER PORT ON RT. SIDE OF HOOD

(ON ALL BUT "LN" TYPE)

FORD 9000

C SERIES TILT CAB **$5167.**
I.D. # C50 (— —) G30000 UP

Ford

(CONT'D. NEXT PAGE)

FORD = 70-A

FORD

Minihome
INTRO. MID-'69

5 PICKUP ENGS. TO 390 C/D V8.

(LTS STARTS MID-1970, AS '71 MODEL.)

CREW CAB (F MED. DUTY) →

F-SERIES CREW CAB

F-350 CAMPER SPECIAL

F350 CAB/CHASSIS $3111. UP (W/O CAMPER)

LOWER PRICED PICKUPS HAVE "RANGER" PKG. AS OPT. EQUIP.

RANGER XLT INSTRUMENT PANEL

B
70
(CONT'D.)

Hertz Truck Rental

F 100 PICKUP $2638. UP

F

C

W

(THIS VAN STYLE BEGINS 1968)

$2607. UP

ECONOLINE VAN

F   L   C   W (W-9000 IS new)
HEAVY-DUTY

302-cubic-inch V-8 OPTIONAL (205 HP)   F-100

4x4's AVAIL.

71
A

240 CID 6 STD. (140 HP)

$2904. UP

W SER. HAS new SMALLER "FORD" NAME IN FRONT.

new GRILLE WITH FEWER HORIZ. PCS.

F SERIES I.D. # F10 (-)(-) J70000 UP

(CONT'D. NEXT PAGE)
Ford =70B, 71A

FORD
Styleside

SPORT CUSTOM

SPORT CUSTOM

CUSTOM

71 B
(CONT'D.)

Flareside

Platform-Stakes
$3018. UP (¾ TON)

Chassis-Cab models are offered for mounting van and other special-purpose bodies. Frame rails are straight and parallel behind cab, except for a slight kickup over the rear axle, for easy body installation and low loading heights. Chassis-cowl and windshield models are also offered on F-350 Series. Chassis-windshield on F-250.

F350
135" OR
159" WB

interior

(CARGO VANS IN ECONOLINE SERIES)=**$2873.** UP

Club Wagons (BELOW)

$3465. UP   I.D. # E11(A)(—)K00000 UP

Camper Special CONVERSION

(105.5" wb.)   (123.5" wb.)
AVAILABLE IN 2 LENGTHS (ABOVE)

CLUB WAGON, CUSTOM OR CHATEAU MODELS

Club Wagon

105 ½" WB

123½" WB
STATION BUS

DOUBLE REAR DOORS

CHATEAU

E110 CLUB W.	$3678.
E120 CUSTOM	3903.
E130 CHATEAU	4052.
E210 CLUB W.	3758.
E220 CUSTOM	3983.
E230 CHATEAU	4133.
E310 CLUB W.	3914.
E320 CUSTOM	4139.
E330 CHATEAU	4289.
V8 ENG.	$126. EXTRA

FORD=71-B

FORD

ECONOLINE VANS
I.D. # E14 (—)(—)
M40000 UP
$2749. UP   V8 ENGINE =
123½" WB $124. EXTRA $118. EXTRA

L SERIES

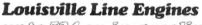

STANDARD CAB
(L SERIES)

Short conventionals with exclusive tilting front end

Louisville Line Engines
up to 534 cu.in. gasoline
up to 927 cu.in. diesel

(*new* LT-880 *and* LNT-880 DUMP TRUCKS
INTRO. EARLY 1972 WITH 475 CID GAS V8s)

72 A

new GRILLE (LT. F)
WITH FEWER
VERTICAL PCS.

F-100
LT. DUTY

Over 1,000 big trucks

C SERIES
CUSTOM CAB

$**2804.** UP

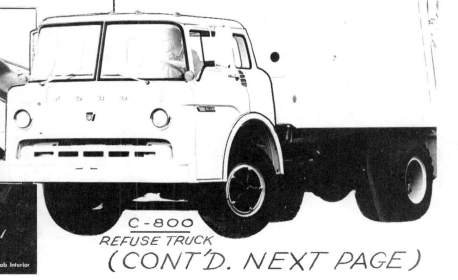

Custom Cab Interior

C-800
REFUSE TRUCK
(CONT'D. NEXT PAGE)

FORD

Ford W-Series tractor

SLEEPER CAB ↙

"DRESS-UP" PAINT PKG. AVAIL. OPTION FROM 5-72. ↓

Choice of 19 popular Diesels

W-Series

EARLY '72 CAB (2 VIEWS)

Spacious super cab—

WOODGRAIN INSTRUMENT PANEL, BEIGE STEERING WHEEL and PADDED ENGINE COVER STANDARD AS OF 5-1-72.

ALUM. CAB OPTION. ON W, WT

72B (CONT'D.)

The newest Ford
W-9000 Series

FORD 73-75

C-Series $5848. UP

DIESEL V8s AVAIL. (522, 573 or 636 C.I.D.)

ALL F TYPES GET NEW GRILLE, 1973.

(EARLIEST 1973 "W" SERIES RETAINS OLD GRILLE)

CAB (MED. F)

F-700 DUMP

BRIGHT METAL GRILLE

NEW EXTERIOR SHEET METAL ON F-500-750 and F-6000-F-7000 ('73)

F-750

('74)

WITH WHITE GRILLE (ABOVE) (F-250 ¾-T., F-350 1-T., F-500 1½-T., F-600 2-T., ETC.) (CREW CABS. AVAIL. ON 1973 F-600 THROUGH F-750, and F-250 and F-350)

RESTYLED W SERIES INTRODUCED SPRING, 1973, WITH GRILLE SIMILAR TO LOUISVILLE (L) MODELS.

MANY NEW MECHANICAL IMPROVEMENTS IN REDESIGNED LIGHT F TYPES

('73) F-100 $2899. UP

(CONT'D. NEXT PAGE)

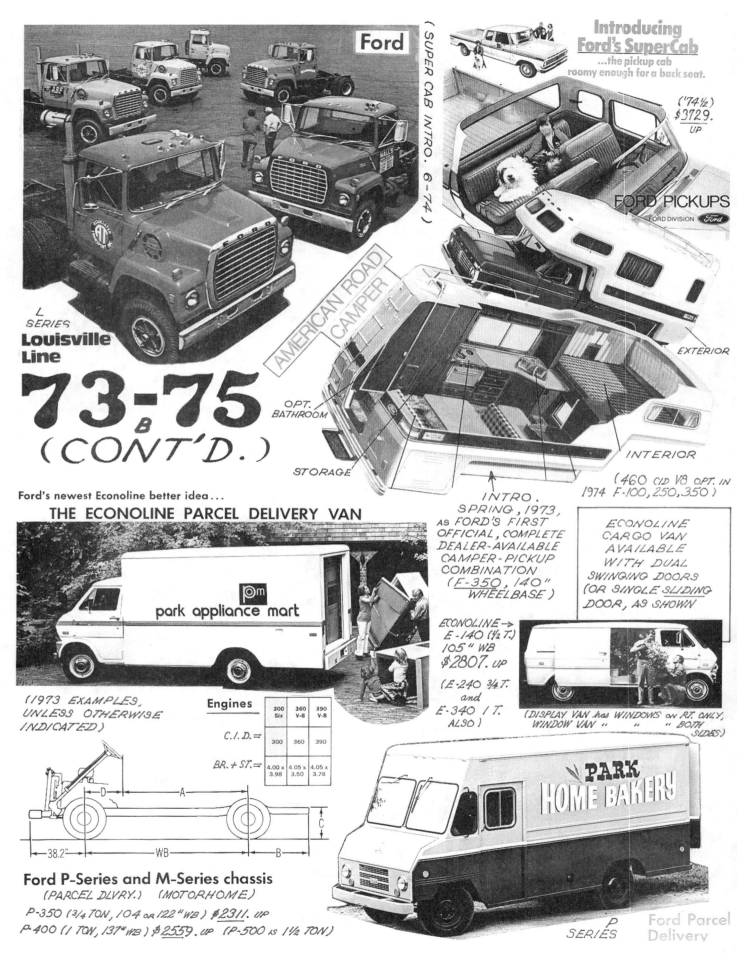

Ford

(SUPER CAB INTRO. 6-74)

**Introducing
Ford's SuperCab**
...the pickup cab
roomy enough for a back seat.

('74½)
$3729.
UP

FORD PICKUPS
FORD DIVISION *Ford*

L
SERIES
**Louisville
Line**

73-₈75
(CONT'D.)

AMERICAN ROAD CAMPER

OPT.
BATHROOM

STORAGE

EXTERIOR

INTERIOR

(460 CID V8 OPT. IN
1974 F-100, 250, 350)

INTRO.
SPRING, 1973,
AS FORD'S FIRST
OFFICIAL, COMPLETE
DEALER-AVAILABLE
CAMPER-PICKUP
COMBINATION
(F-350, 140"
WHEELBASE)

ECONOLINE
CARGO VAN
AVAILABLE
WITH DUAL
SWINGING DOORS
(OR SINGLE SLIDING
DOOR, AS SHOWN

Ford's newest Econoline better idea...
THE ECONOLINE PARCEL DELIVERY VAN

pm
park appliance mart

ECONOLINE →
E-140 (½ T.)
105" WB
$2807. UP

(E-240 ¾ T.
and
E-340 / T.
ALSO)

(DISPLAY VAN has WINDOWS on RT. ONLY,
WINDOW VAN " " " BOTH
SIDES)

(1973 EXAMPLES,
UNLESS OTHERWISE
INDICATED)

Engines

	300 Six	360 V-8	390 V-8
C.I.D. =	300	360	390
BR. + ST. =	4.00 x 3.98	4.05 x 3.50	4.05 x 3.78

**PARK
HOME BAKERY**

38.2"   WB   B

D   A   C

Ford P-Series and M-Series chassis
(PARCEL DLVRY.)   (MOTORHOME)
P-350 (¾ TON, 104 or 122" WB) $2311. UP
P-400 (1 TON, 137" WB) $2559. UP (P-500 IS 1½ TON)

P
SERIES

Ford Parcel
Delivery

168

C SERIES TILT CAB $8207.

Ford

LN

F-150. Runs on any kind of gas.
F-100 FROM $3827.

300 CID 6 OR 3 DIFF. V8s.

F L

76-77

new ↑
GRILLE/HEADLT. DETAILS (LIGHT F SERIES)

2 TON LN-600 $7415.

New! Long 118" BBC Louisville Line tractor

New LTL-9000

('76 PRICES and MODELS ILLUSTR.)

W-SERIES LINEHAULER

W. 82" BBC SLEEPER CAB (52" BBC AVAIL. ALSO)

F-100 PICKUP

...4-wheel and 2-wheel drive ('78)

New GRILLE (LIGHT/MED. F SERIES)

78-79

F, L, LN, LNT, LTL, C, and CL SERIES

1978 **Club Wagon** $7491. UP

CL-9000 C.O.E.

NEW heavy-duty truck

| 1978 F SERIES I.D. # F10 (H) (-) AA 0000 UP (FROM $4350.) |
| 1979 " " " " F10 (G) (-) DC 0000 UP (FROM 5766.) |
| 1978 ECONOLINE " " E10 (B) (-) AA 0000 UP (FROM 4537.) |
| 1979 " " " E10 (B) (-) DC 0000 UP (FROM 5658.) |

FORD=76-79

F-100 PICKUP

('81)

PICKUP WHEELS

POLYSTEEL RADIAL GOODYEAR

PICKUP DASH

FORD'S OUT FRONT. ('81)

1981

FORD TRUCKS

Ford TRUCKS

HEAVY TRUCKS.

FORD

FLARESIDE

1961

GAS OR DIESEL!

PICKUP

NEW RESTYLED MEDIUM/HEAVY

F-SERIES

WITH ADVANCED 8.2L "FUEL PINCHER" DETROIT DIESEL POWER.

F-600, F-700, F-800

80-81 A

(81)New 4.2L (255) V-8 engine.

DDA 8.2L Fuel Pincher Diesel

FORGED ALUMINUM WHEEL ('81)

SUPERCAB

('81 EXAMPLES ILLUSTRATED)

CUSTOM CAB

CAB

FORD F-SERIES.

(CONT'D. NEXT PAGE)

Built Ford Tough

FORD

Ford Club Wagon—

CLUB WAGON
I.D. #s
VARY,
ACCORD. TO
VARIOUS
SIZES, ETC.

1980

('80)

124"
WB

CHATEAU VAN

SUPER VAN
$10,613.

(138" WB, 15 PASS.) ('80)

1980 ECONOLINE
I.D. # =
E10 (E) (-)
0A 0000 UP

Standard Instrument Panel

80B-81
(CONT'D.)

$9172. UP

('81)

Econoline
School Bus.

Econoline
Commercial Stripped
Chassis Model.

ECONOLINE

Instrument Panel.
(CHATEAU)
"KING OF CLUBS"
PACKAGE = $4605.

SOLAR INSTALLATIONS

$6748.
UP

ENGINES =
300 CID 6, OR
V8s OF
302, 351,
400 OR
460 CID

('81)

('81)

1981 ECONOLINE
I.D. # =
1FMDE 04
(-) (-) B (-)
A 00001

1981

ECONOLINE CHASSIS
(CUSTOM CARGO BOX)

FORD ECONOLINE VAN

Medium and Heavy

C

LN

Tough new F-700 4x4!

82

F-SERIES.

Chassis-Cab Models.

11,000 LB. MAX. GVWR

Chassis Cab shown

America's Truck. Built Ford Tough!

NEW OVAL "FORD" EMBLEM ON GRILLE (LT. "F" SERIES)

232 CID V-6 STD. IN F-100 (EXCEPT IN CALIFORNIA)

SCHOOL BUS

B-600 B-700

SCHOOL BUS

(GAS, LP GAS OR DIESEL)

DETROIT DIESEL (ABOVE) OR LIMA 370 or 429 CID V8.

BUS USES "FUEL PINCHER" 8.2 L

STYLESIDE

ECONOLINE FROM $7676.

Ford = 82

172

Ford

C-Series

REFUSE TRUCK

REFRIG. TRUCK

C-SERIES

C-Series
CAB TILTS
FOR SERVICING

SCHOOL BUS

School Bus Preparation Package
A School Bus Body Builders
Preparation Package is available
on the 138-in. wheelbase Econoline
Commercial Cutaway model

AS BEFORE,
VARIOUS
TYPES OF
SCHOOL
BUSES, VANS
AVAILABLE.

F-SERIES

('83)
F-350   137" WB
$9352.

F-350
CHASSIS-CABS   w. 137 or 161" WB

F-100s FROM $7349.
117" OR 133" WB
ON F-150

4WD
4 CYL.
FROM
$8677.
('83)
RANGER 4WD

83-
85
A
(CONT'D.
NEXT
PAGE)

RANGER *is new COMPACT 4-CYL. PICKUP (ABOVE)*

(INTRO. DURING 1982 AS A 1983 MODEL
R10C, R10A, OR R11A I.D. #,
PRECEDED BY 1FT-( )-D-# FOLLOWS
(2-WHEEL DRIVE $6877. UP) 108 or 114" WB
('83)

(FORMERLY A
MODEL NAME IN
F-100 SERIES)

I.D. #S:	
1983	1FT-( )-D #
1984	1FT-( )-E #
1985	1FT-( )-F #

FORD = 83 - 85 A

173

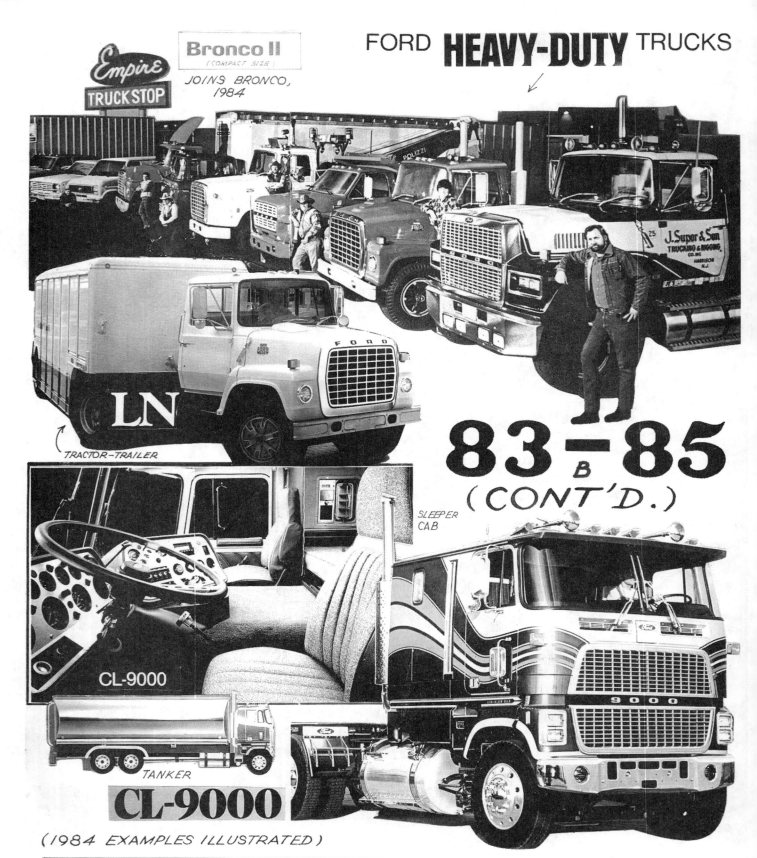

Bronco ll
(COMPACT SIZE)
JOINS BRONCO, 1984

Empire TRUCK STOP

LN
TRACTOR-TRAILER

83-85
B
(CONT'D.)

SLEEPER CAB

CL-9000

TANKER
CL-9000

(1984 EXAMPLES ILLUSTRATED)

ECONOLINE VAN I.D. #s =
  1983 —— 1FT-(EO4Y)-D-#   (ALSO (E14Y) E150 SERIES; (E24Y) E250; (E34Y) E350
  1984 ——————— -E-
  1985 ——————— -F-

FORD=83-85B

Ranger **Ford**

Ranger STX

WITHOUT GRILLE GUARD

EMBLEM NEAR EDGE OF GRILLE

('87)

4 CYL. V6 or DIESEL 4 CYL.

SUPERCAB F. SER. $12590. UP ('86)

STD. F. SER. FROM $10691. ('86)

86-87

$11953. UP (F. SER. '87)

F-Series 4x2/4x4

FORD TRUCKS
AMERICA'S TRUCK BUILT FORD TOUGH

F SERIES

WITH BLACK GRILLE

BRIGHT GRILLE

88

F SERIES RESTYLED FRONT END

F SERIES FROM $10963. (6) 10176. (V8)

HVY WITH SLEEPER CAB

RANGER
new GRILLE

89

XLT

4 or V6 $8093. UP

89-90

new GRILLE ON AEROSTAR IN 1989

WAGONS FROM $13470. ('89) 14487. ('90)

XL new STD. SERIES IN 1990.

HIGHEST-PRICED 1990 AEROSTAR "EDDIE BAUER"
$21207. A-3I-U EXTEND.

HEAVY TRUCKS ('90)

Club Wagon
FROM $14751. ('86)

138" WB

124, 138, 158 or 176" WB

6, V8 or V8 DIESEL (VAN and F-SERIES PICKUP)

1986 MODELS ILLUSTRATED, UNLESS OTHERWISE DESIGNATED

Econoline Van
(CHOICE OF SLIDING OR HINGED SIDE DOORS.)

new
Aerostar Wagon/Van **86-88**

4 CYL. or V6 ('86~87) 119" WB

V6

$12420. UP ('88)

(THIS STYLE OF FORD VAN CONTINUES THRU 1991.)

Econoline Van

$7288. UP → **RANGER**

BRONCO II FRONT END SIMILAR TO RANGER

GRILLE CLOSE UP

F SERIES $10592. (6) 13132. (V8)

RANGER GRILLE $8354. UP ('90)

(new 4x4 Explorer
4 DR. VERSION OF BRONCO.)

F-150

90-91

AEROMAX 120 new FOR 1991

116.8" WB (133" OPT.)

FORD ☰ 86~91

175

FREIGHTLINER

MFD. BY FREIGHTLINER CORP., PORTLAND, OREGON (A SUBSIDIARY OF CONSOLIDATED FREIGHTWAYS)

ESTABLISHED 1939, BUT NO REGULAR FULL PRODUCTION UNTIL 1947.

C.F.R.*

47

EARLY CONVNT'L. (RARE!)

* CONSOLIDATED FREIGHTWAYS REBUILT; MODIFIED OLDER FAGEOL.

"AS IS" USED EXAMPLE SHOWN

new INSIGNIA-NAMEPLATE IN 1951, AS SALES AND SERVICE TAKEN OVER BY WHITE

WHITE FREIGHTLINER

FREIGHTLINER" IS ONLY NAME ON GRILLE INSIGNIA

50

6-CYL. BUDA OR CUMMINS DIESEL ENGINES, BUT WITHIN A FEW YRS., VARIOUS OTHER ENGINES AVAIL.

53

new GRILLE; NAMEPLATE NOW ON CAB FRONT, ABOVE GRILLE.

TILT-CAB MODEL INTRO. 1958.

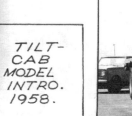

6-CYL., 638 CID CATERPILLAR "1674" DIESEL (270 HP @ 2200 RPM) AVAILABLE ('67.)

61

(OPTIONAL QUADRUPLE HEADLIGHTS AVAIL. DURING 1960s.)

66

TRIPLE AXLES AVAIL.

PRODUCTION DURING 1960s	
1960	931
61	1242
62	1928
63	3053
64	3854
65	4993
66	6704
67	5226
68	7162
69	8674

68

1968 WINDSHIELD WIPERS MOVED TO A LOWER POSITION ON CAB FRONT

HALF-CAB

70

FREIGHTLINER = 47~70

Freightliner

9 CAB LENGTHS FROM 48" TO 104" BBC

48 51 63 72 75 81 96 104

71

White-Freightliner builds more cab body sizes than any other truck manufacturer. Choose from three non-sleeper and six different sleeper cab sizes, including a double bed model and a top mounted sleeper. If your crew numbers more than two men, try our 104 inch, 4-door crew cab for size.

new VENT SLOTS

WHITE FREIGHTLINER

The Road's Too Long For Anything Less

STD. ENG. IS 6-CYL. CUMMINS 585 CID DIESEL NTC-290 (290 HP @ 2100 RPM)

DASH

72 -73

SOME '71-STYLE TRACTORS AVAIL. THROUGH '76.)

The hydraulic 90° tilt cab is nothing new to White Freightliner. In fact, we were the first to develop it. And in the years since, we've improved it to the point of perfection. In seconds, the cab is tilted to a full 90°, or stops and locks anywhere in between. Our tilt cab gives you the ultimate in access and ease of service.

new GRILLE, new STYLE of NAMEPLATE (SOME MODELS. '72.)

('72) RADIATOR FILLER UNDER TILTING NAMEPLATE

FREIGHTLINER = 71~73

Freightliner

CONVENTIONAL
WITH FIBERGLASS
TILT-HOOD

WHITE
FREIGHTLINER

FINAL USE OF
COMBINED
White Freightliner
NAME

74-75

NEW
CONVENTIONAL

JOINS C.O.E.
MODELS

FREIGHTLINER = 74-75

FREIGHTLINER

"WHITE" PREFIX NAME NO LONGER APPLIED.

STD. C.O.E.

↗ THIS STYLE OF C.O.E. "POWERLINER" AVAILABLE FALL, 1973.

WHITE AFFILIATION CEASES IN 1977.

76 ON

1978 TYPES: FLC-12042-T; FLC-12064-T; FLC-12064. COEs: FLT-6342-T; FLT-7564-T; FLT-6364. POWERLINER COEs: FLP-6342-T; FLP-7564-T; FLP-6364 (250-600 HP DIESEL ENGINES)

CONVENTIONAL

(The **CF** Company)

('83) C.O.E.

SHOWN WITH INSIGNIA OF PARENT COMPANY ↙

DAIMLER-BENZ ACQUIRES FREIGHTLINER IN 1981.

80s

AVAILABLE WITH **2 OR 4** HEADLIGHTS

('84)

CONVENTIONAL

FREIGHTLINER = 76 ON

(SINCE 1912)

FWD Trucks

FWD CORPORATION
CLINTONVILLE, WIS. 54929

4-wheel drive

MODEL B

TOWN PLEAS VALLEY YORK

('27)

WITH SNOW PLOW ('28)

MODEL B HAS OWN 4-CYL. ENG. IN 1927. SMALLER 1½-TON "H" (with 121" WB) INTRODUCED, USING 4-CYL. WISC. ENGINE.

1920s

1929 MODELS:

		ENG.
H, HT	2 TON 120" WB	4 CYL. WISCON.
B, M	3, 3½ 124	6 OWN ENG
U-6	3½ 148	6 WAUKESHA
MF6, X6	5, 5½ 170	6 "

(HORIZONTAL LOUVRES, LONGER HOODS)

SHORT CONVENTIONAL

C. 34

HIGH PLACEMENT OF HEADLTS. ON SOME TYPES

('39)

1930s

(CONVENTIONALS)

(ABOVE) H SERIES
(1½ TO 3 TON MODELS)
85 HP AND UP

"SU" (4-5 TON)
"YU" (5-6 TON)

COLO. S.H.D. N° 200-B

('38-42)

('38)

132" WB

1½ TON "HS"
LIGHT-MEDIUM DUTY
282 CID 6 (85 HP @ 3200 RPM)

C.O.E.

('37-'39)

T-40

6-CYL. WAUKESHA ENGINES

('39)

FWD = 1920s - 1930s

180

FWD "D" SUFFIX ON MODEL NUMBER
MEANS *DIESEL - POWERED*.
('46 ON)

('40)

T-32 (138" WB, 7.8 - 4.1 GR)
$3995. 6-CYL.
(91 HP @ 381 CID
2100 RPM) "MKR" WAUKESHA ENG.

1940 WAUKESHA 6-CYL. ENGINES USED:
# BK	282 CID	85 HP @ 3200 RPM	IN MODELS HS, T26
MKR	381	91 @ 2400	IN HH6, T32
MZR	404	96 @ 2400	CUA, CU
SRLR	462	112 @ 2400	SUA, SU
SRKR	517	126 @ 2400	MJ5, MJ6, MJ6X6, T40
RBR	677	152 @ 2400	M7, M6X6, T45

ALSO, HERCULES 6 CYL., 935 CID ENGINE (HXE)
IN MODEL M-10 (198 HP @ 2000 RPM)

1940s

MILITARY

WORLD WAR II ('46)

CUMMINS DIESEL ENGINES
AVAILABLE IN SOME
POSTWAR MODELS.

36th Year

48
MODELS: HA, HR, HG,
SU, M7, M7-D,
M10-D
6-WH.-DR.: M6X6, M6X6D
320-779 CID WAUKESHA GAS OR 844 CID
BUDA DIESEL ENGINES (104-186 HP)
(ALL 6-CYL.) 132-182" WB

YU, ZU, M10 GAS-POWERED
MODELS ADDED FOR 1949.
ZU has 188 HP @ 2600 RPM.

FWD = 1940s

FIRE TRUCK

('52)

FWD

6-WHEEL-DRIVE H6×6
ADDED FOR 1950.

('54)

50-57

('54)

1954 MODELS : 141, 170, 220, 223-D, 262,
264-D, M262, M264-D,
T273, T285, T286, T284-D, T288-D, 323,
324, 324-D, 327-D, 365, 366, 368-D, A369,
408, 409, 406-D, 409-D, 509, 506-D, 509-D,
ALSO, 6-W-D MODELS with 6, L6, or G6
PRECEDING MODEL NO.
HERCULES, WAUKESHA, GMC or CUMMINS
ENGINES (6-CYL., EXC. for CERTAIN 4-CYL.
GMC DIESELS. 6-CYL. GMC DIESELS ALSO.)
97 to 240 HP

NUMEROUS MODELS ADDED
TO FWD LINE DURING 1950s.

('55)
TERACRUZER
8 × 8
DRIVE
⟶

The first FWD 8x8 Teracruzers built for commercial service have been delivered to the Pak-Stanvac Petroleum Project in East Pakistan. The highly specialized Teracruzers and specially built trailers are being used to haul full loads of oil well drilling equipment and supplies in monsoon climate areas inaccessible to conventional vehicles.

The secret of the Teracruzer's maneuverability lies in its unique eight-wheel drive system, its superior articulation, its small turning radius, the very low ground pressure which results from the special characteristics of the design, and the ability to adjust immediately to changing terrain conditions by automatically deflating and inflating each tire separately from the cab.

1957 MODELS : 140; U-150;
181; 182;
202; 232; 233D; 284;
M284D; M284; 284D;
285; 285D; M285; 305;
326; 324D; 327D; 367;
368D; S326; S324D;
408; 409; 406D;
409D
6-WHEELERS have 6,
R6, T, TS, C6 or CS6
PREFIXES

DUETZ,
INT., GMC, CUMMINS OR WAUKESHA ENGINES
USED (240 to 779 CID, 3, 4, 6 or 8 CYLS.,
102 to 240 HP IN 1957.

('57)

FWD = 50 ~ 57

182

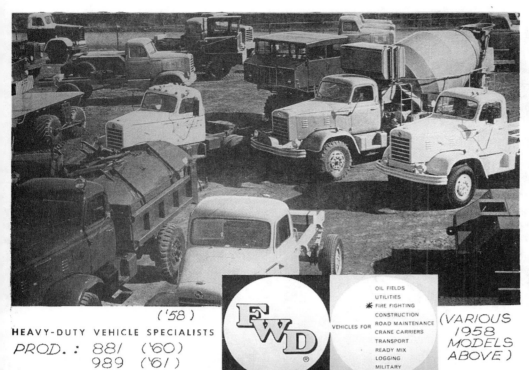

58-59

3, 4, 6, 8 CYL. MODELS with GMC, INT., CUMMINS DIESEL, WAUKESHA, or DEUTZ AIR-COOLED DIESEL ENGINES. 213 TO 779 CID 102 TO 240 HP

130" TO 161" WB

VEHICLES FOR:
- OIL FIELDS
- UTILITIES
- ✳ FIRE FIGHTING
- CONSTRUCTION
- ROAD MAINTENANCE
- CRANE CARRIERS
- TRANSPORT
- READY MIX
- LOGGING
- MILITARY

('58)

HEAVY-DUTY VEHICLE SPECIALISTS

PROD. : 881 ('60)
989 ('61)
1,029 ('62)
827 ('63)

(VARIOUS 1958 MODELS ABOVE)

PRODUCTION :
1,227 ('58)
1,067 ('59)

TRACTIONEER MODELS FIRST APPEAR IN 1958.

EARLY TO MID –
1960s

1,123 ('64)
1,496 ('65)
1,619 ('66)

✳ STARTING MAY 1, 1962, FWD NO LONGER BUILT NON-MILITARY COMPLETE FIRE TRUCKS, BUT SUPPLIED F.T. CHASSES FOR OTHER MFRS., SUCH AS SEAGRAVE. FWD BOUGHT SEAGRAVE IN 1963 AND CONTINUED TO PRODUCE SEAGRAVE FIRE TRUCKS.

"TRACTIONEER" MIXER TRUCKS

('66)

MODEL C6-6461

FLATBED WITH FREIGHT RACK

FWD=58~MID-60s

183

MIXERS

LATER
1960s

with T.L. SMITH 10-YARD MIXER

MODEL C88-4479
8-WHEEL DRIVE
(ABOVE)

FRONT
DETAILS OF
CONVENTIONAL
(TYPE WITH
OPEN GRILLE)

PROD. :
1, 251   ('67)
1, 233   ('68)
1, 403   ('69)
1, 093   ('70)

MIXER TRUCKS OF
VARIOUS
WHEEL ARRANGEMENTS
ARE
ILLUSTRATED.

FWD ══ LATER 1960s

('70)

150 TO 300 HP GAS,
OR 130 TO 300 HP
DIESELS
(6 OR V-6)

FWD CORPORATION

SLEEPER CAB
IN
"Big Tilt" COE

('70)

WITH
CUMMINS
NH-230 DIESEL ENG.
(230 HP @ 2100)
OTHER ENGS. AVAIL.

tractioneer

6X6

(ABOVE)

70-71

ON

"FORWARD

mover"

MODEL B5-2116
6 × 4
LIGHTWEIGHT
(FOR MED./HVY. USE)

"FWD" ON
DIFFERENTIAL

CF C.O.E.
HAS
FIBERGLASS/PLASTIC
BODY SHELL and FENDERS
(METAL DOORS)

DESIGNED FOR MIXER/
DUMPER SERVICE
(AS
ILLUSTR.
AT
UPPER
RT.)

"FWD"
ABOVE
GRILLE

"FORWARD
MOVER"
NAMEPLATE
IS
ON HOOD.

CAB/CHASSIS OF
"FORWARD MOVER"
MODEL B5-2116 6×4 LTWT.

CF ('71)

FWD = 70~71 ON

B, LB **FWD** ('72)

B & LB SERIES

C

C SERIES

D

D SERIES

C5-2178

C5-2178

CB 4×4 ('74)

tractioneer 4×4 truck

RB 4×4 ('74)

tractioneer

TRACTOR

FWD adds conventional and COE tractors

('72)

116" BBC

CA-64 CONVENTIONALS

WITH MERCURY 30" SLEEPER BOX

HEAVY-DUTY
WITH AFTER-COOLED CUMMINS 350 DIESEL ENGINES

SINCE **72**

84" BBC WITH SLEEPER CAB   CO-64   ('72)

1978 LINE INCLUDES RB and CB CONVENTIONALS OR DF (C.O.E.) W. DIESEL ENGINES OF 195 TO 350 HP MANY CUSTOM-BUILT VARIETIES IN RECENT YEARS.

CF SERIES

DF SERIES

CF   DF

C SERIES ALL-WHEEL DRIVE ('74)
WITH LOW BED DUMP BODY and HYDRAULICS FOR PLOWING OPERATIONS.

FWD = SINCE 72

186

GARFORD

(1909–1933)
GARFORD MOTOR TRUCK CO., LIMA, OHIO

CHASSIS PRICES LISTED

3½ Ton "77-D" 162" WB $4390 ('21)

2-TON "70-H" 144" WB $3450. ('21)

5-TON "68-D" 162" WB $5200. ('21)

1¼ TON "25" 135" WB $2290.

Garford 5-ton Truck

"51-D" 4-CYL. 25-29 PASS. BUS CHASSIS 187" WB $4350. ('24)

1920s

1-TON "15" 132" WB CHASSIS ('24) $1590.

"KB" 17-PASSENGER COACH 6 CYL., 180" WB CHASSIS ('25)

(3⅜" x 5" BORE and STR.) 32 x 6" TIRES

GARFORD BUS ('25) SINGLE-DOOR STYLE

GARFORD GREYHOUND 17-PASS. PARLOR CAR BUS 180" WB ('26)

MULTI-DOOR STYLE

1½-2 TON "30" 144" WB 4 CYL. ('28)

MODEL 50 2½ TON ('26) 156" WB

RELAY MOTORS BUYS GARFORD, SEPT., 1927.

CHASSIS $2690.

MERGER

GARFORD GREYHOUND 19-PASS. PARLOR CAR BUS ('28) 180" WB

('29)

COMMERCE-GARFORD-SERVICE 2 TON "40-Z" (RELAY TRUCK SIMILARLY STYLED)

GARFORDS SALES IN 1929 AMOUNT TO ONLY ABOUT 100 UNITS.

DECEMBER, 1932: RELAY GROUP GOES INTO RECEIVERSHIP. CONSOLIDATED MOTORS BUYS ASSETS.

GARFORD

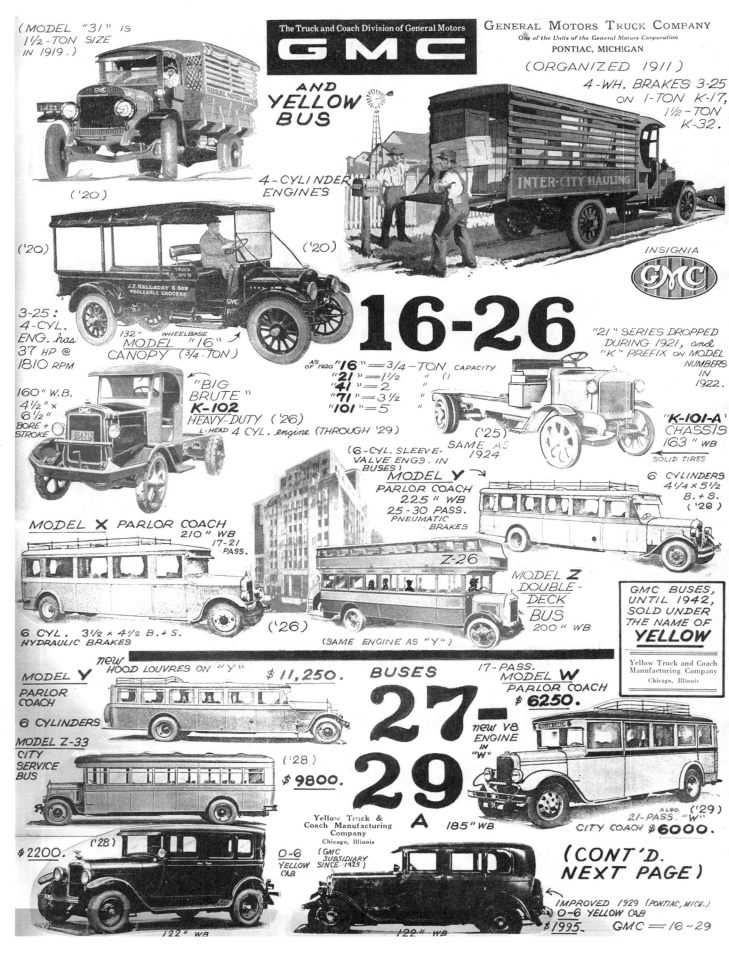

(MODEL "31" IS 1½-TON SIZE IN 1919.)

('20)

The Truck and Coach Division of General Motors
GMC
AND YELLOW BUS

4-CYLINDER ENGINES

GENERAL MOTORS TRUCK COMPANY
One of the Units of the General Motors Corporation
PONTIAC, MICHIGAN
(ORGANIZED 1911)
4-WH. BRAKES 3-25
ON 1-TON K-17,
1½-TON K-32.

('20)

('20)

INTER-CITY HAULING

INSIGNIA
GMC

3-25:
4-CYL.
ENG. has
37 HP @
1810 RPM

132" WHEELBASE
MODEL "16"
CANOPY (¾-TON)

16-26

AS OF 1920 "16" = ¾-TON CAPACITY
"21" = 1½ " (1
"41" = 2 "
"71" = 3½ "
"101" = 5 "

"21" SERIES DROPPED DURING 1921, and "K" PREFIX ON MODEL NUMBERS IN 1922.

160" W.B.
4½" × 6½"
BORE + STROKE

"BIG BRUTE"
K-102
HEAVY-DUTY ('26)
L-HEAD 4 CYL. engine (THROUGH '29)

('25)
SAME AS 1924

"K-101-A"
CHASSIS
163" WB
SOLID TIRES

6 CYLINDERS
4¼ × 5½
B. + S.
('26)

(6-CYL. SLEEVE-VALVE ENGS. IN BUSES)

MODEL **Y**
PARLOR COACH
225" WB
25-30 PASS.
PNEUMATIC BRAKES

MODEL **X** PARLOR COACH
210" WB
17-21 PASS.

Z-26

MODEL **Z**
DOUBLE-DECK BUS
200" WB

GMC BUSES, UNTIL 1942, SOLD UNDER THE NAME OF
YELLOW
Yellow Truck and Coach Manufacturing Company
Chicago, Illinois

6 CYL. 3½ × 4½ B. + S.
HYDRAULIC BRAKES

('26)

(SAME ENGINE AS "Y")

new HOOD LOUVRES ON "Y"
$11,250.

MODEL **Y**
PARLOR COACH
6 CYLINDERS

MODEL Z-33
CITY SERVICE BUS

('28)
$9800.

BUSES
27-29
A

17-PASS.
MODEL **W**
PARLOR COACH
$6250.

new V8 ENGINE IN "W"

185" WB

Yellow Truck & Coach Manufacturing Company
Chicago, Illinois

O-6 {GMC SUBSIDIARY SINCE 1925}
YELLOW CAB

ALSO ('29)
21-PASS. "W"
CITY COACH $6000.

$2200.
('28)

(CONT'D. NEXT PAGE)

IMPROVED 1929 (PONTIAC, MICH.)
O-6 YELLOW CAB
$1995.
GMC = 16~29

122" WB

122.4" WB

188

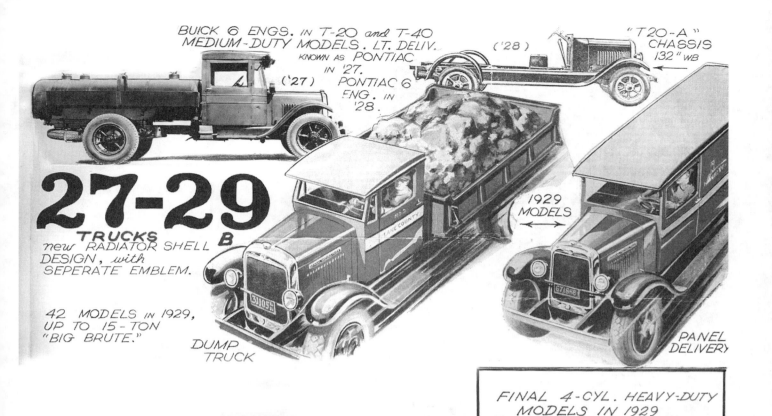

BUICK 6 ENGS. IN T-20 and T-40
MEDIUM-DUTY MODELS . LT. DELIV.
KNOWN AS PONTIAC
IN '27.
PONTIAC 6
ENG. IN
'28.

('28)

"T20-A"
CHASSIS
132" WB

('27)

27-29
TRUCKS B
new RADIATOR SHELL
DESIGN, *with*
SEPERATE EMBLEM.

42 MODELS IN 1929,
UP TO 15-TON
"BIG BRUTE."

DUMP
TRUCK

1929
MODELS
→

PANEL
DELIVERY

FINAL 4-CYL. HEAVY-DUTY
MODELS IN 1929

1½ TON Range $960

2 TON Range $1545

1 TON Range $745

2½ TON Range $1845

¾ TON Range $695

3 TON Range $2080

½ TON Range $625

3½ TON Range $3035

1½ TON Range $1265
Super-power

4 TON Range $3795

six-cylinder

Service Station
OF 1930,
WITH
30
T-60-B
TANKER

AC 221

PETROLEUM CO. INC.

395 *choices*

THIS
"T-60-B"
3½-TON
TANKER *has*
94 HP ENG.

5 TON Range $5885
Six-wheeler

TRACTORS up
to 15 Tons

UNION COAL CO.
COAL

"T-82-A" 4-TON
DUMP TRUCK
94 HP

(CONT'D.
NEXT PAGE)

GMC = 27~30

189

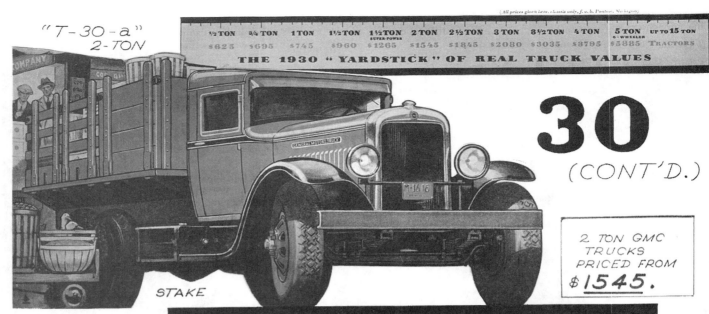

"T-30-a" 2-TON

½ TON	¾ TON	1 TON	1½ TON	1½ TON SUPER-POWER	2 TON	2½ TON	3 TON	3½ TON	4 TON	5 TON 6-WHEELER	UP TO 15 TON TRACTORS
$625	$695	$745	$960	$1265	$1545	$1845	$2080	$3035	$3795	$5885	

THE 1930 "YARDSTICK" OF REAL TRUCK VALUES

30
(CONT'D.)

2 TON GMC TRUCKS PRICED FROM $1545.

STAKE

PANEL DELIVERY   (T 31 and T-45 HAVE 257.5 CID 6, 76 HP @ 2500 RPM)

The Truck and Coach Division of General Motors

GMC

ALL MODELS with 6 CYLINDERS (THROUGH '54)

31-32

('31) 1½ - 2 TON "T-19-a" WITH 200.3 CID 6, 60 HP

MODEL "U" BUS ('32)

9-32: new GMT "400" ENG. (400.9 CID 6) 112½ HP @ 2800 RPM, FOR T-61, T-83, 6-WHEEL T-90

ABOVE: "T-26" ('31) 2-3 TON RANGE

SEPT., 1931: new "T-18" INTRODUCED, WITH SIMILAR SPECIFICATIONS TO "T-19."

GMC = 30~32

33

CAB (new "AIRPLANE-TYPE" DASH GAUGES)

EXTERIOR VISOR ELIMINATED ON SOME 1933 MODELS

OCT., 1932

new "221" (221.4 CID) O.H.V. 6 ENG. has 69 H.P. @ 2800 RPM, REPLACES EX-PONTIAC "200" SERIES L-HEAD TYPE IN T-18 (1½-2 TON) and T-23 (2-3 TON) (JAN., 1933)

EARLY MODEL (ABOVE) (with OVAL REAR WINDOW)

T-23 (2-3 TON, 131" WB and up)

"GMC" ON BUMPER

NO HEADLIGHT TIE BAR ON LT. and MED. DUTY.

A NEW GMC 3-TON TRUCK

C.O.E.

DUAL REAR WINDOWS

3 new C.O.E.s IN 1934.

"331" and "400" ENGINES have WATER PUMP RE-LOCATED at FRONT END OF FAN PULLEY.

HEAVY-DUTY DUMP

6 CYL OHV, 69 HP

$925. (CHASSIS)

PEERLESS STAGES (CALIFORNIA)

MODEL **722** PUSHER-TYPE

YELLOW COACH

34

SOME MODELS RESTYLED. new GRILLES.

new 1934 "450" ENGINE has 120 HP @ 2300 RPM.

1½-2 TON

70 HP

CHASSIS **$595.**

A Combination of Features Never Before Offered in a Truck at This Price

NOTE THAT FRONT DOOR IS SET BACK BEYOND FRONT AXLE.

69, 76, 94, 110, 120, 128 or 149 HP 6-CYL. TRUCK ENGINES

HVY. DUTY MODELS : T-18 (1½-2 T.); T-23, T33L (2-3 T.); T-33 (3-3½ T.); T-43, T-43T (3½-4½ T.); T-51 (4-5½ T.); T-51W, T51H, T-61 (5-6½ T.); T-83 (5-7½ T.); T-84 (7-9 T.); COEs : T-73 (3-3½ T.); T-75 (5-6½ T.); T-78 (7-9 T.); 6-WHEELERS : T954R (9-11 T.); T-1204R (12-15 TON)

$625. ~ **$9490.** PRICE RANGE

GMC = 33 ~ 34

GMC

MFD. BY THE GMC TRUCK and COACH DIVISION of GENERAL MOTORS CORP.

1½-2 TON **T-16** / CAB

NEW for 1935,
HYDRAULIC BRAKES ON ALL LT. and MEDIUM-DUTY GMC TRUCKS
SLOPING GRILLE
FENDER-MOUNTED HEADLIGHTS

IN ADDITION TO "T-16" and "T-18," MODELS ALSO INCLUDE :

T-23	2½ to 3 TON	221 CID	
T-33	3 to 4½	257	
T-43	3½ to 5	"	$1795
T-46 (H)	4 to 6½	331	2625
T-51 (W,H)	4 to 6½	"	3095
T-61	5 to 6½	400	4395
T-83	6 to 8	"	5185
T-84	7 to 10	450	5760
T-84-SX	7½ TON	"	

C.O.E. MODELS :

T-73 (H)	3 to 4½ TON
T-74 (H)	3½ to 5½
T-75 (T,H)	5 to 13
T-78 (T)	7 AND UP

(1935 SPECS.)

note VARIATIONS IN GRILLES and HOOD LOUVRES

35 T SERIES

DUMP TRUCK 2 to 3 ton **T-18**

140" W.B. (UP TO 164" AVAIL.)
221 CID
6 CHASSIS FROM $777.

"T-16" EARLY MODEL with 1934-STYLE CAB ROOF

213 C.I.D., 6 CYL. L-HEAD engine IN "T-16" 1½-2 TON 131" W.B. (UP TO 157" AVAIL.)

ALL BUT "T-16" MODELS have 6-CYL. OVERHEAD-VALVE ENGINES of 221, 257, 331, 400 or 450 C.I.D.

new **T-46** 5 TON INTRO. JULY, 1934 WITH "331" ENGINE 94 HP @ 2500 RPM $2135. and up

"DUAL-PERFORMANCE" 2-SPEED REAR AXLES (5.14 and 7.15 GEAR RATIOS) AVAILABLE ON LATE '35 1½-2-TON MODELS

note "GMC" ON BUMPER

"T-16" LATER MODEL 1½-2-TON with "BLISTER" VISOR on CAB, and SMALL VERTICAL HOOD LOUVRES and 84 H.P. @ 3500 RPM FROM $976. (TACOMA, WASH.)

CAPACITIES UP TO 22 TONS

192

new 239 CID 6 IN T-18, T-18 H.
also 257, 286, 331, 400
and 450 CID 6-CYL. ENGINES.

The Truck and Coach Division of General Motors
GMC

213 CID 6
IN T-14

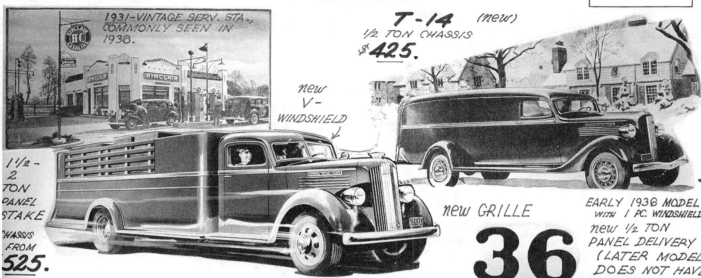

T-14 (new)
½ TON CHASSIS
$425.

new V-WINDSHIELD

1931-VINTAGE SERV. STA.,
COMMONLY SEEN IN
1936.

1½-2 TON PANEL STAKE CHASSIS FROM 525.

new GRILLE
36

EARLY 1936 MODEL
WITH 1 PC. WINDSHIELD
new ½ TON
PANEL DELIVERY
(LATER MODEL ?
DOES NOT HAVE
"BLISTER VISOR
ABOVE
WINDSHIELD.)

MODEL 719
325 GMC/YELLOW "719"
BUSES BLT. FOR
GREYHOUND LINES

"DUAL PERFORMANCE"
REAR AXLES NOW AVAIL.
IN 1½ TO 6-TON RANGE

CAPACITIES
UP TO
15 TONS

"HELMET-TOP" CAB

C.O.E PANEL-STAKE

new "DUAL TONE" COLOR DESIGNS

300 "720" and "725"
REAR-ENG. DOUBLE
DECK BUSES BLT.
1936 TO 1938. (160 FOR
NYC, 140 FOR CHICAGO.)

3 MODELS OF
2-WHEEL UTILITY
TRAILERS AVAIL.
FROM GMC (ALSO
IN '38)
{ OPEN EXPRESS
SCREEN-SIDE "
STAKE

new LOW-PRICED 1½-TON C.O.E.
TRUCK ($830., f.o.b., for
chassis and cab;
$635., f.o.b., chassis only.)

37

PICKUPS and
PANELS ON
112 OR
126" WB

(INTRO. LATE '36)

The GREYHOUND LINES

INTER-CITY BUS
(BLT. FOR
GREYHOUND)
GM/YELLOW
"743"
(1250 BLT., '37-'39) '36 "719"
SIMILAR, BUT WITH VERTICAL VENTS
BY DESTINATION SIGN.)
TRUCK
CAPACITIES UP TO 12 TONS

GMC=36~37

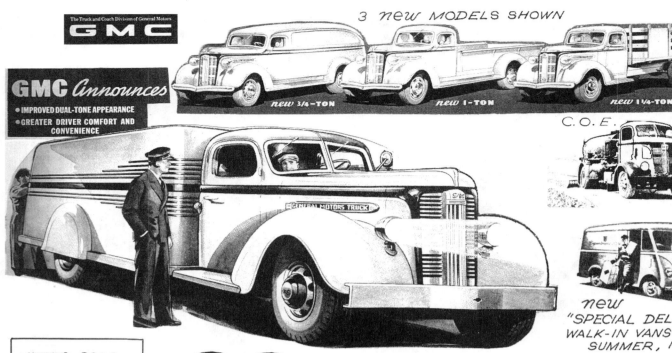

The Truck and Coach Division of General Motors

GMC

GMC *Announces*
- IMPROVED DUAL-TONE APPEARANCE
- GREATER DRIVER COMFORT AND CONVENIENCE

3 new MODELS SHOWN

new 3/4-TON   new 1-TON   new 1¼-TON

C.O.E.

new "SPECIAL DELIVERY" WALK-IN VANS AVAIL. SUMMER, 1938.

new 3-DOOR, 5-MAN CAB ON UTILITY LINEMAN'S SPECIAL C.O.E. MODEL

38
(HOOD LOUVRES ELIMINATED)
GRILLE SLIGHTLY CHANGED
CAPACITIES UP TO 15 TON

YELLOW CITY BUS ('38~42 TYPE)

GMC/YELLOW "743" BUS BLT. FOR

The GREYHOUND LINES

new C.O.E. MODELS (1½ TO 8 TONS)

new 10-12-15-TON DUMP MODELS AVAIL. AUGUST, 1939.

C.O.E.

THE TRUCK GMC OF VALUE

new GRILLE →

39

new "228" GMC O.H.V. ENGINES IN ½-TON (80 H.P. @ 3000 RPM)

New **TRUCKS**

O.H.V. 7 New **ENGINES** "SUPER-DUTY"

12 New **DIESELS** 3½ TONS and up

New **SYNCRO-MESH** TRANSMISSION ON MEDIUM AND HEAVY-DUTY MODELS

GMC=38~39

194

BLT. BY GMC's YELLOW COACH DIV., THIS FAMOUS "SILVERSIDES" INTER-CITY BUS INTRODUCED APRIL, 1940, CONT'D. TO END OF THE DECADE. MOST SOLD TO GREYHOUND LINES, REPLACED 1936~1939 STYLE. 591 BLT. 1940~41, 2000 MORE IN 1947~48.

PDG-3701 IS EARLY 33' TYPE. 3751 IS 35'

BUS

GMC

The Truck and Coach Division of General Motors

GMC/YELLOW BUSES AVAIL. WITH GASOLINE OR DIESEL ENGINES.

BALL-BEARING STEERING OPTIONAL IN MEDIUM and HEAVY-DUTY MODELS.

LT. and MEDIUM-DUTY MODELS: (TO 1½-TON)

AC-100
AC-150
AC-251
AC-252
AC-300
AC-350
SPEC. DELIV. (C.O.E.)
AF-310   "
AF-350   "

HEAVIER MODELS ALSO AVAIL. *

New DIESELS (6-CYL.)

new 40 SEALED-BEAM HEADLIGHTS

PARKING LIGHTS ON FENDERS ARE New

"RIDER-EASE" CABS WITH "QUICK VISION INSTRUMENT PANELS "POWER PAK" PISTONS 6 CYL., 80 H.P. @ 3000 RPM (LARGER ENGINES ALSO)

C.O.E.

C.O.E.s FROM $868.

* CAPACITIES UP TO 15 TONS

new 6-WHEELERS

AS OF JULY, 1940 = new ½-TON DELIVERY VAN and 2 new 1-TON VANS ("BAKERS' DELIVERY" VAN has ALL-FLAT FLOOR.)

195

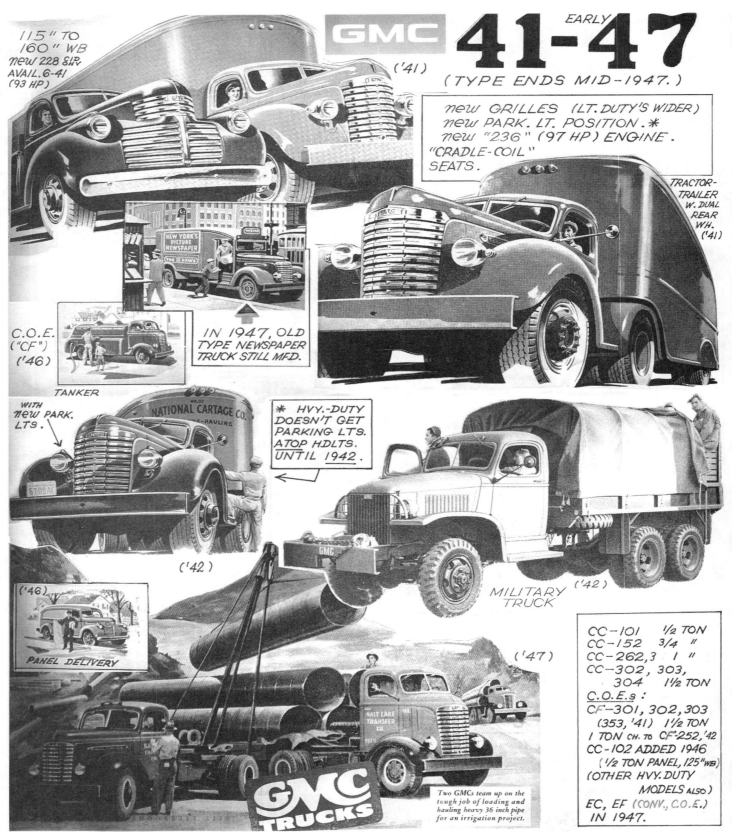

115" TO 160" WB
new 228 6 cyl.
AVAIL. 6-41
(93 HP)

GMC 41-47 EARLY

('41)

(TYPE ENDS MID-1947.)

new GRILLES (LT. DUTY'S WIDER)
new PARK. LT. POSITION.*
new "236" (97 HP) ENGINE.
"CRADLE-COIL"
SEATS.

TRACTOR-TRAILER W. DUAL REAR WH. ('41)

C.O.E. ("CF") ('46)

IN 1947, OLD TYPE NEWSPAPER TRUCK STILL MFD.

TANKER

WITH new PARK. LTS.

* HVY.-DUTY DOESN'T GET PARKING LTS. ATOP HDLTS. UNTIL 1942.

('42)

MILITARY TRUCK ('42)

('46) PANEL DELIVERY

('47)

GMC TRUCKS

Two GMCs team up on the tough job of loading and hauling heavy 36 inch pipe for an irrigation project.

CC-101   ½ TON
CC-152   ¾ "
CC-262,3 1 "
CC-302, 303,
    304   1½ TON
C.O.E.s :
CF-301, 302, 303
    (353, '41) 1½ TON
1 TON CH. TO CF-252, '42
CC-102 ADDED 1946
    (½ TON PANEL, 125" WB)
(OTHER HVY. DUTY
    MODELS ALSO)
EC, EF (CONV., C.O.E.)
IN 1947.

CONVENTIONAL (ABOVE)	1941	1942~1945	1946	1947
½ TON SUBURBAN —	$875.	875.		1219.
PICKUP —	648.	641.	879.	927.
PANEL —	730.	723.	1052.	1020.

C.O.E. (ABOVE)

½ TON	115" WB
¾ "	125" "
1, 1½ T.	134; (160, 178" WB ALSO, 1½ T.)

GMC = 41~47

GMC

INTER-CITY BUS
GREYHOUND. ('48)

New GMC Postwar Cab ('48)

REAR WINDOW VISION INCREASED 60%

DOOR OPENINGS FOUR INCHES WIDER

3-POINT CAB MOUNTING AND RUBBER STABILIZERS

SEATING WIDTH INCREASED 8 INCHES

73 INDIVIDUALLY WRAPPED SPRINGS

TUBULAR FRAMED ADJUSTABLE SEATS

WINDSHIELD VISION INCREASED 20%

FAMOUS BALL BEARING STEERING

EASIER CLUTCH PEDAL ACTION

CIRCULATING FRESH AIR VENTILATION

PD - 4103 ('49-53)
TRAILWAYS

GMC's new cabs circulate fresh air by a revolutionary ventilating system. And you can have forced air heating and defrosting, too, if desired.

FC 101 PICKUP $927. ('48)

DIESEL COACHES—In 1938, less than 200 Diesel-powered motor coaches were in operation. By 1948, the number had multiplied to over 18,000. GMC Diesel coach production has accounted for more than 90 per cent of the industry's total.

New

"FC" SERIES

48-53

TOTALLY RESTYLED LT. DUTY 1948 MODELS INTRO. SUMMER, 1947.

4 and 6 CYL. DIESEL ENGINES ALSO AVAIL. 1948.

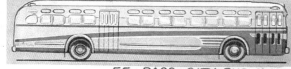
55-PASS. CITY BUS ('49)
(note SMALL "STANDEE WINDOWS" ABOVE SIDE WINDOWS)

'48~53 PICKUP FRONTAL STYLING SIMILAR TO THIS MODEL, BUT 1 LESS HORIZONTAL PIECE IN GRILLE.

('50)

DIESELS RESTYLED LIKE OTHER GMCs IN 1950. HEAVY-DUTY GASOLINE MODELS RESTYLED ALSO. PRE-1950 TYPE DIESEL SHOWN AT RIGHT ——→

DIESEL TRUCKS—In 1938, less than 500 Diesel trucks were in service. By 1948, the number had jumped to more than 12,000. In recent months, GMC has produced nearly 30 per cent of the industry's total. Shown is a GMC six-cylinder, 200-horsepower Diesel tractor.

GMC Diesel trucks are powered by engines of the same basic design as the Diesel locomotives which pull many of the nation's finest, fastest trains. This advanced and exclusive GM 2-cycle design cuts Diesel weight without sacrifice of power, thus permitting greater payloads. It also provides outstanding fuel economy, low maintenance costs, exceptional dependability and long life. GMCs are the only Diesel trucks offering a choice of four- and six-cylinder engines . . . specially engineered Diesel chassis . . . a selection of eight series of models. And, more important, GMC has had unequalled experience in equipping vehicles with these modern, time and money saving Diesel power plants.
GMC TRUCK & COACH DIVISION • GENERAL MOTORS

GM GENERAL MOTORS COACH

GMC TRUCKS

GMC=48~53

197

LOAD CLEARANCE ANTENNA

PANEL TRUCK

SUBURBAN

('55)

HEAVY DUTY

TRACTOR-TRAILER (C.O.E.)

1070B

FLEET CARRIER CORP.

170T

('54)

Greyhound

HWY. TRAVELER

TRAILWAYS

$1732. UP

('56)

1954 CANOPY EXPRESS (137" WB)

GMC

54-59

Greyhound

SCENICRUISER

('54)

6 OR V8   HYDRA MATIC A/T AVAIL.

$1846. UP

1957 has new GRILLE

GREYHOUND

CITY TRANSIT BUSES ALSO AVAILABLE

MODEL 374 FLATBED ('59)

('57)   MODEL 0/60

TRUCK PRODUCTION: 64,216 ('58)
77,473 ('59)

NEW GRILLE ON 1958 LT. DUTY

(NO BUMPER PODS ON '59 LT. DUTY)

1958

1958 $1929. UP

('58-59)

189 H.P.
DR-860 DIESEL

860

D-860

GMC

('59)

59-63

new 72" BBC C.O.E. TILT-CABS ('60) FROM 19,500 LBS. G.V.W.

('59)

BELOW: "NEW LOOK" RESTYLED CITY TRANSIT BUS FOR 1960 s

TYPE AVAIL. 1959-1977

NOTE LOW WINDSHIELD

DLR-8000 LIGHTWT. ALUMINUM TILT-CAB (with 6-71 SE GMC DIESEL ENGINE)

New

('63)

('63)

('60)

AT RIGHT, SHOWN WITH LOAD OF LARGE NEWS-PRINT PAPER ROLLS →

CAPACITIES UP TO 60 TONS

SUBURBAN

van

C.O.E. HEAVY TRACTOR

('60)

| GMC PROD. : 77,473 ('59) |
| 104,310 ('60) 74,996 ('61) |
| 89,789 ('62) 101,234 ('63) |

GMC=59~63

BOTTLER'S TRUCK

GMC

UTILITY

GMC PROD.:
110,521 ('64); 136,705 ('65)
127,294 ('66)

TRACTOR/TRLR.

Medium-Ton Trucks

new "TORO-FLOW" DIESEL ENG. AVAIL.

64-68

DUMP TRUCK ('64)

TILT-CAB C.O.E.

('64)

DOUBLE ROOFED CAB

('65) WOOD FLOOR

305 CID V6 (A GMC EXCLUSIVE)

new

('66)

MOULDINGS ON HOOD

6-CYL. INCR. TO 155 HP IN 1966.

"GMC"

4 HDLTS.

PRINTED CIRCUIT BEHIND INSTR. PANEL

8.15 x 15" TIRES

TRUCKS
FROM ½ TO 60 TONS

('67)

RESTYLED 1967 PICKUP
(175 or 220 HP IN V8s)

1967 GMC PROD.: 130,659

211 CU FT. LOAD SPACE
(168" TOTAL LENGTH)

GMC's Handi-Van.

(STARTS '64)

4 CYL. (90 HP)
OR 6 CYL. (140 HP)

1968 GMC PROD.: 148,479

SCHOOL BUS

1966 GMC Model SV4019

200

PICKUP

GMC

Stake Model

Steel Tilt Model

TILT CAB
AND
CHASSIS
FROM
$**5389.**
('72)

3/4 TON
STAKE
FROM:
$**2986.**-('69)
$**3176.**-('72)

P.D-4107 ('69)

69-72
A

(1972
EXAMPLES
SHOWN)

Conventional

GMC SPRINT
STARTS 1971

INTERIOR

195,
217 OR
229
HP
('72)

Series 7500
Conventional

401 OR 478 CID
V6 GAS ENG.
OR 318 CID
DETROIT DIESEL
6V-53N ENGINE
(ILLUSTRATED)

('72)

The Truck People from General Motors

FRONT END OF **GMC "SPRINT"** PICKUP-
CAR

6 OR
V8

('72)
FROM
$**3019.**

PICKUPS	$ 2438.	C SERIES	(1969)
priced	2630.	CE "	(1970)
	2832.	" "	(1971)
FROM	2804.	" "	(1972)

GMC=69~72 A

(CONT'D. NEXT PAGE)

GMC

Series 9500

Conventional Heavy Duty (CONT'D.)

WITH OPTIONAL GRILLE GUARD →

69-72B (1972 EXAMPLES SHOWN)

9500

ASTRO 95 Tilt Cab
C.O.E.

ASTRO 95

Available RPM and MPH Sangamo instruments are located in bezels provided for standard tach and odometer. Both units are placed for rapid reading.

INTERIOR VIEWS (ABOVE)

GMC "JIMMY" VERSION OF CHEV. "BLAZER" INTRO. 1970, AT $2377. UP (104" WB, 6 CYL.)

GMC "SPRINT" VERSION OF CHEV. "EL CAMINO" INTRO. 1971, AT $3019. UP (116" WB, V8)

GMC=69~72 B

GMC

('74) STAKE
Cab & Chassis

3500
←THIS GRILLE USED 1973-1974 ONLY

← 1975 TO 1976 - STYLE GRILLE (LT. DUTY)

4-wheel and 2-wheel drive

REAR DETAILS (ACCESSORY BOX CAP)

('79)

JIMMY

PASSENGER VAN

('79)

CARGO VAN

CONVENTIONAL
Series 5000, 6000 and 6500   ('73)

C-3500
('79)

('73)

73-79

INTERIOR   ('74)

9500 Conventional

GMC = 73-79

('76)

ASTRO 95

GMC

DRAGFOILER

('80)

BRIGADIER
WITH 2
HEADLIGHTS

(1977-78 STYLE PICKUP)

('78)

C.O.E. ('79) (ABOVE)

76-79

1979 PICKUP (HEADLIGHT FRAME JOINED TO " OF PARK. LIGHT DIRECTLY BELOW)

RADIATOR ORNAMENT

HEAVY-DUTY TRUCKS

HAVE "GMC" NAME ATOP or ABOVE GRILLE.

GMC introduces the first really new heavy-duty conventional in years.

1977 SLOGAN: "GET TRUCKIN' - GET A GMC."

1978: "NOTHIN' GOES TRUCKIN' LIKE A GMC."

DASH

GEN'L. INTRO. DURING SUMMER OF 1976. note 4 HEAD-LIGHTS.

BUDD ALUMINUM CAB. FIBERGLASS HOOD and FENDERS.

General ('76½)

new

'79 SLOGAN:

GMC
Trucks are what we're all about.

CREW CAB
$9018.
UP ('81)

GMC PICKUPS

SPARE TIRE and WHEEL
CARRIED BELOW
PICKUP BOX

WIDESIDE

$6679.
UP ('81)

HORIZONTAL GRILLE PC.
PAINTED IN 1980.

DASH   (SIERRA CLASSIC)

Sierra Classic instrument panel.

SIERRA
WIDESIDE
4-W-D

('80)

GASOLINE AND DIESEL
ENGINES

CAT 3208
V8 DIESEL ENGINE

BLACK BUMPER
ON SOME '80 MODELS

STD. VAN DASH

1981 EXAMPLES
ILLUSTR., UNLESS
OTHERWISE INDICATED.

TOP KICK

('81)

HEAVY-
DUTY

80-81

RALLY (PASSENGER)
VAN

VANDURA
CARGO VAN
110" or 125" WB

4.1 L. 6
(105 HP) or
5.0 L. V8 (160 HP)
(5.7 L. V8 AVAIL.)

1979-1983
SLOGAN

GMC TRUCKS ARE WHAT WE'RE ALL ABOUT.

GMC

S-15 DASH

4 CYL. (1.9 L.)

82 HP @ 4600 RPM

UP TO
39 MPG (HWY)
28 MPG (EPA)

S-15

(**NEW** COMPACT SERIES) $**6704.**
UP

V-6 (2.8 L.)

110 HP @ 4800 RPM

5 - SP. OVERDRIVE AVAIL.

S-15 REAR

118" WB

108" WB

82
A

DASH (FULL-SIZE PICKUPS)

FULL-SIZE PICKUP FROM $**7297.**

FENDERSIDE

NOTE:
SOME '82 PICKUPS DO NOT HAVE PARK. LTS. BELOW HEADLTS.

NEW 6.2 V8 DIESEL AVAILABLE

QUALITY BUILT FOR VALUE

(CONT'D. NEXT PG.)

GMC-82 A

GMC

"HEAVY HAULER"
WIDESIDE with DUAL REAR WHEELS

RALLY $10710. UP

82B
(CONT'D.)

VANS

FROM $9359.
CAB & CHASSIS
W. STAKE BODY

RALLY CAMPER SPECIAL CHASSIS

WITH UTILITY BODY (ABOVE)

125 OR 146" WB

MAGNAVAN $10973. UP
ALUMINUM VALUE VAN

$7470. UP **VANDURA**

WALK-IN "STEP VANS"

STEEL VALUE VAN

STEP-VAN ENGINES:
6 CYL. (4.8 L.)
(115 HP @ 3400 RPM)
V8 (5.7 L.)
(160 HP @ 3800)
V8 (7.4 L.)
(210 HP @ 3800)
DIESEL V6
(6.2 L.)
(135 HP @ 3600)
GMC = 82 B

$12731. UP

207

FULL SIZE PICKUP

('83)

new GRILLE

PICKUPS FROM
$7551. ('83)
7918. ('84)

GMC
A truck you can live with.

5000-6000-
7000 SERIES
(6000 WITH
DUMP BODY IS
ILLUSTR.)
('83)

'83 PICKUP V.I.N.= 1G (C or T)-014F-D-#
    1984 "   "   "   " "E""

VANDURA CARGO VANS
FROM $7738. ('83); $8114. ('84)

83-84

S-15 SIMILAR TO 1982 TYPE, PRICED
FROM $6750. ('83); $6815. ('84)

('84)

RALLY VAN (A.K.A. RALLY WAGON) 110" OR 125" WB
250 CID 6 (120 HP) OR 305, 350 CID V8s
379 CID DIESEL V8   160, 165 HP)
(130 OR 135 HP)

('84)

**VANDURA SEATS 16 STUDENTS
OR 12 ADULTS**

TRANSIT BUS

**VANDURA SPECIAL
SEATS UP TO 20 STUDENTS**   ('84)

GMC A truck you can work with.

**P-3500 FC CHASSIS
SEATS UP TO 30**

('84)

DETR.
DIESEL.
6V-
92TA,
OTHERS
AVAIL. IN

LOWER
BUS~
VAN
ON
STEP~
VAN
CHASSIS
→

BRIGADIER   ('84)
SHORT CONVENTIONAL

(1984 STEP-VANS
$13537. UP)

GMC=83~84

208

GMC PICKUPS
FULL-SIZE MODELS

(ABOVE)
CAB/CHASSIS
WITH
VAN,
UTILITY,
OR WRECKER
BODY

1985 MODELS ILLUSTRATED, UNLESS OTHERWISE INDICATED.

(SAFARI MINIVANS INTRO. 1985)

85

FROM $8297. ('85)
($9807., WEST COAST)

-86

INSTRUMENT PANEL OF SIERRA CLASSIC WITH BRUSHED PEWTER-TONE CLUSTER FACE

C SER.

LT. DUTY HAS new GRILLE and new HEADLIGHT SETTING.

('86)

$10444.

$6456.

FOR ENGINE CHOICES, SEE CHEVROLET 1985 LT. DUTY.

The compact S-15 Pickup takes its place next to the full-size pickup as a truck just right for the job.

Sierra Classic instrument panel with brushed, pewter-tone instrument cluster face

(MEDIUM-DUTY MODELS SIMILAR TO CHEVROLET'S)

ALUMINUM CABS IN ASTRO and GENERAL HVY.-DUTY.

CUMMINS DIESEL ENGS. AVAIL. IN HEAVY-DUTY TYPES BELOW.

STD. BLACK INSTR. PANEL

C-3500 CREW CAB w. DUAL RR. WHEELS

C.O.E. ASTRO

STEEL-CAB SHORT CONVENTIONAL BRIGADIER

CONV. GENERAL

SIERRA CAB/CH. W. DUMP BODY (DUAL REAR WHEELS)

CUSTOMER PROVEN GMC

209

GMC

(ASTRO-BASED) CARGO MINIVAN (SAFARI) 111" WB (4 CYL. or V6)

V6 or V8 VANDURA 110" 125" or 146" WB

PASSENGER MINIVAN SAFARI $12043. ('87) 111" WB

FROM $10900.

$13084. UP

$12861. ('88) $13746. ('89)

S-15 $8049. UP

FINAL SET OF V.I.N. #s PRECEDED BY H ('87) J ('88) K ('89) L ('90), AND SO ON

$8049. UP ↗

RALLY $15393. UP

87-89

1989 EXAMPLES and PRICES, UNLESS OTHERWISE INDICATED.

JAN., 1988 = VOLVO WHITE and GMC HEAVY TRUCK OPERATIONS MERGE, CREATE VOLVO GM HEAVY TRUCK CORP. (LIGHTER GMC TRUCKS EXCLUDED)

OFFICIAL TRUCK AT THE 1988 Indianapolis 500 THE 72nd - MAY 29, 1988

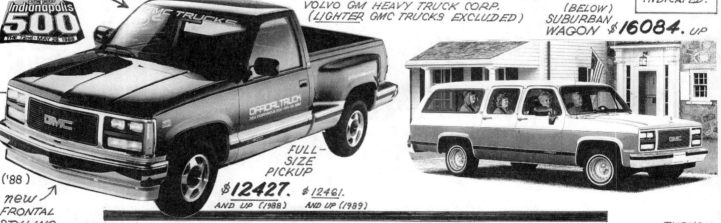

(BELOW) SUBURBAN WAGON $16084. UP

FULL-SIZE PICKUP $12427. AND UP (1988) $12461. AND UP (1989)

('88) new ↗ FRONTAL STYLING SINCE 1987

90

SLIGHT CHANGE IN HEADLIGHT DESIGN

THOUGH NOT CLEARLY SEEN IN EA. ILLUSTRATION, "GMC" APPEARS ON CENTER OF GRILLES.

RALLY

FULL SIZE PICKUP $13465. UP

$17056. UP

VOLVO-GM ALLIANCE ENDS (1995)

GMC = 87~90

210

MFD. BY
GRAHAM BROTHERS
(1919 ~ 1928)
EVANSVILLE, IN. and DETROIT, MI.

STARTING 1921, <u>DODGE BROS. CHASSIS</u>; SOLD BY DODGE DEALERS

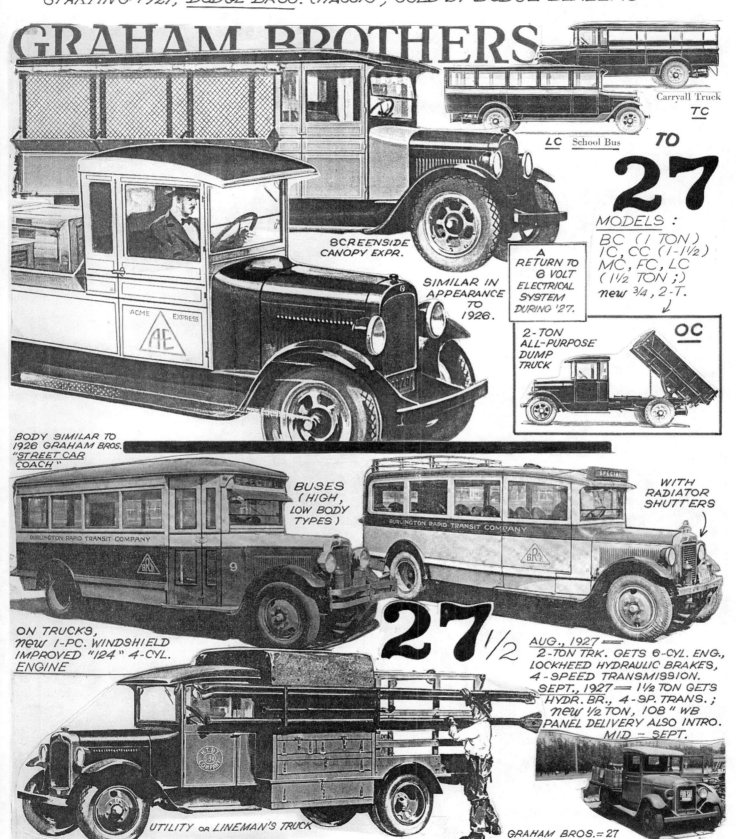

GRAHAM BROTHERS

Carryall Truck
TC

LC School Bus

TO

27

MODELS:
BC (1 TON)
IC, CC (1-1½)
MC, FC, LC (1½ TON;)
new ¾, 2-T.

SCREENSIDE CANOPY EXPR.

SIMILAR IN APPEARANCE TO 1926.

A RETURN TO 6 VOLT ELECTRICAL SYSTEM DURING '27.

2-TON ALL-PURPOSE DUMP TRUCK

OC

ACME EXPRESS AE

BODY SIMILAR TO 1926 GRAHAM BROS. "STREET CAR COACH"

BUSES (HIGH, LOW BODY TYPES)

WITH RADIATOR SHUTTERS

BURLINGTON RAPID TRANSIT COMPANY

BURLINGTON RAPID TRANSIT COMPANY

SPECIAL

27½

ON TRUCKS, new 1-PC. WINDSHIELD IMPROVED "124" 4-CYL. ENGINE

AUG., 1927 =
2-TON TRK. GETS 6-CYL. ENG., LOCKHEED HYDRAULIC BRAKES, 4-SPEED TRANSMISSION.
SEPT., 1927 = 1½ TON GETS HYDR. BR., 4-SP. TRANS.; new ½ TON, 108" WB PANEL DELIVERY ALSO INTRO. MID - SEPT.

UTILITY or LINEMAN'S TRUCK

GRAHAM BROS. = 27

GRAHAM BROTHERS

ASSEMBLY LINE

28

108" WB and up

MODELS: (EARLY '28)
SD (1/2 TON;)
DD, DDX (3/4 TON;)
BD, ID, IDX (1 TON;)
MD, MDX, LD, LDX (1 1/2 TON;)
OD, ODR, ODX, TD, TDR, TDX,
ED, EDR, EDX (2 TON)

CHRYSLER CORP. PURCHASES DODGE BROS., SPRING, 1928.

2-TON MODELS have 6-CYL. DODGE 3 1/4 × 4 1/2 ENGINES.

$4060.

ALL MODELS 6 CYL., AS OF SUMMER, 1928

SOME AVAIL. WITH ATTACHED SET OF HORIZONTAL SHUTTERS (ON THIS STYLE OF RADIATOR)

5101-M

21-PASSENGER BUS (STREET CAR COACH) 162" WB 6 CYLS. (1926-1927 SIMILAR, BUT WITH 158" WB and 4-CYL. ENG.)

DODGE BROS. HAD OWNED A LG. SHARE OF GRAHAM BROS., AND IN 1927 BOUGHT THE REMAINDER. THE 3 GRAHAM BROS. (JOS., ROBT. and RAY) THEN BOUGHT PAIGE, and IN 1928 INTRODUCED GRAHAM-PAIGE CARS.

FACTORIES AT DETROIT; EVANSVILLE, IND.; STOCKTON, CALIF.

R.W. ADAMS

MODELS BUILT LATE '28 CONSIDERED "1929."

STARTING JAN., 1929, ALL DODGE BROS. TRUCKS SOLD WITH DODGE BROS. OR FARGO NAME.

PANEL

1929 FARGO "CLIPPER" 9-PASS. METAL BODY WAGON (w. DOUBLE REAR DOORS) (FARGO PANEL DLVRY. SHOWN IN "MISC." SECTION)

FARGO

$1075.

SEE ALSO: DODGE

GRAHAM BROS. = 28

212

GREYHOUND Lines

WORLD'S · GREATEST MOTOR · COACH · SYSTEM

1918 PREDECESSOR TO GREYHOUND BUS LINES (MESABI'S FLEET)

IN ADDITION TO GREYHOUND PAGES, SEE ALSO: GMC, MCI.

EARLY PICKWICK SPLIT-LEVEL COACH

PICKWICK STAGES

('28)

"OBSERVATION PLATFORM" LOOK OF REAR END SHOWS A STRONG RAILROAD INFLUENCE.

TO 32

1931 ROUTES IN USA

('29)

PICKWICK'S SPECIAL NITE COACHES INTRO. FALL, '28. GREYHOUND ABSORBED PICKWICK IN 1930.

MOST '27-'30 MODELS BLT. BY WILL MOTORS CORP., MINNEAPOLIS, MINN.

PICKWICK NITE COACH

53-PASS. DOUBLE DECK WITH REST ROOM FAC., FOOD AVAIL. ON BUS

THESE ODD BUSES IN REGULAR SERVICE UNTIL 1933.

SERVICE IN 1931:

These Greyhound Lines Serve the Nation

CENTRAL · GREYHOUND
E. 11 St. & Walnut Ave., Cleveland, Ohio
PENNSYLVANIA · GREYHOUND
Broad St. Station, Philadelphia, Pa.
ATLANTIC · GREYHOUND
601 Virginia St., Charleston, W. Va.
EASTERN · GREYHOUND
Nelson Tower, New York City
CAPITOL · GREYHOUND
405 American Bldg., Cincinnati, Ohio
RICHMOND · GREYHOUND
412 E. Broad St., Richmond, Va.

PACIFIC · GREYHOUND
9 Main St., San Francisco, Calif.
PICKWICK · GREYHOUND
917 McGee St., Kansas City, Mo.
NORTHLAND · GREYHOUND
509 6th Ave., N., Minneapolis, Minn.
SOUTHLAND · GREYHOUND
Pecan & Navarro Sts., San Antonio, Tex.
SOUTHEASTERN · GREYHOUND
101 N. Broadway, Lexington, Ky.
PROVINCIAL · TRANSPORT
1227 Phillips Square, Montreal, Que.

FINAL WILL BUSES DELIV. TO GREYHOUND JANUARY, 1931. THEN GMC'S YELLOW DIV. TAKES NEW BUS ORDERS.

SOME PICKWICK NITE COACHES WITH AERODYNAMIC SHROUD OVER RADIATOR, AND ADDITIONAL PORTHOLES ALONG THE SIDE.

PICKWICK NITE COACH

('31)

GREYHOUND LINES

NEW YORK — PHILADELPHIA — CHICAGO — KANSAS CITY — DENVER — LOS ANGELES

THE ABOVE TYPE IS THE FIRST MOST-COMMONLY-SEEN GREYHOUND BUS SINCE THE COMPANY BEGAN.

(ABOVE) YEARS AHEAD OF THEIR TIME IN PASSENGER CONVENIENCES, THESE PICKWICK DOUBLE-DECK OVERNIGHT BUSES WERE UGLY IN APPEARANCE AND VIRTUALLY EXTINCT. GREYHOUND = TO 32

GREYHOUND

BUSES BLT. BY GMC/YELLOW and OTHER MANUFACTURERS FOR GREYHOUND (BUS) LINES

GOOD SCENES OF THESE BUSES IN THE 1934 COLUMBIA FILM, "IT HAPPENED ONE NIGHT" (AVAILABLE ON VIDEO!)

INTERIOR

33-34

('33)
6 CYLS.
707 CID
250" WB

GMC/YELLOW "Z-250"

DECORATIVE "OBSERVATION PLATFORM" RAILING CONT'D. TO 1934.

Gas ENG.

GREYHOUND'S FINAL OLD-FASHIONED CONVENTIONAL TYPE WITH ENGINE and HOOD IN FRONT

GMC/YELLOW "843"

34-36

NEW "STREAMLINED"

('34)

New

719 REAR
('36) VARIATIONS

743 ('37)

THIS EARLY TYPE has VERTICAL VENT SLOTS ('36) ON EITHER SIDE OF DESTINATION SIGN.

GMC/YELLOW "719" (LATER MODEL IS "743" note HORIZONTAL VENT SLOTS ON LATER TYPE)

36-40

"719" has 3-PC. REAR WINDOW, and "743" has 2-PC. REAR WINDOW.

GREYHOUND!

325 = 1936 "719s" BLT.
1250 = 1937-39 "743s" BLT.

87 DIESEL BUSES SOLD TO GREYHOUND, 1939.

GREYHOUND = 33~40

GREYHOUND

PDG-3701 ('33')
('40)

EARLY COMPANY PHOTO (ABOVE)

FRONT TOP DETAILS ('44)

New

DIESEL

New Super-Coach!

Enjoy perfected air-conditioning as you travel *"This Amazing America"* by GREYHOUND

THESE "SILVERSIDES" **SUPER-COACHES** PRODUCED BY GMC 1940-1953 WITH A FEW MINOR CHANGES DURING THOSE YEARS.

('40)

UNTIL 1942, BUILT BY YELLOW COACH DIV. OF GENERAL MOTORS CORP. (SUBSEQUENTLY, GMC TRUCK and COACH)

EARLY MODELS OF 3701 SERIES DO NOT HAVE OPENING SIDE WINDOWS. REPLACED BY 35' MODEL 3751/4151.

("YELLOW" NAME ON BUSES MFD. BEFORE 1943; GMC ON POST-'43 BUSES)

40 -46

DIESEL BUSES SOLD TO GREYHOUND (LISTED AT BOTTOM OF PAGE)

(NO NEW BUSES FOR GREYHOUND IN 1943-44, BECAUSE of MILITARY PRIORITIES.)

GMC

('46)

FULL-LENGTH DRIVER'S-SIDE VIEW

1946 INTERIOR, W/O VENT and HEATER DUCT PERFORATIONS.

DIESEL BUSES SOLD TO GREYHOUND:	1940 = 367	1945 = 440
	1941 = 288	1946-
	1942 = 348	1947 = 1518

THESE "SILVERSIDES" MODELS WON THE MOST PUBLIC FAVOR of ANY GREYHOUND BUS!

GREYHOUND = 40~46

215

GREYHOUND

45-PASS. SUBURBAN TYPE

('47)

new TYPE FRONT BUMPERS

47 -49

37-PASS. INTERCITY TYPE (WINDSHIELD RECESSED)

33-PASS. DOES NOT HAVE THIS EXTRA CENTER WINDOW

1
2
3
4

1 - PACKAGE RACK
2 - VENT AND HEATER DUCT PERFORATIONS
3 - SOLEX WINDOWS (NON-GLARE SAFETY GLASS)
4 - HEADREST COVERS

9 - HVY. LUGGAGE COMPT. OPENS FROM SIDE

5 - ARMRESTS EACH SIDE
6 - LEVER FOR ADJUSTING RECLINING SEAT
(note CHANGE IN STYLE OF SEAT ARMS SINCE 1946 VIEW ON PRECEDING PAGE.)

These Greyhound features add up to the smoothest most relaxed ride on American Highways

1949 INTERIOR

FOOT REST

8

5

6

('49)

('49)

7

FABRIC-COVERED FOAM RUBBER

GREYHOUND

('49)

49 -51

('50) **GMC**
PDG - 4151 (35')
has
SHORTER SIDE WINDOW
JUST BEYOND DRIVER'S
SECTION.
(1949 ON, OTHER TYPES OF
LARGE INTERCITY BUSES ALSO
AVAIL.
FROM GMC)

DRIVER'S COMPARTMENT ('51)

('51)

DETAILS OF INTERIOR (1951)

GREYHOUND=49~51

GREYHOUND

GMC 4104 TYPE
(INTRO. DURING '53) WITH AIR SUSP.

54
TO
EARLY
60s

NEW
the *Scenicruiser*®

INTRODUCED 1954

←(FIRST *new* "SPLIT-LEVEL" BUS IN 20 YRS.!)

GMC
"PD-4501"
SCENICRUISER

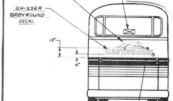

GH-165-5" WHITE NUMBERS
GH-234R DOG 36"
GH-226R GREYHOUND DECAL
12"
4"

GMC TRUCK & COACH DIVISION

IN THIS PHOTO, ON-BOARD REST ROOM is AT THE FOOT OF STAIRWAY, TO THE RIGHT. (PD-4501)

4104 INTERIOR "HIGHWAY TRAVELER"

GREYHOUND = 54~EARLY '60s

218

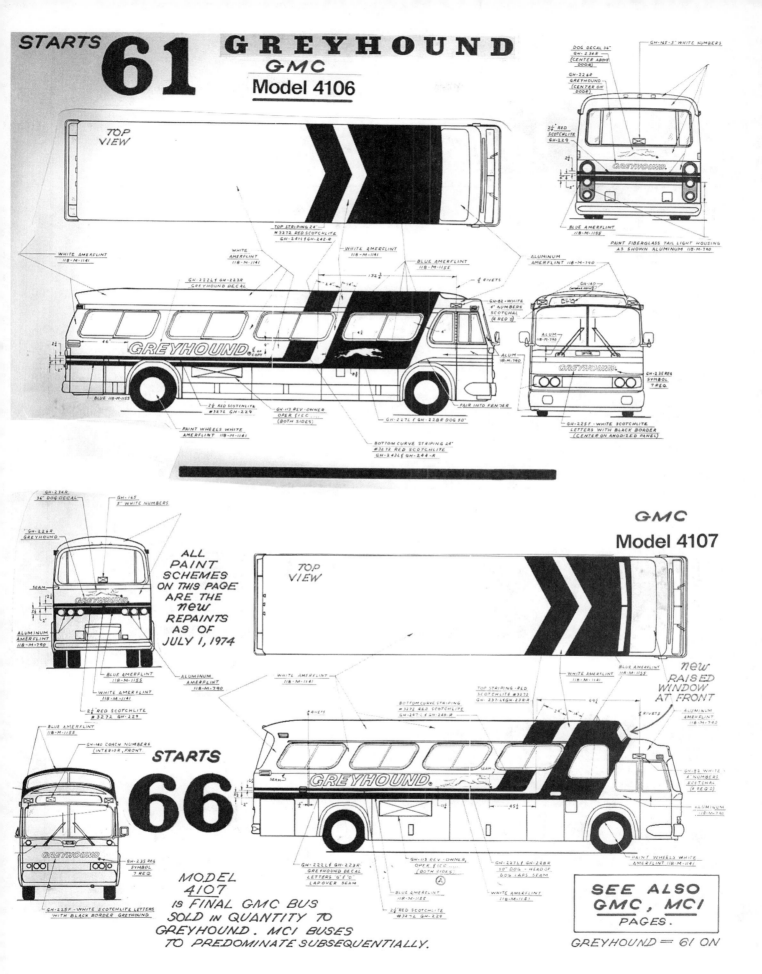

STARTS **61** **GREYHOUND**

GMC
Model 4106

TOP VIEW

ALL PAINT SCHEMES ON THIS PAGE ARE THE *new* REPAINTS AS OF JULY 1, 1974

GMC
Model 4107

new RAISED WINDOW AT FRONT

STARTS **66**

MODEL 4107 IS FINAL GMC BUS SOLD IN QUANTITY TO GREYHOUND. MCI BUSES TO PREDOMINATE SUBSEQUENTIALLY.

SEE ALSO GMC, MCI PAGES.

GREYHOUND = 61 ON

HUDSON *Six*

(TRUCKS = 1938 – 1947)

MFD. BY HUDSON MOTOR CAR CO., DETROIT

6 CYL. 88 OR 100 HP ('36)

115" WB $560.

TERRAPLANE 6

PICKUP (3/4 TON)

new HYDRAULIC BRAKES IN 1936, WITH MECHANICAL SAFETY RESERVE SYSTEM

90 PANEL DELIVERY

$808.

HUDSON 6

SERIAL # 90-101 UP (90 SER.)
OR 98-101 UP (98 SERIES)

39

HUDSON CARS BUILT FROM 1909 TO 1957. TERRAPLANE TRUCKS REPLACED BY HUDSON TRUCKS AFTER 1938.

1/2 -TON MODEL "90" (86 HP) 112" W.B. (REPLACES 1938 "112" SERIES)

note DIFF. BETWEEN "90" and "98" GRILLE

CAB PICKUP

$651.

98 CLOSE-UP FRONT DETAILS

3/4 -TON "BIG BOY" MODEL "98" 119" W.B. (96 HP)

$695.

---

new 113" W.B. ON 1/2 -TON MODEL "40"

SERIAL # 40-101 UP

40

1940 PRICES

"40" PICKUP	$671.
"40" PANEL	828.
"48" PICKUP	715.
"48" PANEL	884.

new 125" W.B. ON 3/4 -TON "BIG BOY" MODEL "48."

new BROAD, LOW GRILLE
new SEALED BEAM HEADLIGHTS

TYPICAL OF MANY "AS IS" UNRESTORED TRUCKS THAT HAVE BEEN FOUND.

HUDSON-to 40

HUDSON *Six*

(new SEDAN CARRYALL PRICED AT $1022.)

Van

C.O.E.
MODEL "10"
"ALL-PURPOSE DELIVERY"
116" W.B.
92 HP (98 HP OPTIONAL)
"VACUMOTIVE" DRIVE
PLYWOOD FLOOR (5-PLY)
STARTS 9-40

BODIES 3" LONGER

(new HEAVY-ARMORED X-TYPE *frame)*

REAR DETAILS

41

PICKUP
3/4 TON MODEL **18**
PICKUP *and*
SEDAN CARRYALL *have*
98 HP *and* 128" WB

SER. # FROM C-10101 *or* C-18101

1/2 TON MODEL **10**
PICKUP *has*
116" WB, 92 HP
FROM $782.

---

6 CYL.
175 CID
92 HP @ 4000 RPM

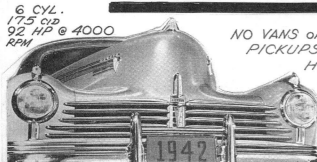

1942

NO VANS *or* PANEL TRUCKS *in* HUDSON LINE.
PICKUPS ONLY (THROUGH 1947, FINAL YR. FOR
HUDSON TRUCKS) (SERIAL # T-20101 UP)

42-45

new GRILLE

1/2 -TON "C-20"
has 116" W.B.
$828.

3/4 -TON "C-28"
has 128" W.B.
$872.

HUDSON's
TRUCK STYLING
SIMILAR TO HUDSON
CARS!

REAR DETAILS

46

MODEL "58"

102 H.P.

new GRILLE CONCAVE NEAR CENTER

3/4-TON ONLY AFTER END OF 1945.

$1244.

128" WB (THROUGH '47)

$1338.

47

MODEL 178

STYLING SIMILAR
TO 1946, BUT
'47 *has* new
HEAVIER CHROME
FRAME AROUND
MEDALLION
ABOVE GRILLE.

pickup

(SCENE OUTSIDE FACTORY)

(HUDSON CARS TOTALLY
REDESIGNED FOR 1948 BUT TRUCK DISCONTINUED.)
HUDSON 41~47

THE HUG CO., HIGHLAND, IL.

HUG

(1922 ~ 1942)

C.J. HUG, FOUNDER

28

(APRIL, 1927)

MODELS : 20 (1½ T;) 60, 25, C60 (2T;) 84, C84 (2½ T;) 40, 86 (3T;) 90, C90 (3½ TON)

("20" NOT LISTED AFTER 1928.)

1929 MODELS : 22 (1½ T;) 26, 60, 66 (2T;) 81, 84 (2½ T;) 40, 86 486 (3T;) 90 (3½ TON) (ALL 6 CYL. EXC. 60, 81, 84.)

SPEED TRUCK

with new COUPE CAB BY
THE GENERAL WOODWORK CORPORATION
Cincinnati, Ohio

37 TO 126 HP IN 1931.

Model "42"
6 CYL. 298.2 CID
86 HP

3 Ton Commercial Express
143" TO 201." WB

← "XPRES 6" MODELS

BUDA ENGINE IN
Model "43"
6 CYL. 428.4 CID
107 HP
6.8 TO 1 G.R.

29-32

32 MODELS : ('32)
22, 23, 60 (2T;) 61, 85, 85D (2½-3T;) 41, 42,

67, 85-6, 85D6 (3T;) C87, 87M (3½ T;) 43 (3½-4T;) C97, 97 (5 TON;) 6-WH.: 97-6 (5T;) 98-6 (7½ T;) 99 (10 TON)

33

MODELS : 23, 63 (2T;) 41S, 42, 42K, 70 (3 TON;) 43, 87K (3½ T;)

43L, 87Q (5T;) 99 (10 TON, 6-WHEELER)

HYDRAULIC BRAKES

146" TO 201" WB

3½ Ton Commercial

34

new 97-L (5 TON) IN 1934.

new MODELS IN 1935 ('35-'36 MODELS)

35 ON

12D (1½ TON, ADDED 1936.)
15A, D, T (1¾-2½ T;) 19A, D, T (2½-5T;) 23S, A, T (2½-5T;) 41S (3T;) 42A, T (3-6T;) 43A, T (4-8T;) 70 (3T;) 87K (3½ T;) 87Q; 43L (5T;) 97L (7½ TON) 6-WHEELERS : 97 LD (7½ T;) 99 (10 TON) new 4WD MODELS ('36): 43-4; 87K4; 87Q4

('36)

ROADBUILDERS

Model 87K Hug Roadbuilder with 5-yard Hug scoop type body, designed for dirt moving and 3-batch houling.

Model 87Q Hug Roadbuilder equipped with 6-yard Hug scoop type body and especially designed for dirt and rock moving.

Model 97L Hug Roadbuilder with 8-yard Hug rock type body, for dirt and quarry operations.

BUDA 6-CYL. ENGINES CONT'D. IN MODELS 23S and up.

NO CAB ENCLOSURE ON ABOVE 87Q MODEL

REAR-ENGINE BUS CHASSIS INTRO. 1938

new WAUKESHA 6-CYL. ENGINES IN MODELS UP TO 19T (1935 ON.)

HUG 28 ~ 35 ON

HUG

**THE HUG CO.
HIGHLAND, ILLINOIS
1922 ~ 1942**

new WAUKESHA 6-CYL. ENGINES IN MODELS UP TO 19T (1935 ON)

35-37

6 ~ CYL. BUDA ENGINES CONTINUED IN MODELS 23 S and up

new DIESELS AVAIL.

87-Q

5 TON

4 CYL., 831 CID CATERPILLAR DIESEL ENGINE (77 HP @ 850 RPM) IN 6-WH. "954 FR" 18-TON.

HUGE 6 CYL., 1246 CID DIESEL CATERPILLAR ENG. (125 HP @ 850) IN 20-TON 4WD "100."

"QUARRY SPECIAL" 10-TON "99"

99-S

(1937 EXAMPLES SHOWN AND LISTED)

MODELS :
12D (1½T;) 16A; 15D, T (1¾-2½T;) 19A, D, T; 23S, A, T (2½-5T;) 41S (3T;) 42A, T (3-6T;) 43A, T (4-8T;) 70K (3T;) 87K (3½T;) 43L, 87Q (5T;)
    6-WHEELERS : 97L, LD (7½T;) 99 (10 TON)
4-W-D : 43-4; 87K4; 87Q4   (2 DIESELS : SEE TOP OF PAGE)

REAR

('37)

98-MB

(WAUKESHA ENG.)

"HUG LUGGER" C.O.E. 10-TON MODEL 16 WITH 468 CID CAT. DIESEL ENG.

('38)

('39)

38

MORE DIESELS ADDED '38: (BUDA, CUMMINS, and CATERPILLAR - POWERED DIESELS : D42; D43 (L); (T) HC; D70K; D8, 8; 16; D98, D998 (6 WH.)

COMMERCIAL SERIES 42-T (3-6 TON)

1939 : BUDA GAS ENGINES REPLACED BY WAUKESHA. CATERPILLAR DIESELS CONTINUE

39

MODEL 42-T (SINCE '35)

1940 CHASSIS PRICES : $1875. – $8900.

40-42

FINAL HUG STYLE → (SEE ALSO REO.)

REO BODY USED ('42)

IN '41, MODELS REDUCED TO 85W ('42;) 87W; 92U; D92U; 98; D98 ('41 6-WH. : 99; D99; 995; D995

51-6, CB7P NEW FOR '42

"COMMERCIAL BUILDER DESIGN" CB7P

HUG 35~37

(SINCE 1907) INTERNATIONAL

MFD. BY INTERNATIONAL HARVESTER CO., CHICAGO, IL.

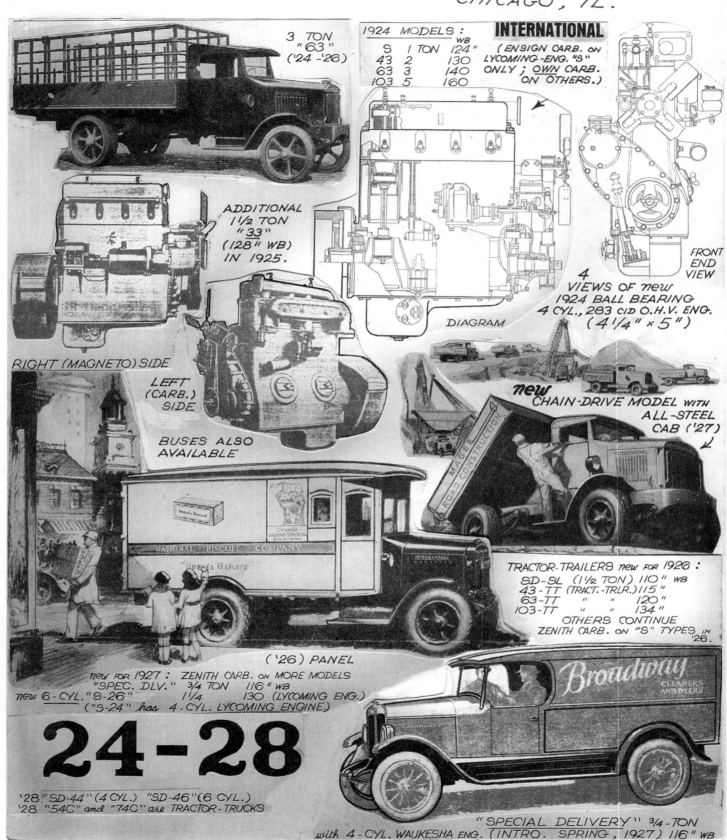

3 TON "63" ('24-'26)

1924 MODELS:

		WB	
S	1 TON	124"	INTERNATIONAL
43	2	130	(ENSIGN CARB. ON LYCOMING-ENG. "S" ONLY; OWN CARB. ON OTHERS.)
63	3	140	
103	5	160	

ADDITIONAL 1½ TON "33" (128" WB) IN 1925.

DIAGRAM

FRONT END VIEW

4 VIEWS OF new 1924 BALL BEARING 4 CYL., 283 CID O.H.V. ENG. (4¼" x 5")

RIGHT (MAGNETO) SIDE

LEFT (CARB.) SIDE

BUSES ALSO AVAILABLE

new CHAIN-DRIVE MODEL with ALL-STEEL CAB ('27)

NATIONAL BISCUIT COMPANY "Uneeda Bakers"

('26) PANEL

TRACTOR-TRAILERS new for 1926:
SD-SL (1½ TON) 110" WB
43-TT (TRACT.-TRLR.) 115"
63-TT " " 120"
103-TT " " 134"
OTHERS CONTINUE ZENITH CARB. ON "S" TYPES IN '26.

new for 1927: ZENITH CARB. on MORE MODELS "SPEC. DLV." ¾ TON 116" WB
new 6-CYL. "S-26" 1¼ 130 (LYCOMING ENG.)
("S-24" has 4-CYL. LYCOMING ENGINE.)

24-28

'28 "SD-44" (4 CYL.) "SD-46" (6 CYL.)
'28 "54C" and "74C" are TRACTOR-TRUCKS

Broadway CLEANERS AND DYERS

"SPECIAL DELIVERY" ¾-TON with 4-CYL. WAUKESHA ENG. (INTRO. SPRING, 1927) 116" WB

INTERNATIONAL

6-Cylinder TYPES

have "6" IN MODEL NUMBER (AS IN "SF-36," etc.)

1929 PRODUCTION = 50,000

1929 MODELS: SD (¾-TON;) 6 Sp. (1-TON;) S-24, S-26 (1¼-TON;) SL-34, SF-34, SF-36, SL-36 (1½-TON;) SD-44, SD-46, SF-46 (2-TON;) HS-54, HS-54C, 54, 54C (2½-TON;) 74, 74C, HS-74, HS-74C (3½-TON;) 104-C, HS-104-C (5-TON)

"HS" PREFIX MEANS HALL-SCOTT 4-CYL. ENGINE.

INTERNATIONAL SIX-SPEED SPECIAL

The 2-Speed Axle

ZENITH CARB. ON ALL MODELS

29 BUS

BRINK'S ARMORED TRUCK

BRINK'S EXPRESS CO. OWNED MORE THAN 500 INTERNATIONAL TRUCKS (AS OF OCT., 1930.) INT'L. ARMORED TRUCKS HAVE BULLET-PROOF WINDSHIELD and 2-THICKNESS STEEL IN BODY.

HIGH STAKE VAN

2 HEAVY-DUTY MODELS ILLUSTRATED HERE

30 A

5-SPEED TRANSMISSIONS AND SPIRAL-BEVEL DRIVE (ON SOME MODELS)

DUMP TRUCK

1930 PRODUCTION = 29,000

(CONT'D. NEXT PAGE)

COMPANY-OWNED BRANCHES AT 176 POINTS (181 BY JUNE, 1930)

INTERNATIONAL = 29~30

new 3/4 -TON "SPECIAL DELIVERY" PANEL TRUCK (8-30)

THE AVENUE SHOP

30 × 5 TIRES
ON LIGHT TRUCKS

SPEC. DLV. and AW-1 have
4 CYL., 173 CID
WAUKESHA "XA" ENGINE
with 30 HP @ 2700 RPM,
AS DOES 1-TON
6-Sp. SPEC.

STEEL-
SPOKED
WHEELS

130" WB

B 30 (CONT'D.)

MOVING
VAN

INTERSTATE
TRANSPORTATION CO

SIMILAR
MODEL SERIES
TO 1929, IN EARLY '30,
with
WAUKESHA 4, LYCOMING 4 and 6,
and HALL-SCOTT 4-CYL. ENGINES.

3/4-TON "AW-1," 1½-TON "AL-3" and
"A-5" TRACTOR-TRUCK MODELS
INTRODUCED SUMMER, 1930.

1920s STYLING CONT'D.
ON HEAVY-DUTY OF
EARLY '30.

OWN INTERNATIONAL 279 CID 6-CYL. ENGINE IN
new "A-5" '30½
3-TON

156-210" WB
65 HP @ 2800 RPM
34 × 7 TIRES
5-SPEED TRANSMISSION

A-5

W-3

new 3½-TON "W-3"
has 160-235" WB,
HALL-SCOTT "152"
4-CYL., 390 CID
ENGINE (60 HP
@ 1800 RPM)
(SAME ENGINE IN
3½-TON "HS-74"
and "HS-74-C"

36 × 6

40 × 12 "W-3"

SOME ENGINES WITH
OVERHEAD VALVES
and REMOVABLE
CYLINDERS

DOUBLE-REDUCTION
HERRINGBONE DRIVE
IN "W" SERIES

INTERNATIONAL = 30-B

31

INTERNATIONAL

AMERICAN INSTITUTE LAUNDRY PS 51-7

VAN

1½-TON "6-SPEED SPECIAL" IMPROVED FROM '30 TYPE.

A-4

2-TON "A-4" has 145" WB, 32 × 6 TIRES, and OWN "FBB" 6-CYL., 3⅝" × 4½" ENGINE with 65 HP @ 2800 RPM.

S.S. PIERCE CO · IMPORTERS · GROCERS

OPEN-SIDED CANOPY EXPRESS (POPULARLY KNOWN AS "PEDDLER'S WAGON")

BALTIMORE & OHIO R.R.

3-TON
A-5

W-3

"W-3" RATING UPPED TO 5 TONS IN 1931.

INTERNATIONAL TRUCKS

SHOWN ABOVE = SPECIALIZED TYPE OF FLATBED BODY WITH PIPE DERRICKS

183 COMPANY-OWNED BRANCHES IN U.S.A. and CANADA

INTERNATIONAL = 31

INTERNATIONAL

A-3
LOWER EDGE OF
WINDSHIELD
ARCHED

INTRO. 7-31:
4-SPEED **A-2** MODEL
with
RECTANGULAR WINDSHIELD

new 1½-TON **A-3** (ABOVE)
has 6-CYL. 3¼" × 4½" LYCOMING
L-HEAD "9AH" ENGINE
(54 HP @ 2700 RPM)
5.50/6.00 × 20"
TIRES

136" OR
160" WB

(12-31)

32
A

A-2

(ABOVE)
1½-TON A-2, B-2 WITH 136" W.B.
4 CYL. WAUKESHA
"XAH" 3⅝" × 4½"
ENGINE (39 HP @ 2400 RPM)
5.50 × 20" (F)
6.00 × 20" (R)
TIRES

A-6
3-TON STAKE
(BELOW)

3-TON
"A-5" and "A-6" have OWN
6-CYL., 3⅝" × 4½"
"FBB" ENGINE (67 HP @
2600 RPM.)

← 34 × 7 TIRES

INTERNATIONAL TRUCKS

MODEL	TONS	W.B.	CYLS.	H.P.
A-1	¾	136"	4	(LIKE A-2, B-2)
A-2, B-2	1½	"	4	39 @ 2400 RPM
A-3, A-3½, AL-3	"	136" UP	6	
A-4	2	145"	6	67 @ 2600 RPM
W-1	2½	148"	4	59 @ 1800 RPM
A-5, A-6	3	156"	6	
W-2	3½	148"	4	59 @ 1800 RPM

ALSO, W-3 5 TON 160" WB 4 CYL. (69 HP @ 1800 RPM.)

6 CYL.
5-TON

6-Cylinder

NEW!

SHIP
The UNIVERSAL Way

Models **A-7** and **A-8**
New

(INTRO. 2-32)
DELCO-
REMY
IGN.

NEW!

A-7
has OWN
"FDB" 4½" × 5½"

ENGINE
(117 HP @
2200 RPM)

A-8 has
OWN "FEB" 5" × 5½"
ENGINE (136 HP @ 2100
RPM)

160" WB
(STROMBERG
CARB. ON A-8)

(CONT'D.
NEXT PAGE)

WITH
EARLY TYPE OF
SLEEPER CAB

INTERNATIONAL = 32

228

INTERNATIONAL

32 (CONT'D.)

INTERNATIONAL TRUCKS

TELEPHONE LINEMAN'S TRUCK
A-3 (1½-TON)

INTERESTING EXAMPLES OF SPECIALIZED BODY TYPES

"EAT ICE CREAM"

ICE CREAM MAKERS OF AMERICA

ICE CREAM FREEZER TRUCK

Illustration shows 3-ton Model A-5, 190-in. wheelbase chassis with mechanically refrigerated body.

A-5 (3-TON)

FLAT RADIATORS CONT'D.   113" TO 225" WBs

33

N.R.A. PARTICIPANT LATE IN 1933

NRA MEMBER WE DO OUR PART

no VISOR ON "D-1"

OTHER MODELS : M-2 (1-TON;)
A-2, B-2, A-3, A-3½, AL-3
(1½-TON;) B-4, A-4 (2-TON;)
A-5, A-6 (3-TON ;)
W-2 (3½-TON;) W-3 (5-TON;)
A-7 (5-7½-TON ;)
A-8 (7½-TON)

WILLYS-BUILT new ½-TON "D-1"
6 CYL., 70 HP OWN "D" ENGINE
(3⁵⁄₁₆" × 4⅛")

FROM **$360.**

Here It Is! PICKUP 113" WB

The New Half-Ton, 6-Cylinder International Model D-1 Truck.

INTERNATIONAL = 32~33

INTERNATIONAL TRUCKS

SINCE 1907

INTERNATIONAL HARVESTER COMPANY
(INCORPORATED)
606 So. Michigan Ave. Chicago, Illinois

INTERNATIONAL

6 CYL. 78½ HP

WIRE WHEELS ON 1934 PICKUP 5.25 x 18 TIRES

UNSKIRTED FENDERS ON HVY. MODELS

2-TON AND 3-TON TRUCKS

('34) (A-TYPE)

H.J. HEINZ CO.
RICE FLAKES
BAKED BEANS
BOTTLED VINEGARS
PURE FOOD 57 PRODUCTS
H.J. HEINZ CO. 57 VARIETIES

TRUCKS TO 7½ TONS IN 1934.

C-1

11½ TON C55 F

('36)

New STYLING ON MOST (LT.) '34 MODELS.

'33 MODEL DESIGNATIONS CONT'D. IN 1934, and 11½-TON, 6-CYL. "B-3" ADDED. 4.18 TO 8.5 G.R. 4 and 6 CYL., IN 1935. 42 TO 140 HP

PANEL 113" WB

34-36 (EARLY 1937 ALSO)

RESTYLED C SERIES

INTERNATIONAL

New ½-ton ('34)

1936 MODELS:
C-1, C-5 (½ T.); M-3 (1 T.)
C-20, C-30, CS-30 (1½ T.); C-35, CS-35
(1½-2 T.); C-40 (2-3 T.); C-50 (3-4 T.);
C-55 (3½-4½ T.);
C-60 (4-5 T.);
A-7 (5-7½ T.);
A-8 (7½ T.);

½ T. PICKUP $565. ('36)

PICKUP REAR DETAILS ('34)

all WITH OWN 6-CYL. ENGINES, EXC. 4 CYL. WAUKESHA IN C-5, M-3 and C-20.

'36 C-1 has OWN "HD" 213 CID 6 (79 HP @ 3400)

D SERIES 37-40 A

INTERNATIONAL

new "D" SERIES (INTRO. MARCH, 1937)
(COMPLETELY RESTYLED)

INTERNATIONAL STATION WAGONS
113" WB

('40)

PANEL

½-TON "D-2" PICKUP
113" OR 125" W.B.
(¾ TO 1-TON "D-15" has
130" W.B. and HORIZONTAL
RIBS ON BOX SIDES.)

INTERNATIONAL EMBLEM

D-2 $620. ('38)

(FINAL "C" MODELS IN 1938)

The ALL-STEEL CAB is a feature in every new International. The one-piece top, the sides, the back and cowl panels, are welded into the complete cab frame. Rubber mountings wherever cushioning is needed. This is the roomy, well-appointed de luxe cab.

1938 MODELS:
C-1; C-5, D-2, D-5, C-15,
D-15, C-20, C-30,
CS-30, D-30, DS-30,
C-35, CS-35, D-35,
DS-35, C-40,
CS-40, D-40,
C-50, D-50,
C-55, C-60,
D-60, DR-60,
DR-70, A-8.
(ALSO e.U.S. 1½ T.
D-300, DS-300.
(PLUS SEVERAL
6-WHEEL MODELS)

TRACTOR-TRAILER MOVING VAN

PANEL-STAKE

1½-TON "D-30"
D-30

WITH
128" WB   155" WB   173" WB
$858. $913. $968.
(1938 PRICES)

$788.

¾ TON
D-15
('39)

DUMP TRUCK

NOTE HORIZONTAL RIBBING ON "D-15" PICKUP BOX

$750. ('39)

ALL 1939-1940 MODELS have "D" PREFIX (EXCEPT A-8.)
D-5 ONLY 4-CYL. MODEL (132 CID WAU., 33 HP @ 2800 RPM.)
(OWN 6-CYL. ENGINES IN OTHERS.)

33 TO 140 HP IN 1940.

(CONT'D. NEXT PAGE)

INT'L. 37-40 A

Heavy-Duty* Internationals

*Heavy Duty means all-trucks rated at 2-ton and over.

(BELOW)

NABISCO. BOUGHT AN AVERAGE OF 200 INT'L. TRUCKS PER YEAR IN 1930s →

D~15 3/4-TON PANEL

NATIONAL BISCUIT COMPANY

('38)
$878.

('40)

↑ SOME HEAVY-DUTY MODELS HAVE CENTER PROTRUSION IN LARGE, PAINTED BUMPER (AS ABOVE.)

HIGHEST-PRICED INT'L. 6-WHEELER IS AR-626-F @ $12,500. ('40)

GOLDEN GATE INTERNATIONAL EXPOSITION HORTIC

37-B-40 (CONT'D.)

('39)

6 WHEELER TRACTOR-TRAILER

FUEL OIL

ROGERS OIL CO.

('39)

STREAMLINED TANKER

International Truck sizes range from Light Delivery units up to powerful Six-Wheelers. Diesel-powered models in 12,000 to 42,000-lb. carrying capacities.

WINDSHIELD OPENS →

('38)

JACK'S COOKIE CO. TAMPA ORLANDO MIAMI

N° 28

Jack's COOKIES

C.O.E.s ON NEXT PAGE

TRACTOR-TRAILER (WITH VAN TRAILER)

INTERNATIONAL

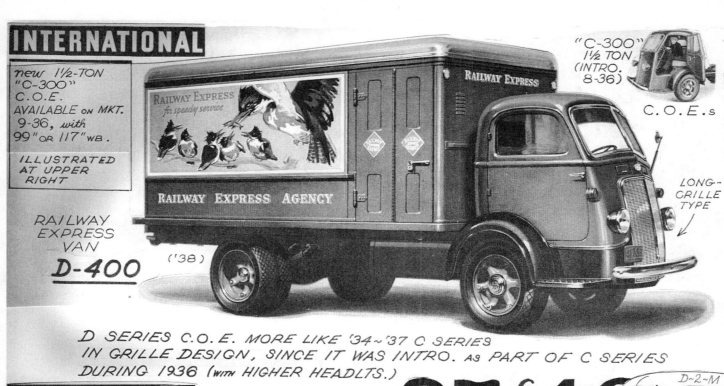

new 1½-TON "C-300" C.O.E. AVAILABLE on MKT. 9-36, with 99" OR 117" WB.

ILLUSTRATED AT UPPER RIGHT

RAILWAY EXPRESS VAN
D-400
('38)

"C-300" 1½ TON (INTRO. 8-36) C.O.E.s

LONG-GRILLE TYPE

D SERIES C.O.E. MORE LIKE '34~'37 C SERIES IN GRILLE DESIGN, SINCE IT WAS INTRO. AS PART OF C SERIES DURING 1936 (WITH HIGHER HEADLTS.)

CAB-OVER-ENGINE
VARIATIONS

"D-300"
('40)
13,200-lb. G.V.W.
$715. and up (CHAS.)

232 CID 6 CYL. 81 HP @ 3200 RPM

37ᶜ40
(CONT'D)
C.O.E.
HEAVY~DUTY
"D~500" (18,800 lb. G.V.W.)
"DR~700" (26,900 " ")

(G.V.W. = GROSS VEHICLE WT.) COMBINED WEIGHT OF TRUCK and LOAD

METRO VAN (LATE '40) 2/3 CID 6

INSIGNIA
INTERNATIONAL

new TYPE OF "D-400" ('40) GRILLE (NOTE = GRILLE DOES NOT EXTEND AS FAR DOWNWARD AS ON OTHERS ILLUSTRATED.)

1940 TYPE

16,200-lb. G.V.W.

New Model D-400

INT'L. 37-40 C

233

K-1-M OR K-3-M THRU '46
METRO VAN
102" WB
6.00 × 16 TIRES

"Green Diamond" 6-CYL. 82 HP ENG. IN '42 VAN (4.18 G.R. IN 1/2-TON) 4.875-6.5 G.R. IN 3/4-1-TON VAN

INTERNATIONAL HARVESTER COMPANY

THIS EMBLEM APPEARS ABOVE GRILLE

INTERNATIONAL

New **K** SERIES

RESTYLED

HVY. DUMP

WITH TANDEM AXLES

PANEL ('41)

4- CYL., 33 HP "D-5" CONT'D. INTO 1941. AT START OF '41, 51 MODELS and 166 WHEELBASES!

41-46

TRUCK–TRACTOR (3 TO 4 TON)

DIESEL MODELS AVAILABLE

('41)

HEAVY DUTY

"K" MODELS IN 1942: 82 TO 140 HP K-1 THROUGH K-8, K-10, KR-11; C.O.E.s IN K-5, K-7, K-8, KR-11 LINE. 160"-WB A-8 STILL AVAIL. (BUT NOT IN 1946.)

6-CYL. ENG. (SOME O.H.V. TYPES AVAIL.) 13 TYPES IN 1948, 214 TO 1090 CID

CAB ('41)

"RED DIAMOND" **ENGINE**

USED IN K~8, K9~8, KR~11, KS~11

('45)

82 TO 148 HP IN '46.

1946: K~1~M and K~3~M new

6 CYL.

C.O.E. WITH NEW 2-PC. SPLIT GRILLE

D-500 C.O.E.

TANKER

INT'L. 41~46

INTERNATIONAL

21 BASIC MODELS IN 1947

PICKUP

HEAVY-DUTY

KB-8-F

KB-8-F—for mixing and transporting concrete.

THIS EMBLEM *INTERNATIONAL* IDENTIFIES GREAT TRUCKS

BOTTLER'S TRUCK
KB-6

"KB-8"

K-8
(GAS)
('47)

↑ or DIESEL (WEST COAST '46 MODELS SIMILAR.

note THE BOXY CAB STYLE.)

6-WHEELERS ('47) INCLUDE:
KB-6F-4R; KB-8F-4R; KB-11F-4R;
W-4064-H (SAME ENGINE AS
W-3042-H)

"KBR-12"
TRUCK-
TRACTOR

"KBR-11"

LOG
TRUCK-
TRACTOR
"W-6564-OH"

new "KB" SERIES

47-49

"KB" PREFIX STARTS 1947

new GRILLE, OTHER CHANGES
82 TO 322 H.P. ENGS.
13 DIFFERENT ENGINES IN 1948,
FROM 214 TO 1090 C.I.D.
Cummins DIESEL ENG. AVAIL.,
'48 ON

LARGEST MODEL
IS "W-3042-H,"
with 749 CID Cont.
S-6749 6-CYL. ENG.
(254 HP @ 2600 RPM

STATION
WAGON

KB-1 IS
½ TON PICKUP
$1030. (113" WB)
1188. (125" WB)
('47-48 PRICES)
KB-2 = ¾ TON
KB-3 = 1 TON

('48)

INTERNATIONAL-METRO COACH—auxiliary bus for limited passenger transport.

METRO COACH
PASSENGER
BUS-VAN (RARE)
(above)

1½ TON
KB-5
(ILLUSTR.)

EMBLEM
SET IN TOP
OF GRILLE.

INTERNATIONAL

INTERNATIONAL

1/2-TON PICKUP PRICES FROM $1378. ('50)
$1438. ('51-52)

1/2-TON PANEL PRICES FROM $1360. ('50) $1478. ('51-52)

LT.-DUTY MODELS
L-110 1/2-TON, 115"-127" WB
L-112 3/4-T., 127" WB
L-120 HD 3/4-T., 127" WB
L-130 1-TON 134" WB

PANEL

New L Series.
50-52

TOTALLY RESTYLED, WITH new 1-PC. WINDSHIELD, 2-PC. REAR CAB WINDOW, new GRILLE (new 115" MINIMUM WB)

DETAILS OF CAB VENT SYSTEM

Now-International Roadliners offer 3 types of power

GASOLINE, DIESEL and LPG! ('52)

HVY. DUTY

L-185, 195 ROADLINER HEAVY DUTY HAS 157" W.B.

BOTTLER'S TRUCK

new 220 CID, 101-HP O.H.V. 6-CYL. ENGINE IN LIGHT TRUCKS (STARTING 1950.)

IN 1951, ONE MILLION USED INTERNATIONAL TRUCKS WERE STILL IN SERVICE (MORE THAN 1/2 OF INTERNATIONAL'S TOTAL OUTPUT SINCE 1907!

CAB

130" TO 172" WB ON 1 1/2-TON L-150 MODELS (STAKE) 1950 PRICES = $1919. TO 2045.

(ABOVE) WITH VAN BOX BODY ON CAB/CHASSIS

METRO VAN AVAIL. WITH 102" OR 115" WB

INTL. 50~52

new "IH" CORPORATE TRADEMARK ADDED TO GRILLE.

INTERNATIONAL HARVESTER

MILK TRUCK ('54)

AVENUE DAIRY

53-55
RESTYLED "R" SERIES

RAISED SIDE SECTIONS ARE OPTIONAL.

R-110
1/2-TON PICKUP $1607. ('55)

WHEELBASES FROM 115" TO 195"
1/2-TON R-100 LIGHT DUTY JOINS
1/2 TON R-110 "HVY.", 1955,
PRICED AT $1539.

"LCFD-405" HEAVY
"HIGHBINDER" HIGH CAB
SHORT-BBC STARTS 1954.

HYDRA-MATIC OPTION, 1955

MILITARY HAULER

DASH

"S-100" LT. DUTY FROM $1662.
"S-110" FROM $1735.

new "S" SERIES

56
(and EARLY 1957)

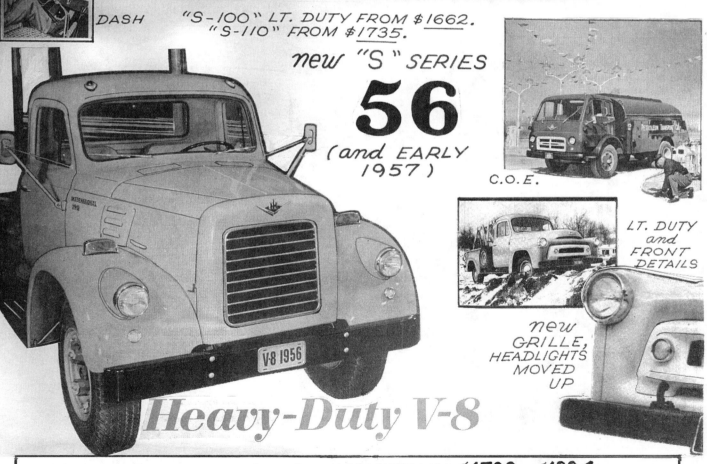

C.O.E.

LT. DUTY and FRONT DETAILS

INTERNATIONAL 190

V-8 1956

new GRILLE, HEADLIGHTS MOVED UP

Heavy-Duty V-8

3/4 TON "S-112" and "S-120" PICKUPS (127" WB) **$1789.; $1884.**
1 TON "S-130" PICKUP (134" WB) **$2007.**
1 1/2 TON "S-150" STAKE (130-172" WB)
2 TON STAKES AVAIL. with 187" OR 195" WB)

AUTOMATIC TRANS. AVAILABLE IN SOME MODELS

INTL. 53~56

INTERNATIONAL® A-LINE LIGHT-DUTY TRAVELETTE

REAR DETAILS

6-Passenger Capacity!
3-Door Cab!
2 Full Width Seats!

New

3/4 ~ 1 TON CAPACITY

A~120 $3254.

← 129" WB

EXTRA DOOR ON RIGHT SIDE

COMPACT CITY DLVRY.

48" SIGHTLINERS

C.O.E.

REFRIGERATOR TRUCK

IH

6-PASS. TRAVEL CREW CAB WITH UTILITY BODY

trucks

← note EXTRA WINDOWS BELOW DASH LEVEL.

SCHOOL BUS (CHASSIS MFR.)

('58)

DUMP

1 OR 1½ TON STAKE

Multi-Million-Mile diesels.

Golden Anniversary MODELS

Stake or platform-body models.

Powerful, dependable six-wheelers.

PANEL DLVRY. and TRAVELALL WAGON HAVE 2 DOORS ON PASSENGER'S SIDE, and JUST 1 DOOR ON DRIVER'S SIDE.

(57½)

57½-58

"A-100" LT. DUTY TOTALLY RESTYLED, $1905. UP

Conventional tractors for biggest jobs.

Extra-rugged off-highway models.

114" WB

A-100 $2364.

WITH 240 CID O.H.V. 6-CYL. ENGINE 114" WB (PICKUP STYLING SIMILAR TO TRAVELALL ABOVE.)

190 CONV. TRACTOR WITH TANKER

PRODUCTION: 81,213 ('58)

60110

238

ABOVE:
SIGHTLINER ACO V8
(THIS TYPE AVAIL. 1959 TO 1965.)

TANDEM-AXLE

HEAVY-DUTY V8 TRACTOR TRLR. (RT.)

MEDIUM-DUTY STAKE (CONVENTIONAL OR ALL-WHEEL DRIVE AVAIL.)

A pickup with a back seat! New Travelette takes 6 passengers, plus full-size pickup loads.

TRAVELETTE P.U. (6' BED)

OIL FIELD HVY. DUTY

6-CYL. ENGS. WITH 220, 240, 264, 282 OR 308 CID

TRAVELALL

$2659. UP

EVANS

SPECIAL TRIM OPT.

C.O.E. TRACTOR-TRAILER

B-110 ½ TON
(8½' BED, 126" WB)

$2094.

V8 ENGINE OPTIONS
266 CID (154.8 HP)
304 CID (193.1 HP)
345 CID (197.6 HP)

new **59** A
B SERIES
new GRILLE and new QUADRUPLE HEADLTS.

BLACK BACKGROUND AROUND FRONT EMBLEM (SEE ARROW)

B-100 ½-TON PICKUP (7' BED)

$2045. 114" WHEELBASE

1959½ PICKUP has 6 CYL. 141 HP ENG. (V8, AUTO TRANS. OPTIONAL)

1959 PRODUCTION = 143,231

(CONTINUED NEXT PAGE)

INT'L. 59-A

239

INTERNATIONAL

"TRAVELETTE"
B-120
6-PASS. PICKUP
129" WB
6' BED
~~129"~~
$3401.

BC-150
CAB-FORWARD
(C.O.E.) STAKE
has 149" WB
$2995.   V8
OPTIONAL

('59½)

59 B
(CONT'D.)

new
"METRO MITE"
VAN
MODEL
"80"
4-CYL.
(new
COMPACT
LIGHTWEIGHT
SERIES)
WT.= ONLY
2800 lbs.
STEEL BODY
with UNITIZED
CONSTRUCTION
13' OVERALL
LENGTH
66" INTERIOR
HEIGHT, and
66" WIDTH

96" WHEELBASE   **$2251.**

IT'S BIG!
(A BIG 200 CU. FT. OF LOADSPACE)

WILL IDLE
MORE THAN
7
HOURS
ON JUST
ONE
GALLON
OF
GAS!

6-CYL. METRO
PARCEL DLVRY.
VANS CONTINUE
102", 115", 123"
OR 134" WB
$3092. TO
$3842.

INT'L. 59-B

REAR
DETAILS

240

DUMP TRUCK

BC~150
1½-TON C.O.E.
STAKE TRUCK
$3091. UP
(149" WB

TANKER

METRO MITE "80"
4 CYL.

new ROUND PARK. LTS.

$2251.

C.O.E.
TRACTOR-
TRAILER

B~100 (7' BED)
PICKUPS FROM
$2151.
Pickup Truck

W/O REAR BUMPER

60

PRODUCTION:
119,696

WITH REAR
BUMPER

6 CYL.:		
220 CID,	112 HP
240 "	141 "
264 "	153 "

new OPTIONAL
154.8 HP
V8
AVAIL.

RESEMBLES
1959,
BUT
WITH
new SILVER
BACKGROUND
AROUND
FRONT
EMBLEM

TRAVELALL
$2845. UP

MILK DELIVERY TRUCK
RETAINS 1956 PICKUP
STYLING!

INT'L. 60

241

('61)

'61 MODELS START 11-1-60, have SUFFIX "—1" FOLLOWING SERIAL NUMBER. '62 STARTS 11-1-61, WITH SUFFIX "—2" FOLLOWING SERIAL NO.

new LOADSTAR CONV. ('62)

EVACUATION ROUTE

C.O.E. ('62)

C.O.E. ('62)

('61)

C-100 PICKUPS PRICED FROM
$2187. ('61)
2190. ('62)

PRODUCTION:
142,816 (1961)
147,283 (1962)

C-100 PANEL	$2502.
" TRAVELALL	2792. up
C-110 PICKUP	2248.
C-120 "	2403.
C-130 "	2486.

(1961)

PICKUP

AS OF NOV. 1, 1960, ALL 1961 INTERNATIONALS HAVE THE SUFFIX (—1) FOLLOWING SERIAL #.

61-62

new RESTYLED "C" MODELS

LT. DUTY MODEL PICKUPS and TRAVELALL WITH new WIDE CONCAVE ANODIZED ALUMINUM GRILLE and HEADLIGHT TRIM

39 DIFFERENT PICKUP MODELS, INCLUDING new C-130 ALL-WHEEL DRIVE

'62 SCOUT (INTRO. '61)
2-W-D FROM $1751.
(4-W-D OPTIONAL)

INTL. 61~62

242

SPECIAL PRESSURIZED GASES TANKER

HOPPER TRUCK

C.O.E. WITH LONG-DISTANCE MOVING-VAN BODY

MIXER

new type INTER-CITY FREIGHTER

HEAVY-DUTY DUMP

SLEEPER-CAB ('64) INTERIOR (LONG-CAB C.O.E.)

54" SHORT CAB C.O.E.

63 -64

6 or V8
4 DOOR TRAVELALL
$2705. ('64)
119" WB

new GRILLE on PICKUP and TRAVELALL

1963 SERIES STARTS NOV. 1, 1962 WITH SUFFIX "-3" FOLLOWING SERIAL #.

compact 6-ft. body...

C-900 ('63½)
(new) COMPACT PICKUP
WITH 4 CYL. 93.4 HP "COMANCHE" ENGINE (ALSO USED IN SCOUT)

900
107" WB

C-1000 PICKUP FROM $2093.

('64) PICKUP WITH CAMPER

LT. DUTY IN C-900, C-1000, C-1100 and C-1200 SER.

METRO VANS (4 CYL.)
CM 80 (96" WB)
$2400.
CM 110 (102" WB)
$2700.
(6 CYL. METRO VANS ALSO)

PRODUCTION:
168,296 ('63)
166,892 ('64)

MODEL 1100
4 × 4

INTL. 63~64

243

1/2 TON = C-900, C-1000, C-1100
3/4 TON = C-1200
1 TON = C-1300
1 1/2 TON = C-1500
2 TON = C-1600

INTERNATIONAL

2 TYPES SHOWN ↘
pickup

SPARE TIRE and WHEEL STORED UPRIGHT. ↙

C SERIES
65
NEW GRILLE WITH VERTICAL PCS. (LT. DUTY)

CONVENTIONAL

LT. and. MEDIUM CONVENTIONALS:
1/2 TON PU 7' 119"wB $2097.
" TRAVELALL " 2705.
" PANEL 7' " 2427.
" TRAVELALL (C-1100) 2731.
" PU 8 1/2' 131"wB 2155.
" TRAV. PU 6' 140" 2769.
3/4 T. PANEL 7' 119" 2550.
" TRAVELALL " 2854.
" PU 8 1/2' 131" 2278.
" TRAV. PU 6' 140" 2893.
1 TON PU 8 1/2' 131" 2362.
" STAKE 9' DUALS 134" 2593.
1 1/2 T " 12' 156"wB 3167.
2 TON STAKE WITH 12' BED 151"wB
$3678.

You don't have to share cab space with a gas tank. You keep all that room for people. We tuck the tank under the cab of INTERNATIONAL pickups. Which makes our pickups safer, too.

C.O.E.

ALSO C-900 1/2 T. COMPACT PICKUP (4 CYL., 107"wB) = $1952.

Pick your own power—93 to 193 hp—from our 4, 6 and V-8 engines. They're tough, responsive, economical. Naturally, they're built for trucks only.

New full-width flip-hood service accessibility eliminates need to work inside the truck

new International
METRO
multi-stop trucks
(VANS)
(RESTYLED)
7' TO 18'8" BODIES
FROM **$2372.**

INTL. 65

244

6 or V8

C.O.E.

FINAL 4-CYL. 900-A

$1980.

PROD. 170,385

(1966 MODELS START WITH 11~1~65 REGISTRATIONS)

1000 A

Pickup

66A SERIES

new GRILLE

ON LT. TRUCKS, CENTER STRIP RUNS ACROSS FULL WIDTH OF GRILLE.

½ TON	1000-A	PICKUP (7' BED)	$2138.	METRO VANS
"A"	" 1100-A	" (8' ")	2200.	M800, M1100
SERIES	1100-A	TRAVELETTE (6' ")	2810.	(4 CYL.)
	1200-A	(¾-TON MODELS)	2319. UP	6 CYL.:
	1300-A	(1-TON ")	2359. UP	M1200, M1500
				(V8 OPT.)

1967 PRODUCTION: 167,940

B SERIES

67-68

C SERIES

new CAMPERMOBILE PICKUP

LT. DUTY FROM $2126. ('67) 2440. ('68)

1967 I.D. # 1000-B UP

CO-LOADSTAR

TILT-CAB

('68)

V-8 diesel

TRAVELALL $2841. ('67) $3146. ('68)

1968 PROD.: 145,549

INTL. 66~68

245

NOTE THE ODD SIDE WINDOWS

INTERNATIONAL HARVESTER

('69) with 16-SPEED SPICER TRANSMISSION

new GRILLE (LIGHT DUTY)

LT. DUTY FROM $2623. ('69) $2795. ('70)

new D SERIES

69-70

IH

TRAVELALL

PRODUCTION:
160,255 ('69)
155,353 ('70)

('70)

TRANSTAR "400"
(CONVENTIONAL) SIDE and FRONT VIEWS

INTERNATIONAL

('70)
CONV. CAB

"8V-71" DETROIT DIESEL ENG. IN TRANSTAR

IH "DVT-573-B" DIESEL V-8 ENGINE with 230 HP. (260 or 285 HP AVAIL.) CUMMINS ENGINE AVAILABLE

C-O Transtar

SEVERAL VARIETIES OF CONVENTIONAL and C.O.E. HEAVY-DUTY MODELS, (VARIOUS CAPACITIES,) MOST WITH "STAR" SUFFIX IN MODEL NAME: FLEETSTAR, LOADSTAR, CARGOSTAR, UNISTAR, ETC.

SHORTEST WB ON 4-CYL METRO VAN NOW 108" (M1100) $3446. (6 CYL. and METROS ALSO.) INTL. 69~70

(LT. DUTY)
new TAIL-LIGHTS

MODELS 1010
and up

STD. PICKUPS
FROM
$2920.

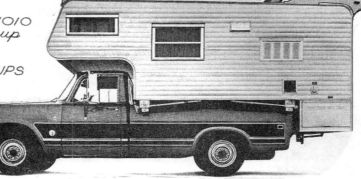

camper pickup

We haven't had a model year since 1907.
Not because we couldn't have done it along with everyone else.
But because we didn't believe in it. Whenever we found a way to change something for the better, we did it right away.
As the early leader of one of our biggest automotive manufacturers once stated, "...the primary function of an annual model introduction is to create a certain dissatisfaction with previous models."
Now, change for the sake of change might win you customers in the Fall. But it's hard to keep their confidence when you tell them they've made a $3,000 mistake ten months later.
So we've never had a model year. Until now.
Because of the need to include certain scheduled safety features, we had no reasonable alternative but to begin having model years.
So we have a 1971 INTERNATIONAL Pickup.
And because so many people look for certain changes in the forthcoming year's models, we've added a few.
A new grill. New hubcaps. A different tailgate treatment. New rocker panel trim. And several new colors.

71 A

LT. DUTY
RESTYLED

"INTERNATIONAL"
NAMEPLATE ON
DRIVER'S SIDE OF
MESH GRILLE.

LT. DUTY
ENGINES:
V-304
193.1 HP @ 4400 RPM
173 NET HP @ 3900

V-345
196.7 HP @ 4000
182.3 NET HP @ 3800

V-392
253 HP @ 4200
235.9 NET HP
@ 3600 RPM

FLEETSTAR
INTERIOR

The attractive, well equipped cab features easy-reading, individually illuminated and fully-calibrated instruments with air core magnetic voltmeter, fuel, water, temperature, oil and pressure gauges for the greatest accuracy and long-life reliability.

FLEETSTAR® D

(CONT'D.
NEXT PAGE)

4 CYL. METRO VAN (108" WB) $3790.
6 CYL. (119, 127 OR 134" WB) $4305. UP

INTL. 71~A

choice of IH quality-built gas or diesel engines. Up to 285 horsepower.

For maximum cargo-hauling capacity, you have a short 90 or 92-inch BBC. So you can pull 45-foot trailers in 55-foot states. GVW'S from 25,500 to 54,000; GCW'S from 50,000 to 65,000.

WITH MIXER BODY

new T-415 5-SPEED MANUAL and new 451 and T-454 AUTO. TRANS. AVAIL. MID-1971.

FLEETSTAR A 71 B
(CONT'D.)

Loadstar

4200	MAKE	MODEL	DESIGN	GROSS BHP @ RPM.
Std.	Detroit	8V-71NE V8	W/N—55 Inj.—Naturally Aspirated	260 hp @ 1950
Opt.	Detroit	8V-71N V8	W/N—60 Inj.—Naturally Aspirated	290 hp @ 2100
Opt.	Detroit	8V-71N V8	W/N—65 Inj.—Naturally Aspirated	318 hp @ 2100
Opt.	Cummins	V-903 V8	Naturally Aspirated	320 hp @ 2600
4300				
Std.	Cummins	NH-230	Naturally Aspirated	230 hp @ 2100
Opt.	Detroit	6-71N	W/N—65 Inj.—Naturally Aspirated	238 hp @ 2100
Opt.	Cummins	NHCT-CT	Turbo-charged Custom Torque	240 hp @ 2100
Opt.	Cummins	NHC-250	Naturally Aspirated	250 hp @ 2100
Opt.	Cummins	N-927	Naturally Aspirated	270 hp @ 2100
Opt.	Cummins	NHCT-270	Turbo-charged	270 hp @ 2100
Opt.	Cummins	NTC-335	Turbo-charged	335 hp @ 2100
Opt.	Cummins	NTC-350	Turbo-charged	350 hp @ 2100
Opt.	Cummins	NTA-370	Turbo-charged (Aftercooled)	370 hp @ 2100
Opt.	Detroit	12V-71NE V12	W/N—55 Inj.—Naturally Aspirated	390 hp @ 1950
Opt.	Detroit	12V-71N V12	W/N—60 Inj.—Naturally Aspirated	434 hp @ 2100

TRANSTAR SPECS.   **(C.O.Es ON NEXT PAGE)**
(HOOD TILTS FORWARD)

FLEETSTAR D

(INTRO. MID-SEASON)

Transtar 4200 and 4300 heavy

(71½)

Fleetstar D offers five big-bore diesels. Choose Cummins or Detroit Diesel 6's from 218 HP to 270 HP.

1½ TON STAKE   156" WB   MODEL 1510 = **$3807.**
2 TON   "   151" "   MODEL 1600 = **$4226.**

INTL. 71-B

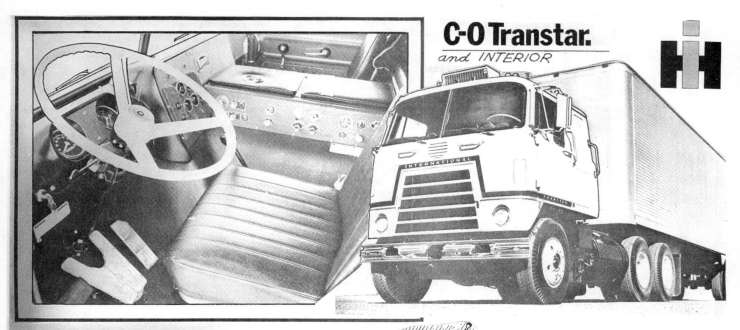

C-O Transtar.
and INTERIOR

V-304	Gas	193 HP
V-345	Gas	197 HP
V-392	Gas	253 HP
VS-401	Gas	206 HP
VS-478	Gas	234 HP
VS-549	Gas	257 HP
DV-462B	Diesel	160 HP
DV-550B	Diesel	180 HP
6V-53N	Diesel	195 HP
DV-550B	Diesel	200 HP

CHASSIS
DETAILS,
(SHOWING
PLACEMENT
OF ENGINE)
(CARGOSTAR
C.O.E.) →

71c
(CONT'D.)
C.O.E.

INTERNATIONAL

Cargostar.

10 MODELS OF CARGOSTAR:

Model CO-1610A
GVW Rating: 19,500 to 24,000 lbs.
Engine Type: Gasoline—Standard: V-304;
Largest: V-345.

Model CO-1710A
GVW Rating: 22,000 to 27,500 lbs.
Engine Type: Gasoline—Standard: V-304;
Largest: V-392.

Model CO-1750A
GVW Rating: 22,000 to 27,500 lbs.
Engine Type: Diesel—Std.: DV-462B.

Model CO-1810A
GVW Rating: 24,000 to 35,000 lbs.
Engine Type: Gasoline—Standard: V-345;
Largest: V-392.

Model CO-1850A
GVW Rating: 24,000 to 35,000 lbs.
Engine Type: Diesel—Std.: DV-550B (180HP);
Largest: DV-550B (200HP).

Model COF-1810A
GVW Rating: 37,000 to 46,000 lbs.
Engine Type: Gasoline—Standard: V-345;
Largest: V-392.

Model CO-1910A
GVW Rating: 27,500 to 35,000 lbs.
Engine Type: Gasoline—Standard: VS-401;
Largest: VS-549.

Model CO-1950A
GVW Rating: 27,500 to 35,000 lbs.
Engine Type: Diesel—Std.: DV-550B (180HP);
Largest: DV-550B (200HP).

Model COF-1910A
GVW Rating: 39,000 to 46,000 lbs.
Engine Type: Gasoline—Standard: VS-401;
Largest: VS-549.

Model COF-1950A
GVW Rating: 39,000 to 46,000 lbs.
Engine Type: Diesel—Std.: DV-550B (180HP);
Largest: DV-550B (200HP).

TILT-CAB CO 1600 2~TON STAKE
101" WB 12' BED
CAB and CHASSIS PRICE, f.o.b. $5305.

INTL. 71-C

Heavyweights of our Light-Duty Line

Power steering and brakes are especially helpful with all-wheel drive when hauling heavy loads.

Models 1310 and 1510

MODEL 1310, shown above with dump bed which is ideal for contractors, landscapers, cemeteries, municipalities, and many other uses. Wheelbases are 131 inches for 8-foot regular or Bonus-Load pickup bodies, 134 inches for 9-foot regular pickup, dump, stake or platform bodies, 156 inches for 12-foot stake, dump, platform or van bodies. GVW ranges up to 10,000 pounds.

LT. DUTY HAS *new* GRILLE

Direct-reading gauges are standard on all International vehicles. No idiot lights.

1972

72 A

CONVENTIONAL *TRANSTAR*

4200

LT. DUTY OR LOADSTAR OFFERS OPTIONAL 345 CID OR 392 CID V8s

Loadstar

A new optional fiberglass hood and fender assembly tilts forward so a serviceman can walk right up to the engine.

1-TON "1310" PRICED FROM $3186.

1½-TON "1510" FROM $4022.

CONTINUED NEXT PAGE)

INTL. 72-A

250

This year you can equip your new FLEETSTAR A truck with any of four dependable diesels. Including 180 and 200 HP International V-8's. Or 225 HP Cummins* or Cat* engines. Or, you could choose one of the time-proven IH gasoline engines. Here your choice includes seven models. Ranging from our 193 HP Six to our big 285 HP V-8.

'72 2050 OR F-2050 FLEETSTAR NOW OFFERS 225 H.P. V8

AVAIL. WITH FIBERGLASS ← TILT HOOD

Cat 1160 Diesel Engine | **Fleetstar A**

AS ALTERNATE CHOICE.

90 OR 92" BBC CAB

72 B
(CONT'D.)

Lightweight Western Mixer Chassis from International

8500 M *new* ('72 ½)

WITH 107" BBC, 1160 CAT. DIESEL ENG.

VIEW OF IHC FACTORY ASSEMBLY LINE IN BACKGROUND

INTERNATIONAL

(C.O.E. ON ⟶ NEXT PG.)

TRAVELALL 1010 (½ T.) = $3769.
1110 (½ T.) = 3656.
1210 (¾ T.) = 3783.
119" WB   V8 $161. EXTRA
ON ALL

INTL. 72~B

251

CARGOSTAR INTERIOR

IH

72 C
(CONT'D.)

C-O TRANSTAR 4070A

6 V6
V8 OR V12
(ALL
DIESEL)
(195 TO
434
HP)

INTERNATIONAL

new
BUMPERS

CO 1610 A and OTHERS
CARGOSTAR

6 CYL. OR V8
4, 6, V6 OR
V8 DIESEL
(193 ~ 253
HP)
89 TO 192"
WHEELBASE

106
TO
184"
WB

WITH
JIFFLOX DOLLY PULLS
SINGLES AND DOUBLES

C.O.E.
MODELS

UNISTAR CO 744 4-WHEEL DRIVE
6, V8 OR V12 (ALL DIESEL)
121~131"   260 TO 434 HP
WB

INTL. 72~C

252

105,569 LIGHT TRUCK SALES

INTERIOR

TRAVELALL
FROM $3729.

PICKUP FROM $2791.

FRONTAL STYLING OF PICKUP SIMILAR TO TRAVELALL.

73

FLEETSTAR'S IHC INSIGNIA MOVED FROM FRONT OF HOOD, BACK TO COWL.

Transstar 4200/4300.

TON CAP'Y.	SERIES
1/2	1010, 1110
3/4	1210
1	1310
1 1/2	1510
2	1600

AT RT. → DIESEL ENGINE DESIGNATED ON MODEL # NAMEPLATE (ON SIDE OF HOOD)

INTERNATIONAL

TRANSTAR 4200

new BUMPER

FLEETSTAR 2070-A

(CONT'D. NEXT PAGE)

INT'L. 73-A

253

SCHOOL BUSES
(VARIOUS IHC CHASSIS TYPES)

73 B
(CONT'D.)

* 6-CYL. METRO VANS

MS 1210	125"WB	$4956.
"	137 "	5078.
MS 1510	" "	6204.

* (V8 ENGINE $113. EXTRA)

Paystar 5000

new F-5010 MIXER INTR. 73½, WITH GAS VS-549 ENG. (227 HP) (1ST GASOLINE POWERED MODEL IN THE PAYSTAR 5000 LINE.)

BUSES ILLUSTR. THIS PAGE:
"PUSHER" (FLAT-FRONT) TYPE=(UPPER LEFT)
CONVENTIONAL (PROTRUDING HOOD)=(CENTER, LEFT and RT.)
TRAVELALL MODIFICATION =
(UPPER RIGHT)

CO 1600 2-TON TILT-CAB C.O.E. (101" WB) FROM $5661.

INT'L. '73~B

**Model 200
Four-Door Travelette**

$**4093.**

1974
I.D. #
4 (H) I (A)
ODHB UP

Model 500
Chassis & Cab

½-TON MODELS DO NOT
HAVE THESE ROOF
CLEARANCE
LIGHTS.

1974

74

**new GRILLE (LT. DUTY
and CARGOSTAR)**

½ TON	100 SERIES FROM	$3258.
3/4	200	3526.
1½	500 CH./CAB	4230.
2	1600 CH./CAB	4773.

CARGOSTAR

TANKER
(ABOVE)
REFUSE TRUCK
(RIGHT)

150 HP V-345
ENGINE STD. IN
MODEL CO-1610B,
CO-1710B,
CO-1810B,
COF-1810B

180 HP DV-550B
ENG. STD. IN
CO-1850B,
CO-1950B,
COF-1950B

186 HP VS-401 ENG.
STD. IN CO-1910B,
COF-1910B
(OTHER ENGS. AVAIL.,
INCLUDING
CATERPILLAR.

INTL. 74

255

1975 LT. DUTY SIMILAR TO 1974, BUT ½-TON NOW IS "150" SERIES (FROM $3952.)

75-77

NEW ('75)

TRANSTAR II (STARTS MID-1974)

new SQUARED HEADLT. BEZELS

37,630 LIGHT TK. SALES IN 1975

TRANSTAR 4100 "CONCO"
(<u>CON</u>= CONVENTIONAL
<u>CO</u>= CAB-OVER) COMBINATION

PLEASE NOTE: PICKUPS, TRAVELALLS, VANS, LIGHT-DUTY TYPES NOT LISTED AFTER 1975, BUT "<u>SCOUT</u>" and HEAVY-DUTY MODELS CONTINUE.

LOADSTAR, FLEETSTAR A, <u>PAYSTAR</u>, 9, <u>TRANSTAR</u>, C.O.E. CARGOSTAR and <u>CO-TRANSTAR II</u> TYPES AVAIL. (DIESEL ENGS. ONLY, IN <u>UNDERLINED</u> MODELS.)

78

GAS OR DIESEL ENGS. (150-430 HP)

NEW "S" SERIES

↑ CO-TRANSTAR

...truck is an "S", ...answer is yes.

NEW

IH **INTERNATIONAL TRUCKS** The common sense solution.

IH **79** **Eagle** *C.O.E.*

IH INTERNATIONAL WE BUILD YOUR KIND OF TRUCK.

SERIES **MEDIUM TRUCKS**

The new 9.0 liter Money-Back Diesels.
(WITH DIESEL ENGINE, $2980. EXTRA)

FINAL
1½ TON CAB/CHASSIS/DR
V8 CONVENTIONAL (140" WB)
$10567.

C.O.E.
2-TON TILT-CAB
CAB/CHASSIS $11536.
/DR

FINAL 1980
4-CYL. SCOUT (100" WB)
FROM $8342.
(ALSO 118" WB, V8 OR
6 CYL. TURBO DIESEL)

(BELOW)
4300 CONVENTIONAL
('81)

80-84 A

(BELOW)
new EAGLE
C.O.E.
('81½)

(CONT'D. NEXT PAGE)

**We're not giving in.
We're going on.**
(1982-83 SLOGAN)

('81)

MIXER   ('84)   DUMP

*FINANCIAL DIFFICULTIES
INTERRUPTED PRODUCTION
FOR A TIME
(1981-1982)*   ('80)

80-84 B
(CONT'D.)
medium diesel trucks
('84)

*FINAL
GAS
TYPES,
1984*

*XL
C.O.E.*

6.9 LITER DIESEL

ALSO AVAILABLE:

**our 9.0 liter and our
DT-466 engines.**

The economy 9.0 liter.
Unsurpassed fuel efficiency.
The 9.0 liter at 165 and 180
h.p. offers fuel efficiency
that can double that
of comparable gas
engines. It can even
save you money if
you use it for as little
as 8,000 miles a year.
And because it's built to
meet International's rugged
durability standards, the 9.0 liter
is even available with an industry
exclusive 36 month/75,000
mile warranty.

The premium DT-466.
Number one's #1. It's the
engine designed especially to
operate efficiently and economically for years and years. At 180
and 210 h.p., the proven DT-466
is the only American
built in-line six cyl-
inder diesel with
wet-type cylinder
sleeves. This
allows for in chassis
rebuilding which saves
time. Saves money. And
adds to resale value.

*IN
1982,
IVECO
BLT.
new
"T"
SERIES
FOR
IHC
(AN
IVECO
TRUCK
WITH
"INTER-
NATIONAL"
NAME.)*

The commitment
is forever.   *('84)*

*FINAL GASOLINE-POWERED
MODELS (FOR THE NEXT
FEW YEARS) = 1984.*

*HEAVY-DUTY MODELS and BUS
CHASSIS UNITS ONLY,
1981 ON.
(CONVENTIONAL or C.O.E.)*

INTL. 80-84 B

all-new LONGNOSED CONV. 9370 REPLACES THE TRANSTAR 4200 and 4300 SER.

NEW

85 -90

"EAGLE" CAB (9370 CONVENTIONAL)

PREMIUM 9370
CONVENTIONAL (STARTS 8-84)

WITH FACTORY-INSTALLED AERODYNAMICS PACKAGE (WIND SHROUD, ETC.) AVAILABLE

note TAPERED REAR FRAME RAILS ON 9370 CONV.

9370 INTERIOR DETAILS

TOGGLE SWITCHES REPLACE ROCKER SWITCHES

UNIQUE MODULAR GAUGES CAN BE PULLED OR TWISTED OUT OF THE HINGED DASH PANEL.

DIESEL ENGINES ONLY, AFTER 12-1-84.

9670 C.O.E.

('89)

note HORIZONTAL GRILLE PCS. ON THIS 1989 MODEL

AS OF FEB. 20, 1986, INTERNATIONAL HARVESTER BECOMES **NAVISTAR** INTERNATIONAL CORP. FOR A FEW YEARS.

new CONVENTIONAL AVAIL. IN 9370, F-9370 and EAGLE TANDEM VARIETIES.

9370 CONVENTIONAL

TO 1940~41 JEEPS BLT. BY AMERICAN BANTAM OF BUTLER, PA. (note UNIQUE FRONTAL DESIGN) (SEE LOWER LEFT CORNER OF PAGE)

46 HP

4 CYL 112 CID CONTINENTAL ENG.

JEEP

(SINCE 1941) WILLYS-OVERLAND, INC., TOLEDO, OHIO UNTIL 1962

HORN
WIPER
MIRROR

DASH ('42) (WILLYS / FORD)

LIGHTS
CHOKE
BEAMS
IGN.
HAND THROTTLE
PANEL LIGHTS
GAS GA.
OIL GA.
SPEEDO
TEMP. GA.
AMPS.
STARTER
HAND BRAKE
INFO. PLATES

4-wheel drive

MILITARY JEEP KNOWN AS "G.P.W. ¼ TON 4 × 4 TRUCK."

4-CYL. L-HEAD ENG. 134.2 CID 6.48 COMPR. 60 H.P. @ 3600 RPM

FORD-BUILT MILITARY JEEP ('42)

80" WB

$ **965.** WARTIME PRICE

'WILLYS ENGINES

(MILITARY MODELS ONLY, UNTIL 1946) 6-CYL. ALSO AVAIL., STARTING 1948.

WILLYS BUILT MOST W.W. 2 JEEPS, BUT FORD ALSO PRODUCED EXACT COPIES, TO HELP MEET THE EMERGENCY DEMAND.

1940s NEW

½ TON **Jeep Pickup** $732. 2-W-D

118" WB AVAIL. 1948

2-W-D (ABOVE)

4-W-D

('47)

104" WB ON PICKUPS, PANEL DLVRY., 1947

104" WB

BAR B RANCH

STATION WAGON INTRO. 1946. (ALL-STEEL) $ **1565.** ('47)

FRONT

TRANSMISSION	TRANSFER CASE
R 2	OUT ◯ LOW
N	IN ◯ ◯ N
1 3	◯ HIGH
	FRONT AXLE DRIVE AUX. RANGE

DISENGAGE FRONT AXLE DRIVE WHEN OPERATING ON DRY HARD SURFACED ROADS

4-W-D SHIFT PATTERN ('42)

WILLYS-OVERLAND MOTORS
TOLEDO, OHIO
MAKERS OF AMERICA'S MOST USEFUL VEHICLES
(1948-1949 MODELS on NEXT PAGE)

(THE FINAL 1941 AMERICAN BANTAM JEEPS BORE A CLOSER RESEMBLANCE TO THE WILLYS MILITARY MODEL.)

JEEP ~ 1940s

48 -49

'Jeep' Trucks

1 TON PICKUP **$1346.** ($1650. WITH 4 WHEEL DRIVE)

('48)

1 TON STAKE TRUCK (RARE)

(118" WB ON 1 TON MODELS)

$1410. ($1712. W. 4WD)

$1765. 6-CYL. STARTS 1948

JEEPSTER

new 1950 JEEPSTER INSTRUMENT PANEL

6.50 x 15" TIRES

('50) **$1390.**

FUEL · OIL · AMP · TEMP

Jeepster

EARLY **1950s**

new "CRISS-CROSS" GRILLE PCS., 1950

1953 IS WILLYS-OVERLAND'S 50TH ANNIVERSARY

4-W-D AVAIL. ON "UNIVERSAL JEEP" RETAINS 1940s GRILLE

('53)

4-W-D PICKUP

"4 WHEEL DRIVE" DESIGNATION ON SIDE OF HOOD

('51)

4 CYL. 134.2 CID WILLYS

PANEL DELIVERY (RARE) 104½" WB 4-W-D OPTIONAL

STATION WAGON (A.K.A. "STATION SEDAN")

('53)

4-W-D OPTIONAL

HURRICANE F-HEAD ENGINE

72 HP @ 4000 RPM COMPRESSION RATIO 7.4-TO-1

JEEP = 1948 ~ EARLY 1950s

'Jeep'

New style!

4 CYL.
81" WB
74" PICKUP
BOX LENGTH

INTRODUCED 1957,
CONT'D. TO 1963

75 HP @
4000 RPM

7.00 x 15" TIRES

New 'Jeep' / Forward Control
4-Wheel-Drive / FC-150

LATER

1950s -62

$1979.

CJ-5 JEEP

('58) LARGER FC-170 103" WB 6 CYL. (1958) $2857.

'Jeep'
4-WHEEL-DRIVE VEHICLES BY **WILLYS** KEEP AMERICA ON THE MOVE

RETAIL SALES

JEEPS =
7739 ('58)
10,576 ('59)

JEEP TRUCKS =
14,765 ('58)
20,050 ('59)

('58)

STATION WAGON
$2378. ($2901. 4-W-D)
(1958 PRICES)

4.89 OR 5.38 GEAR
RATIO
(OVERDRIVE AVAIL.)
('61)

BELOW:
EARLY '60s TYPE
STATION WAGON
$1995.
('61)

new
"ROCKET"
SIDE TRIM
and
1 PIECE
WINDSHIELD
and
TAILGATE
WINDOW

JEEP = LATER 1950s ~ 62

ALL NEW 'JEEP' WAGONEER

('63)

A/T OPTIONAL $3332. ('63)

"WAGONEER" (110" W.B.)
(REPLACES 1962 WILLYS JEEP SERIES)
4 WHEEL or 2 WHEEL DRIVE

improved

('63) CJ UNIVERSAL JEEP

DJ DISPATCHER
IS LOWEST-
PRICED JEEP,
AVAIL. TO 1965

63-65

WAGONEER
FROM $3279. (4WD) (2 DR.)
" $3332. (ILLUSTR. 4 DR.)
NEW "TORNADO" ENGINE (AMERICA'S
ONLY OVERHEAD-CAM ENGINE IN 1963)
140 HP 6 (4 CYL. ALSO AVAIL.)

PICKUP has
HI-TORQUE 6
OR 250-HP V8

OPTIONAL
camper

66
A

New Idea
in Sports Cars... **'Jeep'**
Tuxedo Park Mark IV
with 4-wheel drive

For those who want a new and different sports car with a captivating flair, the 'Jeep' Tuxedo Park Mark IV is the only answer. Stylish as a sports car, tough as a truck, the Tuxedo Park combines complete vehicle versatility with a lively new appearance and a hot new 160 horse-power V-6 engine option. World-famous 4-cylinder Hurricane engine standard.

'Jeep' Gladiator

TUXEDO PARK

New 'Jeep' V-6!
(160 HP)
(OR "HURRICANE" 4)

81"
OR
101" W.B.

The Flying 'Jeep'
Universal
with 4-wheel drive

DJ
2-W-D
PRICED
FROM $1699.
CJ (4WD) $2225. UP

(CONT'D. NEXT PAGE)

V6 ENGINE = $185. EXTRA

JEEP = 63~66A

with 'Jeep' 4-wheel drive.

HYDRA-MATIC A/T OPT.

$2650.

DOUBLE SWING-OUT REAR DOORS

AVAIL. SINCE 1964   110" WB
JEEP PANEL DELIVERY
HIGH-TORQUE 6
OR 250 HP "VIGILANTE" V8 ENG.

'66 (INTRO. SEPT. 1965)

'Jeep' Wagoneer

You've got to drive it to believe it! See your 'Jeep' dealer.

WAGONEER GETS new WIDE GRILLE

DASH INTERIOR

WAGONEER PRICES $2791.~$3780.

66 (CONT'D.)
B

new 'Jeep' Super Wagon-eer

The Most Unusual
Luxury Wagon Ever Built

Even the roof of the Super Wagoneer is elegant. The smartly textured, padded vinyl covering is hand fitted, and especially treated for durability. Further enhancing the attractiveness of the 'Jeep' Super Wagoneer is a chromium luggage rack that easily supports anything from safari equipment to resort luggage.

WAGONEER CORNER TAIL LIGHTS

NEW V-6 ENGINE

You've Got To Drive It To Believe It!
Visit Your **Jeep** Dealer for a
Traction-Action Demonstration Drive in one of the "Unstoppables"
from **KAISER Jeep CORPORATION**
Toledo, Ohio 43601   JEEP = 66 B

264

COMMANDO

RESTYLED JEEPSTER ("COMMANDO") RETURNS (1ST TIME AVAILABLE SINCE 1953)

new 'Jeepster'
4-wheel drive fun cars

134.2 C.I.D. F-HEAD 4-CYL. "HURRICANE" ENGINE (75 H.P. @ 4000 RPM) OR 225 C.I.D. "DAUNTLESS" OVERHEAD-VALVE V-6 (160 H.P. @ 4200 RPM) 4-WHEEL-DRIVE (AUTO. TRANS. AVAIL. AS OPTION WITH V-6 ENGINE.) POWER-OPERATED TOP OPTIONAL.

JEEPSTER ORIGINALLY INTRODUCED IN 1948 BY WILLYS.

('67)

T.V. and FILM STAR DANNY THOMAS APPEARED IN VARIOUS 1967 JEEPSTER ADS

11-MONTH SALES FIGURES:
1967 = 36,004
1968 = 34,329

101" W.B.

$2466. and up ('67)

67-69

MFD. BY KAISER JEEP CORPORATION TOLEDO, OHIO

"GLADIATOR" PICKUP

'Jeep' Wagoneer.

$3648. UP ('67)

INTERIOR (WAGONEER)

('69)

('67)

6 OR V8

CAMPER INTERIOR (SLEEPS 4)

OCT., 1969: AMERICAN MOTORS CORP. BUYS KAISER JEEP

WITH CAMPER UNIT DETACHED

New family camper for your 'Jeep' Universal.

(CJ-5 with V6 ENGINE)   ('69) $2247. UP (W/O CAMPER)

Jeep. The 2-Car Cars.
KAISER Jeep CORPORATION

265

JEEP NOW BUILT BY AMERICAN MOTORS

The toughest 4-letter word on wheels.
Jeep Products from American Motors

sporty new Gladiator ('70)

$3516. UP ('70)
232 CID 6 (135 HP) OR 350 CID V8 (230 HP) IN WAGONEER and PICKUP ('71)

pick up

GLADIATOR

120" OR 132" WB (126" WB ALSO IN 1970)

V8

110" WB ('71)

The Jeep Wagoneer—
the 4-wheel drive family wagon
$4284. UP ('70)

70-71

UNIV. CJ JEEP has SAME ENGINE CHOICES AS COMMANDO. ('71)

UNIVERSAL JEEP

"Jeep guts"

$3197. UP ('71) 134.2 CID 4 CYL. F HEAD ENGINE 75 HP @ 4000 RPM

OPT. 225 CID V8 160 HP @ 4200

81" OR 101" WB

101" WB ('71)

The Jeepster Commando—

1972 is FINAL YEAR KNOWN AS "JEEPSTER" COMMANDO

STD. 232 CID 6 IN UNIVERSAL JEEP ('72) (100 HP @ 3600 RPM)
OPT. 258 CID 6 (110 HP @ 3500) OR 304 CID V8 (150 HP @ 4200)

PICKUPS FROM $3328.

PICKUP GRILLE (SINCE 1970) "GLADIATOR" NAME NO LONGER USED ON JEEP TRUCK.

72
NO MORE 4-CYL. MODELS

RESTYLED '72 COMMANDO $3257. UP

(175 HP @ 4000 RPM) 360 CID V8 OPTIONAL IN COMMANDO PICKUP

WAGONEER $4398. UP

UNIVERSAL JEEP

$2475. UP

Toughest 4-letter word on wheels.
Jeep

PICKUP has SAME 3 ENGINE CHOICES AS WAGONEER

Jeep
Toughest 4-letter word on wheels.

INTERIOR

This pickup comes with new passenger car interiors and rugged Jeep guts.

120" OR 132" WB

3. This $200.00 Cargo Cap at no extra cost

CAP HAS 45" JALOUSIE WINDOWS AND SCREENS LOCKABLE LIFTGATE WITH SAFETY GLASS

STD. PICKUP $3353. UP

232 OR 258 CID 6 CYL. ENG. (100 HP) (110 HP) IN COMMANDO (V8 OPT.)

104' WB

O.H.V. 6 and V8 ENGINES

WITH WOODGRAIN PANEL

258 CID 6 (110 HP @ 3500) OR 360 CID V8 (175 OR 195 HP) PLAIN SIDES

WAGONEER 110" WB

6 CYL. COMMANDO RDSTR. $3355. WAGON 3506. PICKUP 3382. ($126. EXTRA FOR V8, 304 CID 150 HP @ 4200 RPM)

73

Jeep Introduces Automatic 4-Wheel Drive.

QUADRA-TRAC—Someday all 4-wheel drive vehicles may have a system like it...Jeep Wagoneer has it now.

'73 Jeep Wagoneer.
$4501. UP

CJ 3086. UP

DJ 5 OR CJ 5 = 84" WB CJ 6 = 104" WB (SAME ENGINES AS COMMANDO)

SUPER JEEP

WITH 258 CID 6 OVERSIZE L78 x 15 POLYGLAS WHITEWALL TIRES

NEW (RENEGADE V8 SUPER JEEP AVAIL. 1-73)

Toughest 4-letter word on wheels.

Jeep

'73

Jeep

New Cherokee

'74

6 CYL.

360 OR 401 CID V8s AVAIL.

INSTRUMENT PANEL

WAGONEER

• Automatic Transmission—equally at home on the highway or on rough terrain.
P R N D 2 1

109" W.B. $5857. UP

109" W.B. CHEROKEE $4602. UP (REPLACES COMMANDO)

CJ-5 FROM $3899.
RENEGADE

304 CID V8
IMPROVED BRAKES

ROLL BAR INCLUDED

CJ-6 has 104" W.B. $3995.

CJ-5 84" W.B.

304 CID V8 OPT.

PICKUP 258 CID 6 AVAIL.

119" OR 131" W.B. $4167. UP

EASY OPEN TAILGATE

Jeep

REAR DETAIL

Only Jeep Pickups offer Quadra-Trac™

Quadra-Trac is the new automatic 4-wheel drive system the experts are raving about. And only Jeep Pickups offer it. This new system delivers 4-wheel drive super-traction to the wheels the instant you need it. No need to get out and lock hubs, no shift lever to fuss with. Quadra-Trac is an exciting option that makes the toughest trucking smoother than ever before.

Whether you choose Quadra-Trac or our famous standard 4-wheel drive the

hauling's easier because both are the product of over 30 years of rough-road experience.

Add 'em up: The rugged dependability that Jeep has come to stand for—axles, suspension, body—all hanging together super-tough to do most any job you put it to, and Quadra-Trac, the premier 4-wheel drive. That adds up to one sweet pickup.

For fun or profit, Jeep Pickups are a little more equal than all the rest.

Jeep /| Cherokee
From a Subsidiary of
American Motors Corporation

('75)

"a Jeep-and-a-half"

$5280. UP

Jeep wrote the book on 4-wheel drive.

('75) Jeep /| CJ/5 $4456. UP

Introducing the Jeep CJ/5 in "Jeans"

(UPHOLSTERED IN LEVI'S JEANS MATERIAL, IN BLUE OR TAN)

$6499. ('76)

Jeep Honcho

Mucho Macho

Jeep /| Pickup
From a subsidiary of
American Motors Corporation

75-76

The New Jeep CJ-7

94" W.B.

RENEGADE

('76)

Jeep wrote the book on 4-wheel drive.

$4566. UP

Jeep /| CJ-7
From a Subsidiary of
American Motors Corporation

Jeep Wagoneer

$7531. UP

('76)

A/T, 360 CID V8, POWER STEER., FRONT DISC BRAKES

JEEP = 75~76

Jeep Wagoneer

4-DR.
WAGONEER
"CUSTOM WAGON"
109" W.B. $8053.

BY 1977, JEEPS ALSO MFD. IN INDIA,
and 20 OTHER FOREIGN COUNTRIES!

Jeep
**we wrote the book
on 4-wheel drive.**

77

PICKUPS FROM
$6283.

Cherokee
"CHIEF"

2-DR.
FROM
$6924.
$7024.
(4-DR.)
REAR
DETAILS

OPT. 360
OR 401 CID
V8s

CJ-7

94" Long wheelbase
and a tuned suspension
give a smoother ride

Jeep CJ-7

$4970.
UP

A removable
hard top with
steel doors and
roll-up windows
is optional for
extra protection
in bad weather

The golden eagle
comes to Jeep country

CJ-5 FROM
$4870.

REAR

Jeep Quadra-Trac®
delivers power to all
wheels...automatically
so you don't have to
get out and
lock hubs

Extra room in the back
so you can haul more
of your gear

The
golden
eagle
Limited Edition
Jeep CJ's

new
GOLDEN EAGLE
AVAIL. IN EITHER
CJ-5 OR CJ-7
SERIES.
TAN LEVI'S TOP,
EAGLE HOOD DECAL,
GOLD-COLORED
WHEELS

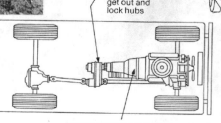

An automatic transmission is optional.
If you want it

JEEP = 77

270

(CHEROKEE "CHIEF" PACKAGE OPT.)

Jeep

CJ "RENEGADE"
$4995. UP
258 CID 6

(304 CID V8 OPT. AT $186. EXTRA)

CJ 5 = 83½" W.B.
CJ 7 = 93½" W.B.

78

We wrote the book on 4-wheel drive.

('78½ WAGONEER LTD. INTERIOR)

109" WB
CHEROKEE 4 DR. $7992.
2 DR. "S" (2 DR. $7886.)
$8332.

WAGONEER
$8760.

Introducing the Jeep Wagoneer *Limited*

$11,413. →
(INTRO. LATER IN 1978)

('78½)

(1979 ADVERTISED WITH THESE WHEELS, BUT WITH NEW GRILLE AS BELOW)

WAGONEER LIMITED
$13,621.

SAME GRILLE ON 1979 PICKUP ↓

79- 81

new GRILLE IN '79

('81)

(1979 PICKUPS $8201. UP)

WAGONEER
16 MPG EPA
21 MPG HWY

new "SCRAMBLER" JOINS JEEP LINE IN 1981 (103" WB)
$7998.

JEEP = 78~81

Jeep

1982 WAGONEERS $13,232. UP

1982 CHEROKEES FROM $11,517. (2-DR.) $13,315. (4-DR.)

1982 PICKUPS FROM $10,494.

82-83 CJ

SPECIAL SALE PRICE $6995. (CJ-7) (REG. $8180.) ('83)

CJ-5 FROM $8174. ('83)

('82)

CHEROKEE CHIEF

CJ-7 AVAILABLE FOR $158.87 PER MONTH!* 11.9% INTEREST (JAN., 1983)

*AFTER 20% DOWN PAYMENT

Why drive a car when you can afford a Jeep?

Jeep Corporation
At over 1,500 Jeep Dealers.

$12,268. ('84)

CHEROKEE.
4 CYL. OR V6

TAILGATE DETAIL

COMANCHE PICKUP ('86) $9713. UP

84-86

$15,471. UP STD. WAGONEER ('86)

4x4

FULL 1986 LINE, INCLUDING 4WD EAGLE (ARROW)

COMANCHE "X"

JEEP = 82~86

Only in a Jeep

WAGONEER LIMITED 101.4" WB

Wagoneer Limited

$20,799. ('87) $22,325. ('88)

87-88

1987 WRANGLER REPLACES CJ JEEP 94" WB (4 OR 6 CYL.) $9194. UP

COMANCHE PICKUPS FROM $10,107. ('87)

(BLT. BY CHRYSLER CORP, 1988 O/N)

CHEROKEE $15,071. ('87 4-DR.)

GRAND WAGONEER 108.7" WB

$24,521. ('87)

Grand Wagoneer

Jeep Eagle

Only in a Jeep

101" WB

NOW JEEP HAS CHRYSLER MOTORS 7/70*

* 7 YEAR, 70,000 MILE WARRANTY

('89)

CHEROKEE has SAME 4 OR 6 CYL. ENGINES AS PICKUP

('90)

2 DR. CHEROKEE $16,609. TO $26,125. ('90)

89 -90

WAGONEER LTD. has 242 CID 6 (177 HP)

360 CID V8 (144 HP)

$27,040. ('89) $28,455. ('90)

Jeep Grand Wagoneer

4 DR.

$11,162. UP ('89)

Jeep Comanche

150 CID 4 (121 HP) OR 242 CID 6 (177 HP)

$8995. ('89)

Jeep Wrangler

150 CID 4 (117 HP) OR 258 CID 6 (112 HP)

AS BEFORE, 2 OR 4 DR. CHEROKEES

273

KENWORTH

(REPLACES GERSIX TRUCK)

KENWORTH TRUCK CO., SEATTLE, WA.
(KENWORTH MOTOR TRUCK CORP., UNTIL 1973)

OLD FACTORY (BELOW)

🔲 KENWORTH

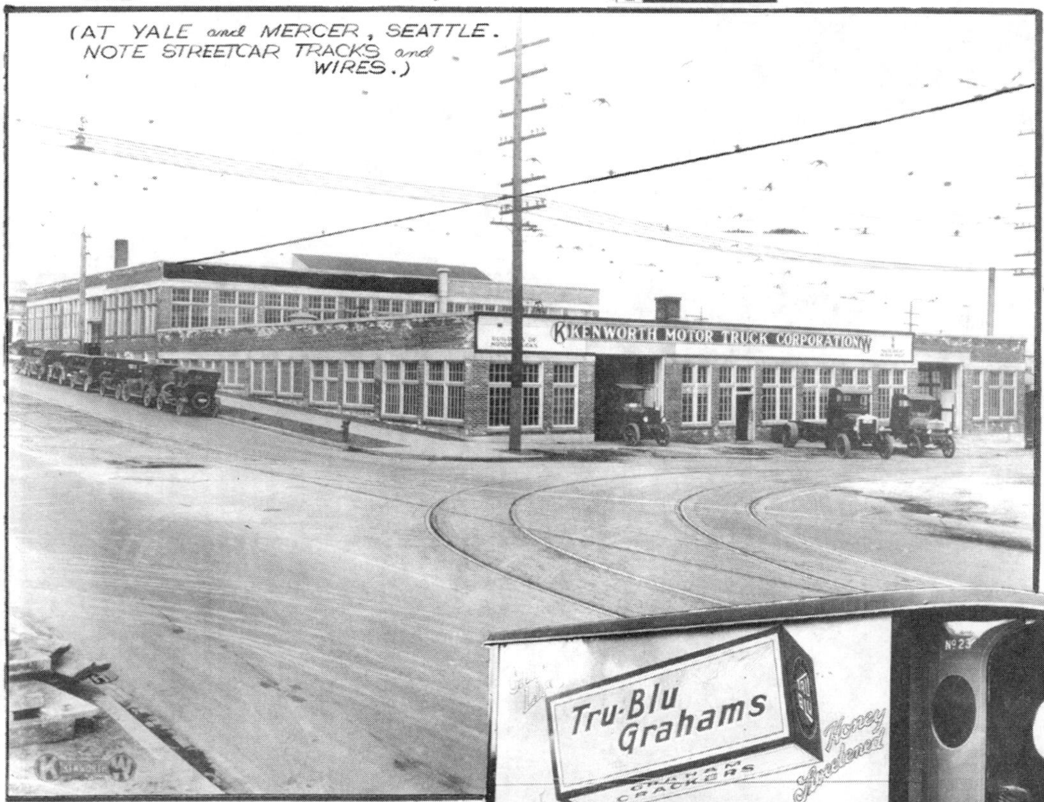

(AT YALE and MERCER, SEATTLE. NOTE STREETCAR TRACKS and WIRES.)

TO

26

4 - CYLINDER BUDA ENGINES (SIZES VARY, ACCORDING TO TRUCK MODEL.)

KENWORTH NAMED FOR FORMER GERSIX DIRECTORS HARRY W. KENT and EDGAR K. WORTHINGTON

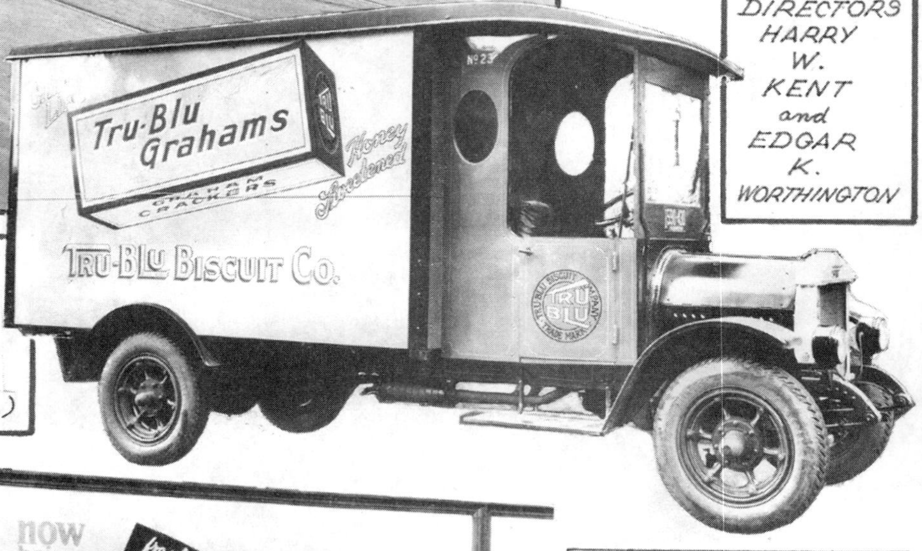

5 MODELS IN 1926:
"OS-OL" = 1 to 1½-TON 131" W.B.
"M" = 2   150"
"KS" = 3   160"
"L" = 4   170"
"RS" = 5   178"
(LONGER W.B. AVAIL. ON "O" TYPES.)

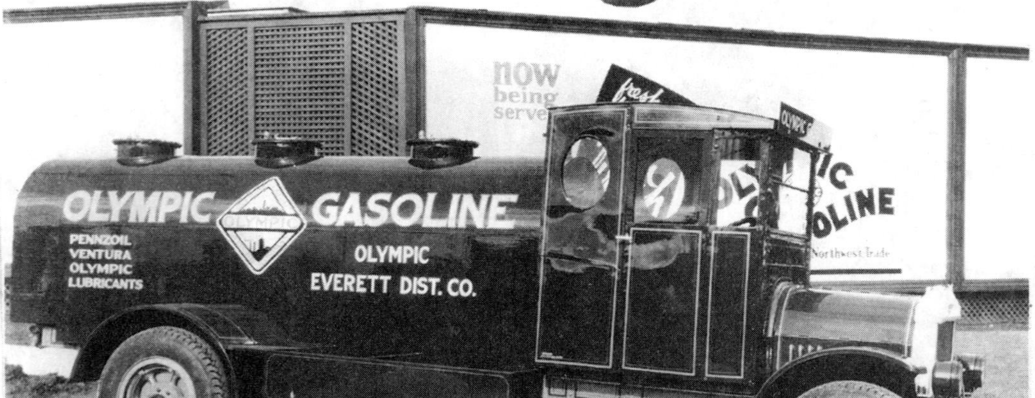

Tru-Blu Grahams — Honey Goodness
GRAHAM CRACKERS
TRU-BLU BISCUIT CO.

OLYMPIC GASOLINE
PENNZOIL VENTURA OLYMPIC LUBRICANTS
OLYMPIC EVERETT DIST. CO.

now being served

ROBT. BOSCH IGNITION ON 2 TO 5-TON MODELS; REMY ON OTHERS. REMY STARTER and GENERATOR ON ALL.

ZENITH CARB. ON 2 TO 5-TON MODELS; STROMBERG ON OTHERS.

THIS TYPE STILL AVAIL. IN 1927.

KENWORTH = 26

new CABS

new HIGHER-PLACED
HEADLAMPS

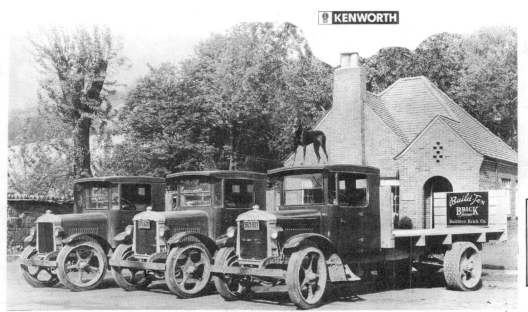

27

new SLANTING
SINGLE GROUP of
HOOD LOUVRES
(on TRUCKS
ILLUSTRATED
AT LEFT.)

MODELS
AVAILABLE
DECEMBER, 1927:

MODEL	TONS	W.B.	CYL.	GEAR RATIO
A	1	131"	4	6.0
A6	1½	140	6	7.8
G	2	150	4	7.75
J	3	160	4	7.75
N	4	170	4	8.75
S	5	178	4	8.75

('28)

VS-107

28

RADIATOR and
HOOD DETAILS

29

A TYPICAL
"VISIBLE
SUPPLY"
GAS STATION
PUMP OF THE
LATE 1920s

KENWORTH SPLIT LEVEL MOTOR BUS
USED FOR INTERCITY SERVICE
ACROSS WASHINGTON STATE

ELLENSBURG   WENATCHEE
YAKIMA   PORT ANGELES
SEATTLE — CROSS STATE ROUTE — SPOKANE

(OPTIONAL WHEELBASES
AVAIL. ON ALL MODELS.)

45	1½ TON	152" WB	BUDA WTU ENGINE	4 CYLINDERS
55	2	163	BUDA HS-6	6
D	2½	158	BUDA KBU-1	4
J	3	172	BUDA EBU	4
G	3	172	BUDA DW-6	6
N	4	170	BUDA YBU	4
S	5	178	BUDA BTU	4
10-TON	10	181	WAUKESHA GU	4

KENWORTH ═ 27~29

KENWORTH

1930 MODELS:

Model	Ton	WB	Cyl.	Engine	CID	H.P.	@ RPM
"70"	1 TON	140-152" WB	6-CYL.	CONT. eng.	214.7 CID	61 H.P.	@ 3000
"100"	1½	164-182"	6	BUDA	241.6 CID	57 H.P.	@ 2500 (75 H.P. IN '31)
"125"	2	157½-183"	6	HERC.	298 CID	67 H.P.	@ 2400
"145"	2½	158½-184"	6	HERC.	339 CID	74 H.P.	@ 2400
"184"	3	164-206"	6	HERC.	360.8 CID	76 H.P.	@ 2600
"185"	3	183¼-211"	6	HERC.	428.4 CID	94 H.P.	@ 2200
"N"	4	170"	4	BUDA			(REPL. BY "240" IN '31.)
10-TON		181"	4	WAUKESHA			
"345"	10-T., 6-w.	245" WB	6-CYL.	HALL-SCOTT	706.8 CID	150 H.P.	@ 2000
"165"	3-TON	158-171" WB		(ENGINE LIKE "184")			
"205"	3½	172-223"		572.5 CID BUDA 6 CYL.,		114 H.P.	@ 1900

"240" 4 TON 170-221" WB
1.53 CID HERC. 6 CYL., 99 HP
@ 2200 (103 HP IN 1931)

30-32

OPT., 1932 =
CUMMINS
DIESEL ENG.
100 HP 4 cyl.

('32)

(10-TON
MODELS NOT LISTED IN 2-28-31
"AUTOMOTIVE INDUSTRIES.")

new FOR 1931:
"85" 1¼-TON 140" WB 6-CYL. CONTINENTAL
"18-E" engine (3⅜"×4") 61 H.P. @ 3000
"220" 3½-TON 194" WB 6-CYL. HALL-SCOTT
"160" engine (4¼"×5½") 105 H.P. @ 2000
(OTHER MODELS CONTINUED FROM '30.)

('33)
MILK TRUCK

1933 MODELS: 86, 88, 101-B, 89,
127, 90, 146-B, 166-B, 166-A, 186,
241, 241-A,B,C; 6-WH.,
10-TON: 186-SDT,
241-SDT, 346-A,B,C,
386-C

33

ALL 6-CYL., with BUDA,
HERCULES, OR
HALL-SCOTT ENGINES. 141-240" WB
1½ TO 10-TON CAPACITIES

6 CYL. GAS (2 TO 7 TON)
ENGINES, AS BEFORE (7 TO 10
TON
6-
WHEELERS)

34

*new KENWORTH-BUILT
TRUCK CABS, 1935*

"D-146" REPORTEDLY
KW's FIRST STOCK
1935 DIESEL MODEL.

(1937 C.O.E.
ILLUSTRATED)

35

ADDITIONAL DIESEL MODELS, 1936

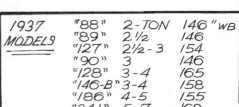

36 -37

6 CYL. (ALL)
HERCULES ENG.
(BUDA,
HALL-SCOTT OR
CUMMINS
DIESEL ALSO)

('37)

1937	"88"	2-TON	146" WB
MODELS	"89"	2½	146
	"127"	2½-3	154
	"90"	3	146
	"128"	3-4	165
	"146-B"	3-4	158
	"186"	4-5	155
	"241"	5-7	169
	"241-A"	"	169
	"241-C"	"	174

('37) CONVENTIONAL

468 CID 112 H.P. @ 2200
707 CID 125 H.P. @ 1800

CID	H.P.	@ RPM
282 CID	83 H.P.	@ 2500
282	83	2500
360	90	2400
282	83	2500
360	100	2400
393	103	2600
453	98	2200
529	110 H.P.	@ 2200

Truck 🛡 **KENWORTH**

38

KENWORTH
BUSES *
('38)

1938 MODELS :
"88" (146-200" W.B., HERC.282 CID 6, 5.8-6.8 G.R.)
"89" (SAME W.B. and 83 HP ENG., 6.16-7.4 G.R.)
"127" (154-202" W.B., HERC.360 CID 6, 6.16-7.4 G.R.,
90 HP @ 2400 RPM)
"90" (146-200" W.B., HERC.282 CID 6, 6.8-7.8 G.R.,
83 HP @ 2500 RPM)
"128" (165-206" W.B., HERC.360 CID 6, 6.8-
7.8 G.R., 100 HP @ 2400 RPM)
"146-B" (158-206" W.B., BUDA
393 CID 6, 6.8-7.8 G.R.,
103 HP @ 2600 RPM)
"525," "526" (168-204" W.B.,
BUDA 525 CID 6, 135 HP @ 2200)
"241-A" (169-228" W.B., HALL-
SCOTT 468 CID 6, 6.02-8.5 G.R.,
112 HP @ 2200 RPM)

CUMMINS-ENGINED DIESELS :
(NO. OF CYLINDERS IN PARENTHESIS)
"505" (4;) "506" (4;)
"507" (4;) "511" (6;)
"519" (6;) "521" (6.)

6-WHEELERS :
(D = CUMMINS DIESEL)
"89-SBT;" "127-SBT;"
"146-SBT;" "346-C;" "386-C"
"508" (D;) "509" (D;)
"510" (D;) "512" (D;) "513;"
"514" (D;) "520" (D;)
"522" (D;) "523" (D;)
"524" (D;) "527;" "528."

*=BUSES AVAIL. FROM LATE 1920s TO LATE 1950s.

6-CYL. GAS ENGINES ;
4 and 6-CYL. DIESELS

39

83 TO 150 HP RANGE
282 TO 672 CID RANGE. IN '39 KW LINE,
NO HALL-SCOTT ENGINES LISTED.

EARLY

$2739.-$9410.
IN 1940

1940s

DURING W.W. 2, KENWORTH BUILT
MILITARY VEHICLES, THE M-1 and M-1A1
WRECKERS and BOMBER NOSE ASSEMBLIES.
COMM'L. PROD. FACILITIES MOVED TO YAKIMA, WA.

1940 =
new UPRIGHT
RADIATOR
SHELL,
CONT'D.
SINCE THEN.

1944 = KENWORTH
BECOMES A WHOLLY-OWNED SUBSIDIARY OF PACIFIC CAR
and FOUNDRY CO.
(LATER **PACCAR**.)

(CIRCA '47)

TANKER TRUCK AND TRAILER

1946 = KENWORTH MOVES
TO NEW FACTORY IN
SEATTLE.

(46~47)

KENWORTH 38~EARLY 40s

KENWORTH

1946 - ACQUIRED FACTORY
SHOWN IN
BACKGROUND

WITH
6-CYLINDER
DIESEL OR
GAS
ENGINES

47

"521" DIESEL (6¾ TON CAP'Y.)
161-215" W.B.
CUMMINS "HB-6"
ENGINE   672 CID
200 HP @ 2100 RPM
6.42 - 7.84 G.R.

"522" DIESEL (15 TON)
187-245" W.B.
SAME ENG. AS ABOVE,
BUT 150 HP @ 1800 RPM

"587" GAS   (9¾ TON)
150-215" W.B.
BU-LO-525 ENGINE   525 CID
135 HP @ 2200 RPM

WESTINGHOUSE
AIR BRAKES

ALSO 6-WHEEL
MODELS "523,"
"524," "528,"
"532," "548,"
"552." CUMMINS
"HB-6" DIESEL
ENGINE IN
ALL BUT
"528"
(WITH 135-HP
"BU-LO-525"
ENGINE)
and
"532"
(WITH "6MZR"
WAUKESHA ENG.
404 CID, 112 HP
@ 2500 RPM)

6-WHEELERS
have 186-255"
WHEELBASE,
DEPENDING ON
MODEL.

10.00 × 20 TIRES
(UP TO 11.00 × 22 AVAIL.)

KENWORTH ~ 47

KENWORTH

SHORT CONVENT'L. TANKER

INFLAMMABLE

"521" DIESEL CONT'D., BUT RATED AT 150 HP @ 1800 RPM.

6 – WHEELERS INCLUDE :
"522" (4-WH. IN '47)
"523"
"524"
"528"
"548"
"552"
"825"
"829"

48

ALL with 150-HP "HB-6" CUMMINS DIESEL ENGINES EXCEPT "528" and "829"

new "585" has ENGINE SIMILAR TO FORMER "587," BUT WITH 150 HP @ 2200 RPM.

DON E. KEITH

KENWORTH ~ 48

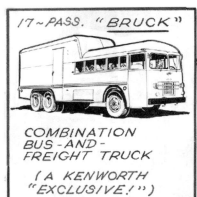

17~PASS. "BRUCK"

COMBINATION BUS-AND-FREIGHT TRUCK

(A KENWORTH "EXCLUSIVE!")

WITH 136-HP HALL-SCOTT ENGINE

🔲 KENWORTH

DUMP TRUCK (WITH DUMP BOX IN RAISED POSITION)(SHOWING HYDRAULIC LIFTS.)

49A
Gas &
Diesel Trucks

CAB AND CHASSIS TRUCK TRACTORS AT RIGHT, AND BELOW

CONVENTIONAL
HEAVY-DUTY

"521" DIESEL
6-CYL., 621 CID
CUMMINS ENGINE
(150 HP @ 1800 RPM)
161"-215" W.B.
6.42 TO 7.84 GEAR RATIO

"585" GAS-POWERED
6-CYL., 525 CID
BUDA ENGINE
(150 HP @ 2200 RPM)
150"-215" W.B.
6.14 GEAR RATIO

(CAB-OVER-ENGINE 1949 MODELS ON NEXT PAGE)

WITH FACTORY VIEWS (ABOVE, and TOP RIGHT)

KENWORTH 49-A

KENWORTH MOTOR TRUCK CORPORATION

A PAIR OF ADDITIONAL FACTORY VIEWS ON THIS PAGE, INCLUDED IN THESE OFFICIAL KENWORTH PHOTOS

C.O.E.

49B (CONT'D.)

KENWORTH MOTOR TRUCK CORPOR

INDUSTRIAL HAULER TRACTOR

WITH ONE-MAN CAB

RARE!

KENWORTH 49-B

6-CYL. ENGINES

■ KENWORTH

50-52

1951 SPECS.:

521 (D) 165~255" WB
672 CID (150 HP @ 1800 RPM)
585 (SAME WBs AS 521)
554 CID (188 HP @ 2600 RPM)
6~WHEELERS: 522,
523, 524, 548, 552,
584, 825, 829, 888.
(ALL DIESELS,
EXCEPT 585
and 829.)

('50)

1953 MODELS:
521; 584 (ENDS '53);
585 (188 HP WAUKESHA
GAS ENGINE) *
801 (200 HP CUMMINS
DIESEL)

ON CONVENTIONAL,
"KENWORTH" NAME
MOVED FURTHER
FORWARD ON HOOD
IN 1953.

NEW CAB-BESIDE-ENGINE MODEL
(CBE)
(SEE 1955
ILLUSTRATION)

53-54

1953 6~WHEELER MODELS:
522; 523~4R; 524~4R;
548~4R; 552~4R;
825~4R; 829~4R (WITH
WAUKESHA GAS ENGINE) *
(STD. ENG. IS 150 HP,
672 CID CUMMINS
DIESEL.)

('53)
TANKER / TRAILER

* = HAS 200 HP LE ROI
ENGINE IN 1954

NOTE DIFFERING DETAILS IN THESE
1954 C.O.E. TYPES.

848~4R,
849~4R,
and
850~4R
ARE
NEW IN
1954.

153 1/4" and
LONGER WBs

('54)

...There's more
WORTH in KENWORTH

('54)

WITH
SPECIAL
1/2 CAB
TRACTOR
CBE
(CAB-
BESIDE
ENGINE)

NEW MODELS: 801, 802, 802~A

55

"521" NO
LONGER
LISTED;
OTHER
REGULAR MODELS
CONTINUED.

KENWORTH 50~55

KENWORTH

4 HDLTS.
OPTIONAL
('58)

GIANT-SIZED MODEL 953 OF
1958 had CUMMINS NTC-350
ENGINE, COST OVER $100,000.!

('56)

CONVENTIONAL

56-58

('60)

C.O.E.
TRACTOR

(11.00 x 22" TIRES ON ALL
BUT 3 LARGEST
'59 MODELS WITH
24" TIRES)

('61)

DIESEL   GASOLINE
CUMMINS OR HALL-SCOTT 6-CYL. ENGINES
401 TO 743 C.I.D. (180 TO 232 HP) ('59)
MODELS 905, 908, 909, 921, 985 (GAS),
922, 923, 924, L924, 925,
928 (GAS), 929 (GAS),
552, 848, 849

59-62

new = QUADRUPLE
HEADLIGHTS

1962 = ALL '59 CUMMINS
DIESEL MODELS STILL AVAIL.,
BUT GAS MODELS NOT
LISTED.

('61)

MODEL
"S"
(SHORT
HOOD)

('61)

CONVENTIONAL CAB/CHASSIS (ABOVE)

KENWORTH 56~62

63

KENWORTH

C.O.E.
Tractor

new "MULTIPLE
CHOICE" GAS PUMP
OF '63 (NORWALK)

heavy

64

TANDEM-AXLE TANKER AND
TRAILER

65

6-WHEELER
WITH WRECKER
BODY (RARE)

KENWORTH 63~65

KENWORTH

66-67

('66)

CONVENTIONAL

C.O.E.

11-MONTH SALES FIGURE:
1967 = 2648

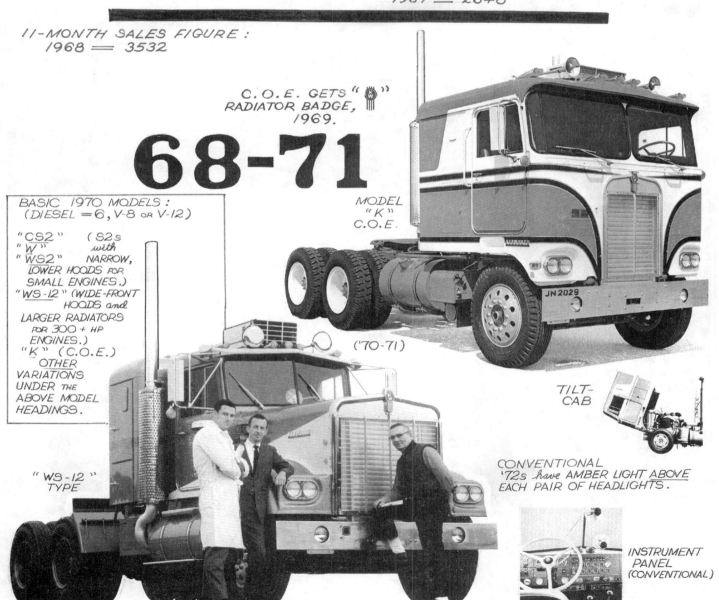

11-MONTH SALES FIGURE:
1968 = 3532

C.O.E. GETS " 🖐 "
RADIATOR BADGE,
1969.

68-71

MODEL
"K"
C.O.E.

BASIC 1970 MODELS:
(DIESEL = 6, V-8 OR V-12)

"CS2" (S2s
"W" with
"WS2" NARROW,
LOWER HOODS FOR
SMALL ENGINES.)
"WS-12" (WIDE-FRONT
HOODS and
LARGER RADIATORS
FOR 300 + HP
ENGINES.)
"K" (C.O.E.)
OTHER
VARIATIONS
UNDER THE
ABOVE MODEL
HEADINGS.

('70-71)

TILT-
CAB

"WS-12"
TYPE

CONVENTIONAL
'72s have AMBER LIGHT ABOVE
EACH PAIR OF HEADLIGHTS.

INSTRUMENT
PANEL
(CONVENTIONAL)

SYMBOL ON CONV. SINCE 1940s, ON C.O.E. SINCE 1969.

KENWORTH
CONVENTIONALS

Construction Truck C-500 (STARTS SUMMER, '72)

SINCE 1972 A

W-900 IS STD. TYPE CONVENTIONAL.

"BRUTE" (STARTS SUMMER, '72) (note GRILLE GUARD)

('83)

Fifty years old and still setting the pace.

The FIRST factory-installed diesel engine in a motor truck.

The FIRST extruded aluminum frame.

The FIRST aluminum disc-type wheels.

The FIRST gas turbine powered truck in scheduled freight service.

The FIRST threaded spring pins and bushings in a motor truck.

The FIRST dual drive torsion spring bogey.

The FIRST grille/condenser air conditioning system.

The FIRST tilt hood in an American motor truck.

The FIRST piano-hinged bulkhead type door.

The FIRST tilt-out instrument panels.

('73)

KENWORTH
"FAMOUS FIRSTS"
innovations
(AS OF 1973)

NEW 1976½ VIT-200 has AERODYNAMIC ROOFLINE WITH 2ND (UPPER) SLEEPER CAB WINDSHIELD (AVAIL. AS C.O.E. OR CONVENTIONAL)

IN THE 1980s, SQUARE HEADLIGHTS ON SOME MODELS

(C.O.E.s ON NEXT PAGE)

KENWORTH~72 ON (A)

LOW-CAB MIDDLEWEIGHT "PD" ('72)

KENWORTH

UP TO 250 HP ('74)

C.O.E. MODELS

('74)
LOW-CAB MIDDLEWEIGHT Kenworth Hustler

↑ REAR (WITH TRIPLE BACK WINDOWS) (SINGLE BACK WINDOW TYPES ALSO.)

K-100 TYPE

SINCE 1972 (CONT'D.) B

K100E (new) ('85)
SUPERSEDES FORMER K-100

new ACCESS DOOR FOR W.W.

AERO-DYNAMIC SHROUD OVER CAB HELPS TO CONSERVE FUEL IN 1980s. K-100 and K-100 "AERODYNE" C.O.E.s AVAIL. 1978, WITH 228 TO 450 HP DIESEL ENGS.

THIS TYPE STARTS 1985

KENWORTH ~ 72 ON (B)

Kleiber

MFD. AUTOMOBILES ALSO, 1924 TO 1929

(1914–1937)
HEADQUARTERS AT
SAN FRANCISCO, CALIF.

KLEIBER MOTOR CO.

| 4-CYL. CONTINENTAL ENGINES | STROMBERG CARBURETOR |

LONGER WBs ON ALL BUT "AA" (AS OF 1920) BOSCH IGN.

11th and Folsom Sts.
SAN FRANCISCO

1800 E. 12th St.
OAKLAND

11th and San Pedro Sts.
LOS ANGELES

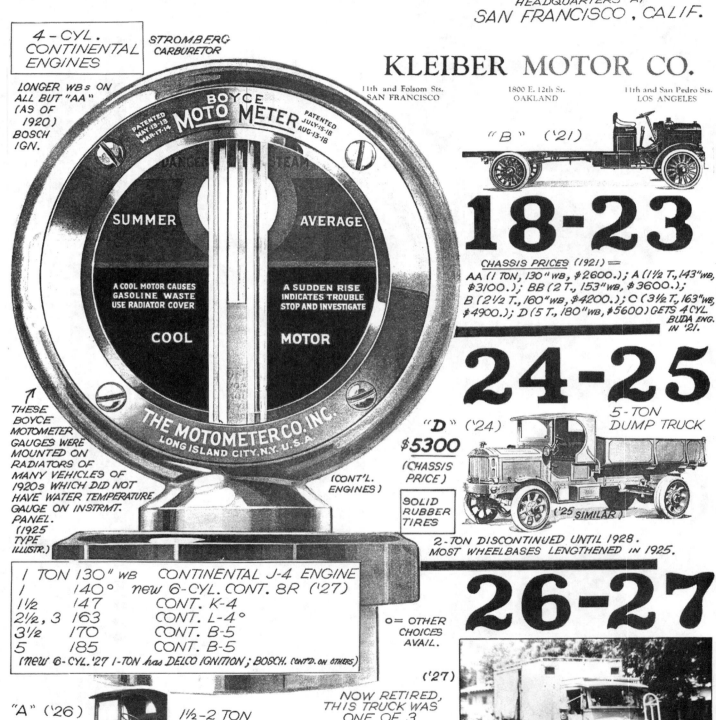

"B" ('21)

18-23

CHASSIS PRICES (1921) =
AA (1 TON, 130" WB, $2600.); A (1½ T., 143" WB, $3100.); BB (2 T., 153" WB, $3600.);
B (2½ T., 160" WB, $4200.); C (3½ T., 163" WB, $4900.); D (5 T., 180" WB, $5600) GETS 4 CYL. BUDA ENG. IN '21.

24-25

"D" ('24)
$5300
(CHASSIS PRICE)

SOLID RUBBER TIRES

5-TON DUMP TRUCK

('25 SIMILAR)

2-TON DISCONTINUED UNTIL 1928. MOST WHEELBASES LENGTHENED IN 1925.

↑ THESE BOYCE MOTOMETER GAUGES WERE MOUNTED ON RADIATORS OF MANY VEHICLES OF 1920s WHICH DID NOT HAVE WATER TEMPERATURE GAUGE ON INSTRMT. PANEL. (1925 TYPE ILLUSTR.)

(CONT'L. ENGINES)

1 TON	130" WB	CONTINENTAL J-4 ENGINE
1	140°	new 6-CYL. CONT. 8R ('27)
1½	147	CONT. K-4
2½, 3	163	CONT. L-4°
3½	170	CONT. B-5
5	185	CONT. B-5

(NEW 6-CYL. '27 1-TON has DELCO IGNITION; BOSCH. CONT'D. ON OTHERS)

o = OTHER CHOICES AVAIL.

26-27

"A" ('26)   1½-2 TON

('27)

NOW RETIRED, THIS TRUCK WAS ONE OF 3 KLEIBERS KNOWN TO BE IN ACTIVE SERV. IN CALIF. AS THE 1970s BEGAN. →

1½-2 TON SPEED TRUCK

CHASSIS $2450.

147" WB MECHANICAL BRAKES, EXPANDING ON REAR AXLE

Kleiber 28

3/4 TON	136"WB	6 CYL.	5.36 GR
1½	158	6	6.42
2	147	4	7.75
2	170	6	6.42
2½ SPEED	190	6	7.75
2½	163	4	7.75
3	163	4	
3 SPEC.	163	6	new BUDA "BUS" ENG.
3½	170	4	8.75
5	185	4	10.3

MODELS ('29):

3/4 TON	121"WB	6 CYL.	CONT.	46 HP ('30)
1, 1½	140	6	CONT.	50 HP ('30)
2°	147°	4	CONT. K4	
2° (SPEED)	170°	6	CONT. 8R	55½ HP ('30)
2½,3 (SPEED)	190°	6	CONT. 6B°	
3°	163°	4	CONT. L4	
3 (SPECIAL)	163	6	BUDA "BUS"	
4 (new)	202	6	BUDA "BUS"	° = OTHER
3½,5	185°	4	CONT. B5	CHOICES AVAIL.

('29) KLEIBER'S FINAL CARS WITH CONT'L. 6 OR ST. 8 ENGINES

29-30

6 CYL. ENGINES ONLY IN 1930 (46 HP and up)

170" WB CHASSIS $2450.

('29) 2-TON SPEED

new # 31 NUMERICAL MODELS:

51 (1 TON;) 52 (1½ TON;)
54 (2 TON;) 64, 56 (2½ TON;) 65, 58 (3 TON;)
657 (4 TON;) 66 (5 TON)
CONTINENTAL AND BUDA ENGINES (6 CYL.)
(58 TO 126 HP)
(6-WHEELERS: SAME MODELS AS IN 1932 (SEE BELOW)

32-33

80	1½ TON	140"WB	CONT. 18E ENGINE	61 HP @ 3000 RPM
100	2	158	BUDA H-260	75 HP @ 3000
120	2½	170	BUDA	86 HP @ 3000
140	3	180	CONT.	74 HP @ 2400
210	3½	190	CONT. 20-R	89 HP @ 2400
225	4	202	CONT. 21-R	102 HP @ 2400 (ENDS '32)
260	5	206	BUDA GF6	126 HP @ 1850

'32 6-WHEELERS: 22DD 5T; 28DD, 34DD, 34DDT (REPLACED '33 BY 280, 340, 340T)

Kleiber

KLEIBER ALSO SOLD **STUDEBAKERS** DURING THE 1930s.

new DIESELS IN 1934

34-37

MODELS		140" to 210" WBs	6 CYL.	
		new		
80	1½-2 TON	HERCULES "JXB"	(263 CID, 68 HP @ 2800) 5.14
100	2-3½	SAME, BUT RATED	70 HP @ 3000 5.81 GR
120	2½-4½	CONT. "E601"	(318 CID, 80 HP @ 2700) 6.17
140	3-5½	CONT. "18R"	(339 CID, 90 HP @ 2700) 6.84
210	4-6	CONT. "21R"	(427 CID, 118 HP @ 2500) 7.25 GR
KD-4	4	CUMMINS 4 CYL.	(448 CID, 83 HP @ 1800) 5.5 GR
KD-6	6	CUMMINS 6 CYL.	(672 CID, 125 HP @ 1800) 5.5 GR

6-WHEELERS ('35-37):

81	5 TON	HERC. "JXB"	5.14 GR
121	7	CONT. "18R"	6.17
141	9	CONT. "21R"	6.84

KLEIBER

LECTRA HAUL

(SINCE 1963)

UNIT RIG EQUIPMENT CO.

MODELS M-85 and M-100

700 HP @ 2100 RPM IN CUMMINS "VT-12-700" OR DETROIT "16V-71NT" DIESEL ENGS.

400-GALLON FUEL TANK

21.00 × 49 OR 24.00 × 49 TIRES

(MFD. OIL FIELD EQUIP. and VARIOUS OFF-ROAD VEHICLES SINCE 1935.)

16'8" (16'10") EMPTY
16'3 (16'5) LOADED

29'4" (29'6")

15'11" (16'1") EMPTY
15'6" (15'8") LOADED

8'3' (8'3')   15'0" (15'0')
32'4" (32'4')

(M-100 DIMENSIONS IN PARENTHESES)

STARTS **66**

CAB INTERIOR

FORWARD
NEUTRAL
REVERSE

↙ FRONT WHEEL DETAIL

20' HIGH, 43' LONG, WITH *new* ACCESS STAIRWAY TO CAB, and GUARD RAILING

('70)

STARTS

M-200

200-250 TON CAPACITY

69

NEW!

ELECTRO-MOTIVE V-TYPE DIESEL ENG. (8 CYL.) 9 1/16" × 10" BORE and ST. 1650 HP @ 900 RPM

36.00 × 51
50-PLY TUBELESS TIRES

LECTRA HAUL

MACCAR

(1912-1935)

MACCAR TRUCK CO., SCRANTON, PA.

(ORIGINALLY MAC-CARR CO., ALLENTOWN, PA., 1912-1913)
FOUNDED BY JACK MACK — ONE OF MACK BROS. WHO
BEGAN MACK TRUCK CO. — AND ROLAND CARR.)

('21)
4 CYL.
4 1/2" x 6"
BORE + STR.

3 1/2 - TON CHASSIS
174 OR 186" WB
36 x 5 SOLID TIRES
4-SPEED TRANS.

Chassis

('24)

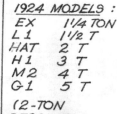

1924 MODELS:	
EX	1 1/4 TON
L1	1 1/2 T
HAT	2 T
H1	3 T
M2	4 T
G1	5 T

(2-TON
BECOMES
MODEL VI IN
1925.)

G1 5-TON
DUMP
TRUCK
162" WB
2-WHEEL BR
7-SPEED
TRANSMISSION
$5350.

('25) (4 CYL.)
5" x 6"
BORE and STR.

NEW 6-CYLINDER
ENGINES (BUDA
and WISCONSIN)
AVAIL. IN 1926.

H1 3 TON
162" WB
4 CYL. (4 1/4" x 6" BORE and STR.)

('26)
(6 CYL.)

H3 3
TON
SPEC.
TRUCK
(TANKER)
186" WB

1920s

46 2-TON MOVING
VAN 180" WB
4-SP. TRANS.

('28)

2-WHEEL
BRAKES

1929 MODELS:			
36	1 1/2 TON	$1950.	
46	2 T	3100.	
64	3 T, 4 CYL.	3800.	
66	" 6 CYL.	4100.	
84	4 T, 4 CYL.	4100.	
86	" 6 CYL.	4400.	
G	5 TO 6 TON	5100.	

NEW TANDEMS and
6-WHEELERS AVAIL. 1929.

46 2-TON TANKER
150" WB

('29) FOLLOWING A
1929 MERGER,
MACCAR A

30-35

PRODUCT OF MACCAR-SELDEN-HAHN CORP.,
ALLENTOWN, PA.

86-A
5 TO 8 TON
CAB AND CHASSIS

NOTE
HORIZONTAL
HOOD
LOUVRES

('30)

LITTLE
CHANGE
IN DESIGN
AFTER 1930.

$1330 to $5950
CHASSIS PRICE RANGE
IN 1933.

1933 MODELS and ENGINES		
100	1 1/2-2 TON	BUDA H-260
40A	2 1/2-4 T.	" H-298
180	3-5 T.	" K-393
60A	4-6 T.	" BA-6
66A	"	HERCULES YXC3
220H	"	WAUKESHA 6SRK
220W	"	" "
86-A	5-8 T.	" "

Maccar

ESTABLISHED 1902
(IN BROOKLYN, N.Y.
UNTIL 1905)

MACK

MACK TRUCKS, INC.,
ALLENTOWN, PA.

5½ - 7 TON
AC CAB-
CHASSIS
('28)

$5500.

FAMOUS "AC" TYPES
INTRODUCED 1916

FACTORY BRANCH
MACK TRUCKS
TRUCKS

BJ ('27)
HORIZONTAL
HOOD LOUVRES
THROUGH
1929.

MACK'S
FIRST
HIGH-SPEED
6 - CYL. MODEL.

LATER
1920s

AC
"BULLDOG"
TYPES

AB   2½ - 3 TON
      4 CYL.
WITH DUAL
REDUCTION DR.
$3850.
($450. LESS WITH
CHAIN DRIVE)

146½ OR 164½" WB   ('28)

4 CYL. = 60 HP @ 2200 RPM
6 CYL. = 75 HP @ 2600 RPM
(1931 SPECS.)

(WITH
WINDSHIELD
ATTACHED)
('26)

NOTE THE CHAIN DRIVE ON
"AC" MODELS ILLUSTRATED
ABOVE.

('26)

AL →

MOVING
VAN

(MACK BUS
ALSO USED
THIS
CHASSIS)

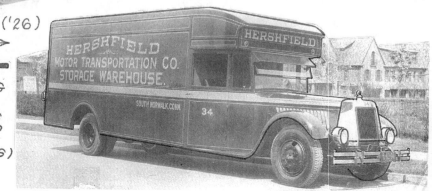

HERSHFIELD
MOTOR TRANSPORTATION CO.
STORAGE WAREHOUSE.
SOUTH NORWALK, CONN.   34
HERSHFIELD

1½ - TON MODEL "BB"
(INTRO. LATE 1928)
IS FIRST WITH HYPOID
GEAR REAR AXLE.

MACK = LATER 1920s

BUSES

('25)

25-PASS.
CITY-TYPE BUS (AB)
4-CYL. 196" WB
CHASSIS $**4250**.
WITH BODY $**7000**.

622 "AL" TRUCKS, BUSES
BLT., 1926~1929.

($11,500. COMPLETE)
29-PASS. PARLOR CAR BUS
6-CYL., 233" WB 34 × 7 TIRES

AL

('25)
(ALSO AVAIL. 1925 W.
230½" WB CHASSIS,
8-DOOR SEDAN
BODY (24-PASS.)
$**8850**.
COMPLETE, W. BODY)

29-PASS. CITY BUS
4-CYL., 225" WB
34 × 7 TIRES $4750. (CHASSIS)
BODY $3250.
EXTRA

1928 and 1929
GAS-ELECTRIC TYPES
ALSO AVAIL.,
$6388~8436.,
CHASSIS PRICE
('28)

AB 29-PASS. CITY BUS
225" WB CHASSIS = $**4750**.
$**8000**.
WITH BODY

('26)

('28)

6-CYL.,
25-PASS. PARLOR CAR
BUS (233" WB)
(2-WHEEL BRAKES
UNTIL END
OF 1928)
AL

AB

25-
31

CENTER-AISLE
INTERIOR
VIEWS (BC MODEL)

('29)
new
4-WH.
BRAKES

AB 29-PASS.
CITY BUS
$**8000**.
WITH BODY

LEFT
SIDE

('30)

BC

(6-
CYL.
126-
HP
BK
ALSO
BLT.
IN
EARLY
'30s,
AS
WELL AS
4-CYL.
AB.)

RIGHT SIDE

"BC"
6-CYL.,
29-PASS.
INTERSTATE BUS

(STREETCAR-TYPE
BODIES AVAIL.
1931~1933)

6-CYL. (126 HP) **BK** ALSO BLT. IN EARLY 1930s,
AS WELL AS 4-CYL. **AB**

3,813 "AB" MACK BUSES
BUILT, 1925~1934.

411 "BC" MACK BUSES
BUILT, 1929~1937.)

MACK ═══ 25~31

BC 6 CYL. 100 HP @ 2300 RPM

('30-31)

AB

('30-31)

AK 6 CYL. OR 4
(4 CYL. AVAIL. W. CHAIN OR SHAFT DRIVE)

('30-31)

BG 6 CYL. 75 HP @ 2600 RPM

EARLY **1930**s

NEW bus

A

AC

('32)

PORTLAND LINES INC.
PORTLAND LINES INC. Newark N.J.

note 6 DOOR-TYPE VENTS ON SIDES OF HOOD. (ABOVE ILLUSTR.)

3½ TON

('33)

(ABOVE) **BT** 40-PASS. *CITY TRANSIT BUS* (87 BLT., 1931-1934) ('31)
(*CL* IS SHORTER, 30-PASS. VERSION)

MODELS

BB 1928-32 1½ TON, 4 CYL.
BC 1929-33 3-4 T., 6 CYL.
BF 1931-39 (1179 BLT.)
BG 1929-37 1½ T., 6 CYL.
BJ 1927-33 4 T., 4 OR 6 CYL.
BL 1929-36 (502 BLT.)
BM 1932-41 (3030 BLT.)
BQ 1932-37
BX 1932-40 (3032 BLT.)
BG BUS 1931-37 (87 BLT.)
BK BUS 1929-34 (544 BLT.)
CG BUS 1933-37 ('76 BLT.)
CL BUS 1932-37 (441 BLT.)
CQ BUS 1934-41 (886 BLT.)
CR BUS 1934-43 (275 BLT.)

(CONT'D. NEXT PAGE)

"*BOULDER DAM*" MACK HEAVY DUTY DUMP TRUCK ('33~'34)

MACK — EARLY 1930s

Mack

BL VAN ('30-31)

← BC CAB-AND
CHASSIS (IN
FOREGROUND)

APRIL, 1930
MACK
FACTORY PHOTO
(AT LEFT)

BJ
RACK ↗ ('30-31)
6 CYL.
126 HP @ 2200
RPM

BJ DOUBLE TANKER RIG ↗

note THE MACK
BULLDOG FIGURE
ON RADIATOR CAP
OF TRUCK
SHOWN BELOW

EARLY
1930s (CONT'D.)
B

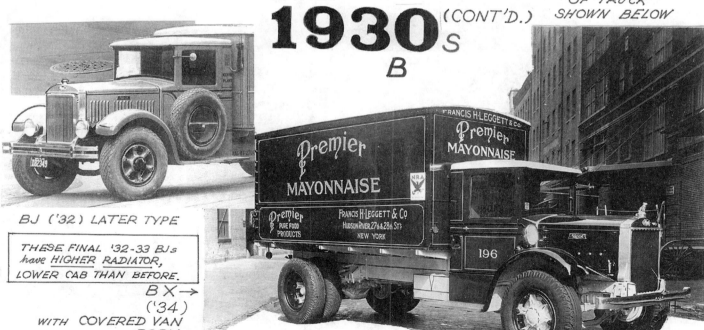

BJ ('32) LATER TYPE

THESE FINAL '32-33 BJs
have HIGHER RADIATOR,
LOWER CAB THAN BEFORE.

BX →
('34)
WITH COVERED VAN
BODY

Premier
MAYONNAISE

Francis H·Leggett & Co
Hudson River 276 & 284 Sts
New York

Premier
PURE FOOD
PRODUCTS

196

(1933: 1ST MACK C.O.E.s AVAIL. SINCE 1916)
("CH" and "CJ")

MACK — EARLY 1930s - B

MODELS:

MACK TRUCKS, INC.,
ALLENTOWN, PA.
WESTERN BRANCH FACTORY
(SINCE 1966) IN
HAYWARD, CALIF.

MODELS:

Model	From	To	WB		CID		HP @	RPM	G.R.		T
CB	1941	1950									
CH	1934	1941	126"-180" WB	415 C.I.D.	108	HP @	2800		6.54	9.82 G.R.	3½-5½ T
CJ	1933	1941	126 180	468	118		2400		6.54	8.92	4½-7
DE	1939	1942									
EB	1936	1941									
EC	1936	1941									
ED	1938	1944	120½-136" WB	210 C.I.D.	67	HP @	3000 RPM				
EE	1938	1950	133 175	253	75		2800		5.14 - 5.66 G.R.		
EF	1938	1951	133 192	271	78		2800		4.85	6.80	
EG	1938	1950	133 193	290	85		2800		4.86	6.80	
EH	1936	1950	158 194	310	90		3000		4.44	7.40	
EJ	1937	1938	158 194	288	84		2800		4.86	6.80	
EM	1937	1943	158 194	310	90		3000		5.43	6.33	
EQ	1937	1950	158 194	354	100		2800		6.31	8.64	
ER	1936	1941	146 194	310	90		3000		7.7	13.1	
ES	1938	1940	144 210	354	100		2800		9.3	13.0	
ETX	1950	ONLY									
EXBX	1940	ONLY									
FC	1936	1947									
FG	1938	1942									
FH	1937	1941	160 172	468 C.I.D.	118	HP @	2400 RPM	7.48			
FJ	1938	1943									
FK	1938	1941									

1938-1939 SPECS. LISTED
(CH, CJ = 1936 SPECS.)

TO 12.4 G.R.

HP 1936 ONLY
19 THROUGH 125 (1937-1955)

BUDA OR CUMMINS DIESEL ENGINES
OPTIONAL IN FINAL AC "BULLDOG" MODELS.

LATER
1930s

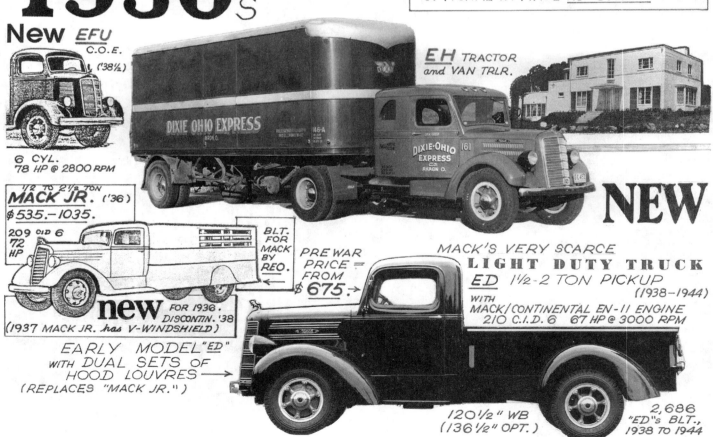

New **EFU** C.O.E. ('38½)
6 CYL.
78 HP @ 2800 RPM

EH TRACTOR and VAN TRLR.

DIXIE OHIO EXPRESS 146-A

DIXIE-OHIO EXPRESS CO. AKRON, O. 161

NEW

½ TO 2½ TON
MACK JR. ('36)
$535.-1035.
209 CID 6
72 HP

BLT. FOR MACK BY REO.

new FOR 1936.
DISCONTIN. '38
(1937 MACK JR. has V-WINDSHIELD)

EARLY MODEL "ED"
WITH DUAL SETS OF
HOOD LOUVRES →
(REPLACES "MACK JR.")

PRE WAR PRICE = FROM $ 675. →

MACK'S VERY SCARCE
LIGHT DUTY TRUCK
ED 1½-2 TON PICKUP
(1938-1944)
WITH
MACK/CONTINENTAL EN-11 ENGINE
210 C.I.D. 6 67 HP @ 3000 RPM

120½" WB
(136½" OPT.)

2,686
"ED"s BLT.,
1938 TO 1944

MACK'S TRADITIONAL "BULLDOG" TRADEMARK (USED AS HOOD ORNAMENT SINCE MID-1930s.)

PANEL STAKE

CH C.O.E. ('38)

LATER
1930s - 40
(CONT'D.)

EHUT CAB-FORWARD →

INTRODUCED SPRING, 1938 WITH OTHER *new* CAB-FORWARD MODELS: EEU, EFU, EGU, FHU, EMU *and* EQU. HYDRAULIC BRAKES, *with* MECHANICAL BRAKES *on* 2 LARGEST MODELS.

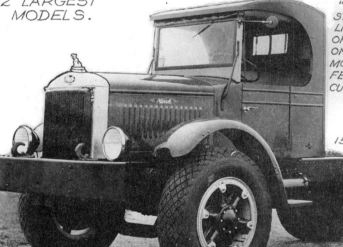

MOVING VANS TRACTOR/TRAILERS WITH SLEEPER-TYPE CABS

"FN" STYLED LIKE TRKS. OF 1920s! ONLY VISIBLE MODERN FEATURES: WHEELS, BULLDOG MASCOT, CURVED DOOR HANDLES, OVAL EMBLEM.

"FN" ONLY 150 BLT., 1940-1941.

CHAIN-DRIVE CAB-AND-CHASSIS

6-CYL. C.O.E.
EC (79 HP @ 2300 RPM)
EB (92 HP @ 2300 RPM)
(RESEMBLE '33-4 CJ, CH)

EC, EB = TRAFFIC TYPE " C.O.E. (INTRO. 1936)

MACK~LATER 30s~40

1 TO 30 TONS IN 1940.

LYON VAN LINES — LET LYON GUARD YOUR GOODS

Model LF (SCALE MODEL OF "LF" ILLUSTR.)

(12,453 LF TRUCKS BUILT, 1940 TO 1953)

Mack

(ABOVE) LF (T) TRACTOR IS **New**

MODELS:

Model	From	To
FN	1940	1941 (REPLACED BY FT)
FP	1940	1942
FT	1941	1950
FW	1941	1949
HT	1941	1943
LF	1940	1953
LH	1940	1953
LJ	1940	1956
LM	1940	1956
LP	1941	1942
LR	1943	1964
LT	1947	1956
LV	1948	1961
LW	1947	(1 ONLY)
MR *	1940	1942
NB, ND	1940 ONLY	
NH	1940	1941
NJU	1941 ONLY	
NM	1940	1945
NN, NQ	1942 ONLY	
NO	1940	1945
NR	1940	1945
NW	1941 ONLY	
SD, SE, SF, SG	(1941-1942)	
SH	1941 ONLY	
T-8 — T-54	(1945-1951)	
CB	1941	1950

LMU (NEW NAME FOR CH, 1941)
LJU (NEW NAME FOR CJ, 1941)

BUSES; FIRE TRUCKS; MARINE ENGINES VARIOUS TRUCKS (1-45 T.)

MACK BUILT A WIDE VARIETY OF MILITARY VEHICLES FOR THE WAR EFFORT SUCH AS:

1940s

AIRCRAFT SEARCHLIGHT TRUCK; 3/4 TRACK; PRIME MOVER FOR "LONG TOM" GUN; NAVY HELIUM-HAULER TRUCK; PONTOON BRIDGE CARRIER; HEAVY-DUTY WRECKER; MILITARY CONSTRUCTION TRUCK; AIRFIELD CRASH TRUCK; NAVY FUEL TRUCK; FIELD DYNAMOMETER TRUCK; NAVY BUS; MILITARY FIRE TRUCK; 10-TON 6 × 4 PERSONNEL CARRIERS TANKS (30-T.);

* = MR IS A C.O.E. DELIVERY TRUCK.

Mack TRUCKS 1 TO 45 TONS

3-AXLE TRACTOR ('47)

('49)

('49)

CIVILIAN FIRE-TRUCK USUALLY *has* CHROMED RADIATOR SHELL →

MACK = 1940s

ILLUSTRATED
WITH

BARTLETT SKYLIFT... 16'6"
BARTLETT MAKES 21 LIFTING MODELS
FOR TOP AND IN-FRAME INSTALLATIONS
In 50,000# and 100,000# Capacities

Mack

MOVING VAN TRLR. ('51)

WITH HYDRAULIC SKYLIFT (REAR VIEW)

('51)

KOREAN WAR MILITARY VEHICLES

('51-'53)

A20U (1951-1952) IS A REVIVAL OF FORMER EFU C.O.E.

G744

More Fleets Use
BARTLETT HYDRAU. LIFT 5th WHEELS Than Any Other

THIS TYPE SKYLIFT WAS ADVERTISED 1971-72 BUT COULD BE USED WITH OLDER TRUCKS, AS SHOWN HERE.

EARLY 1950s
A

A SERIES REPLACES E, IN 1950.

SMITHTON CONCRETE MATERIALS CORP.

('50)

WITH MIXER BODY
1950 SLOGAN ⟹ "MODERNIZE WITH MACK"

MODELS:

A20	1950	1954
A30	1950	1953
A31		1953 ONLY
A40	1950	1953
A50	1950	1953
A51	1950	1953
A52	1951	1953
A54	1952	1953
A55	1952	1953
B20	1953	1960
B30	1953	1965
B31	1953	1960
B41	1953	1954
B42	1953	1965
B43	1954	1965
B50	1953	1955
B60	1953	1963
B61	1953	1966
B62	1954	1958
B63	1954	1958
B70	1953	1966
B71	1953	1958
B421	1954	1965
H60	1953	1954
H61	1952	1957
H62	1954	1958
H63	1954	1958
W71	1953	1958

B61 1953 1966 =(ILLUSTRATED ON NEXT PAGE)

TRANSIT BUS * ('51)

W71-ST C.O.E. DIESEL 6-WHEELER INTRO. SPRING, 1953. (DESIGNED "FOR WEST COAST OPERATIONS."

H61 1952 1957 =(ILLUSTRATED ON NEXT PAGE)

('52)

DUMP TRUCK

(CONTINUED ON NEXT PAGE)

* =(ACTUAL PHOTO OF BUS ON NEXT PAGE)

MACK ~ EARLY 1950s (A)

ACTUAL PHOTO OF MACK
CITY TRANSIT BUS
(BELOW)

MACK

with the economy of Mack diesel power!
Hydraulically controlled...

More room—greater comfort. Note arrow showing staggered seating arrangement —how shoulders overlap, providing at least 4 inches more effective aisle space for the standing passenger yet giving additional space, more comfort for those sitting.

Other important features: Thermostatically-controlled fresh air heating and ventilating system distributes fresh air throughout the bus—even temperature—no drafts. Hydraulic torque converter drive achieves smooth starting and acceleration . . . sensitive edge hydraulic automatic door controls assure greatest safety . . . fluorescent nonglare lighting for passenger appeal . . . wider entrance and exit doors for faster, safer loading and unloading of passengers.

('50)

EARLY
1950s
(CONT'D.)^B

Bus

B61 T

WITH SLEEPER CAB ↗
ENGINE CHOICES ('52) INCLUDE 158 HP GAS (IN
A-54S, T, ETC.) AND 165 HP DIESEL (IN A-55T, ETC.)

Mack
...outlasts them all!

H61 T

C. O. E.
TRACTOR ('52)

BECAUSE OF
THEIR HIGH-SET
CABS, THE
H-60 TYPES
(AS H61 T, AT
RIGHT,) WERE
NICKNAMED
"CHERRY
PICKERS." →

H61 T 1001 - 1052 C 6907.

GLASS
RACK
←

← GLAZIER'S
PANEL STAKE

MACK MODELS OFTEN OVERLAP

MACK~EARLY 1950s (B)

D SERIES C.O.E. ('55) CAB RAISES FOR EASY SERVICING →

Mack

SCHOOL BUS ('55)

TRACTOR / TRLR.

new IMPROVED *B SERIES* STARTS SUMMER, 1953 (RESTYLED) WITH *new* ENGINES and SUSPENSION

TRANSIT BUS ('55)

54 -55

(IN A TYPICAL TRUCK STOP OF 1955)

MODELS STARTING IN 1955 :							
	B-64	58	B-73, B-75	66	D-42	58	
	B-65	58	B-733, B-753	66	D-44	57	
	B-613	66	B-81	66	H-64	59	
B-33 (TO 1965)	B-653	58	D-20	57	H-65	58	
B-44 58	B-655	('55 ONLY)	D-30	58	H-628	('55 ONLY)	

MACK 54~55

Mack TRUCKS

BUS #2101 (1956½ MODEL, BELOW,) has 672 C.I.D. DIESEL ENG., WITH 170 HP @ 2100 RPM and AIR SUSPENSION

(1957 EXAMPLES ILLUSTRATED)

('57)

W/O REAR SIDE DOOR ↙ ('57)

2 TYPES of TRANSIT BUS

REAR SIDE DOOR

56-57

VARIOUS MODELS OF LATER 1950s ARE LISTED AT LOWER LEFT, WITH DATES.

('56½)

note 2 TYPES OF CITY TRANSIT BUSES (WITH OR WITHOUT REAR SIDE DOOR) ↑

MODELS OF LATER 1950s

B46	1958	1965
B66	1958	1965
B67	1957	1965
B72	1956	1965
B77	1958	1964
B80	1956	1965
B83	1956	1966
B85	1956	1964
B86	1957	1959
B87	1956	1964
LY	1958	1962

ALSO INTRO. DURING LATER 1950s:
B426, B473, B633, B673, B813, B833, B853, B873, B8136, G73, G75, G733,

G753, G773, H67, H69, H613, H633, H653, H673, H693 N42, N44, N60, N61, N613

note GRILLE GUARD ON CONVENTIONAL MODEL ABOVE

MACK 56-57

('58)

Mack TRUCKS

VARIOUS H-60 C.O.E. TYPES RESTYLED 1954, CONTINUED TO 1962. (EXAMPLE AT TOP LEFT)

('58)

1955 TO 1958 PRESIDENT OF MACK TRUCKS, INC. (PETER O. PETERSON) HOLDING MODEL OF MACK "AC" "BULLDOG" TRUCK

58-59 A

2 VIEWS

1958 INTERCITY "DEMONSTRATOR" BUS (ONE OF A KIND)

('58) C.O.E., newer-style

('58)

new 1959½ G SERIES C.O.E. has ALL-ALUMINUM CAB WITH FLAT FRONT. GRILLE and HEADLTS. LIKE TYPE AT UPPER LEFT OF THIS PG. 205 TO 262 H.P. DIESEL ENGINE CHOICES

B-61 THERMODYNE DIESEL CONVENT'L.

(CONT'D. ON NEXT PAGE)

MACK 58~59 (A)

HEAVY-DUTY
TRACTOR-TRAILER
(164 TONS GROSS)
('57-'58)

INTER-
CITY
BUS

58-59

(CONT'D.)

PROD.:
14,308 ('58)
17,027 ('59)
14,438 ('60)

PROD.:
9,012 ('61)
13,988 ('62)
16,012 ('63)

60-65

G.O.E.

('60)

('62)

('62)

PRODUCTION: 14,173 ('64)
20,269 ('65)

MODELS INTRO. BETWEEN 1960 and 1965:

R607 to 640, R715, R719,
R737, R609R, R615R, U401 to U615, B13, B23, B37 (1 ONLY,)
B45, B47, B53, B57, B68, B79,
B331, B332, B334, B422, B424, B428, B462,
B576, B615, B755, B815, B4226, B4626 (1 ONLY,)
C607, C609, C611, C615, FC13, FC23, G72, G77,
H68, H81, H813, N68, N422, N442,
18, 20, 25, 30, 32, 40, 45, 50, 60, 65, 70,
DM607, DM815, F607, F609, F611, F615,
F715, F719, F723, F731, F737, F741, F743, F745,
F749, F759, F763, F765, F600R, F700R, MB401,
MB403, MB410, MB605, MB609, R401, R403, R410
R403R, R763

('64)

MACK = 58~65

UNITIZED FIBERGLASS **CA 361**

UNITIZED FIBERGLASS **U SERIES**

NEW DESIGN MACK COMMANDCAB

OFFSET CAB

Mack TRUCKS

U SERIES & DM 400 · 600 SERIES CAB

PROD.: 19,579

66

MODELS: R608F, R611F, DM403, DM410, DM477, DM609, 6076, DM611, DM615, DM640, DM807 to 811, DM819, DM831-845 DM863, F685, MB402, MB607, R402, R709, R711, R731, R611R, U640 ('66 ONLY)

CAB OVER ENGINE NON-SLEEPER **CA 38**

F MODEL STANDARD NON-SLEEPER CAB

('66)

INTRO. 1967: PK5RP, R685F, CF608, CF719, 100, DM401, 6096, 6116, 6118, DM685, 6856, DM823, DM865, DM885, R685, R723, R773, R685R MB477, R477,

67

Maxidyne®

ENDT- 675 6-CYL. DIESEL ENG. INTRO. 9-67

MACK TRUCKS, INC. ALLENTOWN, PA.

"THE TRUCK CAPITAL OF THE WORLD"

note HORIZONTAL RADIATOR SLOTS

C.O.E.

The Mack FL Western

MACK WESTERN

DM-600 HEAVY DUMP

('67)

PROD.: 16,634 ('67)

new "RL" (at WESTERN FACTORY)

MACK WESTERN HAYWARD, CAL.

"THE TRUCK CAPITAL OF THE WEST"

PROD. : 19,166

68

MODELS
INTRO. 1968 :
FC 607B , CF 611,
CF 685, DM 487,
F 707, F 709, F 711,
F 739, F 773, F 785,
MB 487, MB 611, R 487,
R 607R

(11-MONTH PROD. = 17,488)

ENGINE

Maxidyne*

ENDT864 :

11-MONTH PROD. = 21,348
FULL YEAR = 23,583

- Twin-turbocharged Mack V-8 for highest horsepower requirements.
- 300 hp at 2300 rpm.
- Torque output peaks at 1600 rpm—788 lb.-ft.
- Excellent performance, even when hauling top legal loads at top legal speeds.

69

FL SERIES

MB →

LATER '69
(with
RADIATOR
GUARD)

R
SERIES

FL

MODELS
INTRO.
1969 :
35
F 795
MB 685
R 489
R 739
R 785

note
STYLING
SIMILARITY
BETWEEN
THE
"R"
and
"U"
SERIES.

U SERIES

1969 = MACK BUYS
INTO HAYES TRUCKS
OF
CANADA

MACK = 68~69

306

BULLDOG
HOOD MASCOT →

Mack

70

CLOSE-UP VIEW OF
FRONT
END (R
SERIES)

TOP
DETAILS
OF 6-CYL. DIESEL
"MAXIDYNE"
ENGINE
237 HP

MACK

INTRO. 1970 :

FCR-685B, DM491, DM895,
F761, F819 (1 ONLY,)
R761, R795,
R711R (1970 ONLY,)
R715R (1970 ONLY,) R785R (1970 ONLY,)
R795R, U661 (1970-1971,)
U795, RD795

"R" SERIES

140 TO 380 HP
5 TO 18-SPEED TRANSMISSION

"ALL-AMERICAN"

SOME 1970 MODELS
PAINTED IN RED, WHITE
AND BLUE PATRIOTIC
COLORS, FOR ADVERTISING
PURPOSES.

MACK SOLD MORE DIESEL-POWERED
TRUCKS IN 1970 THAN ANY OTHER
MANUFACTURER. OWN DIESEL 6 OR V8s
(OTHER BRANDS OF DIESEL ENGINES AVAIL. BY
SPECIAL ORDER)

PRODUCTION:
22,057

MACK ~ 70

Mack

TRUCKS

FL700L
FS700L Series

Western

FL700L & FS700L Series

(SOME OF THESE MODELS AVAIL. DURING FINAL MONTHS OF 1970.)

LIGHTWEIGHT "RL" SERIES CONVENTIONAL

Mack Western

Mack western mixer boasts 238 hp engine

RL-600 CHASSIS

new U-700 SERIES

WIDE RANGE OF DIESEL ENGINE OPTIONS 140 HP TO 434 HP

71

C.O.E. F SERIES GETS IMPROVED CAB, AUG., 1971. (F SERIES ILLUSTRATED, TOP LEFT, TOP RIGHT.)

325-hp Maxidyne V-8 diesel
ENGINE

MACK ~ 71

New from MACK

AVAILABLE 375 H.P. DIESEL V8

HEAVY CONSTR. DUMP

The new 375 hp V-8 diesel with companion Maxitorque® 10-speed splitter transmission. An engine-transmission combination for top-performance operations—enough power to easily handle highest gross weight in twin or triple combinations on thruway and Interstate runs.

This V-8 Thermodyne diesel produces more horsepower per cubic inch than any engine ever produced by Mack—and provides the power needed for highest gross loads at the highest sustained speeds.

To go with the new 375 hp diesel, Mack engineering has developed the new Maxitorque 10-speed splitter transmission. With selector mounted at the top of the single-stick shift lever, the air-shifted splitter reduces clutching by 40% for substantially prolonged clutch life.

AS AT RIGHT, SOME 1972 C.O.E.s WITH SOLID RADIATOR FILLER DOOR, and 4 FEWER HORIZONTAL BUMPER SLOTS THAN ON TYPE ILLUSTR. BELOW.

72 A

16000-MILE (OR 300 SHORT-HAUL ENG. HOUR) **EXTENDED SERVICE INTERVAL**

Now offered by Mack Trucks
• Increased oil pan capacity
• Improved oil and water flow

6-CYL. DIESEL ENG.

MACK WESTERN F8795LST C.O.E. SLEEP. TRACTOR

Auto Hauler

(325 HP TURBO V8 DIESEL)

EXTEND. SRV. INTERVAL PKG.
2 SPIN-ON OIL FILTERS.
new " " COOLANT CONDITIONER,
PRIMARY + SECONDARY FUEL FILTERS.
SPLINE-DRIVEN POWER STEER. PUMP.
new AIR COND. COMPRESSOR
3-BELT FAN/ALTERNATOR DRIVE
ETC.

THIS TYPE W. MACK NAME ON GRILLE.

(CONT'D. NEXT PG.)

MACK ~ 72 (A)

the INTERSTATER

COCKPIT-STYLE WRAP-AROUND CONSOLE features the most important advance in instrument configuration in years — the RCCC and SAE-recommended control and instrument grouping, which makes driver change a safer and surer operation. And the new console with rich wood-grain finish is made of steel to provide greater safety, strength and protection.

Mack

INTERSTATER
(90° TILT CAB)

72 (CONT'D.)
B

86" BBC SLEEPER (50" BBC NON-SLEEPER AL-90 AVAIL.) WITH 180-325 HP DIESEL ENGS.

New 36"-wide sleeper

There's more to the new Mack INTERSTATER...

MACK ~ 72 (B)

Mack INTERSTATER . . . ideal for high-mileage, long-haul operations.

Mack TRUCKS

('74 - '75
FL
SIMILAR)

INTERSTATER

WESTERN INTER- STATER (LTWT. C.O.E.)

Mack Western INTERSTATER Series . . . lightweight for maximum payloads

MB SERIES (FOR HEAVY LOCAL DELIVERY SERVICE)

R SERIES CONVENTIONAL

Mack R Series . . . most popular over-the-road conventional tractor.

Mack R Model's new RCCC-SAE console with high-visibility, standard instrumentation arrangement. Note attractive, non-glare beige color scheme.

1974 = MACK SELLS HAYES (CANADA) TRUCK HOLDINGS TO GEARMATIC DIV. OF PACCAR, (WHICH DISCONTINUED HAYES IN 1975.)

DRIVER R IMPROVED

73 -75

CF PUMPER FIRE TRUCK

U SERIES (SHORT 90" BBC)

WITH OFFSET CABS

On August 22, 1972, the 50,000th Maxidyne-Powered Mack Rolled Off the Assembly Line

The 50,000th engine has the same horse-power and performance as the first—the revolutionary Maxidyne that was introduced six years ago

Mack in-line six and V-8 diesels

LIGHTWEIGHT (HVY. DUTY) DM SERIES MIXER

V8 = 285 HP
6 = 237 HP

1973 EXAMPLES ILLUSTRATED

DM SERIES

MACK = 73~75

HEAVY-DUTY CONVENT'L.
R SERIES (RT.)

('76)

CRUISE-
LINER
C.O.E.

MACK
The Greatest Name in Trucks

MACK'S
FIRST
all-new
C.O.E.
SINCE
1962.

EARLIEST (1975½)
CRUISE-LINERS had CIRCLE
MEDALLION AT CENTER OF GRILLE.

('77)

CONVENTIONAL
R,
RD, RL,
RM, RS,
U, DM,
DMM, HMN, MB (LOW TILT (AB) and F, WL and WS
C.O.E.
TYPES
IN 1978,
175 TO
450 HP
DIESELS.

76-79

CRUISE-LINER'S
DIESEL
ENG.

Mack
Maxidyne

WITH
"MAXI-
TORQUE"
POWER
TRAIN

('78)

SUPER-
LINER CONV.
LIVESTOCK CARRIER

MACK = 76~79

MACK ★★★★★

175 HP (OR 210 HP TRACTOR) IN **MID-LINER** C.O.E.

STARTS 1981

MANY OLDER SERIES ALSO CONT'D.

↑ **ULTRA-LINER** STARTS 1983

ALSO AVAIL. WITH 2 ROUND HEADLTS. ↗

<u>MC</u> ('80) (MR SIMILAR)

1980s

Bulldog → HOOD MASCOT CONTINUES

SHOWN WITH SLEEPER CAB ↓

CONVENTIONAL **SUPER-LINER** ('80)

Super-Liner

('84)

950

note : AFTER 1982, FRONT BUMPER OF SUPER-LINER has JUST <u>ONE</u> RECTANGULAR SLOT.

IN 1990, MACK BECOMES A WHOLLY-OWNED SUBSIDIARY OF THE FRENCH MOTOR VEHICLE MANUFACTURER, RENAULT V.I. (VEHICULES INDUSTRIELS.) PRODUCTION CONT'D.

MACK = 1980s

MARMON-HERRINGTON
INDIANAPOLIS, INDIANA

TRUCK PRODUCTION
BEGAN 1931

MARMON
CARS
BUILT BY
MARMON
MOTOR CAR
CO., UNTIL
1933
(EST. 1902)

NAME
OF
TRUCKS
SHORTENED
SIMPLY TO
MARMON
IN 1963
AND SINCE,
EXCEPT FOR
A SHORT TIME
IN 1973 WHEN
"MARMON-
HERRINGTON"
NAME
RE-APPEARED.

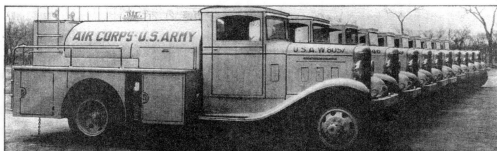

← BUILT
MARCH, 1931
WITH 6-CYL.
HERCULES
ENGINES.

ABOVE:
TRUCK PRODUCTION
BEGINS 1931, WITH THIS FLEET
OF 33 AIRPLANE REFUELING
TRUCKS FOR ARMY AIR
CORPS.

← ON
THESE
EARLY MODELS,
NOTE THE DOOR-TYPE
HOOD SIDE VENTS and ARCHED
SIDE WINDOWS.

TH-320-6
SHOWN WITH MARMON V-16
CAR, FOR SIZE COMPARISON

('32)

1930s

L. TO R.: A.W. HERRINGTON, PRES.;
WALTER C. MARMON, CHAIRMAN;
D. GLOSSBRENNER ; B. DINGLEY

40-Ton, 1200-inch Wheel-
base Truck-and-Trailer
Combination

('32)   new STRAIGHT-TOP WINDOWS, VERT. LOUVRES

Truck-Tractor
(5 TO 7 TON)

190-Horsepower, Six-
Cylinder Motor Drives All
Six Wheels Through a
Twelve-Speed Gearset

885 CID
ENGINE
('32)

6-W-D,
12-SPEED
TRANS.
WESTINGHOUSE
AIR BRAKES
('32-33)

12
MODELS,
2-15 TONS
1932 STYLE STILL BLT. IN 1942!
Marmon-Herrington

STARTING 1935,
MARMON-
HERRINGTON
SUPPLEMENTS ITS
HEAVY-DUTY LINE
BY CONVERTING
FORD TRUCKS
AND CARS TO
SPECIAL ALL-WHEEL
DRIVE LIGHT AND
MEDIUM-DUTY
UNITS.   '39 MARMON-
FORD
ILLUS.

LATER '30s HEAVY-DUTY
LINE KNOWN AS "**C**"
SERIES (6 CYL.,
78 TO 180 HP)

MARMON-HERRINGTON ~ 1930s

314

MARMON-HERRINGTON

HEAVY MARMON TRUCKS OF EARLY 1940s
SIMILAR IN APPEARANCE TO 1932 MODELS

('41)

('42)

('42)
MARMON-
FORD TRUCK
4-W-D
CONVERSIONS
('40-STYLE)

EARLY
1940s

1940 PRICE RANGE :
$ __1557.__ (LD-4)(FORD V8)
$ __16,105.__ TO (DDS-D-1000)
(WITH 6-CYL., 707CID
HERCULES DIESEL ENGINE
176 HP @ 1800 RPM)

MILITARY VEHICLES

('42)

ARMORED
CAR

ARMY
TANK

4-W-D ARMY WINCH TRUCK ('40)

('45)

"LOCUST"
AIRBORNE
TANK

War Service

MARMON-HERRINGTON ~ EARLY 1940s

MARMON-HERRINGTON

('48)

TELEPHONE LINE TRUCK (CONVERSION OF FORD) 4-W-D ('44)

('46)

SINCE 1948, SAN FRANCISCO PURCHASED 174 M-H TROLLEY (ELECTRIC) BUSES.

TANKS, ARMORED CARS, ETC., DURING WW2

SOME EARLIER MODELS SEEN WITH 2-PC. WINDSHIELD 4-W-D or 6-W-D

NOTE EXTRA DRIVE AXLE IN FRONT

VAN

('45)
Front-Wheel-Drive

New
"DELIVR-ALL" TRUCK (FRONT WHEEL DRIVE)

(AVAILABLE 1945 TO 1952.)

All-Wheel-Drive ('50)

new RANGER V-8
FORD 4-W-D CONVERSION

('50)
VAN

139 TO 212 HP, 1959

1940s
AND LATER

1959 MODELS: 104, 504, 604, 704, 804
C704, C754, C804, C854.
6-WHEELERS: T756, T806
ALL WITH FORD 6 or V8 ENGINES, 4WD
(SCHOOL BUS CHASSIS UNITS ALSO AVAIL.)

new

CHICAGO, M-H TROLLEY BUS FLEETS IN INDIANAPOLIS, COLUMBUS, CLEVELAND, DAYTON, CINCINNATI, YOUNGSTOWN, MILWAUKEE, K.C., SHREVEPORT, NEW ORLEANS, S.F., DENVER, LITTLE ROCK, PHILADELPHIA, DAYTON-OAKWOOD (AS OF 1950)

STARTS 4-50

MARMON-HERRINGTON

631

TROLLEY BUS AVAIL. 1946 TO 1955, AGAIN IN 1959.

('50) 27 or 31-PASS. TRANSIT BUS (GAS)
(REPLACES FORD BUS)

200

BLT. 1950 TO 1955

Marmon-Herrington 1940s AND LATER

MARMON-HERRINGTON

(and *MARMON*) (1963 ON)

(TILT-CAB) "HDT" SLEEPER C.O.E.

ALL-ALUMINUM CABS

4-W-D FORD CONVERSIONS AND SCHOOL BUS CHASSES DURING '50s and '60s.)

(INDIANAPOLIS PRODUCTION UNTIL 1963) COMPANY ACQUIRED BY SPACE CORPORATION IN 1964.

special-use truck

('70)

IN ADDITION TO BUILDING OWN UNITS MARMON-HERRINGTON ALSO CONVERTS FORD, CHEVROLET, GMC, DODGE and INTERNATIONAL CHASSIS UNITS TO ALL-WHEEL DRIVE.

"CHDT" CONVENTIONAL (CHOICE OF VARIOUS 6, V-6, V-8, V-12 DIESEL ENGINES): CATERPILLAR, CUMMINS, DETROIT)

1970s ON

('72)

391 CID FORD INDUSTRIAL V8 ENGINE. (4-W-D) ALSO AVAIL. IN 4×2, 6×4, 4×4 and 6×6 DRIVE.

FACTORY IN LEBANON, INDIANA. HEADQUARTERS AT GARLAND, TEXAS (and DALLAS) 1964 ON

C.O.E. ('76½)

('76½)

Marmon Designs Sleeper Box

('76½)

new 86" ALUMINUM SLEEPER CAB (LATE '73) SIMILAR TO 76½

CONVENTIONAL

NEW HEADQUARTERS AT MARMON MOTOR CO., DALLAS, TEXAS, 1970s

CUMMINS NTC-350 ENG.
1981 = MONSANTO "SPRAY-GUARD" RAIN-FLAPS STD. on PREMIUM TRACTORS.

MARMON TRUCKS DISCONTINUED IN 1997.

MARMON HERRINGTON ~ 1970s on

MOTOR COACH INDUSTRIES, INC.
The Mark of Responsibility
Pembina, North Dakota

ORIGINATED 1937 IN CANADA ; PEMBINA, N.D. FACTORY OPENED 1963.

MC-1 (1959-1961)

MC-2 (196 -1963)

MCI

64-65
Model MC-5 Challenger. ('64-65)

BUS
Greyhound

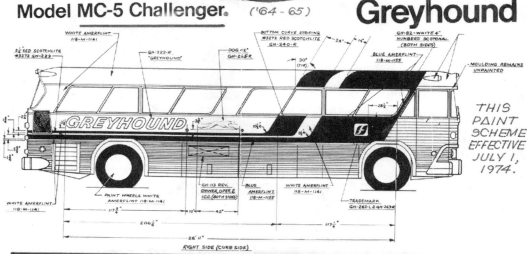

THIS PAINT SCHEME EFFECTIVE JULY 1, 1974.

RIGHT SIDE (CURB SIDE)

65-70

MC-5A ('66-'67)

• 1965 and 1966 Model MC-5A "Challengers®", equipped with air conditioning. Lavatory. Air-suspension ride. Reclining seats.

MCI MC-5C

MC-5 VARIATIONS CONT'D. DURING THE 70s.

MCI ADVERTISING SLOGAN ('78)

MCI so far ahead it's all alone!

261" WB 35' LONG DIESEL V8 252 HP ('72)

MC-5B (1971) 1972

35' MC-5C ('78)

MCI = 64~70s

('67)

MC1

Model MC-6 Supercruiser®

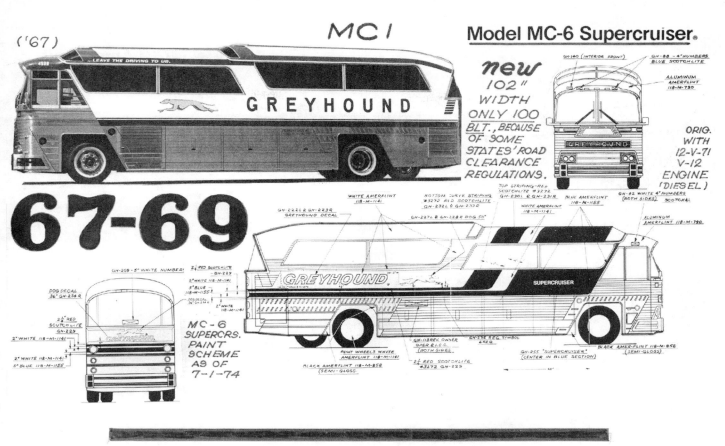

new 102" WIDTH ONLY 100 BLT., BECAUSE OF SOME STATES' ROAD CLEARANCE REGULATIONS.

ORIG. WITH 12-V-71 V-12 ENGINE (DIESEL)

67-69

MC-6 SUPERCRS. PAINT SCHEME A9 OF 7-1-74

('72)

Model MC-7 Super 7 Scenicruiser®

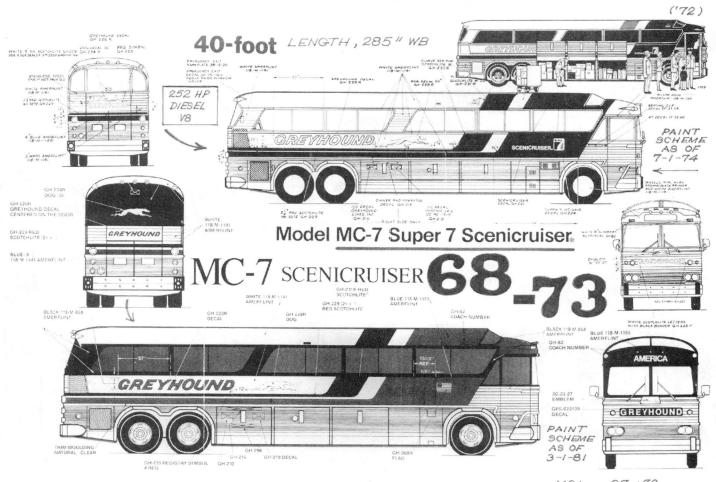

40-foot LENGTH, 285" WB

252 HP DIESEL V8

PAINT SCHEME AS OF 7-1-74

MC-7 SCENICRUISER 68-73

PAINT SCHEME AS OF 3-1-81

MCI — 67~73

MCI

40' Model MC-8 Americruiser.

WHITE 5" NUMBER SCOTCHLITE GH209 USE EDGE SEALER '3M' No 3950

DOG DECAL 36" No GH234R

FLAT BLACK FINISH

67"

FLAT BLACK FINISH

WORD "GREYHOUND"

WHITE AMERFLINT 118-M-1141

DOG 50" LG RIGHT SIDE

FLAT BLACK FINISH

27"

TOP STRIPING ROOF

WHITE AMERFLINT 118-M-1141

BLUE AMERFLINT 118-M-1155

ALUMINUM AMERFLINT 118-M-790

WHITE 4" NUMBERS SCOTCHCAL GH82

BUS NUMBER 4" SIDE & FRONT

FLAT BLACK FINISH

PANEL EDGE

AMERICRUISER

FLAT BLACK FINISH

EMBLEM

GREYHOUND

93 DECAL

SEATING CAPACITY DECAL

FLAG - RIGHT SIDE

GREYHOUND DECAL No GH22GR

2" WHITE AMERFLINT 118-M-1141

RED BAND ON SCREEN TO MATCH RED SCOTCHLITE No 3272 BOTH SIDES

2½" RED SCOTCHLITE No 3272 GH 229

OWNER & OPERATOR

PHOENIX ARIZONA

CURVE STRIPING SIDE RIGHT HAND

WHITE AMERFLINT 2" BAND 118-M-1141

DECAL-AMERICRUISER

98"

BLUE AMERFLINT 8" BAND 118-M-1155

WHEELS, RIMS & HUBS PERMA-PLATE PRIMER & WHITE AMERFLINT 118-M-1141

WORD "GREYHOUND" REGISTRY SYMBOL

PAINT SCHEME ABOVE AS OF 7-1-74

MC-8 CRUSADER

MCI MC-8

A

B

FLOOR LINE

STEP DOWN

35.00" CLEAR OPENING

46.50 CLEAR OPENING

84.00" INSIDE

B

WEAVER COACH WORKS
ELKHART, INDIANA
(MODIFICATION)

('78)

WITH GMC 8V-71 DIESEL ENGINE

TMC DIV. STARTS 1973, ROSWELL, N.M.

CRUSADER

CHARTER

CRUSADER

73-78

MCI
MC-8 AMERICRUISER

PAINT SCHEME BELOW AS OF 3-1-81

TOP VIEW

MC-8 TOP & SIDE

FLAT BLACK FINISH 118 M-858

WHITE 6 NO. SCOTCHLITE GH209 USE EDGE SEALER 3M NO. 3950

DOG DECAL 36 NO. GH234R

WHITE AMERFLINT 118-M-1141

2" WHITE AMERFLINT 118-M-1141

GREYHOUND

2½" RED SCOTCHLITE NO. 3272

8 BLUE AMERFLINT 118-M-1155

MOULDING NOT PAINTED

FLAT BLACK FINISH 118-M-858

GREYHOUND DECAL NO. GH322

GH235 REGISTRY SYMBOL 4 REG.

FLAT BLACK FINISH 118-M-858

67"

FLAT BLACK FINISH 118-M-858

WHITE 118-M-1141 AMERFLINT

RED SCOTCHLITE GH231R

27"

WHITE AMERFLINT 118-N-1141

16

BLUE AMERFLINT 118-M-1155

GREYHOUND DECAL GH323 GH324R DOG (50)

CURVE STRIPING SIDE RIGHT HAND GH233R

GH82

MC-8 FRONT & BACK

WHITE 4 NUMBERS SCOTCHCAL GH82

BLUE 118-M-1155 AMERIFLINT

3F-33-61

3F-33-54

DOG EMBLEM 3C-33-27

FRONT GREYHOUND PANEL IS-261 thru 269

FLAT BLACK FINISH 118

AMERICA

GREYHOUND

GREYHOUND

PANEL EDGE

¼"

11½"

¼"

RED BAND ON SCREEN TO MATCH RED SCOTCHLITE NO. 3272 BOTH SIDES

2½" RED SCOTCHLITE NO. 3272 GH 229

GH210 GH219 GH216

WHITE AMERFLINT 2 BAND 118-M-1141

BLUE AMERFLINT 8 BAND 118 M-1155

GH266 GH268R

993.16

WHEELS, RIMS & HUBS PERMA-PLATE PRIMER & WHITE AMERFLINT 118-M-1141

FRONT

MCI = 73~78

320

MCI

REAR DETAILS

5 WHITE NUMBERS
SCOTCHLITE GH 208
USE EDGE SEALER
3M. NO. 3950

36 DOG DECAL NO. GH-234R

WHITE DUPONT
IMRON N8015U

ALL PAINT & SCOTCHLITE
BANDS CONTINUE AROUND
REAR

GREYHOUND DECAL NO. GH-322

('79)

MCI **MC-9**

A   8

FLOOR LINE

STEP DOWN

92.00 CLEAR
OPENING

41.50
CLEAR
OPENING

54.00
INSIDE

MC-9 CRUSADER II

79 ON

(STARTS 12-78)

MC-9 AMERICRUISER

WITH
DETROIT DIESEL 8V-71
OR 6V92-TA
11.50 × 20 TIRES (TUBE TYPE)
OR 12.5 × 22.5 TUBELESS

PLEASE NOTE:
PLACEMENTS OF SCOTCHLITE DECALS ON ROOF AND
SIDE BELT AREA ARE OPTICALLY ADJUSTED BY
APPROX. 5

4 WHITE NUMBERS
SCOTCHCAL GH 82

AMERICA

BLUE DUPONT IMRON
N8016U

GREYHOUND

FRONT GREYHOUND PANEL
3R-35-261 THRU 265

BLACK

MLDGS. INCLUDING
MNTG. FLANGE PAINTED
BLACK TO MATCH
WINDOW AREA
SEMI-GLOSS BLACK
DUPONT IMRON 99U
FLAT CATALYST

WORD GREYHOUND
GH-323

WHITE DUPONT IMRON
N8015U

50 LONG RIGHT SIDE DOG

RED SCOTCHLITE
NO. 3272

30

26

16

13 3/8"   4"
12 1/4"

WHITE DUPONT
IMRON N8015U

BLUE DUPONT IMRON
N8016U

4 WHITE NUMBERS
SCOTCHCAL GH 82

BLACK

FLAG

GREYHOUND

AMERICRUISER 2

MOULDING NOT
PAINTED

DECAL-SEATING
CAPACITY

**PAINT SCHEME
AS OF 3-1-81**

RED BAND PAINTED ON
TO MATCH RED SCOTCHLITE
NO. 3272 BOTH SIDES

47 1/4"

3R-33-59
3R-33-60
3R-33-61

3R-33-103

REGISTRY SYMBOL
3R-33-74

332 3/4"

AMERICRUISER DECAL
WHITE SCOTCHCAL GH-266
BOTH SIDES

WHEELS RIMS & HUBS
PERMA-PLATE PRIMER
& WHITE DUPONT
IMRON N8015U

FRONT
/ LEFT
SIDE
VIEW

AMERICA

GREYHOUND

AMERICRUISER 2

GREYHOUND

THIS TYPE IN REGULAR
SERVICE IN
MID-1980s
(FROM 1985
GREYHOUND
ADVERTISEMENT.)
↓

NEW

MC-96 A3
(3 AXLES)
OR MC-96 A2 (2 AXLES)

THE NEW MCI

SPECIAL

A NEW STANDARD FOR THE INDUSTRY

AMERICRUISER 2

84 ON

MCI
The Mark of Responsibility

MURTY BROS.

MFD. BY
MURTY BROS.,
PORTLAND, OREGON

ESTABLISHED
1949

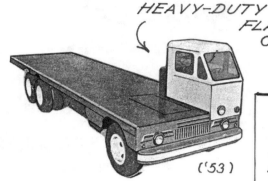

HEAVY-DUTY
FLAT-TOP
CARGO TRUCK
(TYPE OF
1952~1956)

DESIGNED FOR
CARRYING PIPE,
LUMBER, OTHER
LONG LOADS THAT
WOULD NORMALLY
REQUIRE A TRACTOR
AND SEMI-TRAILER.

10-TON with
SINGLE-AXLE DRIVE
has 25' DECK and
179" TURNING WB.

('53)

15-TON DUAL-AXLE DRIVE MODEL
has 30' DECK and 204" WB

Nash MOTORS
CO.,
KENOSHA,
WISCONSIN

NASH

TRUCKS MFD.
1917~1929;
1947~1949
(CARS MFD.
1917~1957)

47-49
6 CYL.

NASH TRUCK
STYLING
SOMEWHAT
SIMILAR TO
1947 NASH
CAR.

('49)

CAB / CHASSIS
MODEL WITH WRECKER BODY
ATTACHED

MURTY BROS. / Nash

(*ESTABLISHED 1917*)

OSHKOSH (MOTOR) TRUCK CORP.,
OSHKOSH, WI.

OSHKOSH

2-TON MODEL B STAKE $3500.

130" WB

18 →

4 CYL. HERSCHELL-SPILLMAN ENG. IN EARLY TYPE ABOVE

4-WHEEL DRIVE

4 SP. TRANS.

← **25** ON

4-CYL. HERCULES ENGINES IN 2½-TON "B" TYPES.

2-TON "AW" and "AAW" (130", 165" W.B., WISC. ENG.)
2½-TON "BO" and "BBO" (146", 165" W.B.
4-TON "F" (146" W.B., WAUKESHA ENG.)
('25)

(1928 "R" EXPRESS 1½-TON AVAIL. *with* 4-CYL. HERCULES OR 6-CYL. WISC. ENGINES.)
(4 CYL. IN '27.)

4-WHEEL DRIVE,
4-WHEEL STEER
FIRST OF RUBBER-TIRED EARTHMOVERS TO GO INTO PRODUCTION.

MODEL "TR" (INTRO. 1933)

32-35

'32 MODELS			
"L"	2½ TONS	70	H.P.
"H"	3 "	73	"
"HC"	3½ "	90	"
"HXC"	4 "	106	"
"FHX"	5 "	112	"

(H.P. DETERMINED @ 2000 RPM.)
6-CYL. HERCULES ENGINES IN ALL MODELS.

146" W.B.
STANDARD ('32)

953A
DEALER WIS. 32

(1½-2-TON "JSW," "JSB" MODELS AVAIL. 1933.)

Nº 3

The "Oshkosh" Maintainer

AVAIL. 1935-1939

OSHKOSH === TO 35

OSHKOSH
MOTOR TRUCK CORP.,
OSHKOSH, WISCONSIN

OSHKOSH

(ESTABLISHED 1917)

35-36

6-CYL. HERCULES ENGINES
(263 TO 855 C.I.D.)

CAPACITIES UP TO 10 TONS

DIESEL ENGINES AVAILABLE IN HEAVY TRUCKS.

'35 MODELS

Model	Capacity
"JB"	1½-2 TONS
"JC"	2 "
"WLD," "WLX"	3 - 3½ "
"B3S," "B3D"	3½ - 4 "
"C3S," "C3D"	4 - 5 "
"FC"	5 "
"FB"	5 - 6 "
"FD"	6 - 7½ "
"BG3"	7½ - 10 "
"GD"	10 TONS

68 - 180 H.P.

146" STD. W.B. ON ALL BUT 165" W.B. "BG3" and "GD," BUT LONGER WHEELBASES (165"-201") AVAIL. on VARIOUS MODELS.

("J" SERIES INTRO. DURING 1935)

36 ON

7.00 × 20" TIRES

10-TON "GD" with SNOWPLOW

2-TON MODEL IS "JCB" IN 1936, has 153" W.B. and HERCULES 282 C.I.D. ENGINE (73 H.P. @ 2800 RPM)

('37)

1940 RANGE:
FROM $2885. "JCB"
TO $10,400. "GD"
VARIOUS 6-CYL. HERC.
ENGINES, 85 TO 199 HP

WARTIME MODEL "W-700"

TRUCKS ILLUSTRATED WERE SHIPPED TO PANAMA

45

and EARLY POSTWAR YEARS

OSHKOSH 35 ON

OSHKOSH

PRE-WAR
STYLING
CONTINUED
ON CERTAIN
OSHKOSH MODELS

48

DURING LATER
1940s, new
6-WHEEL-DRIVE
MODELS, BLT.
FOR OIL FIELDS,
SUGAR CANE
HARVESTING,
ETC.

THIS POSTWAR-STYLE
GRILLE (W/O CHROME)
ALSO FOUND ON 1945
CABLESS 4WD TRACTOR →

49

(W SERIES)
MODEL W-312 TO
MODEL W-1602 BDH

HERCULES, CUMMINS,
BUDA, HALL-SCOTT
ENGINES USED
(ALL 6-CYL.,
404 TO 893 CID
139 TO 295 HP)

GAS AND
DIESEL MODELS

4-W-D
AND
6-WHEELERS

OSHKOSH-HOWE
FIRE TRUCK

50

OSHKOSH = 48 ~ 50

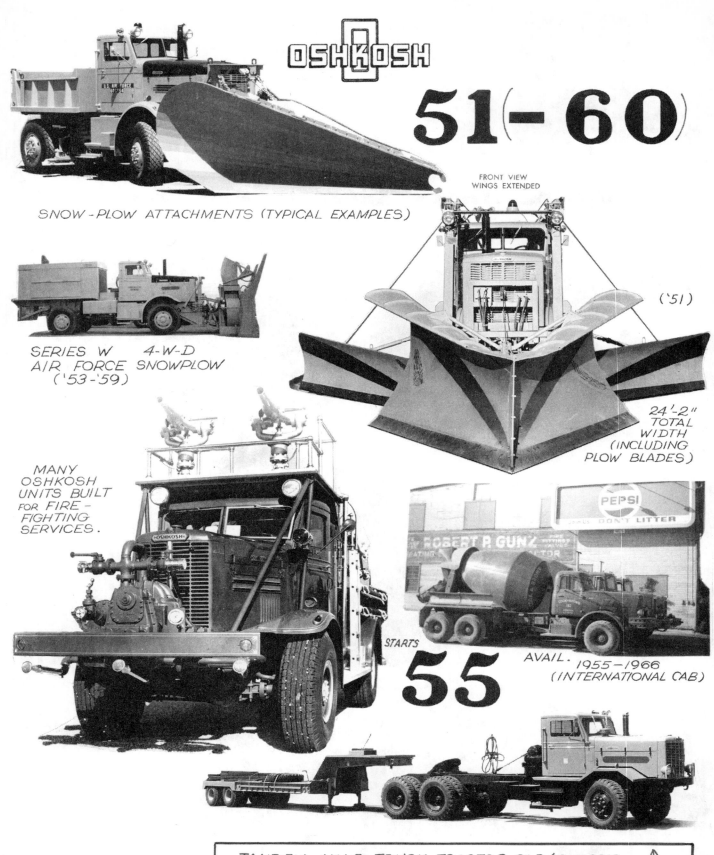

OSHKOSH

51(-60)

SNOW-PLOW ATTACHMENTS (TYPICAL EXAMPLES)

FRONT VIEW
WINGS EXTENDED

('51)

SERIES W   4-W-D
AIR FORCE SNOWPLOW
('53-'59)

24'-2"
TOTAL
WIDTH
(INCLUDING
PLOW BLADES)

MANY
OSHKOSH
UNITS BUILT
FOR FIRE-
FIGHTING
SERVICES.

PEPSI
DON'T LITTER

ROBERT P. GUNZ

STARTS

55

AVAIL. 1955-1966
(INTERNATIONAL CAB)

TANDEM-AXLE TRUCK-TRACTOR CAB/CHASSIS
WITH SPLIT-LEVEL FLATBED TRAILER (ABOVE)

OSHKOSH = 51 ~ 60

326

6 CYL. GAS or DIESEL ENGINES

OSHKOSH

57-62

AMERICAN

6-CYL. INTERNATIONAL, CONTINENTAL, HALL-SCOTT or DIESEL CUMMINS ENGS.

('59)

LONG-HOOD MIXER TRUCK

UTILITY

NEW

MANY OSHKOSH TRUCKS CUSTOM-BUILT FOR SPECIAL PURPOSES. THIS MODEL SOLD TO COAST GUARD.

UNIQUE *new* FORWARD-SLANT WIND-SHIELDS DESIGNED TO PREVENT GLARE and BUILD-UP OF SNOW ON GLASS.

61

new U-44-L "BIG CHIEF" ALL-WHEEL-DRIVE CONVENTIONAL TRACTOR INTRO. 1962 (LONG HOOD, AS ON OTHER MODELS SHOWN HERE)

62

SERIES R

WITH CATERPILLAR DIESEL ENGINE

SERIES C (6×6) (ABOVE)

63

HEAVY-DUTY LOGGER

65

E.J. HERZOG LOGGING COLUMBIA FALLS

note THE GRILLE GUARD

OSHKOSH = 57~65

66

OSHKOSH

SERIES C (new BROADER NOSE)
CONCRETE BLOCK CARRIER
(STYLE SIMILAR UNTIL 1974)

69

SPECIAL BODY
WITH HIGH-REACH BOOM

WITH PLOW

150 TO 270 HP
IN
VARIOUS MODELS

70

CATERPILLAR 1100 OR 1600
DIESEL ENGINES *
IN

NEW
"E" SERIES
(BEGINS 1970)
117~165"
WB

new E SERIES has 50~GAL. FUEL TANK on LEFT SIDE,
PLUS OPTIONAL 50~GAL. TANK
on RIGHT SIDE, MAKING A
100~GAL.
CAPACITY
POSSIBLE.

G SERIES
ARE
6 × 6
TILT-CABS
(C.O.E.)

HAULER TRACTOR
(5 TO 13-SP. FULLER
TRANSMISSIONS)

* 175 TO 270 HP
OSHKOSH = 66~70

MODELS AS OF 10-71:

		DRIVE
P	SERIES	(4 × 4)
R		(6 × 4)
C		(6 × 6)
F		(6 × 6)

F-2 (6 × 6, EXCEPT
  F-2360 and F-3838,
  WHICH ARE 8 × 8,
  and F-3860, WHICH
  IS 10 × 10.)
E SERIES (4 × 2,)
  EXCEPT E-1234
  and E-1244
      (6 × 4)
ALL DIESELS, EXC.
P-2023, AVAIL. w.
GAS OR DIESEL ENG.

MIXER

VARIOUS TYPES
OF UTILITY
BODIES AVAIL.
BY SPECIAL
ORDER.

1970s

('75)

210 - 350 HP
SIMILAR TYPE
P SERIES
SNOW BLOWER
CONTINUES IN
1980s, BUT
WITH UPPER
SECTION OF
HOOD PAINTED
FLAT BLACK
(TO REDUCE
SUN GLARE IN
DRIVER'S CAB.)

P SERIES
SNOW BLOWER
(**H SERIES** SIMILAR)

OSHKOSH = 1970s

FOR THE MARINES

MK 48 LOGISTICAL VEHICLE SYSTEM) (LVS) TRUCK

HEMTT* ('84)

* (HEAVY EXPANDED MOBILITY TACTICAL TRUCK)

OSHKOSH

HOLDS FIREFIGHTING FOAM and WATER (note THE 2 HOSE-GUNS ON UNIT.)

L, M 9 SERIES FIRE TRUCKS AVAIL.

1980s ON

J SERIES
HEAVY TRANSPT. (ABOVE)

('83)

REAR (T SERIES)

B SERIES REFUSE-COLLECTION TRUCKS AVAIL. 1990 TO 1994

(ABOVE)

T SERIES
AIRPORT CRASH / FIRE / RESCUE

V SERIES FORWARD CONTROL BUS CHASSIS AVAIL. (210 H.P.)

NEW S SERIES CONCRETE CARRIER AND MIXER CHASSIS MIXER (9 SERIES) INTRO. 1983.

BELOW : HEAVY TRANSPT., CONSTRUCTION, OR UTILITY TYPE

F SERIES

REAR

T SERIES DASH

OSHKOSH = 1980s ON

330

PETERBILT

(SINCE 1939)

(HEADQUARTERS LATER IN NEWARK, CALIF.)

AL PETERMAN BOUGHT FAGEOL FROM STERLING IN 1939.

EARLY 1939 MODEL WITH GRILLE ↙

Peterbilt MOTORS COMPANY
10700 MAC ARTHUR BOULEVARD   OAKLAND, CALIFORNIA

39-49

12-SPEED TRANSMISSIONS

EARLY MODELS HAVE CIRCULAR HOLES IN BUMPER.

new MODELS START 1949: 280(DD); 6-WH.: 350, 360, 370, 380, 390

('48)

1946 SPECS.: 6-CYL. CUMMINS "HB-600" DIESEL ENGINE with 150 HP @ 1800 RPM 672 CID (THROUGH '53)
6-WHEELER MODELS:
344 DT
345 DT
354 DT
355 DT
ALSO
270 DD (4-W-D)
(1947 and 1948 ONLY)

165" WB and up

RADIATOR GUARDS STILL AVAILABLE

('50)

1951 = new RED OVAL RADIATOR EMBLEM

50-55

(1949 TYPES CONTINUE)

"ALL-ALUMINUM" CONSTRUCTION AVAIL.

('52)

ALUMINUM CAB STD. ON C.O.E. MODEL, INTRO. 1950.

LIVESTOCK CARRIER   ('52)

SOME EARLY C.O.E.s have RADIATOR STYLE LIKE '55, (ILLUSTR. LOWER RT.)

MODELS 281 and 351 ADDED FOR 1955.

C.O.E.

STARTING 1954, IMPROVED CUMMINS DIESEL "NHB-600" ENGINE with new 743 CID, new 200 HP @ 2100 RPM.

('55)

PETERBILT = 39~55

331

Peterbilt CLOSER VIEW OF CONVENTIONAL

('56)

VARIOUS OPTIONAL WBs AVAILABLE

CHOICE OF MODELS REDUCED FOR 1956:

MODEL		
280	175" WB	5.91 – 6.51 GEAR RATIO
280 C.O.E.	114	" "
281	165	" "
6- WHEELERS :		
350	193	6.16 – 6.80
360	198	" "
381	194	10.16
350 C.O.E.	135	6.16 – 6.80
351	190	6.16 – 7.35
360 C.O.E.	135	6.16 – 6.80

INSTR. PANEL HINGED, IN DELUXE CAB (RT.)

CAB

NEW STYLE

SPECIFICATIONS CONT'D. THROUGH 1959, BUT 280 C.O.E. MODEL NO. CHANGED TO 281 FOR 1958.

ALL '59 MODELS WITH 6-CYL. CUMMINS NHB 600 743 CID DIESEL ENGINES 200 HP @ 2100 RPM

56-59

PETERBILT BOUGHT IN 1958 BY PACCAR (PACIFIC CAR AND FOUNDRY CO.)

1960: NEWARK, CALIF. FACTORY BEGINS OPERATIONS.

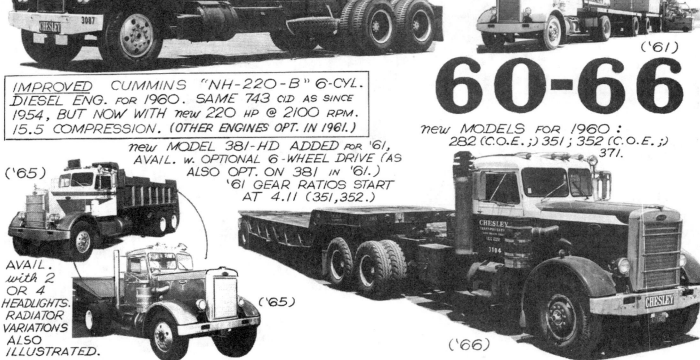

C.O.E. ('60)

new 1960 GEAR RATIOS, FROM 4.41 TO 11.56

('61)

60-66

IMPROVED CUMMINS "NH-220-B" 6-CYL. DIESEL ENG. FOR 1960. SAME 743 CID AS SINCE 1954, BUT NOW WITH new 220 HP @ 2100 RPM. 15.5 COMPRESSION. (OTHER ENGINES OPT. IN 1961.)

new MODELS FOR 1960: 282 (C.O.E.;) 351; 352 (C.O.E.;) 371.

new MODEL 381-HD ADDED FOR '61, AVAIL. W. OPTIONAL 6-WHEEL DRIVE (AS ALSO OPT. ON 381 IN '61.) '61 GEAR RATIOS START AT 4.11 (351,352.)

('65)

AVAIL. with 2 OR 4 HEADLIGHTS. RADIATOR VARIATIONS ALSO ILLUSTRATED.

('65)

('66)

PETERBILT = 56~66

332

new WIDE-RADIATOR TYPE

Peterbilt

CONVENTIONAL

('67)

('68)

C.O.E. "352"
280 HP CUMMINS,
OR OTHERS AVAIL.

('69)

C.O.E.

('70)

"359"

CONVENTIONAL

('71)

comfort and convenience

('71)

LEFT and RIGHT
VIEW of "359"
CONVENTIONAL
with SLEEPER
CAB

DASH (ABOVE)
(CONVENTIONAL)

67-71

11-MONTH
SALES:
1967 = 2066
1968 = 2762
1969 =
(10 MONTH)
3115

SPRING, 1970 = new "PACEMAKER"
C.O.E. MODELS INTRODUCED

('71)

C.O.E.

comfort and convenience
Instruments and controls are arranged for comfort and convenience.

"282"   ('71)

CAB (C.O.E.)

325 OR 375-HP, 6 CYL. CATERPILLAR
DIESEL ENGINES AVAIL. (893 CID)
(CHOICE OF OTHER
ENGINES ALSO)

"352"
with
SLEEPER CAB

PETERBILT = 67~71

('71)

Peterbilt

COMPACT CB C.O.E.
STARTS LATE '70.
COMPACT
CB
('72)

('82)

MODEL
348

INTRO. 1971

slope-nosed Peterbilt mixer

(MODEL 341 DUMP TRUCK ALSO AVAIL.)

ALL DIESELS

ALSO:
281, 351,
288, 289, 358,
359, 381, 383 CONVENTION.
and CB-200, CB-300
C.O.E. TYPES AVAIL. 10-71.

282,
352
TYPE
('72)

C.O.E.
(WITH
DELUXE EQUIP.)

SINCE

1971

54"
TO 110"
BBC
CAB
LENGTHS
AVAIL.

('84)

('84)

MODELS OF
1980s have
SQUARED-OFF
HEADLIGHT
FRAMES.

CONV.
MODELS
289,
359

('73)

DASH. (CONV.)

('74)

Model 200/300

210
TO
262-HP
DIESEL
ENGINES
BY
DETROIT,
CATERPILLAR
OR
CUMMINS.

(218-HP
DETROIT
DIESEL
6172
IS STD.)

CONVENTIONAL
new 20"
WINDSHIELD
WITH NARROW
CENTER POST,
OTHER
IMPROVE-
MENTS
FOR
1973.

C.O.E.

MOST MODELS OF 1970s
CONTINUED INTO 1980s.

PRODUCTION HALTS
1986.

PETERBILT═SINCE 71

NOTE SIDE-
MOUNT SPARE

PLYMOUTH
Trucks and Commercial

(1935 – 1942)
PLYMOUTH DIV. OF
CHRYSLER CORP.

MODEL "PV"
SEDAN DELIVERY
$635.

35

STYLED LIKE
PLYMOUTH CARS.

SUPPLEMENTING
THE REGULAR
LINE OF
DODGE
TRUCKS.

6-CYL. PLYMOUTH
CAR ENGINE

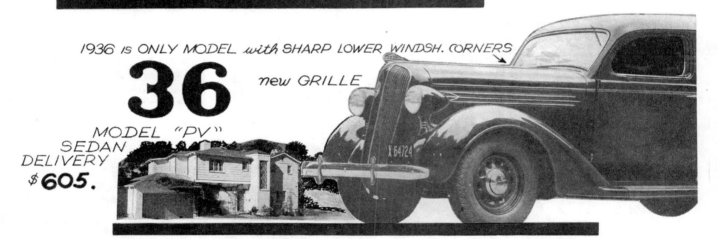

1936 IS ONLY MODEL with SHARP LOWER WINDSH. CORNERS

36

new GRILLE

MODEL "PV"
SEDAN DELIVERY
$605.

MODELS
NOT AS LOW OR WIDE AS EXAGGERATED AD (BELOW) WOULD SUGGEST.

37A

"PT-50" MODELS

AD

ACTUAL PHOTO

PLYMOUTH PICK-UP TRUCK: ½-ton...116" wheelbase...powerful six-cylinder "L-head" truck engine...six-foot steel express body...six-inch X-braced frame with five heavy cross members.

PICKUP IS new FOR 1937.

PLYMOUTH COMMERCIAL SEDAN: 116" wheelbase...powerful six-cylinder "L-head" truck engine...ALL-STEEL body of distinctive modern design...with pay-load space 78" x 54" x 45½"—105 cubic feet.

(CONT'D. NEXT PG.)

NOW
HIGHER and LONGER
THAN PLYMOUTH CAR.
PLYMOUTH = 35 ~ 37

PLYMOUTH

$495.

PICKUP

37 (CONT'D.)

1937 PICKUPS ON ASSEMBLY LINE

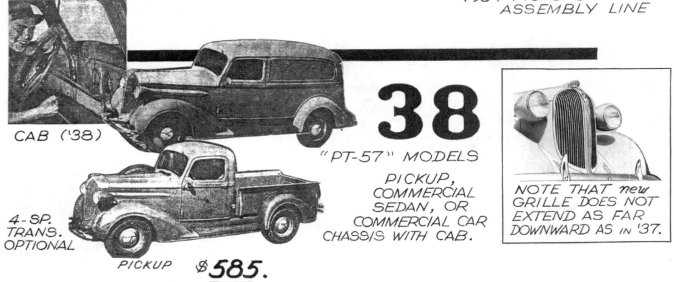

CAB ('38)

4-SP. TRANS. OPTIONAL

PICKUP $585.

38

"PT-57" MODELS

PICKUP, COMMERCIAL SEDAN, OR COMMERCIAL CAR CHASSIS WITH CAB.

NOTE THAT *new* GRILLE DOES NOT EXTEND AS FAR DOWNWARD AS IN '37.

PICKUP REAR VIEW

new DOUBLE REAR DOORS 575.

39

"PT-81" MODELS

ALSO: PICKUP CPE. ('39) AMBULANCE ('39 and '40) 715.

COMMERCIAL CAR →

BEAUTIFUL NEW DISTINCTIVE STYLING

LENGTH EXAGGERATED (IN ORIG. ADVERTISING)
PLYMOUTH = 37~39

PLYMOUTH 40

"PT-105" PICKUP $555.
1/2 T. CH/CAB

$720.

SEDAN DELIVERY

"plymouth" NAME ON TAILGATE CONT'D.

WITH MINOR MODIFICATIONS, 1939 STYLING CONTINUES ON PICKUP (THROUGH '41.)

41

MODEL "P-14-S"

42

"PT-125" PICKUP $593. ('41)
6073 BLT. 1941

ONLY 78 UTILITY SEDANS BUILT IN 1942.

NO PICKUPS IN 1942.

PONTIAC 6

DE LUXE DELIVERY

INTRO. SEPT., 1926

(OAKLAND-PONTIAC DIVISION OF GENERAL MOTORS, PONTIAC, MICH.)
6 CYL. $770.

27

CARTER CARBURETOR
12-GAL. FUEL TANK
4.18 GEAR RATIO

(PONTIAC SEDAN-DELIVERIES AVAIL., 1949-1953.)
(BELOW)

29 x 4.75 TIRES

1928 MODEL ALSO AVAIL.

110" WB

SCREEN BODY

Pontiac
SILVER STREAK

PONTIAC DIVISION of G.M. (OAKLAND NAME DROPPED 1932)

POSTWAR SERIES OF 1949 to 53
← SEDAN DELIVERIES →
STYLED LIKE PONTIAC CARS.
(AS ILLUSTR.)
6-CYL. or STRAIGHT-8

120" WB

PONTIAC $1749. UP
('49)

NEW BODY and 1-PC. WINDSHIELD FOR 1953
('53)

"Dual-Streak" new STYLING

POWELL

(ORIGINALLY ESTAB. 1926; FORMERLY MANUFACTURED MOTOR-SCOOTERS.)

(1954-1956)
POWELL MFG. CO., COMPTON, CALIF.

MID– 1950s

(INTRO. LATE 1954)

117" WB

"SPORT WAGON" PICKUP

87 TO 9.5 HP

$998.

RECONDITIONED 6-CYL. PLYMOUTH ENGINES AND CHASSIS PARTS USED.

RELAY MOTORS CORP., LIMA, OHIO 6 CYLS.

Relay (1927-1933)

(CONSOLIDATED with COMMERCE, GARFORD, and SERVICE TRUCKS.)

BUDA ENGINES USED, BUT CONT. 21-R ENG. IN 5-TON "100-AC" ('30 THROUGH '33.) HERCULES ENG. IN 1933 "230" (5 T.) and "240" (7 T.)

note THE UNIQUE RELAY REAR WHEEL DRIVE MECHANISM.

('28) CONTR. HYDR. BRAKES

↑ 30-A (1½-2 TON) 150" WB

DUMP TRUCK

('28) 70-A (3½ TON) 175" WB note HORIZONTAL LOUVRES

MECH. BRAKES (1928 PROD.: 205)

28 also 50-A (2½ TON) 156" WB

$4950. (CHASSIS)

'29 MODELS : 30-A (1½ T;) 40-A (2 T;) 50-C (2½ T;) 60-C (3 T;) 70-C (3½ T;) 80-C (4 TON) ALSO 20-B (1 T;) S11-B (1½ TON)

'30 MODELS : 15-AA (¾ T;) 15-AB (1 T;) S-11 (1-2 T;) 40 (1½-2½ T;) 50 (2-2½ T;) 60-DA (2½ T;) 60-DB (3 T;) 60-DC (3½ T;) 80 (3-4 T;) 100-AC (5 TON) (6 WHEELERS BELOW)

RADIATOR ('30)

STAKE

29 (PRODUCTION: 511) (CONT. ENG. ALSO IN '31-'32 15AA, '33 15-A.)

30 **31** 50 SW (5 T, 6 W;) 60 SW (7 T, 6 W;) 40 TT; 60 TT (TRUCK TRACT.)

DUAL ENGINES (new) 1931 "300-A" with TWIN LYCOMING STR.-8 ENGINES! 275 HP

V-FRONT ON "300-A"

Westinghouse AIR BRAKES

TANKER ('30)

DEC., 1932 = CO. INTO RECEIVERSHIP, (FOLLOWING PETITION OF HERCULES MOTOR CORP., A CREDITOR.)

NEW OVAL EMBLEM ON RADIATOR INTRO. DURING 1930 SEASON (AS SHOWN ABOVE ON ENLARGED RADIATOR VIEW

IN 1933, A NEW OWNER, (CONSOLIDATED MOTORS) CONTINUES RELAY and GARFORD TRUCKS A FEW MONTHS, AFTER DISCONTINUING BOTH COMMERCE and SERVICE.

RELAY

4.66 GEAR RATIO (4.7, '21)

NO CENTER SIDE CANOPY SIDE SUPPORT ON '15 TO '19 MODELS.

CANOPY DETAILS

REO SPEED WAGON (1904~1967)

REO MOTOR CAR CO. LANSING, MICH.

MODEL "F" 3/4-TON

GRAIN BOX-50 BU. $1625

Express

IDEAL DAIRY TRUCK $1575

TRUCK-FARMERS' DOUBLE DECK VAN $1600

20-21

4 CYLS. (4⅛" × 4½") 128" W.B. 34 × 4½ TIRES

TAXI CHASSIS INTRO. 12-21

22

Canopy Express $1435

MODEL "F" 3/4 - 1¼ TON

Chassis - $1245

SPEED REO WAGON THE GOLD STANDARD OF VALUES

HORN ON LEFT SIDE (UNTIL '23)

JOHNSON CARB.

CYLINDRICAL FUEL TANK IN CAB

SPARE TIRE CARRIER NO LONGER ON LEFT SIDE.

new ½-TON PANEL (WITH 113" WB TAXI CHASSIS) INTRO. 8-23.

NORTHEAST ELECTRICAL SYSTEM

23-24

RESTYLED

GRAVITY FUEL FEED CONTINUES (TO '27)

SPEED WAGON CANOPY EXPRESS

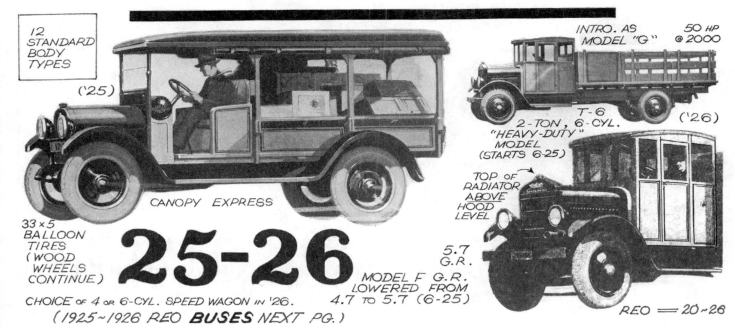

12 STANDARD BODY TYPES

('25)

CANOPY EXPRESS

33 × 5 BALLOON TIRES (WOOD WHEELS CONTINUE)

25-26

CHOICE of 4 OR 6-CYL. SPEED WAGON in '26.

(1925~1926 REO **BUSES** NEXT PG.)

INTRO. AS MODEL "G"

50 HP @ 2000

T-6 2-TON, 6-CYL. "HEAVY-DUTY" MODEL (STARTS 6-25)

('26)

TOP OF RADIATOR ABOVE HOOD LEVEL

5.7 G.R.

MODEL F G.R. LOWERED FROM 4.7 TO 5.7 (6-25)

REO ═ 20~26

339

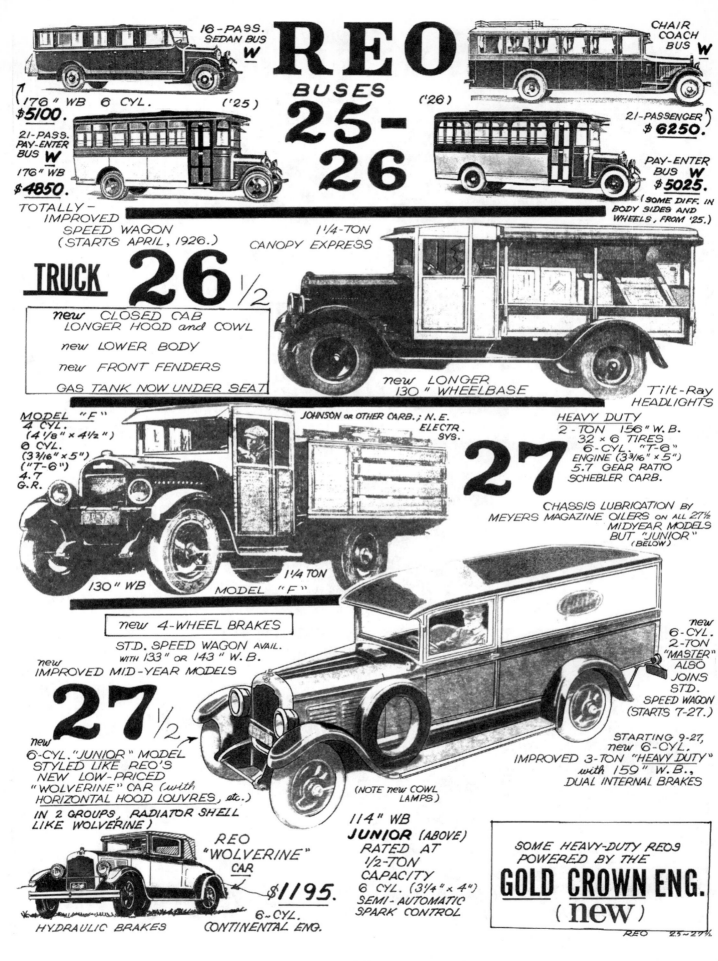

16-PASS. SEDAN BUS W

176" WB 6 CYL.   ('25) $5100.

21-PASS. PAY-ENTER BUS W 176" WB $4850.

REO
BUSES
25-26

('26)

CHAIR COACH BUS W

21-PASSENGER $6250.

PAY-ENTER BUS W $5025.
(SOME DIFF. IN BODY SIDES AND WHEELS, FROM '25.)

TOTALLY-IMPROVED SPEED WAGON (STARTS APRIL, 1926.)

1¼-TON CANOPY EXPRESS

TRUCK 26½

new CLOSED CAB LONGER HOOD and COWL

new LOWER BODY

new FRONT FENDERS

GAS TANK NOW UNDER SEAT

new LONGER 130" WHEELBASE

Tilt-Ray HEADLIGHTS

MODEL "F"
4 CYL.
(4⅛" × 4½")
6 CYL.
(3 3/16" × 5")
("T-6")
4.7
G.R.

JOHNSON or OTHER CARB.; N.E. ELECTR. SYS.

27

HEAVY DUTY
2-TON 156" W.B.
32 × 6 TIRES
6-CYL. "T-6"
ENGINE (3 3/16" × 5")
5.7 GEAR RATIO
SCHEBLER CARB.

CHASSIS LUBRICATION by MEYERS MAGAZINE OILERS on all 27½ MIDYEAR MODELS BUT "JUNIOR" (BELOW)

130" WB

1¼ TON MODEL "F"

new 4-WHEEL BRAKES

STD. SPEED WAGON AVAIL. WITH 133" OR 143" W.B.

new IMPROVED MID-YEAR MODELS

27½

new 6-CYL. "JUNIOR" MODEL STYLED LIKE REO'S NEW LOW-PRICED "WOLVERINE" CAR (with HORIZONTAL HOOD LOUVRES, etc.) IN 2 GROUPS, RADIATOR SHELL LIKE WOLVERINE)

new 6-CYL. 2-TON "MASTER" ALSO JOINS STD. SPEED WAGON (STARTS 7-27.)

STARTING 9-27, new 6-CYL. IMPROVED 3-TON "HEAVY DUTY" with 159" W.B., DUAL INTERNAL BRAKES

(NOTE new COWL LAMPS)

114" WB JUNIOR (ABOVE) RATED AT ½-TON CAPACITY 6 CYL. (3¼" × 4") SEMI-AUTOMATIC SPARK CONTROL

REO "WOLVERINE" CAR

$1195.

HYDRAULIC BRAKES   6-CYL. CONTINENTAL ENG.

SOME HEAVY-DUTY REOS POWERED BY THE

GOLD CROWN ENG. (new)

REO 25-27½

340

28 REO 29

MECH. BRAKES ON ALL BUT "JUNIOR."

SEVERAL BODY VARIETIES ILLUSTRATED

½-TON "JUNIOR" with HYDRAULIC BRAKES $1085.
(LOOKS THE SAME IN 1929,) AS MODEL "BA"?)

6-CYL. CONTINENTAL ENGINE ("16-E") IN ½ and 1-TON ("JR.," "DA," "DC" MODELS)

HYDRAULIC BRAKES ON ADDITIONAL MODELS

3-TON HEAVY-DUTY "GA" 163" W.B. 32 x 6 TIRES →

"TONNER" MODEL "DA" 123" W.B. 30 x 5 TIRES

STANDARD SPEED WAGON "FA" → 137" WB 32 x 6 TIRES HYDR. BRKS.

6-CYL. "GOLD CROWN" ENGINE has CHROME NICKEL BLOCK (AVAIL. IN 1½ TON and up.)

SHIP SAFELY BY MAYFLOWER TRUCK 65 Mayflower Transit Co
NATIONAL HOUSEHOLD MOVERS

OFFICES
NEW YORK   ST. LOUIS
PHILADELPHIA CHICAGO
PITTSBURGH   DETROIT
COLUMBUS   TOLEDO
CLEVELAND   CINCINNATI
WASHINGTON D.C. BUFFALO
NEWARK N.J. INDIANAPOLIS

14 W.B. LENGTHS, 115" TO 179" IN ½, 1, 1½, 2 and 3-TON MODELS.

new, SIMPLER RADIATOR BADGE ON 3-TON "GA" STAKE TRUCK (ILLUSTRATED)

REO "MAYFLOWER" MOVING VAN (LATE '29)
(THIS COULD ALSO BE CONSIDERED AN EARLY 1930 MODEL.)

REO = 28~29

341

14 WHEELBASE LENGTHS, UP TO 210"

REO

PANEL

CONSUMERS LAUNDRY

6 CYL., 268.3 CID ENGINE with 67 HP @ 2800 RPM on 1½-TON, 2-TON, 3-TON MODELS

6-CYL. CONTINENTAL "16-E" IN "JR.15;" REO ENGINES IN OTHERS

30

new "SPEEDWAGON" LETTERING ATTACHED TO RADIATOR CORE.

"JR.15" ½ TON 115" W.B. 6 CYL. 214.7 CID 60 HP @ 2800 4.45 G.R. 6.00 × 18 TIRES
"DF TONNER" 1 TON 135" W.B. 6 CYL. 268.3 CID 80 HP @ 3200 5.2 G.R.
"FA-137," "FE," "FF" 1½ TON 137, 152, 156" W.B. 5.2 G.R.
"FC", "FD", "FH*" 2 TON 152, 168, 142" W.B. 5.7 G.R. 32 × 6.00 TIRES
"GA", "GC", "GD*", "GCS" 3 TON 163, 179, 144, 210" W.B. 6.14, 6.14, 6.85, 6.14 G.R. 32 × 6.00
HIGH-PRESSURE OR BALLOON TIRES
*- AVAIL. AS TRACTOR-TRUCK

METROPOLITAN DELIVERY →

28-45 Passenger School Bus

CAPACITIES TO 7½ TONS (with TRAILERS)

31

MODELS AS IN 1930. FINAL YEAR FOR "JUNIOR 15" ½-TON.

HYDRAULIC BRAKES AND new GRILLE ON LATER 1½-TON MODELS, STARTING 5-31.

EARLY '31 MODEL

MID-YEAR MODEL

STAKE TRUCK (MID-YEAR MODEL)

note THE HORIZONTAL-BARRED RADIATOR QUARD ON ABOVE EXAMPLE.

REO = 30~31

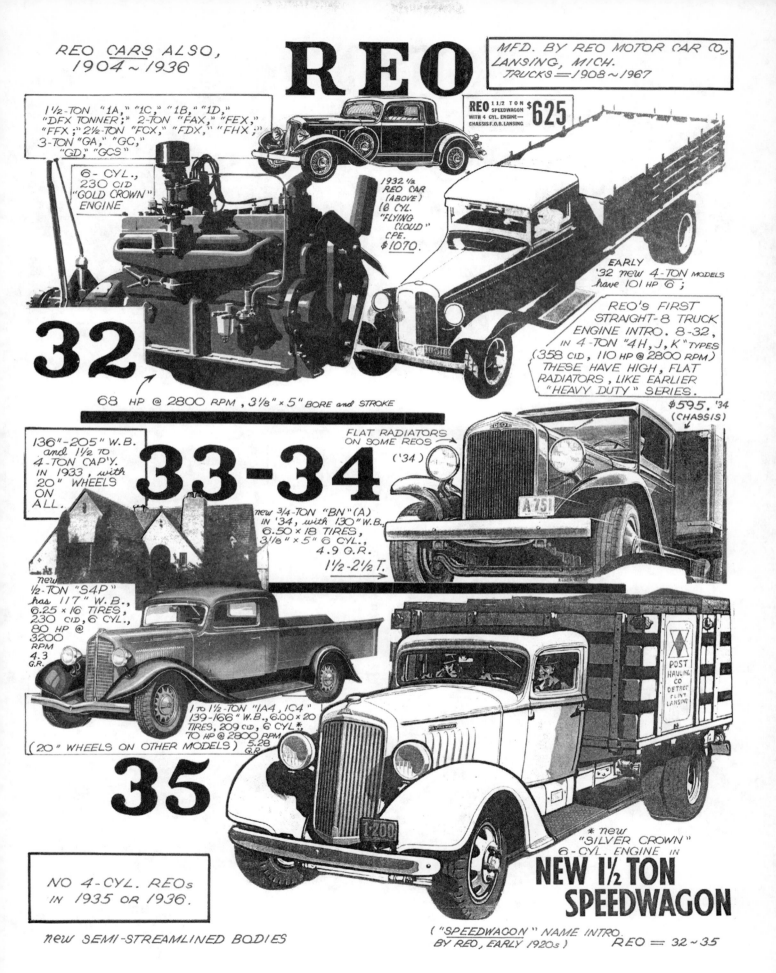

REO

REO CARS ALSO, 1904~1936

MFD. BY REO MOTOR CAR CO., LANSING, MICH.
TRUCKS = 1908 ~ 1967

1½-TON "1A," "1C," "1B," "1D," "DFX TONNER;" 2-TON "FAX," "FEX," "FFX;" 2½-TON "FCX," "FDX," "FHX;" 3-TON "GA," "GC," "GD," "GCS."

REO 1 1/2 TON SPEEDWAGON WITH 4 CYL. ENGINE— CHASSIS F.O.B. LANSING **$625**

6-CYL., 230 CID "GOLD CROWN" ENGINE

1932 ½ REO CAR (ABOVE) (6 CYL. "FLYING CLOUD" CPE. $1070.

EARLY '32 new 4-TON MODELS have 101 HP 6;

REO's FIRST STRAIGHT-8 TRUCK ENGINE INTRO. 8-32, IN 4-TON "4H, J, K" TYPES (358 CID, 110 HP @ 2800 RPM) THESE HAVE HIGH, FLAT RADIATORS, LIKE EARLIER "HEAVY DUTY" SERIES.

32

68 HP @ 2800 RPM, 3⅛" × 5" BORE and STROKE

$595. '34 (CHASSIS)

33-34

136"-205" W.B. and 1½ to 4-TON CAP'Y. IN 1933, with 20" WHEELS ON ALL.

FLAT RADIATORS ON SOME REOS ('34)

new ¾-TON "BN" (A) IN '34, with 130" W.B., 6.50 × 18 TIRES, 3⅛" × 5" 6 CYL., 4.9 G.R. 1½-2½ T.

new ½-TON "S4P" has 117" W.B., 6.25 × 16 TIRES, 230 CID, 6 CYL., 80 HP @ 3200 RPM 4.3 G.R.

1 to 1½-TON "1A4, 1C4" 139-166" W.B., 6.00 × 20 TIRES, 209 CID, 6 CYL., 70 HP @ 2800 RPM 5.28 G.R.
(20" WHEELS ON OTHER MODELS)

POST HAULING CO. DETROIT FLINT LANSING

35

* new "SILVER CROWN" 6-CYL. ENGINE IN

NEW 1½ TON SPEEDWAGON

NO 4-CYL. REOs IN 1935 OR 1936.

new SEMI-STREAMLINED BODIES

("SPEEDWAGON" NAME INTRO. BY REO, EARLY 1920s)   REO = 32~35

343

C.O.E.

REO

IMPROVED
GOLD CROWN
and
SILVER CROWN
ENGINES

36

$445* AND UP

FINAL YEAR THAT
REO ALSO BUILT
AUTOMOBILES.

In repeated tests, a 1936 Reo 2-3 Ton Truck, equipped with the Reo Gold Crown Engine, pulled an 80-ton load without laboring, in snow! A tough job that only a rough truck can perform!

ABOVE:
2~3 TON
STAKE TRUCK

FINAL YEAR FOR 358 CID
STRAIGHT-8 REO ENGINE IN
4 TO 6-TON "4H, J, K, M" MODELS;
REPLACED BY STREAMLINED
'37-STYLE 3 TO 6-TON MODELS
INTRO. JUNE, 1936 (156~190" WB)

'36½~'37 3 TO 6 TON WITH
6 CYL. 428 CID BUDA ENG.
(104 HP @ 2600 RPM)

"6~50," "6~75," "1A4Y" and "1A4(H)"
MODELS CONT'D. 1937 THROUGH 1939.

('37)
REO
CITY
BUS
3P7

new
"Silver Crown"
4 OR 6-CYL.
ENGINES

114" W.B. and up
('37)

PICKUP →

** EXTRA **

PANEL
DELIVERY →

America's Toughest Truck!

('37)

new
STYLING
new V-
WINDSHIELD

37-39

new C.O.E. MODELS
IN 4 WHEELBASES from
105" TO 166,"
with 228 CID
OR 268 CID
"GOLD
CROWN"
6.

STORAGE
and
MOVING

75-00

('38)

FINAL 4-CYL. REOS
("4-50" and "4~75")
IN 1939

SIDE-LOADING
C.O.E. (ADV. 10~37) WITH
"ART DECO" STYLING

REO = 36~39

$656. TO $3350. IN 1940

REO

THIS STYLE CAB ALSO WAS USED BRIEFLY BY HUG TRUCKS.

COWL-HINGED HOOD

SCHOOL BUS

('47)

1941 MODELS (all 6 CYL.):			
19, 19R	228 CID	83 HP	@ 3200 RPM
20	245	89	@ 3100
21, 21R	"	"	"
22, 22R	288	88	@ 2800
23, 23R	310 CID	93	@ 2700
OSL-41, NWL-41	"	"	"

1946 SPECS.:

19	145-165" WB	245 CID	89 HP @ 3100 RPM
20	130-165	288 CID	94 @ 3000
21	130-145	427 CID	127 @ 2600 (CONTINENTAL ENG.)

(C-19 TO C-25 CONT'D. ALSO)

*new MODELS FOR 1940 (**19-A**, ETC.)*

1940s

ASSEMBLY LINE AT LANSING, 1948 (BELOW)

Final inspection for brand new Reo trucks as they roll off the assembly line. From the Reo Model 19 to the giant Model 31, there's a Reo truck to fit the job you want done. See your nearest Reo dealer, now!

37-PASS.

new "FLYING CLOUD" TRANSIT BUS 186" WB INTRO. FALL, 1947. 427 CID 6.

1948 REO HEAVY DUTY
MODELS 30-31
TRACTOR CAPACITY UP TO 76,000 LBS. G.V.W.

1949 ENGINES = (6 CYL.)

245 CID : IN D-19-A ; 119, 119L and 119LS SCHOOLBUSES.

288 CID : IN D21A, 121, 121LS SCHOOLBUSES.

310 CID : IN D21RA, D22A, D22RB, D216*, D226*, 122 and 122L SCHOOLBUSES.

371 CID : IN D23SA	(ALSO OPT. IN SCHOOLBUS)
427 CID : IN D23A, D23RB, D236 *	"
513 CID : IN 30A, D306 *	
602 CID : IN 31A, D316 *	

* = TANDEM AXLES

note DIFFERENT (BOXIER) STYLING OF HVY. DUTY TYPE ABOVE

COMPANY KNOWN AS REO MOTORS, 1940~1957.

REO = 1940s

"EAGER BEAVER" ARMY TRUCK (CAN BE DRIVEN THROUGH WATER.)

STARTS 1949

REO

new F-50 with

new "SUPER GOLD COMET" 1953 6 (160 HP)

new IMPROVED "GOLD COMET" 6 ENGINE (INTRO. '49)

GOLD COMET 292 CID

('51) SCHOOL BUS

('51)

MOVING VAN

GOLD COMET

new V8 ENGINE ALSO AVAIL. (1955) 195 OR 220 HP

('51)

CONVENTIONAL MEDIUM-DUTY

1950s

REO MOTORS, INC.

SUBSIDIARY OF **BOHN** ALUMINUM AND BRASS CORPORATION, FROM 12-31-54 UNTIL BECOMING A DIVISION OF WHITE MOTORS IN 1957.

HEAVY DUMP TRUCK ('55)

REO WORLD'S TOUGHEST TRUCK

GOLD COMET REO 220

UTILITY SS57

SIGNAL TRUCKING SERVICE

REO

H 75 762

REO "ROYALE" POWER MOWERS ALSO

('51)

1950 E-19, E-21, E-22, E-23, ETC. WITH "R-E-O" VERTICAL ON NEW GRILLE. NEW GRILLE AGAIN, IN 1955, AS ABOVE

SUPER V-63 C.O.E. ('56)

1960s

new ready-mix truck
(with a flywheel power take-off)

C (GAS ;) D (GAS ;) E (DIESEL)
and DC (GAS, C.O.E.) SERIES
IN '61 (145 TO 207 HP)
OWN 6 OR V8, ALSO
CUMMINS 6-CYL. DIESEL

C.O.E.

HVY. DUMP TRUCK

REO 6 XF

BEKINS REO

('60)

('62)

MAY 1, 1967: WHITE MOTORS COMBINES ITS SUBSIDIARY DIAMOND T and REO DIVISIONS, CREATING A NEW BRAND OF TRUCK = DIAMOND REO.

REO = '50 ~ '67

346

REPUBLIC

O = OTHER CHOICES AVAIL.

"85" (1½ TON)

new 25-6 3-TON (BELOW)

NICKEL TRIM

new 8.5 RB DUMP TRUCK 110" WB

REAR DETAILS

26

MODELS:

Model	Ton	WB
75	1¼ TON	124" wb°
85	1½	146°
15,15W	2	153
25W,25	3	165°
30,30W	4½	170°
35	5	170°

NOTE TRANSVERSE REAR SPRING IN ILLUSTRATION AT UPPER RIGHT.

REPUBLIC BLT. *1913~1929* BY REPUBLIC MOTOR TRUCK CO. OF ALMA, MI. (ORIG. ALMA MOTOR TRUCK CO., 1913~1914) REPUBLIC ACQUIRED LINN MFG. CO. *(1916~1950)* OF MORRIS, N.Y. IN 1929, BOTH MERGED WITH AMERICAN LA FRANCE (EST. 1910) OF ELMIRA, N.Y. REPUBLIC DISCONTINUED IN U.S.A. IN 1929, BUT AVAIL. IN ENGLAND UNTIL 1931.

LINN TRACTOR *now a division of* Republic Motor Truck Co., Inc.

(AS OF FALL, 1927)

LINN REPUBLIC
TRACTORS-TRUCKS

TYPICAL REPUBLIC RADIATOR SHAPE →

It is significant to note that the acquisition of Linn by Republic makes the Republic line of motorized transportation more complete than ever for serving the haulage requirements of industrial America.

"½ TRACK" 6 CYL., 100 HP, OR 4 CYL., 75 HP

MODELS ('27):

Model	Ton
75,76,76 6	1¼-1½ TON
15,15W	2
50	2
60	2½
25,25W	3
30,30W,35	4½,5

Note the Linn exclusive patented flexible traction-unit.

(ALSO SEE LINN IN "MISC." SECTION, P. 395.)

27-28

Model	Ton	WB
85	2 TON	146" wb°
S25W	3½	165°

(BOTH ADDED FOR 1928)

"76-6" (1½ TON)

150½" WB° ('28)

"60" (2½ TON)

163" WB°

LYCOMING, CONT., OR WAUKESHA ENGINES (AS SINCE '22)

29

"65" (3-TON) 179" WB

"S-25W" (3½ TON) 165" WB°

MODELS:

1¼-1½ TON: 75,75-6,76,76-S; 2-TON: 15,15W,50,88,88-6;
2½-TON: 58,58-6,60,85; 3-TON: 25,25W,65;
3½-TON: S-25W; 4½ TON: 30,30-W;
5-TON: 35

REPUBLIC/LINN

CHASSIS $3695.
(SAME PRICE FOR "65", "S-25W")

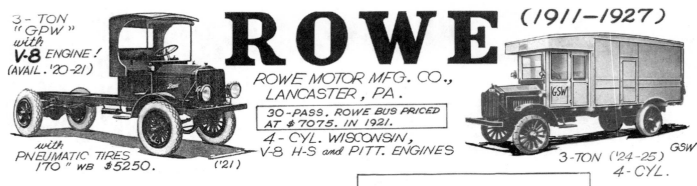

ROWE (1911-1927)

3-TON "GPW" with **V-8** ENGINE! (AVAIL. '20-21)

ROWE MOTOR MFG. CO., LANCASTER, PA.

30-PASS. ROWE BUS PRICED AT $7075. IN 1921.

4-CYL. WISCONSIN, V-8 H-S and PITT. ENGINES

with PNEUMATIC TIRES 170" WB $5250. ('21)

3-TON ('24-25) GSW 4-CYL.

ROWE'S PEAK YEAR WAS 1922, WITH 900 BLT. ROWE ALSO BLT. BUS CHASSIS UNITS.

A FACTORY FIRE IN 1923 HASTENED THE COMPANY'S DECLINE.

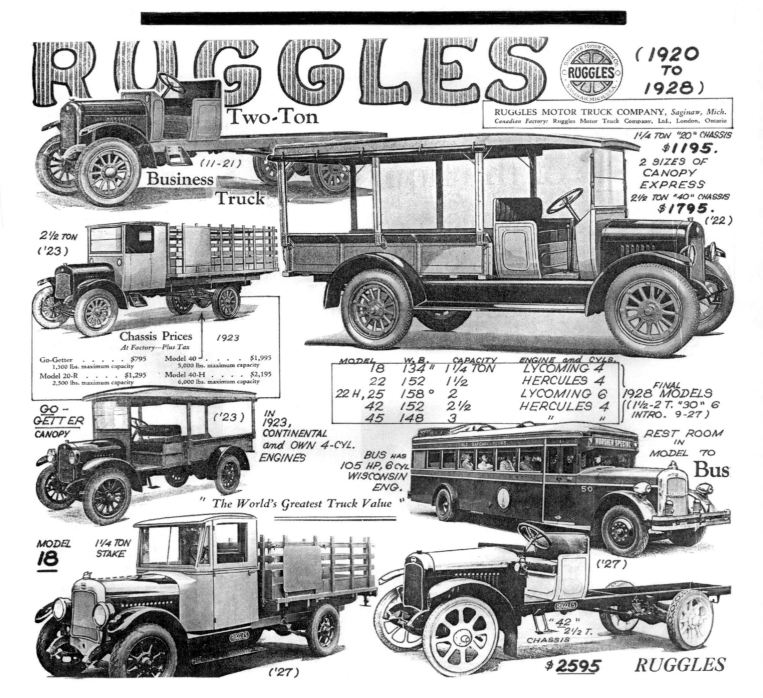

RUGGLES (1920 TO 1928)

RUGGLES MOTOR TRUCK COMPANY, Saginaw, Mich.
Canadian Factory: Ruggles Motor Truck Company, Ltd., London, Ontario

Two-Ton

Business Truck ('11-21)

1¼ TON "20" CHASSIS $1195.

2 SIZES OF CANOPY EXPRESS

2½ TON "40" CHASSIS $1795. ('22)

2½ TON ('23)

Chassis Prices 1923
At Factory—Plus Tax

Go-Getter $795
1,500 lbs. maximum capacity

Model 20-R $1,295
2,500 lbs. maximum capacity

Model 40 . . . . $1,995
5,000 lbs. maximum capacity

Model 40-H $2,195
6,000 lbs. maximum capacity

GO-GETTER CANOPY ('23)

IN 1923, CONTINENTAL and OWN 4-CYL. ENGINES

MODEL	W.B.	CAPACITY	ENGINE and CYLS.
18	134"	1¼ TON	LYCOMING 4
22	152	1½	HERCULES 4
22H, 25	158°	2	LYCOMING 6
42	152	2½	HERCULES 4
45	148	3	" "

FINAL 1928 MODELS (1½-2 T. "30" 6 INTRO. 9-27)

"The World's Greatest Truck Value"

BUS HAS 105 HP, 6 CYL. WISCONSIN ENG.

REST ROOM IN MODEL 70 Bus

MODEL 18 1¼ TON STAKE

('27)

"42" 2½ T. CHASSIS ('27)

$2595 RUGGLES

SCHACHT

THE G. A. SCHACHT MOTOR TRUCK CO.
Factory—Cincinnati, Ohio **(1904-1938)**
(TRUCKS)
New York Branch: Hancock St. and Paynter Ave., Long Island City

3½ TON ('21)

5 TON

4-CYL. ENGS. BUDA (THROUGH '23) WISCONSIN ENGINE ('23 ON)

('21)

('22)

(SOME MODELS WITH 10-SPEED TRANSMISSION)

4-TON "G" ('24)

('25)

SUPER SAFETY BUS

('25)

6 CYL., 201" W.B.

('26)

1½ TON "H" ('24)

SHOWING 2 BODY VARIETIES OF 1½-TON MODEL H

197, 217 OR 237" WB
$5900. (BUS CHASSIS)

CHASSIS $2500.

3-TON MODEL L ('26)

('26)

$3275. ('28)

MFR. KNOWN AFTER 1927 AS THE LE BLOND-SCHACHT TRUCK CO.

2-TON "HS" CAB AND CHASSIS

6 CYL. WAUK. ENGS. IN MOST '29 MODELS
2½-TON "ROADMAKER"

2-TON "JW" VAN

('29)

CONT. and HERCULES ENGINES IN 1931.

(1928-1929 BUS CHASSIS IS KNOWN AS MODEL "N.")

FINAL '37-'38 MODELS (1 TO 15 TON)
8A; 10A; 12A; 15A; 18A; 20A; 25A; 28A; 35A; 40A; 66A; 75A; TRA; TRCU; 115CU; 120CU; 125CU; 128 CU

('37)

6-CYL. HERC. ENGINES
68 TO 148 HP   263 TO 707 CID

STAKE

CAB/CHASSIS

SCHACHT ACQUIRED **ARMLEDER** TRUCK CO. IN 1928.
280 SCHACHTS SOLD IN 1929, 359 IN 1930.

AHRENS-FOX ACQUIRED 1936; SCHACHT FIRE ENGINES STILL AVAIL. IN EARLY 1940s.

SCHACHT

349

(1913~1932)

SELDEN
MODEL 53 VAN

MFD. BY SELDEN TRUCK CORP.,
ROCHESTER, N.Y.
(SELDEN-HAHN MOTOR TRUCK CORP,
ALLENTOWN, PA., 1929~1932)

Selden 24

ALL new MODELS

MODELS:

30-C	1½ TON	137½" WB
33	1½	146
53	2½	154 OR 172
50	2½	149

70	3½ TON	164" WB	(ALSO,
73	3½	168	"52"
90	5	166	BUS)

new 6-CYL.
1¼-TON "PACEMAKER" 20-6
144" WB
('25)

25-26

OLD RADIATOR DESIGN CONTINUES ON HEAVY TKS.
('26)

4-TON
CONTINENTAL   73-B
ENGS. CONTINUE 168-193" WB

ROADMASTER 21-PASS. PAY-ENTER
BUS (6 CYL., 190" WB) ("PACEMAKER"
and "CENTURY" BUS CHASSES ALSO)

new↑
LIGHT 6-CYL.
MODELS AVAIL.

'27 MODELS:

PACEMAKER	1¼ TON
UNIT 34-36	2 *
ROADMASTER	3 *
UNIT 53	3
UNIT	3½-4
UNIT 90	5

* 6 CYL.

('27½) (ILCO-RYAN SAFETY LIGHTS)↓

"47"
(3-4 TON)

('29)

ROADMASTER
CAB and CHASSIS

"37-C"
PACEMAKER
SPECIAL (2-2½ TON)

27 ON

MINOR VARIATIONS IN CAB and HOOD DETAILS

FINAL 4-CYL. MODELS ("25" and "35") IN 1929.

'30 and '31 MODELS: (ALL with 6-CYL. CONT. ENGS.)

7	1 TON	124" WB
17,317	1½	142
UNIT 37	2	151
39-C	2½	164
47-CB	3	151
47-CD	4	151
67-C	5	164
77	5½	170

ROADMASTER
DUMP TRUCK

Culver 3756
Stone 1271

W.J. ELAM & SONS
SAND AND GRAVEL

('28)

SELDEN

SERVICE MOTOR TRUCK CO., Wabash, Ind., U.S.A.   (1911–1933)

BUDA 4-CYL. ENGINES ON ALL (THROUGH '28, EXCEPT 6-CYL. BUDA IN '28 2½-TON "61," and MIDW. 4-CYL. IN '21-'23 ¾-TON "15."

Service MOTOR TRUCK
With the Red Pyramid on the Radiator

(9-20 = EARLY '21 MODEL, PYRAMID ON RADIATOR)

'19 MODELS = 320, 340, 370, 375, 400 (1-5 TON)

('20)

'20 MODELS: 220, 31, 36, 51, 76, 101, (1 TO 5 TON)

NOTE UNUSUAL SHAPE OF DOORS.

FROM 1921 TO 1927, RED PYRAMID ON TOP OF RADIATOR TYPIFIED SERVICE TRUCKS.

Look for the Red Pyramid on the Radiator

SERVICE MOTORS, Inc. Wabash, Indiana
('21)

CANOPY EXPRESS ('21)

Service

1920s

RADIATOR UPPER PAN

'23 MODELS:
12	¾ TON
25	1¼
21	1½
32	2
52	3
72	4
77	4
101	6

"51" (2½ TON) ('21) 160" WB

('23)

OHIO POWER COMPANY

NOTE DISC WHEELS

33, 42, 61, 81 new MODELS for '24 (FALL, '23)

THE E.T. SLIDER CO SAND & GRAVEL

'27-28 MODELS:
25H (1 T;) 34 (1½ T, '26-7;) 61 (2½ T;) 81 (3½ T;) 103 (5 T;) 61, 81, 103 TT MODELS ALSO

"61" 3-TON ('24) 164½" WB

('24-'26 STYLE)

(RELAY MOTORS CORP. TAKES OVER, LATE '26.)

H.Q. IN LIMA, O. 1927 ON

REMOVABLE CYL. HEAD

new '29 MODELS: (20-Z, 25-Z, 8TT-Z, 30-Z, 40-Z, 61-L, 50-Z, 60-Z, 70-Z, 80-Z) have 6-CYL. BUDA ENGINES. 4-CYL. BUDA IN 5-TON "103."

('28) RELAY AFFILIATE

CHASSIS $3215.

61-L (2½ TON) 174" WB

ONLY ABOUT 80 SOLD IN 1928, and 40 IN 1929. SERVICE TRUCKS DISCONTINUED AFTER PARENT COMPANY **RELAY** WAS LIQUIDATED and ACQUIRED BY CONSOLIDATED MOTORS.

Service

KNOWN AS **STERNBERG**
UNTIL 1915.
STERLING
FROM 1916 ON

Sterling
Since 1907 ✱

(1907 TO 1953)

STERLING
MOTOR TRUCK CO.,
MILWAUKEE, WIS.

('20)

OWN 4-CYL.
ENGINES
(TO '22)

7½-TON CHAIN DR.
4 CYL. (5 × 6¼")
174" WB

✱ = REGULAR
PRODUCTION
SINCE 1909.

WHITE
BUYS STERLING,
COMPANY MOVES
TO CLEVELAND, OH.,
NAME CH. TO
STERLING-WHITE, 1952

'20 MODELS :

1½ TON	142" WB	7.0 GR
2½	156	7.70
3½	162	8.75
5 (W)	168	8.80
5 (C)	174	7.04
7 TON	174	7.26

('21)

1920s

4- CYLINDER
WAUKESHA
ENGINES IN '23

EW-20
('26)

ABOVE : ('24)
5 TON CHAIN-DRIVE TRUCK
4 CYLS., CAST IN PAIRS (5×6¼")
2-WHEEL BRAKES   148" WB
HEAVY CHASSIS = $6000.

'26 MODELS :   (OWN 4-CYL. ENGS.)

DW-8	1½ TON	EC-29-7½	7½ TON	
DW-10,12,14	2½	EC-35-34	10	
DWS-14	3	DWS-10T	TT 130" WB	
DW-18X	4	EW-15T	TT 148	
EW-20	4	EW-20T	TT "	
EC-EW-23	5	ECS-24T	TT "	
EWS-25	5	EC-50T	TT "	
ECS 24	5			
EW-EC26-6	6			

DB-8

1½ TON
150" WB
6 CYL.

('28)

DC-25
6 TON
166" WB

4 and 6-CYL. ENGS.
IN '29 ; "OWN" WAU.
ENGS. (IN '29 1½ TON UP)

DB 7
('29)
137, 145
OR 150"
WB

DB7
(1-1¼ TON) has
6-CYL. CONTINENT.
ENG. (3⅜ × 4")
32 × 6 TIRES

DW 18-64
2½ T.
166, 180,
or 148"

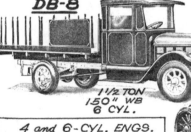

'29 MODELS : DB7 (1-1¼ TON ;) DB8-63 (1½ T ;)
DB 9 (1½-2 T ;) DW12 (2½-3½ T ;)
DW14-64 (3 T ;) DW15 (3½-4½ T ;)
DW18 (4½-5½ T ;) DC21-44
(4 TON, 4 CYL. ;) EW20-44
(5 TON, 4 CYL. ;) EW23 (5½-7 T ;)
EW27 (7-8½ T ;) D619 (4-5 T ;)
D623 (6-7 T ;)
D6 26 (7-8½ T ;)
EC 29 (8½-10 T ;)
EC 35 (10-12 TON

DC 26 64
5½ T.
('29)

EC 29-66A 6-WHEELER ('29)
218" WB   36 × 6 TIRES

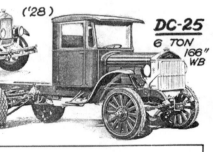

TYPICAL
GAS STATION
OF 1929

(1916-1953)

WITH SOLID RUBBER TIRES UNTIL 1927!

Sterling

LATER 1920s and

1930s

1928 : new 1-TON MODEL, HIGH-SPEED 6 CYL. ENGINES, MULTIPLE TRANS.

(SOLID RUBBER TIRES RETAINED ON A FEW MODELS UNTIL 1931.)

DIESEL MODELS AVAILABLE 1933 !

('30)

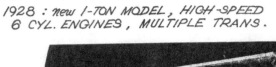

Keystone Stores. NATIONALLY KNOWN GROCERIES

('32)

SHELL

('35)

SHELL OIL TANKERS

1933 MODELS : 1½-TON FB-40 to 12-12½ TON DIESEL FD-195

ALL with WAU. 6-CYL. ENGINES, EXCEPT FD-195 with CUMMINS "H" 6-CYL. DIESEL. ALSO, CONTINENTAL "25-A" 6-CYL. ENGINES IN FB-40, FB-50. 6-WHEELERS ALSO AVAIL., UP TO 16-16½ TON FDT-250.

('36)

('36)

SHELL

C.O.E.

('37)

STARTS 1937 (125 HP (CUMMINS DIESEL)

MODEL **G** C.O.E.

DIESEL **HEAVY DUTY**

STILL USES CHAIN DRIVE

THIS TYPE of "J" INTRO. 12~38, STILL AVAILABLE 1942 (note THE ORNATE GRILLE!) (8 to 12 TON CAP'Y.)

('39) J SERIES $8165. UP

STERLING ACQUIRES FAGEOL TRUCK and COACH CO. IN 1938. SELLS FAGEOL TRUCK DIV. TO AL PETERMAN, 1939.

STERLING = 1930s

1940 MODELS: MB, MC, MD, HC,
HD, JC, JD SERIES
6-WHEELERS: HBT, HCS, HWS,
JWS SERIES
178-251" WB

DIESEL ENGINES AVAIL. IN
MOST MODELS.
$2520.-$15,200. 1940
PRICE RANGE
6-CYL.
WAUKESHA
ENGINES,
320 TO
677 CID
86 TO 152 HP
('40)

Sterling

1940s
ON

HC-250 (GAS)
HC-250H
(DIESEL)
('47)

('46)

4-WHEEL-DRIVE
MODELS ALSO AVAIL.

('50 - '51)
('52-'53
STERLING-WHITE
SIMILAR)

JUNE,
1951:
STERLING
ACQUIRED
BY
WHITE
MOTOR
CO.

('52)

"STERLING WHITE" NAME
ON HOOD VENT
TRIM *

1954 MODELS:
HB-1204 (127" WB)
HA-1304 (160" WB)
HB-1604 (152" WB)
HB-1904 (152" WB)
HB-2254 (CUMMINS
DIESEL MODEL has "D"
SUFFIX)

6-WHEELERS IN
HA, HB, SF, TA
SERIES
ENGINES:
WAUKESHA 6,
CUMMINS 6 (DIESEL) or BUDA 8 (DIESEL)

('52)
MIXER

MODEL DD-5160 (4WD)

* WHITE MOTOR CO. (CLEVELAND, OH.)
BOUGHT STERLING IN 1951, AND IN
1952-1953 STERLING PRODUCTION
MOVED TO CLEVELAND.

STERLING NAME
REVIVED 1973.

(ESTIMATED GRAND TOTAL
OF ALL STERLING TRUCKS
BLT. BETWEEN 1916 and 1953:
APPROX. 12,000)

STERLING = 1940s ON

(1912~1941) **Stewart** MOTOR TRUCK

MFD. BY STEWART MOTOR CORP., BUFFALO, N.Y.

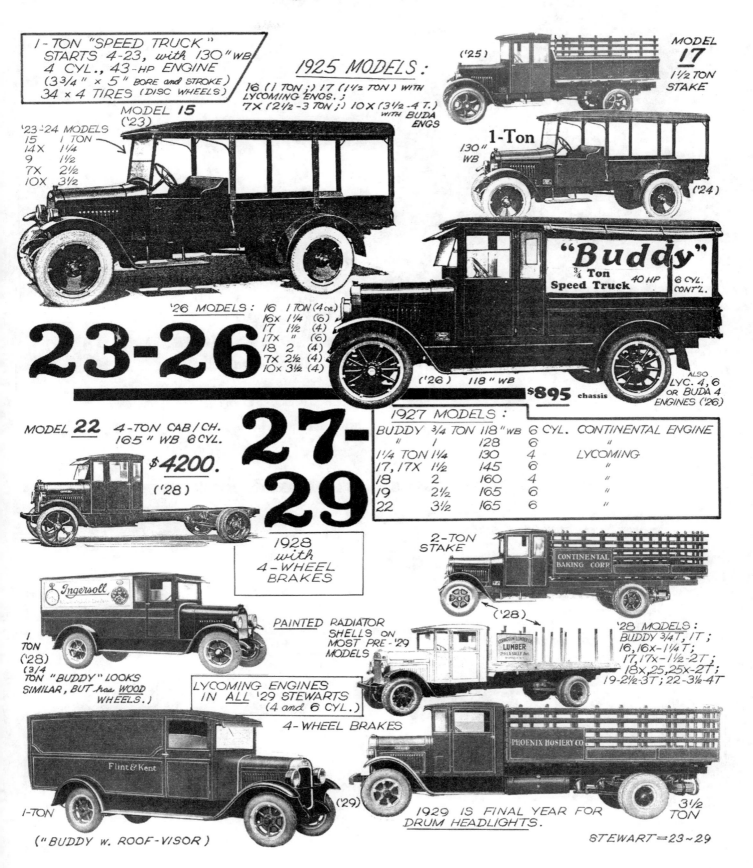

1-TON "SPEED TRUCK" STARTS 4-23, with 130" WB
4 CYL., 43-HP ENGINE
(3¾" × 5" BORE and STROKE)
34 × 4 TIRES (DISC WHEELS)

MODEL 15 ('23)

'23-'24 MODELS
15   1 TON
14X   1¼
9   1½
7X   2½
10X   3½

1925 MODELS:
16 (1 TON;) 17 (1½ TON) WITH LYCOMING ENGS.;
7X (2½-3 TON;) 10X (3½-4 T.) WITH BUDA ENGS.

('25)   MODEL 17   1½ TON STAKE

1-Ton   130" WB   ('24)

"Buddy" ¾ Ton Speed Truck   40 HP   6 CYL. CONT'L.

'26 MODELS:
16   1 TON (4 cyl.)
16x   1¼ (6)
17   1½ (4)
17x   " (6)
18   2 (4)
7x   2½ (4)
10x   3½ (4)

23-26

('26) 118" WB $895 chassis

ALSO LYC. 4, 6 or BUDA 4 ENGINES ('26)

MODEL 22   4-TON CAB/CH.
165" WB 6 CYL.
$4200.   ('28)

27-29

1928 with 4-WHEEL BRAKES

1927 MODELS:

		WB	CYL.	ENGINE
BUDDY	¾ TON	118"	6	CONTINENTAL ENGINE
"	1	128	6	"
1¼ TON	1¼	130	4	LYCOMING
17, 17X	1½	145	6	"
18	2	160	4	"
19	2½	165	6	"
22	3½	165	6	"

2-TON STAKE   CONTINENTAL BAKING CORP.

('28)

Ingersoll

1 TON ('28)
(¾ TON "BUDDY" LOOKS SIMILAR, BUT has WOOD WHEELS.)

PAINTED RADIATOR SHELLS ON MOST PRE-'29 MODELS

LUMBER

'28 MODELS:
BUDDY ¾T, 1T;
16, 16x-1¼ T;
17, 17x-1½-2T;
18x, 25, 25x-2T;
19-2½-3T; 22-3½-4T

LYCOMING ENGINES IN ALL '29 STEWARTS
(4 and 6 CYL.)

4-WHEEL BRAKES

Flint & Kent

PHOENIX HOSIERY CO.

1-TON

("BUDDY w. ROOF-VISOR)

('29)   1929 IS FINAL YEAR FOR DRUM HEADLIGHTS.

3½ TON

STEWART = 23~29

"BUDDY" LT. DUTY DISCONTINUED EARLY IN 1930.

Stewart

30

ALL 6-CYL. EXC. 4-CYL. "30", "40."

PICKUP

CANOPY $695. CHASSIS PRICE

31

31-X →

PRATT & LAMBERT VARNISH PRODUCTS

PANEL

STAKE

30

$695. TO $5700

LYCOMING ENGINES, EXCEPT FOR WAUKESHA 462 CID 6 (100 HP) IN *new* "31-X," "27-X" MODELS.

MODEL,	TON	WB	CID	POWER
30	1 T.	130"	199	50 @ 2600
30X	"	"	185	55 @ 2600
40	1½	"	(SAME AS "30")	
34X	"	145	224	61 @ 2600
28X	1¾	130	"	"
29X	2 T.	145	278	" "
18X	2½	165	310	85
32X	"	"	278	80
33X	3 T.	"	354	90 @ 2750
19X	3½	"	"	"

OTHERS ALSO AVAIL.
new MODELS

| 31X | 5 T. | | 462 | 100 @ 2000 |
| 27X | 6-7 | | " | |

NEW

31 the New 8 Cylinder Model *with* STRAIGHT-8 ENGINE (420 CID, 130 HP LYCOMING) (STARTS 3-31) *with* 12-SPEED TRANS. 9.00 × 20 TIRES

6-CYL., 60 HP "40X" JOINS "40" FOR 1931.

"29XS" (85 HP) REPLACES "29X." "35X" IS *new*

38-8 (3½ TON)

CONTINENTAL, LYCOMING, WAUKESHA ENGS.

FB-30
30 ✱ (FINAL 4-CYL.)
30-X

32

19-X, 38-6, OR 38-8

3½ Ton

1 Ton

ALSO, 2-TON "50-X," "29-XS" 3-TON "36-X," "48-8"

15 Models—57 Wheelbases 1 to 7 Ton— $695 to $6190—6 and 8 Cylinder Motors

40-XA

1½ Ton

5 Ton

31-X DUMP

18-X, 32-X, OR *new* 8-CYL. 58-8 ✱

2½ Ton

27-XS (7 TON)

✱ = STRAIGHT-8 TRUCKS WERE RARE! FEW BRANDS OFFERED THEM.

Tractor and Trailer

27-XS 7 TON

STEWART = 30~32

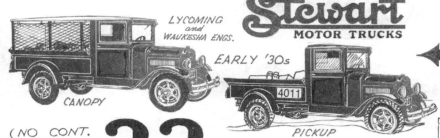

Stewart MOTOR TRUCKS

LYCOMING and WAUKESHA ENGS.

CANOPY

EARLY '30s

4011

PICKUP

BECAUSE OF THE DEPRESSION, MANY MODELS of TRUCKS REMAINED LITTLE CHANGED UNTIL 1935, TO AVOID RE-TOOLING COSTS.

LONGER WHEELBASE CHOICES AVAILABLE ON MOST MODELS.

(NO CONT. ENGINES)

33

3/4-TON =	41X
1 1/2	42X
2	43X, 29XS
2 1/2	32X, 58-8
3	18X, 48-8
3 1/2	19X, 38-6, 38-8
5	31X
7	27XS

JUNE, 1933:
new 1-TON with 6-CYLS., 56 HP, 4-SPEED TRANS., 134" WB.
1 1/2-TON has 62 HP 6, 134" WB.
2-TON 65 HP 6, and 145" WB.

34

41XS (1-TON) new in 1934, AS ARE 44X (1 1/2 TON) and 45X (2 1/2 TON)

OTHER MODELS CONTINUED FROM 1933, SOME WITH INCREASED TON RATINGS.

EARLY '30s STYLE CONTINUES ON ('35) SOME

VENT DOORS ON HOOD

1935 MODELS : (65-130 HP)
41H (1 TON;) 46H (1 1/2 T;) 47H (2 T;)
29XS, 48H (2 1/2 T;) 32X, 58-8,
49H (3 T;) 48-8, 18XS (3 1/2 T;)
38-6, 38-8 (3 1/2-5 T;) 31X (5-6 T;)
27XS (7-8 TON)

("BUDDY" LT. DUTY RETURNS 1935-1937.) (SOME 1935 STEWARTS RESTYLED) ('35)

Dole

35-36

new '36 MODELS

40H (1/2 TON, 4 CYL.;) 60H (3/4 T;)
41H (1 T;) 46H (1 1/2 T;) 47H (2 T;)
48H, 50H (2 1/2 T;) 49H, 32X (3 T;)
58X, 18XS (3 1/2 T;) 38-6, 38-8 (3 1/2-5 T;)
31X (5-6 TON)

60H has new CONTINENTAL 170 CID 6 CYL. ENG. (60 HP @ 2800)

"60-A"

1937 MODELS : 40H (1/2 TON;) 60H (3/4 T;)
(INCLUDING new "A" SERIES) 45A (1 1/2-2 T;) 45AS (1 1/2-2 1/2 T;)
47A (2-3 T;) 50A, 50AS (2 1/2-3 1/2 T;)
49A (3-4 T;) 58X, 18XS (3 1/2-4 1/2 T;)
THE NEW 38-8, 38-6 (3 1/2-5 T;) 31X (5-8 TON)

$595 1 1/2 TON

FINAL 8s IN 1937.

('37)

MORE CONTINENTAL ENGINES IN 1938.

1938 MODELS :
40HC, 60H (3/4 T;)
61A (1-1 1/2 T;)
45A (1 1/2-2 T;)
45AS (1 1/2-2 1/2 T;)
47A (2-3 T;)
50A, 50AS, 50AD
(2 1/2-3 1/2 T;) 49A,
49AD, 51A,

'38 (CONT'D.:)
51AD (3-4 T;) 58A, 58AD, 59A, 59AD
(3 1/2-4 1/2 T;) 38-6 (3 1/2-5 T;) 31X (5-8 TON)

BED EXTENDS FURTHER

37-39 ON

Stewart (DISCONTINUED 1941)*

1939 LINE LISTS 4 new C.O.E. MODELS IN 1 1/2 TO 4 TON RANGE with WAUKESHA ENGINES)

new 31-A CONVENTIONAL RATED at 6-8 TONS.)

* "1941-1942" MODELS 38A, 49A, 58A, 59A REPORTED TO EXIST.

STEWART === 33~39 ON

STUDEBAKER *Trucks*

STUDEBAKER CORP., SOUTH BEND, IND. 1852-1966 (MOTOR VEHICLES BEGIN 1902. TRUCK PRODUCTION SUSPENDED FROM '17 TO '27; CEASES 1964.

"SEMINOLE" 22-PASS. PARLOR CAR BUS 6 CYL. (3⅞"×5") 184" WB 34×7.50 TIRES

28

4-WHEEL MECHANICAL BRAKES

113" WB 4.6 GR 32×6.00 TIRES ERSKINE PANEL DELIVERY ALSO REPORTED.

¾-TON PANEL DELIVERY 6-CYL. 3⅜"×4½" BORE and STROKE

29

1929 ERSKINE "52-B" ½-TON 109"WB CONTINENTAL 9-F 6-CYL. ENGINE (2¾"×4½") 30×5 TIRES
"GD-N" 1-TON 140"WB 3⅜"×4½" 6-CYL. ENG. 30×5 TIRES
"76 Sp." 3-TON 184" 3⅞"×5" 6-CYL. ENG. 34×7.50 TIRES
"75 HD" 3½-TON ALSO   BUS ('29)

'29-'30 has FLAT RADIATOR IN STYLE OF STUDE. CAR (ABOVE.)

30

AS OF JULY, 1930,
THE ¾-TON "GN-P" has 115" WB, 6.00×19 TIRES,
221 CID, 6-CYL. (71 HP @ 3200 RPM) 4.7 GR
1-TON "30" has SAME ENGINE, 4.64 GR,
20" TIRES, 130" WB
1-TON "GK-N" has 146" WB,
248.2 CID 6-CYL. ENGINE,
(76 HP @ 3000 RPM,) 4.64 GR,
30×5 TIRES
1¼-TON "40" has 146"WB,
71-HP ENG., 5.10 GR
2½-TON "77" and "88"
have STRAIGHT-8 ENG.
(337 CID, 115 HP @ 3200 RPM)
with SAME 8-CYL. ENG. IN
3½-TON "99."

EARLY '31 (BLT. '30)

S-20 1½ TON STAKE

new RADIATOR SHELL ON SOME 1931 TRUCKS.

31

S-1	½-TON	114"	WB
40	1¼	146	
S-20	1½	130	
S-50	2	148	
88	2½	184	
99	3½	"	

2-TON S-50 CHASSIS (ABOVE)

6-CYL. ENGINE (70-71 HP) (TO 2-TON) 115-HP STRAIGHT-8 ENGINE CONT'D. IN 2½-3-TON STUDEBAKER TRUCKS.

130" WB

S-20 CHASSIS $695.

AS ILLUSTRATED, CHASSIS UNITS ALSO AVAIL., FOR TO-ORDER BODIES.

STUDEBAKER = 28~31

STUDEBAKER

CHASSIS UNITS MAY
OR MAY NOT
INCLUDE CAB.

6-CYLINDERS 75 HORSEPOWER

32 FROM $695.

			TIRE SIZE
S-1	½ TON	114" WB	5.25 × 19
S-20	1½	130"	6.00 × 20
S-50	2	148"	6.50 × 20
88	2½	184"	7.50 × 20
99	3½	184"	7.50 × 20

(2 TON : $895.– 945.)
3 TON (WITH AUX. TRANSMISSION and
B.K. BRAKE BOOSTER : $1350.–1425.)
(ENGINES AS BEFORE)

1933 SERIAL #
3402001 UP

ALL 6 CYL. (3¼"× 4⅝")
$670.–1425.

33

"S" MODELS

S-2	1½–2 TON	130" WB	6.00 × 20	TIRES	5.66 GR
S-4	1¾–2½	130	6.00 × 20		6.8 GR
S-6	2–3	141	6.50 × 20		ON OTHERS
S-8	3–4	141	6.50 × 20		

note
7 SETS VERT. LOUVRES   LONGER WHEELBASES AVAIL.

SLANTING LOUVRES,
new GRILLE

LONG CAB
TRACTOR

SERIAL # 3350460 UP

RESTYLED "S"

34

MODEL NUMBERS
AND SPECS. AS
IN 1933.

SEMI-SKIRTED
FENDERS

DUO-SERVO
HYDRAULIC
BRAKES

SCHOOL BUS WITH
ALL-STEEL
WAYNE
BODY

WAUKESHA
358 CID 6
110 HP @ 280
(IN W-841)

35

new GRILLE
and HORIZ.
LOUVRES

new "T" SERIES
6-CYL., 230 CID ENGINE
75 HP @ 3200 RPM

"ACE"	1½ TON	(T-230, T-430)
"BOSS"	2	(T-641)
"MOGUL"	2½	(T-683)
"BIG CHIEF"	3	(T-841, W-841)

"ACE" MODEL (ABOVE)   1½ TON "T" CHASSIS:
$625.

Studebaker 32~35

Studebaker

CAB/CHASSIS

4.85 TO 7.8 GEAR RATIOS

73 TO 110 HP

36

1½-TON 2T2 CHASSIS: $595.

ACE, BOSS, MOGUL, and BIG CHIEF MODELS CONTINUE (6-CYL. WAUKESHA ENGINES IN ALL BUT "ACE.")

new C.O.E. "Metro" (OFFERED IN ACE OR BOSS MODELS.)

* "M" AT END OF MODEL NO. MEANS A C.O.E. TYPE.

PAIRS OF HORIZONTAL STRIPS ON 1937 GRILLE

Jackson STORES INC.

(1½-TON J-15 "ACE" CHASSIS: $595.)

37

new! $570.

116" WB

"J" SERIES

J-5	½-TON
J-15 *	1½-2
J-20 *	2-3
J-25 *	2½-3½
J-30 *	3-4

COUPE-EXPRESS STYLED LIKE STUDEBAKER CARS (1937 TO 1939.) NAME REVIVED ON LIGHT 1941 PICKUPS.

new 6 CYL. HERCULES ENGS. REPLACE WAUKESHA (J-20 and up)

INTERIOR

new DIESEL— "J-20-D" TYPES INTRO. JULY, 1937, with 6-CYL., 260 CID HERCULES ENGINES.

C.O.E.

K-15M VAN

(1938 ½ TON K-5 CAB/CHASSIS: $690.)

('38) C.O.E. CHASSIS $695. UP

68-106 HP HERCULES 6 IN "K 20" and LARGER.

K-20

('39)

COUPE-EXPRESS

('38)

K-5 BECOMES L-5 FOR 40 (226 CID 6, 90 HP @ 3400, 4.55-4.82 GR.)

38-40

K-5	½ TON	116" WB
K-10	1 "	1130"
K-15	1½-2	
K-20	2-3	
K-25	2½ 4	
K-30	3-5	

(C.O.E. SHORT-WB VARIATIONS ON 1½ TON and UP, WITH M SUFFIX ON MODEL NO.)

MODELS ('38)

(new 1940 SEDAN-DELIVERY: $736.)

(NO 1940 COUPE-EXPRESS)

STUDEBAKER (NO C.O.E.)

COUPE EXPRESS

Full coupe comfort!
Full commercial car serviceability!

M-15 STD. STAKE

M-16 HEAVY-DUTY TANKER

← $724.

('41)

M SERIES STARTS 3-41

M

41-45

SERIES SIMPLIFIED, USING ONLY STUDE. ENG. 3 MODEL TYPES USE SAME BASIC CAB.

('42)

('43)

197,661 STUDEBAKER MILITARY VEHICLES BUILT, INCL. AMPHIBIOUS "WEASEL": M-29-C.

HOOD OF MILITARY TRUCK HAS A PRONOUNCED DOWNWARD SLOPE. CAB PROFILE SIMILAR TO "M."

(M-5 ½ TON PICKUP: $968.)

1-TON "M-15-28" STAKE AVAILABLE TO CIVILIANS STARTING AUG., 1945

1 TON ('46)

('46: PAINTED GRILLE PLAIN BUMPER

('47)

HVY. DUTY STAKE

46-48

ONLY M-16 HAS 94-HP ENGINE.

POSTWAR "M" SERIES

('47~48 SER. # M5~19053 UP)

NO HUBCAPS ON STD., HVY-DUTY

1 TON

(9' VAN BODY) ALSO AVAIL. AS 8' PICKUP.

(1949 EXAMPLES ILLUSTR.)

SERIAL # R-0001 ('49) R-16001 (1½ T) 1950-1951: R5-42501; R10-20101; R15-10801: 1952:78579; 8355; ¾ T: 31399; 3127

$1262. UP ('49-50)

new 1½-TON with 900-GAL. TANK BODY

2-TON 14' STAKE 171" WB ('49)

TOTALLY RESTYLED FOR 1949

'49 STARTS JUNE, 1948

49-53

112" OR 122" WB

CAB DETAIL

2-TON DUMP TRUCK

1953 SER. # 96238; 7424 (¾ TON: 34250; 5926

STUDEBAKER = 41~53

Studebaker

(3/4-TON $1622. UP)

$1469. and up (LT. DUTY)
(new V8 AVAIL.)

BUS CHASSIS 195" WB

54 RESTYLED
3-R SERIES

Built by Studebaker-Packard...
world's 4th largest full-line producer
of cars and trucks

171" WB

CAB AND CHASSIS WITH VAN BODY

INTERIOR

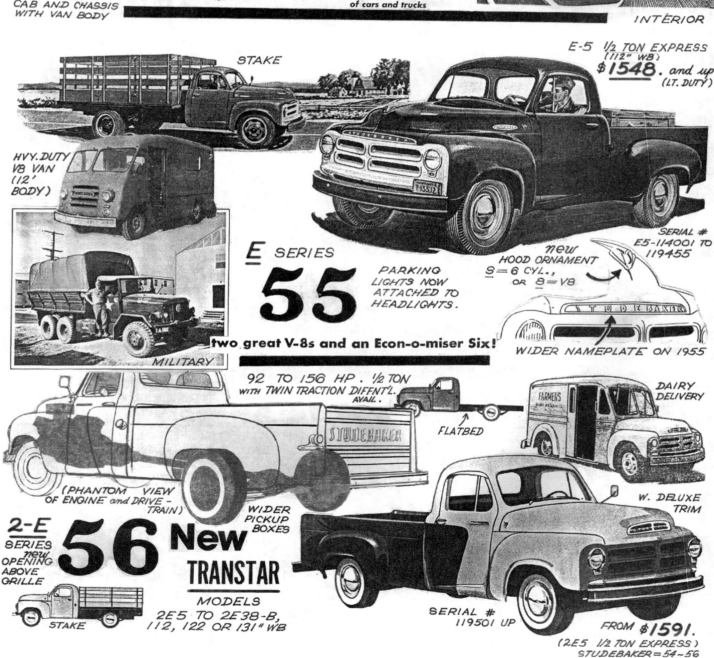

STAKE

E-5 1/2 TON EXPRESS
(112" WB)
$1548. and up
(LT. DUTY)

HVY. DUTY V8 VAN (12' BODY)

E SERIES
55

PARKING LIGHTS NOW ATTACHED TO HEADLIGHTS.

two great V-8s and an Econ-o-miser Six!

SERIAL #
E5-114001 TO
119455

new HOOD ORNAMENT
S = 6 CYL.,
OR 8 = V8

STUDEBAKER

WIDER NAMEPLATE ON 1955

MILITARY

92 TO 156 HP. 1/2 TON
with TWIN TRACTION DIFFNT'L.
AVAIL.

FLATBED

FARMERS

DAIRY DELIVERY

(PHANTOM VIEW OF ENGINE and DRIVE-TRAIN)

WIDER PICKUP BOXES

STUDEBAKER

W. DELUXE TRIM

2-E SERIES
new OPENING ABOVE GRILLE

56 New
TRANSTAR

MODELS
2E5 TO 2E38-B,
112, 122 OR 131" WB

STAKE

SERIAL #
119501 UP

FROM $1591.
(2E5 1/2 TON EXPRESS)
STUDEBAKER = 54~56

STUDEBAKER
½-, ¾-, 1-Ton Models

PROD.: 10,563

TRANSTAR

NEW GRILLE ('57)

57 -58

1958 SERIAL #s BELOW:

E5-125401;
E6-16901;
E11-13001; E14-2801
V8: E7-9301; E12-3601;
E13-2301 and up

Studebaker-Packard CORPORATION

TRANSTAR DASH ('57)

('58)

America's Lowest-Priced Pickup!

('58) REAR

new 1958

Only $1595*

Studebaker Scotsman

TRANSTAR

PROD.: 10,779

AUX. LIGHTS IN GRILLE OF SOME TRANSTAR TYPES IN 1959.
SER. # START WITH
E1-1101;
E3-101;
E11-13501; E14-3101; E16-45301;
V8s: E2-101; E7-11101; E12; E13; E28 SERIES

59

STUDEBAKER NAME ON DOOR

SIMPLE NEW -S- EMBLEM ABOVE GRILLE ON 1959 SCOTSMAN.

PRODUCTION:
12,314 ('60); 7642 ('61);
14,283 ('62);
13,117 ('63);
749 ('64)

SCOTSMAN REPLACED BY

CHAMP ½ ton

FINAL L-HEAD 6s IN 1960. NEW O.H.V. VERSION OF 170 cid 6, 1961.

NEW
light duty

"CHAMP" STYLING SIMILAR TO STUDEBAKER "LARK" COMPACT CARS.

1961 CHAMP AVAIL. WITH NEW "SPACESIDE" WIDE PICKUP BOX FORMERLY USED BY DODGE. FINAL NARROW, 9' BOXES IN 1962, ON "7E" CHAMP. FINAL "8E" CHAMP IN 1963-64.
MODELS E-45A and E-45E DIESELS RESEMBLE TRANSTAR BUT HAVE "DIESEL" DESIGNATION ON UPPER BORDER OF GRILLE. (GM DETROIT DIESEL ENGINE)

(SOME FINAL 1'64I CHAMPS with "STUDEBAKER" NAME ON LOWER EDGE OF GRILLE)

TRANSTAR

60
ON

HEAVY-DUTY
(W. DIESEL ENGINE)

NEW E-35, E-45 TYPE

('63-64) SHORT CONV'T.L. 96" BBC

(NO TRUCK PRODUCTION AFTER 1964)
STUDEBAKER = 57 ON

TERRAPLANE

MFD. BY HUDSON MOTOR CAR CO., DETROIT

(TRUCKS = 1933 - 1938)

CARS ALSO, 1932 ~ 1938 (FORMERLY ESSEX)*

* A.K.A. "ESSEX-TERRAPLANE," 1932 ~ 1933

BUSINESS CAR

('33 STYLED LIKE TERRAPLANE CAR.)

BENDIX MECH. BRAKES

CAB/CHASSIS MODELS AVAIL.

6 - CYL., L - HEAD ENGINE (INCLUDING HUDSON, THROUGH '47.)

212.1 CID

SER. # 373000 UP

34 80 HP

Pickup $515.

112" W.B. (THROUGH '35)

$595.

88 HP

STEEL ROOF ON CAB

35

$675. 3/4-TON SEDAN DELIVERY

PICKUP $545.

SER. # 51101 UP

new BODIES new 2-PIECE V-WINDSHIELD

PICKUP $560.

36

88 HP (100 HP OPTIONAL)

SER. # 61101 UP

new 115" W.B.

HUDSON MOTOR CAR COMPANY SERVICE PARTS

FACTORY and PANEL DELIVERY FLEET

new SMALLER REAR WINDOW IN PICKUP

96 HP @ 3900 RPM $700.

37

SER. # 70101 UP

6.00 x 16 TIRES

new 117"-W.B. MODEL "70" (4.55 G.R.)

new MODEL "78" has 124" W.B., 5.12 G.R. ("BIG BOY")

8,058 SOLD

1938 MODEL KNOWN AS "HUDSON-TERRAPLANE"

SER. # 80-101 OR 88-101 UP

38

96 OR 102 HP

"80" "88" 117-124" W.B.

new HUDSON "112" SERIES IS LOWER-PRICED MODEL with 112" W.B. SER. # 89-101 UP

new SILENT STRAIGHT-THROUGH MUFFLER

SOME 1938 (and all 1939 and LATER) TRUCKS USE THE "HUDSON" NAME.

$900. PANEL

VERSARE

(MFD. 1925-1928 BY VERSARE CORP., ALBANY, N.Y.) (OPERATED 1928 TO 1931 BY CINCINNATI CAR CO.)

A VARIETY OF 4, 6 and 8-WHEELED BUSES and TRUCKS. 8-WHEELERS have ELECTRIC MOTOR AT EACH END, POWERING 4-WHEEL BOGIES. ELECTRICITY GENERATED BY 4-CYL. BUDA ENG. (GAS)

25 -31

8-WHEEL BUSES SOLD TO ALBANY, N.Y.; ALTON, ILLINOIS; MONTREAL, QUEBEC. (33-PASS.)

↗ WITH ARCH ROOF

WITH CLERESTORY ROOF

MONTREAL TYPE

('25) ALTON TYPE

THE ALTON TRANSPORTATION COMPANY   No 2

NEW

"STREETCAR" TYPE BUS (RIGHT) →
INTRO. 1927

C SHERBROOKE

THIS TYPE BUS SOLD TO ALBANY, NYC, MONTREAL, BOSTON, CLEVELAND, SALT LAKE CITY, ETC.

truck

HEAVY-DUTY SIDE DUMP TRUCKS ALSO AVAIL.

IN ADDITION TO PRODUCING ONE OF THE EARLIEST FLAT-FRONT "PUSHER" TYPE (OR "STREETCAR" TYPE) BUSES, VERSARE BUILT SOME OF THE WORLD'S MOST BIZARRE MULTI-WHEELED BUSES and TRUCKS (AS ILLUSTRATED.)

VERSARE

(SINCE 1957)

WABCO
AN AMERICAN-STANDARD COMPANY

69

"35-C" HAULPAK REAR DUMP

LETOURNEAU WESTINGHOUSE, PEORIA, ILLINOIS

Haulpak

OVERLAP OF VARIOUS MODEL TYPES

Model 888B and 777B
GRADER (DETR. OR
('72) CUMMINS ENG.)

(IMPROVED IN 1970, WITH CHOICE OF GM V-12 OR CUMMINS 6-CYL. DIESEL ENG. (GM has 852 CID, 434 HP.)

Haulpak

120-B HAULPAK

('72)

THESE GIGANTIC HEAVY-HAULER TYPES OF DUMP TRUCK SUITABLE ONLY FOR OFF-ROAD SERVICE AT SITES OF HEAVY CONSTRUCTION, LAND GRADING, ETC.

GRADER CAB CLOSE-UP

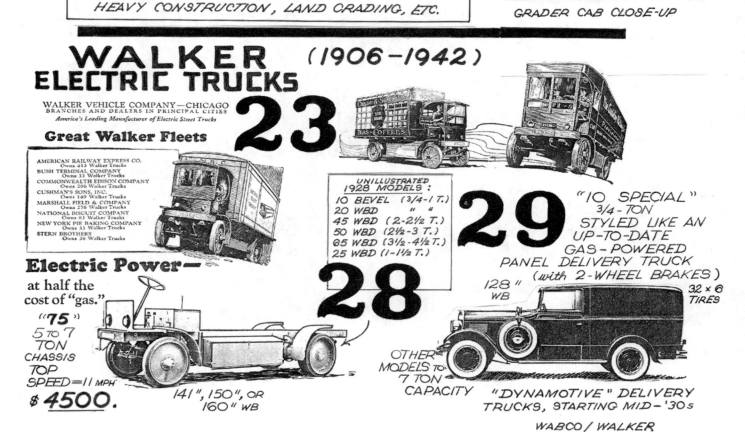

WALKER ELECTRIC TRUCKS (1906-1942)

WALKER VEHICLE COMPANY—CHICAGO
BRANCHES AND DEALERS IN PRINCIPAL CITIES
America's Leading Manufacturer of Electric Street Trucks

Great Walker Fleets

23

AMERICAN RAILWAY EXPRESS CO.
Owns 413 Walker Trucks
BUSH TERMINAL COMPANY
Owns 33 Walker Trucks
COMMONWEALTH EDISON COMPANY
Owns 286 Walker Trucks
CUSHMAN'S SONS, INC.
Owns 149 Walker Trucks
MARSHALL FIELD & COMPANY
Owns 276 Walker Trucks
NATIONAL BISCUIT COMPANY
Owns 83 Walker Trucks
NEW YORK PIE BAKING COMPANY
Owns 33 Walker Trucks
STERN BROTHERS
Owns 38 Walker Trucks

UNILLUSTRATED 1928 MODELS :
10 BEVEL (3/4-1 T.)
20 WBD   "   "
45 WBD (2-2½ T.)
50 WBD (2½-3 T.)
65 WBD (3½-4½ T.)
25 WBD (1-1½ T.)

29

"10 SPECIAL"
3/4-TON
STYLED LIKE AN
UP-TO-DATE
GAS-POWERED
PANEL DELIVERY TRUCK
(with 2-WHEEL BRAKES)

Electric Power—
at half the cost of "gas."

"75"
5 TO 7 TON CHASSIS
TOP SPEED = 11 MPH

28

128" WB

32 × 6 TIRES

$4500.

141", 150", OR 160" WB

OTHER MODELS TO 7 TON CAPACITY

"DYNAMOTIVE" DELIVERY TRUCKS, STARTING MID-'30s

WABCO / WALKER

WALTER

Walter Motor Truck Co.   Sales Office: 605 Fifth Ave., New York

LONG ISLAND CITY; QUEENS, N.Y.
(VOORHEESVILLE, N.Y., 1957 ON)

S
('20-'21)

4-CYL. WAUKESHA ENGINES
(SOMETIMES LISTED AS "OWN ENGINES")

5 TON CHASSIS

FRT
('24-25)
$6500.

$5600.00

MODEL S has 168" OR 192" WB

Walter Patented Automatic Locking Differential and Suspended Drive
EXCLUSIVELY A WALTER ENGINEERING DEVELOPMENT

ELECTRIC MODELS ALSO AVAIL.

"FRT" 15 TO 25 TON TRACTOR TRUCK 100" WB
(THIS TYPE INTRO. MAY, 1923.)

MANY MODELS with FRONT WHEEL DR.

"FH" TRACTOR TRUCK
(11-TON G.V.W. with DUMP BED)
136" WB   ('28-29)
                   $7200.

LONG FRONT OVERHANG AHEAD OF AXLE IS TYPICAL OF MOST WALTER TRUCKS.

('36)

6 CYLS.

(MFR. AT RIDGEWOOD, L.I., N.Y., 1935-1957)

('37)

MAUMEE T-1

6-WAK—Butane Engine
6-WAK—Gasoline Engine
6-WAKD—Diesel Engine   ('53)
6-WAKDS—Supercharged Diesel Engine

WALTER SNOW FIGHTERS
('44)

WAUKESHA
1197 CU. IN. 6-WAK SERIES
ENGINES

with SNOW PLOW

('53)

New Supercharged 6-WAKDS Diesel, with center-mounted turbocharger; 6-cyl., 6¼ x 6½, 1197 cu. in., 352 max. hp.

IN RECENT YEARS, WALTER HAS BUILT SPECIALIZED HVY. DUTY UNITS IN LIMITED PRODUCTION, AND LOW-CAB AIRPORT CRASH TRUCKS IN A STYLE SIMILAR TO THAT OF OSHKOSH.

On the Mesabi Range this 20-tonner hauling iron ore is a Walter Dumper powered by a Waukesha Super-Duty Six 6-WAK Butane Engine

WALTER TRUCKS

(ORIG. WARD LaFRANCE TRUCK CORP.) (EST. 1919)

('45-45)

WARD LaFRANCE
TRUCK DIVISION

GREAT AMERICAN INDUSTRIES, INC.   ELMIRA, NEW YORK (CO. TITLE IN 1945)

Wayne
Wayne Transportation Division
P.O. Box 1447
Richmond, Indiana 47374

SINCE 1931, ALSO MFG. OF SCHOOL BUS BODIES

BUSETTE ('82)

1980s

WITH LUGGAGE RACK

SPECIAL BUS BODIES ON VARIOUS MAKES OF CHASSIS

JAIL BUS

CHEV. OR GMC CHASSIS ON CHAPERONE (MINI)

CHAPERONE™

32-PASS. CITY TRANSIT BUS (ISUZU CHASSIS WITH 130 HP DIESEL REAR ENG. 196.9" WB

1500 SERIES MINI-BUS

MFD. BY WHEELED COACH, ORLANDO, FL.

Wheeled Coach

('84)

1980s
('84)

WARD LaFRANCE / WAYNE / WHEELED COACH

368

MFD. BY
WHITE MOTOR CO.
(WHITE TRUCKS)
CLEVELAND, OH.

White

TRUCKS
SINCE 1901

3/4-TON "15"

133½" WB   34 × 5 TIRES

White 25

OWN 4-CYL. ENGINES CONT'D., with "GK"
3¾" × 5⅛" ENG. IN "15" and "20."
"GR" 4¼" × 5¾" ENG. IN
"40" and "45."

45 D

5-TON "45-D" POWER DUMP TRUCK

156" WB

CHARABANC-STYLE SCENIC BUS

ABOVE:
50-A
BUS

ZENITH CARBS.

26

$4950.
(CHASSIS)

50-A
BUS
198" WB
4 CYL.

32 × 6
TIRES

1926 "15-45" has 10" LONGER
WHEELBASE and LARGER "GR"
ENGINE, UNLIKE STD. "15."

52-GRB
REFUSE
TRUCK →

"GRB"
new
DESIGNATION OF
4¼" × 5¾"
ENGINE.

27

MODEL
"40"
NOW
"40-A"

There is a complete line of White
Trucks to meet every transportation requirement. See these
White models at any of the 33 factory branches or at 300 dealers.

TRUCKS
Model 15—1 ton.........$1,845
Model 20—1¼ ton....... 3,125
Model 56—2 ton......... 3,125
Model 61—2½ ton....... 3,750
Model 64—3½ ton....... 4,650
Model 45—5-½ ton..... 5,100
BUSSES
Model 53—4 cyl. 16 Pass. $4,250
Model 50A—4 cyl. 25 Pass. 5,550
Model 54—6 cyl. 29 Pass. 7,500
THE WHITE COMPANY
Cleveland

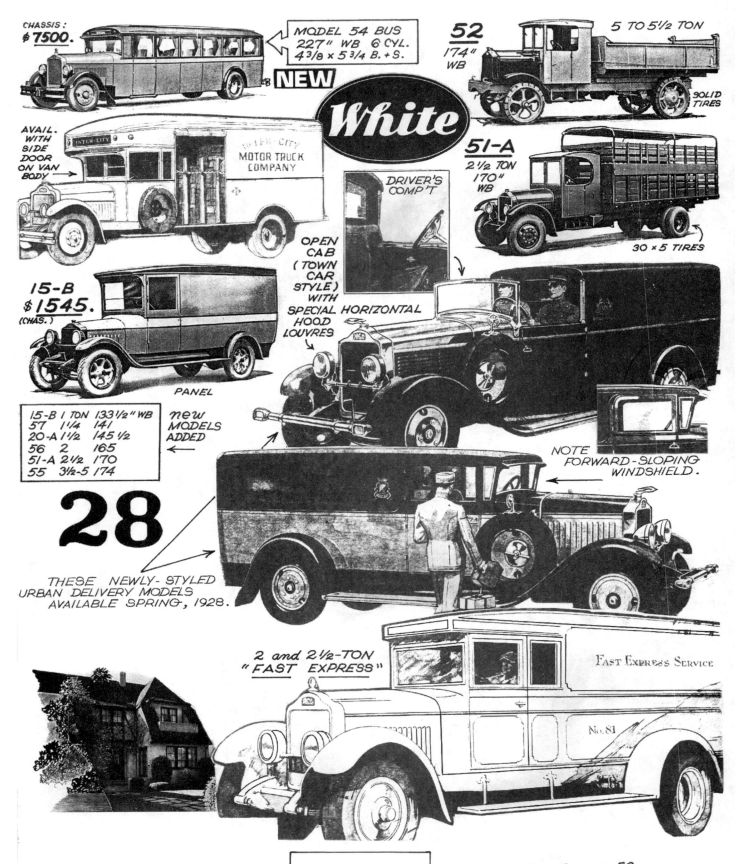

CHASSIS:
$ 7500.

MODEL 54 BUS
227" WB 6 CYL.
4 3/8 x 5 3/4 B. + S.

NEW

White
MOTOR TRUCK
COMPANY

52
174"
WB

5 TO 5 1/2 TON

SOLID
TIRES

AVAIL.
WITH
SIDE
DOOR
ON VAN
BODY →

INTER-CITY

51-A
2 1/2 TON
170"
WB

30 x 5 TIRES

DRIVER'S
COMP'T

OPEN
CAB
(TOWN
CAR
STYLE)
WITH
SPECIAL HORIZONTAL
HOOD
LOUVRES

15-B
$ 1545.
(CHAS.)

PANEL

15-B	1 TON	133 1/2" WB
57	1 1/4	141
20-A	1 1/2	145 1/2
56	2	165
51-A	2 1/2	170
55	3 1/2 - 5	174

new
MODELS
ADDED
←

NOTE
FORWARD-SLOPING
WINDSHIELD.

28

THESE NEWLY-STYLED
URBAN DELIVERY MODELS
AVAILABLE SPRING, 1928.

2 and 2 1/2-TON
"FAST EXPRESS"

FAST EXPRESS SERVICE

No. 81

EXTENDED WHEELBASES
AVAILABLE ON VARIOUS
MODELS

6260 SOLD
IN 1928

4 - CYL. 50-B and 53
BUS CHASSIS UNITS ALSO
AVAIL.
ALSO 6-CYL. EXPERIMENTAL
GAS-ELECTRIC BUS!
WHITE = 28

new "59"
(SUMMER,
'29')

new LOCKHEED HYDRAULIC BRAKES and
new BODY BY BENDER ON "60" and "61."

51-A

4 CYL.
170" WB
CHASSIS
$3750.

2½-TON

new 6-
CYLINDER
L-HEAD
3½" × 4½" ENGINE
IN WHITE SIX "LIGHT DELIVERY" (ABOVE)
(AVAIL. SPRING, 1929.)

"60" = 3-SPEED
"61" = 4-SPEED

"60" CHASSIS
$1850.

29

ALSO, new 6-CYL.
LIGHT-DUTY CHASSIS AVAIL.

"58" 3-TON MODEL ADDED (with 180" and other WBs.)
ALSO, "52-T" and "51-A" TRUCK-TRAILERS.

"52" HVY. DUTY CHAS.
$5100.

FIGURE "W" CENTER BUMPER GUARD
(ON SOME MODELS)

(NOTE ILLUSTRATIONS
BELOW)

1-TON "15-B"
4 CYL., 226.4
CID
31 HP
@ 1600 RPM

30

new
7½-TON
4-CYL.
(56 HP)

"52" and 6-CYL. (75 HP) "59-A."
ALSO "52-T"
and
"51-AT"
TRACTOR-
TRUCKS
ALSO.

"63"
STAKE
(new
MEDIUM-H.
DUTY 2½-TN.)
6-CYL. (396 CID)
75 HP @ 2000
RPM

new 2½-
-TON
"63"
DUMP
TRUCK

29

('30½)

new 3-TON "64" DUMP TRUCK
(518 CID 6) 100 HP @ 2000 RPM
(HEAVY DUTY)

new
2½~TON
63
DUMP
TRUCK

OTHER MODELS :
"60" (1 TON) 260 CID 6 (45 HP @ 1800 RPM)
"57" (1¼-T.) 289 CID 4 (46 HP @ 1700 RPM) ; "20-A" (1½ T.) 226.4 CID 4 (31 HP @ 1600);
"61" (1½-T.) 299 CID 6 (61 HP @ 2000); "56" (2-T.) 289 CID 4 (46 HP @ 1700);
"51-A" (2½-T.) 326.3 CID 4 (56 HP @ 1800); "58" (3-T.) (AS 51-A);
"55" (3½~5T) and "52" (5-T.) (BOTH AS 51-A)

(BUSES ON NEXT PAGE)

WHITE = 29~30

371

25 TO 29 PASSENGERS
38 × 9.00 TIRES (DUAL REAR)

MODEL "54"
BUS INTRO.
12-27, has
"1-A-1" ENG.

227" WB
CHASSIS

White

← INTER-
CITY
BUS
MODEL 54
6 - CYL.
(4 3/8 × 5 3/4 B.+S.)
519 C.I.D. O.H.V.

(1929 PRICES
and SPECS.
LISTED)

29-30
(BUSES)

(VERMONT
TRANSIT
CO.
EXAMPLES
ILLUSTR.
TOP LEFT and BELOW)

ROYAL BLUE
LINES OF
PENNSYLVANIA
EXAMPLE
AT RIGHT

SUBURBAN and
LOCAL TYPE
BUSES

note "W"
ON FRONT
BUMPER

SOME
BODY
BUILDERS
INCLUDE
DECORATIVE
RAILING
AT REAR,
R.R.-
STYLE

MODEL 54 :
7915 LBS. CHASSIS WEIGHT
18000 LBS. GROSS WT.,
WITH BODY and NORMAL
LOAD of PASSENGERS.
METAL-TO-METAL 4-WHEEL
FOOT BRAKES, AIR-
OPERATED. (HAND BRAKE
CONTRACTS ON DRIVESHAFT.)

AS SEEN ON A
NEW ENGLAND
HIGHWAY,
BELOW

THE
MOUNTAINEER

CHASSIS PRICES :

4 - CYL. "53" $**4250.**
(16-21 PASS.)

4 - CYL. "50-B"   **5350.**
(25-29 PASS.)

6 - CYL. "54"   **7500.**
(ILLUSTR.
TOP, LEFT)

"DRUMHEAD" LOGO SIGN *
AT REAR, ON ORNAMENTAL
"OBSERVATION
PLATFORM"

*=SOME WERE
ILLUMINATED
AT NIGHT

WHITE = 29~30 (B)

NEW

"60-K" HOUSE-TO-HOUSE DELIVERY (SUMMER, 1931) TRUCK
6 CYL., HYDRAULIC BRAKES
112" WB and up

White

new 6-CYLINDER HEAVY-DUTY MODELS AVAIL. (with 4-WH. AIR BRAKES or POWER HYDRAULIC BRAKES.

31-32

new HORIZONTAL HOOD LOUVRES (LT. DUTY)

OVERHEAD-VALVE
6-CYL. "620," "630," "640" SERIES MODELS IN MARCH, 1931.

GROSS WEIGHTS = 8,000-40,000 lbs. ('31)

"160-1-2" new for 1931 (1 TO 2 TON) with 138" WB. 4 CYL., 45 HP ENGINE, AS FOUND IN new "210," "211," "212" (1½ TO 2 TON.)

HIGHWAY MOTOR FREIGHT, INC.

('31)

(note DIFFERENCE BETWEEN CAB OF VAN, ABOVE, FROM THAT OF VAN AT LOWER LEFT.)

RETAIL DELIVERY

FAST EXPRESS

HEAVY-DUTY DUMP

CITY OR INTER-CITY VAN

new 1931 6-WHEELERS with 6 CYL., 96 HP ENGS.:
"64 SW 300" (5 TO 7½ TON)
"59 ASW 400" (7½ TO 10 TON) ('31)

1932 MODELS :   ('31)

Model	Tonnage	CYL.	HP
602	(1½ to 2 TON)	6 CYL.	54 HP
611	(2 T)	6	61
161, 162	(1-2 T)	4	45
51-A	(2½ T)	4	54
211, 212	(1½-2 T)	4	45
612	(2½ T)	6	61
620	(2½ T)	6	72
58	(3 T)	4	54
640	(3 T)	6	108
621, 630	(3 T)	6	82
631	(3½ T)	6	82
641	(3½ T)	6	108
642	(4 T)	6	108
643	(5 T)	6	108

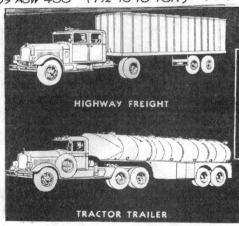

HIGHWAY FREIGHT

TRACTOR TRAILER

6-WHEELERS ALSO

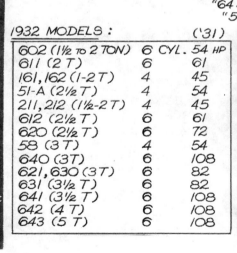

WHITE = 31~32

(ESTABLISHED 1901)

WHITE MOTOR CO., CLEVELAND, OH.

('32 - '33)

33

SUMMER, '33 (K)

MODELS:

60-K, 601, 161 (1¼-1½ T;)
602, 162 (1½-2 T;) 611, 211 (2-2½ T;)
612, 212, 620 (2½-3 T;) 51-A (2½-4 T;)
618, 621 (3-4 T;) 630, 640 (3-4½ T;)
58 (3-5 T;) 631, 641 (3½-6 T;) 55 (5T;)
58-SS (7½ T;) 642 (4-7½ T;) 52 (5-7½ T;)
643 (5-9 T;) 691 (7-9 T;)
6-WH.: 630SW200 (5-6T;) 642SW320 (7-9 T;)
643SW420 (9-11 TON)

$1700.-$16,000.=TRUCK and BUS PRICE RANGE

new "K" SERIES has CAB PLACED FURTHER FORWARD, with ENGINE PARTIALLY PROTRUDING INTO CAB FIREWALL.

ADDED MODELS FOR 1934 (WITH MOST PREVIOUS MODELS CONT'D.)

701 (1¼-1½ T;) 701-A (1½ T;) 702 (1½-2T;) 702-A (2 T;)
612-K (2½-3T;) 618-K, 620-K (3-4 T;) 630-K, 640-K (3-4½ T;) 631-K,
641-K (3½-6 T;) 631-X (7½ T;)   4.73 TO 11.7 GEAR RATIOS

FINAL 4-CYL. CONVENTIONALS ('35)

632-X IS new 10-TON, 215" WB MODEL FOR '35, with 6-CYL., 434 CID ENGINE (105 HP @ 2100 RPM.)
580 CID, 6-CYL. ENG. IS MOST POWERFUL (130 HP @ 2050 RPM) of '35 WHITES, USED IN 640, 640-K, 641, 641-K, 642, 643, and 691 MODELS.

new STYLING FOR 1934 →

34-35

WHITE'S FIRST V-12 "10-AB" ENGINE LISTED FOR 1935. EARLY 465 CID VERSION has 128 HP @ 2600 RPM, FOUND IN MODELS 730 and 731.

54-A STREAMLINED BUS ('35) →

731 C.O.E. V-12 ('35)

WHITE 33~35

374

WHITE

BUS ('37)

ARTICULATED C.O.E. ('37)

MULTI-STOP DLVRY. VAN ('37)

MOST 700 and 600 SERIES MODELS CONTINUED, PLUS 7½-TON 586-GS.

IMPROVED 505 CID V-12 "12AB" ENGINE (143 HP @ 2800 RPM) IN MODELS 730, 730-X, 731, 731-X.

new STREAMLINED 1936 MODELS, STYLED BY ALEXIS DE SAKHNOFFSKY
(ALL MODELS RESTYLED BY MARCH, 1936.)

new CITY TRANSIT BUS MODEL 788 ('38)

IN SOME '36 MODELS UNDER 4 TONS, AN IMPROVED 80 HP ENGINE (RATED 81 HP @ 3000, 270 CID)

PARK BUS '38

36-38 NEW
TOTAL RESTYLING
SO-CALLED "AIR CONDITIONED" CABS

Beautifully designed aero-type instrument panel adds to the de luxe appearance of the cab.

new C.O.E. MODELS ('37)

1937 C.O.E.s: 730, 731, 731-H, 805, 809, 810, 812, 818.

new 900 SERIES 6-WHEELERS ('37) INCLUDE 904, 918, 920, 922, 942, 991.

('37)

STREAMLINED TANKER

FINAL V-12 TRUCKS IN 1938.

68 TO 143 HP IN 1938, 6-WHEELERS TO 16½ TONS.

The new White has been completely modernized with smart streamline styling.

IMPROVED FLOATING RIDE CABS and "SUPER POWER" 6-CYL. ENGINES (6-CYL. ONLY, IN 1939 CONVENTIONALS.)

FROM 76 HP @ 3000 RPM

LONGER WHEELBASES IN 1941; 4.45 TO 9.5 GEAR RATIOS

MID—
39-40s

1940 MODELS 510, 700 800 SERIES and up 95" WB UP

('41)

White

new WA SERIES STARTS 1941.

CONV. 134" and 136" WB

H.T. INC. — HIGHWAY TRANSPORT INC.

STANDARD MOTOR EXPRESS

1½ -10 TON 1941 MODELS:

WA-14	250 CID	90 HP @ 2800 G M
WA-18	270	100 @ 2600
WA-20	318	110 @ 2600
WA-22	362	125 @ 2600
WA-28	and WA-34 ALSO
720	529 CID	133 @ 2400
722	97" and 100 WB C.O.E.s:

(MODEL #S 100 DIGITS HIGHER THAN CORRESPONDING CONVENTIONALS LISTED ABOVE. WA-114 has SAME ENG. AS WA-14, and SO FORTH. 820 and 822 LIKE 720 and 6-WHEELERS: 722 SPECS.) WA-2064, WA-2264, WA-3464, 920, 922 MODELS.

Wm CRAWFORD & SONS

← 99" WB, 4 CYL. AIR-COOLED REAR ENG.

NEW

FOR 1939. (SOME '40-41 WHITE HORSES W/O VERT. FRONT CHROME.)

White Horse

('42) CITY BUS

ORDNANCE PLANT

'41-'42 WHITE HORSE (note CHANGES)

Barclay

CITY TRANSIT BUS ('42) (ABOVE) BECAUSE OF CIVILIAN PUBLIC TRANSPORTATION NEEDS, BUS PRODUCTION CONT'D. DURING WORLD WAR 2.

1941~1942 WHITE HORSE DELIVERY VAN (note CHANGES)

WHITE = '39~MID '40s

White

46

PANEL DELIVERY TRUCK

STAKE

UTILITY LINESMAN'S BODY

LINESMAN'S UTILITY TRUCK w. EXTENDED CAB

C.O.E.

"WHITE HORSE" DELIVERY STILL MFD. (LIMITED PROD.) TO EARLY 1950s.

47-48

TRACTOR/TRAILER COMBINATION

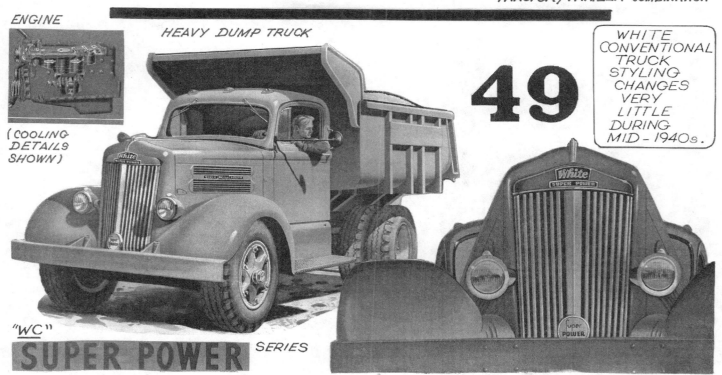

ENGINE

(COOLING DETAILS SHOWN)

HEAVY DUMP TRUCK

49

WHITE CONVENTIONAL TRUCK STYLING CHANGES VERY LITTLE DURING MID-1940s.

"WC" SUPER POWER SERIES

WHITE = 46 ~ 49

WHITE DIESEL POWER

CONVENTIONAL →

HIGHWAY POST OFFICE COACH

('50)

TRANSIT BUS

White

('51)

DIESEL ENGINES *have* 743 CID, 175-200 HP @ 1800 RPM

WHITE 3000

C.O.E.s
3014, 3015, 3016, 3018, 3020, 3022, 3026

SPECIFICATIONS:

16½ TO 27 TONS GROSS VEHICLE WT. 85, 91 OR 109" WB 6 CYL. 318, 340 OR 386 CID 114, 120 OR 135 HP @ 3000 RPM 5-SPEED TRANS.

White SUPER POWER 3000

('51)

EXPRESS MAIN 44

50-53

TILT-CAB DETAILS (INTRO. SPRING, 1949)

White SUPER POWER

CONVENTIONAL

ALL 6 CYL.   CONVENT'L 134" WB UP

1951 MODELS:	(TRUCKS)			
WC-16	298 CID	110 HP @	3100	RPM
WC-18	318	114	@	3000
WC-20	340	120	@	"
WC-22	362	125	@	"
WC-26	386	135	@	"
WC-28	481	170	@	"
WC-32	504	184	@	"

MORE POWER with WHITE MUSTANG ENGINE

184 HP

TRUCK-TRACTORS *have* "T" SUFFIX ON MODEL NO.; DIESELS *have* "D" SUFFIX.

('53)

CONV. WC-24PLT TRACTOR 10.00 x 20 TIRES

WHITE = 50~53

378

COMPACT DIESELS ('54) $12,300.

WITH 6 CYL., 200 HP CUMMINS DIESEL ENG. TILTED 20° TO RIGHT, ALLOWING 2 CYLS. TO BE SET BACK INTO CAB.

WHITE - FREIGHTLINER
(BUILT IN AFFILIATION WITH WHITE MOTOR CO., FROM 1951 TO 1975,) SHOWN IN SEPARATE **FREIGHTLINER** SECTION.

('56)

FLEET OF 225 WHITE 9000's NOW IN SERVICE

DIESELS (ABOVE)

new (AVAIL. IN CANADA)

2000-B
SCHOOLBUS CHASSIS ('56½)

BUS WITH 6-CYL., 298 CID "WHITE MUSTANG" ENG. (110 HP @ 3100 RPM)

54-59

WHITE PROD. ONLY = 12,141 ('58); 15,468 ('59)

COMBINED PROD.:
23,384 ('58)
25,335 ('59)

C.O.E.

new
White "5000"
Cab made of
FIBER GLASS

INTRO. 1959 WITH 335-HP DIESEL ENGINE

2064 TANDEM →

New EMBLEM

"2064" SPECS.

150" W.B.
(155, 160, 165, 170, 175, 180, 185, 190" OPTIONAL W.B.s)
"O.A. 145 ENGINE
331 c.i.a 6
145 HP @ 3200 RPM
7.50 x 20" TIRES
5-SPEED TRANS.

('59)   **GASOLINE POWERED**

WHITE = 54~59

('60)

('69)

('61)

DURING EARLY 1960s, SOME OLDER CONVENTIONAL TYPES CONTINUED.

WORLD LEADER IN HEAVY DUTY TRUCKS
WHITE TRUCKS

('67)

CONVENTIONALS
60-70
A

with MIXER BODY

WESTERN STAR MFD.
IN WHITE'S KELOWNA, B.C. FACTORY (WHICH OPENED 5-67)

('69-70)

('69)

PRODUCTION, 1960 to 1970:

18,389	('60)
19,474	('61)
26,450	('62)
28,161	('63)
21,342	('64)
27,316	('65)
32,422	('66)
24,664	('67)
29,982	('68)
31,520	('69)
22,288	('70)

9000 SERIES TRUCK TRACTOR

(C.O.E.s ON NEXT PAGE)

WHITE = 60~70-A

THE TREND CAB PGS. MOLDED OF "ROYALEX"

White

THIS TYPE DURING MOST OF 1960s, WITH ONLY MINOR CHANGES.

('67)

('69)

60-70

C.O.E.s

COMPACT

B

available with either White Super Mustang gasoline engines or Cummins and Detroit Diesel diesels and a compatible range of transmissions.

PDQ DELIVERY

AVAIL. 1960-1966

('69)

TILT CAB RAISED, SHOWING ENGINE DETAILS

COMPACT SERIES

855 CID 270 HP

('70)

6000 XPEDITOR new

FOR 1970 (EARLY TYPE W. NO SMALL EXTRA LTS. AS SEEN ON LATER MODEL AT LEFT.)

ABC COMPANY

MIXER

VARIOUS 4000 OR
9000 SERIES
CONVENTIONALS
AS OF 10-71.

White

WHITE TRUCKS

CONSTRUCKTOR

Model	BBC
C4364-G	108"
C4664D-G	118"

Stokely·Van Camp
Stokely's
Finest

4000
SERIES
CONV.

OBSOLETE OR
DAMAGED MODELS
CAN BE REBODIED
WITH
CONSTRUCKTOR
GLIDER KIT

M77

71
(and
ON)

"ALLEY CAT"

NATIONAL DISPOSAL SERVICE

REFUSE TRUCK 127" WB
(new)
(STARTS SPRING, '71)

1500, 1600
OR 7000
SERIES
C.O.E.
TYPES
AS OF
10-71.

C.O.E.

REAR
(WEST.
STAR)

W
WHITE
WESTERN STAR

SOME HAVE 2
HEADLIGHTS
INSTEAD
OF
4.

WHITE WESTERN STAR

CAB (WEST.
STAR)

4900 WD, 4864 WD OR
4964 WD SERIES

WHITE "WESTERN STAR" TRUCKS BLT. AT WHITE'S BRANCH FACTORY (OPENED
MAY, 1967, IN KELOWNA, B.C., CANADA.) 637 BLT. 1968; 820 BLT. 1969;
TOTAL OF 2000 BLT. BY MAY, 1970.

WHITE = 71

72½ ON
New

ROAD COMMANDER

(REPLACES 7400 SERIES C.O.E.s)

SINGLE ACCESS DOOR puts the wiper motors and radiator cap right at your fingertips. Also gives you fewer things to go wrong.

TORSION BAR TILT CAB

"ROAD COMMANDER 2" LIGHTWT. STARTS MID-1977.

(BECAUSE OF "ENERGY CRISIS," FUEL-SAVING ("ROAD COMMANDER 2" LIGHTWEIGHT MODEL STARTS MID-1977.)

DURING 1970s and 1980s, CONSIDERABLE OVERLAPPING OF MODELS.

73 ON

ROAD BOSS 2 and WESTERN STAR CONVENTIONALS AVAIL. 1978, 195-475 HP DIESEL ENGINES.

Western Star
(WINDSHIELD HEIGHT INCREASED 2")

(ROAD XPEDITOR 2 and ROAD COMMANDER 2 C.O.E.s ALSO AVAIL. 1978, 195-450 HP DIESEL ENGINES.)

ROAD BOSS
(NEW)

"ROAD BOSS 2" FROM 1977 ON

(C.O.E.s ON NEXT PAGE)

('73)

WHITE = 72½-73

383

WHITE

74
ON
diesel power
CHOICE OF
13 DIFF.
engines.
210 to 335 HP

Inside the Cab
Two inches more headroom
2-Tone padded vinyl interior with
  wood tone dash
RCCC instrument panel — all controls
  standardized
118% bigger speedometer and
  tachometer — easier to read
Quick disconnect dash access panel

ROAD XPEDITOR
new low cab forward

WHITE

ROAD XPEDITOR

ROAD XPEDITOR

(DOOR EMBLEM)

1974 C.O.E.
ROAD
COMMANDER
has
new BUMPER and
GRILLE LIKE THAT of
ROAD BOSS CONVENT'L.

MFD. BY VOLVO WHITE CORP.,
GREENSBORO, N.C.

(DIAGONAL STRIPE ACROSS
GRILLE INDICATES
VOLVO AFFILIATION.)

C.O.E.
84
ON

SLEEPER
CAB

NEW
HIGH CABOVER

WHITE
74~84 ON

WHITE

83 WESTERN STAR

Conventional:

New 84 ON

HAS TANDEM REAR AXLES

Cab features maximum efficiency with wraparound instrumentation (including electric tach and speedometer) and removable instrument panels for easy servicing.

DASH (ABOVE) ('84)

4 RECTANGULAR HEADLIGHTS

new DIAGONAL RADIATOR BAND SHOWS VOLVO AFFILIATION

AERODYNAMIC SHROUD

Integral Sleeper:

CUMMINS FORMULA BIG CAM III DIESEL ENGINE (ALSO IN '84 C.O.E. ON PRECEDING PAGE)
FIBERGLASS TILT HOOD
11R24.5G - 14PR RADIAL TUBELESS TIRES
24.5 x 8.25" WHEELS

100-GAL. RT. SIDE ALUMINUM FUEL TANK

WHITE = 83~84 ON

WILLYS

(1903 TO 1963)

WILLYS-OVERLAND CO., TOLEDO, OH.

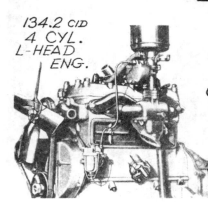

134.2 CID 4 CYL. L-HEAD ENG.

ORIGINALLY **OVERLAND**

REAR DETAILS

COMPLETELY new 1933 MODELS

33-36

"77" SERIES

('33)

WILLYS-OVERLAND TOLEDO, OHIO (BECOMES JEEP AFTER 1945.)

1934 has new WIRE WHEELS, new SEMI-HORIZONTAL HOOD LOUVRES

HOOD VENT DOORS and STEEL ARTILLERY WHEELS ON 1933.

new "BUBBLE" HOOD VENTS IN 1935

WILLYS 77

100" WB (THROUGH '39)

new GRILLE IN 1935

ARTILLERY WHEELS RETURN FOR 1936.

'37 DASH

37-38

(COMPLETELY RESTYLED)

SERIAL NUMBERS :
'37 = 61000 UP
'38 = 65001 UP

new 61-H.P. MODEL "61"

FRONT END RESTYLED (CAR)

TRUCK SERIALS :
"38" 89001 UP
"48" 91751 UP

"440" C.O.E. ALSO AVAIL.

39

1938-STYLE MODEL "48" has 48 H.P. @ 3200 RPM (SINCE '33)

OLD OVERLAND NAME RETURNS FOR 1939 ONLY. (FIRST TIME USED SINCE 1926.)

WILLYS = 33~39

WILLYS 40

"OVERLAND" NAME CEASES.

"WILLYS" NAME ON SIDE OF HOOD (SEE ARROW)

FANCY ORNAMENT

SPLIT GRILLE IN 1940

100" WB, EXC. ON EARLY "441" MODELS LISTED IN 1940.

SC-440
4 CYL.
58 HP
@
3600 RPM
4.7 TO
5.11 G.R.

SCOF-440-P
48 HP @ 3200 RPM
5.11 GEAR RATIO
(OTHERS AVAIL.)

41-42

WILLYS MILITARY **JEEP** STARTS 1941

441   104" WB   **442** →
new GRILLE. HOOD   (LIKE '41)

UNSOLD 1941 and 1942 MODELS (CIVILIAN TRUCKS and CARS) RELEASED (ON A LIMITED BASIS) DURING THE 1943~1945 WARTIME YEARS.

('41)

VAN

THE WALK-IN WILLYS VAN (AT LEFT) IS EXTREMELY SCARCE, AND SELDOM SEEN!

C.O.E. VERSION OF **441** SERIES 104" WB

('41)

(REPLACED 1946 BY **JEEP** VEHICLES)

WILLYS = 1940~42

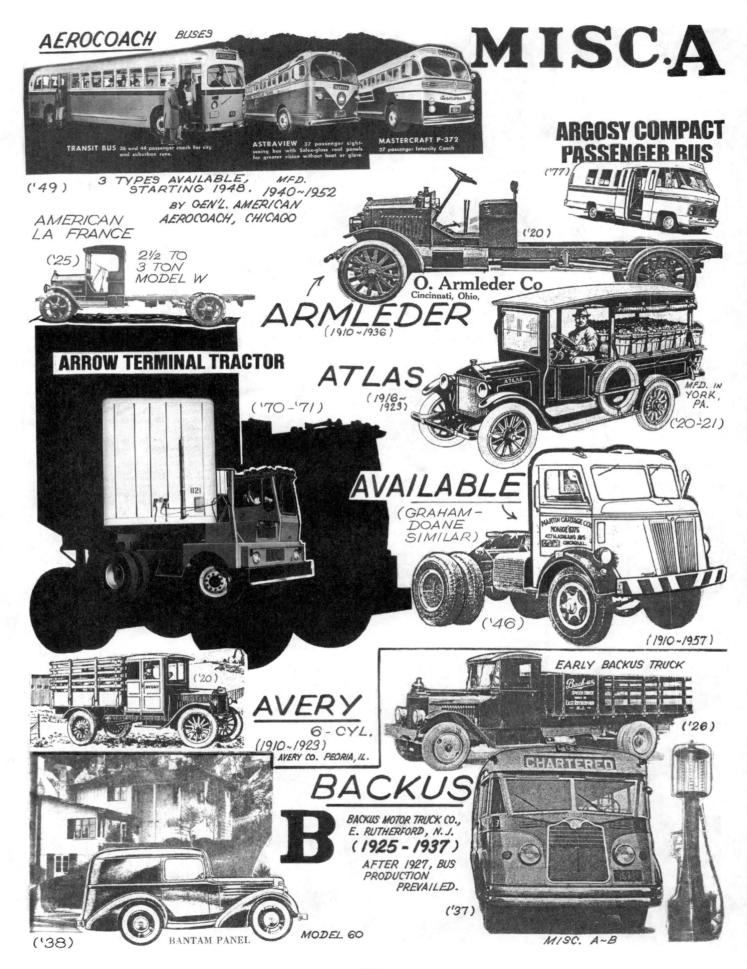

AEROCOACH BUSES

TRANSIT BUS 36 and 44 passenger coach for city and suburban runs.

ASTRAVIEW 37 passenger sightseeing bus with Solex-glass roof panels for greater vision without heat or glare.

MASTERCRAFT P-372 37 passenger Intercity Coach

('49)

3 TYPES AVAILABLE, MFD. STARTING 1948. 1940~1952 BY GEN'L. AMERICAN AEROCOACH, CHICAGO

ARGOSY COMPACT PASSENGER BUS

('77)

('20)

AMERICAN LA FRANCE

('25) 2½ TO 3 TON MODEL W

O. Armleder Co
Cincinnati, Ohio,

ARMLEDER
(1910~1936)

ATLAS
(1916~ 1923)

MFD. IN YORK, PA.

('20-'21)

ARROW TERMINAL TRACTOR

('70-'71)

AVAILABLE
(GRAHAM-DOANE SIMILAR)

('46)

(1910~1957)

('20)

AVERY
6-CYL.
(1910~1923)
AVERY CO. PEORIA, IL.

EARLY BACKUS TRUCK

('26)

BACKUS

B BACKUS MOTOR TRUCK CO.,
E. RUTHERFORD, N.J.
(1925-1937)
AFTER 1927, BUS PRODUCTION PREVAILED.

CHARTERED

('37)

('38) BANTAM PANEL MODEL 60

MISC. A~B

MISC. B

BARROWS

('28)

3½ TON MODEL T-35 — 4 CYL.

BARROWS MOTOR TRUCK CO., INDIANAPOLIS (1927-1928)

(CONT'D.)

('56)

BECK

A CLOSE IMITATION OF GMC'S "SCENICRUISER."

BECK ALSO BLT. OTHER BUSES, 1934-1957.

(1911~1926) BESSEMER 4-TON → ('22)

BIEDERMAN

6-WHEELER (1940s) (1920~1955)

6 × 6, Tractor, Wrecking, Type C-2 (Biederman)

BLAZER

BY CHEVROLET (SINCE 1969)

(C. '34)

→ "BOTTLE" TRUCK, ON 6-CYL. DODGE CHASSIS. TYPICAL OF VARIOUS SPECIAL-BODIED ODDITIES BUILT FOR ADVERTISING PURPOSES.

('81)

BRONCO

BY FORD (SINCE 1966)

('78)

('39)

AS THIS BOOK IS DEVOTED MAINLY TO PICKUPS, HEAVIER TRUCKS, VANS AND BUSES, THERE IS MERELY TOKEN APPEARANCE OF SPORT-UTILITY VEHICLES (S.U.V.s)

Brown

BY BROWN TRUCK + EQUIP. CO. CHARLOTTE, N.C. (1939~1953)

"LS" C.O.E. ('53)

MISC. ══ B

coaches from Champion.

CHEVROLET CHASSIS (DODGE ALSO

('82)

AMERICAN COLEMAN CO., LITTLETON, CO. (EST. 1925)

CLYDESDALE MOTOR TRUCK CO. CLYDE, OH. (1917~1938)

COLEMAN

(EARLY 1960s)

CLYDESDALE

COMET AUTOMOBILE @ DECATUR, IL. (1920~1921)

COMET
4-CYL.
1½-TON
('20)

CONESTOGA ('19-'20)

COMMERCE MODEL "25" 2½ TON ('25)

CRANE CARRIER ('81)
REFUSE TRUCK

CROSLEY
PANEL DELIVERY 4-CYL. ('51)

COOK BROS. ('51)

COOK BROS., LOS ANGELES (1950~1964)

C.T. ELECTRIC
MODEL H-1
½ TON 108" WB
(1908-1928, PHILADELPHIA, PA.)

CUSHMAN "TRUCKSTER" 1960s

Crown
school coach ('71)

('28)

MISC.—C

390

MISC. D

DELCAR
MFD. BY AMERICAN MOTORS INC. TROY, N.Y. (1947~1948)

('20) **MODEL BW**

DEARBORN TRUCKS
BY DEARBORN MOTOR TRUCK CO., CHICAGO, IL. (1919~1924)

('47~'48)
4 CYL., 60" WB

('25) **DE MARTINI**
MFD. BY DE MARTINI MOTOR TRUCK CO., SAN FRANCISCO, CA. (1919~1934)

DIVCO
DIVCO~TWIN TRUCK CO., DETROIT (ESTAB. 1927)

ACME MILK

Divco-Twin ('41)
(4 OR 6 CYL.)

DORRIS MOTOR CAR CO., ST. LOUIS, MO.
2½ TON "K-5" ('26)

DJB ('82)
BRITISH-BUILT
(SINCE 1975)

DORRIS

Capacity Two-Ton
DUTY ('21)
DUTY MOTOR CO., GREENVILLE, IL.
(1920~1922)

DOUGLAS
DOUGLAS TRUCK MFG. CO., OMAHA, NE.
(BUDA 4 OR 6 CYL. ENGS. IN MOST)
(1917~1935)

(BY LOCKHEED)
"DRAGON WAGON"
(8-WHEEL DRIVE)

('72)

MISC.—D

MISC. E-F

EUCLID DIVISION
GENERAL MOTORS CORPORATION
Cleveland 17, Ohio
(EST. 1931)

('72)

EAGLE (EAGLE EMBLEM ON FRONT)
BUS (SINCE 1956) ORIGINALLY BUILT IN BELGIUM. AMERICAN FACTORY OPENED AT BROWNSVILLE, TEXAS IN 1975. MOST BUILT FOR CONTINENTAL TRAILWAYS. ALSO NAMED "GOLDEN EAGLE" and "SILVER EAGLE" SINCE '50s.

('57)

Euclid Equipment
FOR MOVING EARTH, ROCK, COAL AND ORE

FORMERLY
The EUCLID ROAD MACHINERY Co.
CLEVELAND 17, OHIO

(SINCE 1977, EUCLID A SUBSIDIARY OF DAIMLER-BENZ.)

FABCO
FABCO. DIV. of KELSEY-HAYES CO., OAKLAND, CALIF. (SINCE '54) (GAS OR DIESEL)
('72)

UV new for 1972

FARGO
"CLIPPER" 6 CYL. ('29) 3/4 TON (1/2-TON "PACKET" MODEL ALSO in '29) MFD. BY CHRYSLER CORP., DETROIT, SINCE 1928.

FISHER MODEL 16 1-TON (ABOVE)

1 1/2 TON CHASSIS

('26)

from $795 F.O.B. Marion, Ind.

FARMOROAD BY CROSLEY

('51)

1 1/2 TON
Fisher Fast Freight
A SPEEDY 1 1/2 TON TRUCK
STANDARD MOTOR TRUCK CO., DETROIT
(1912~1933)

MODEL C.O. →
$2450. UP

FLEET ARROW (SCREENSIDE DELIVERY)

('28)

('29)

('59) **FOX**

FLEET ARROW
BY PIERCE-ARROW (AVAIL. 1928 TO 1932)

MISC. = E~F

('36)

GAR WOOD (1936~1938)

MISC. G

('75)

SCHOOL BUS

('25)

GILLIG SCHOOL BUS
GILLIG BROS.,
HAYWARD, CALIF.
(SINCE 1932) IN SAN
FRANCISCO
TO '38.

MFD. IN OAKLAND, CA.
1916~1946, AND IN SAN
FRANCISCO, 1946~1948

GRAMM PIONEER BERNSTEIN
(1912~1930)

GRAHAM-DOANE (1946~1948)

('46)   EX-DOANE (1916~1946)

Gotfredson Truck
(1920~1948)
CANADA / DETROIT

('20)

GRAY

('25)

1-TON CHAS.
4 CYL.
(1924 SIMILAR)

('34)   GRASS-PREMIER
(1923~1937)
SAUK CITY, WI.

GUILDER
"JB" 4-TON
ICE CREAM TRUCK
(1924~1936)

J. M. HORTON ICE CREAM CO. INC.
HORTON'S ICE CREAM
NEW YORK

('29)

MFD. BY GUILDER
ENGINEERING CO.,
POUGHKEEPSIE, N.Y.
HERCULES, CONTINENTAL
OR BUDA ENGINES
(TRUCK OR BUS CHASSIS UNITS AVAIL.)

MISC. ═ G

393

MISC. H - J

HENDRICKSON ('39)
CHICAGO and LYONS, IL. (SINCE 1913)

Model 140 Two-Ton Truck

('20)

HUFFMAN
ELKHART, IN. (1919 ~ 1927)

IBEX "FLEXI-TRUC"
MFD. IN SALT LAKE CITY (EST. 1964)
('72)
DETROIT DIESEL 4-53 ENGINE
82" WB
THIS MODEL INTRO. 1970

('30)
(2 VIEWS)

INDIANA (ABOVE, LEFT)
(1911 ~ 1939)

JACKSON MODEL "C-1920"
WITH 4-CYL.
CONTINENTAL ENGINE
(4 1/2" × 5 1/2")
150" WB
4 SP. TRANS.
9.18 GEAR RATIO
(LISTED 9.17, '21)
36 × 7 SOLID TIRES
12 M.P.H. (@ 1027 RPM)
1921 SAME, BUT IS "4WD" MODEL.

Jackson
FOUR WHEEL DRIVE TRUCKS
JACKSON MOTORS CORP., JACKSON, MICH. (1907 ~ 1923)
EISEMANN IGN. and ELECTR. SYSTEM. WITH SELF-STARTER.

"No Hill Too Steep— No Sand Too Deep"

3 1/2 TON "C-1920"

('20)

('33)

J. C. JARRETT MOTOR AND FINANCE CO., COLORADO SPRINGS, COLO. (1921 ~ 1934)
6-CYL. WAUKESHA ENG.

JARRETT

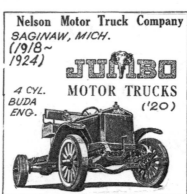

Nelson Motor Truck Company
SAGINAW, MICH. (1918 ~ 1924)
JUMBO MOTOR TRUCKS
4 CYL. BUDA ENG.
('20)

MISC. K-L

KAISER (1946)
60' ARTICULATED BUS

BLT. BY PERMANENTE METALS CORP.
DIV. OF KAISER INDUSTRIES,
PERMANENTE, CALIF. (1 BUS ONLY)
WITH 6-CYL. CUMMINS DIESEL ENGINE.
USED ON SAN FRANCISCO TO LOS
ANGELES ROUTE OF SANTA FE
TRAILWAYS UNTIL 1951.

Swing-away cab for pallet cargo

('71)

KARRY-ALL

('22)
(ELECTRIC)
KELLAND
KELLAND MOTOR CAR CO.
NEWARK, N.J.
(1922~1925)

('66) KW-DART

LECTRA D-100

ELECTRIC truck

('26)

('81)

LEHIGH MOTOR TRUCKS

2 Ton
4 Cylinder Model
$1695
F. o. b. Allentown, Pa.

(1925~1927)

LINN

T-3
8 TON
('44)

LE MOON
1200-D
DIESEL

('38)

MFD. BY NELSON LE MOON TRUCK CO.,
CHICAGO, IL.
(1910~1939)
TOTAL 30-YR. OUTPUT APPROX. 3000,
MOST SALES IN GREATER CHICAGO AREA

UNUSUAL HALF-TRACK
REAR WHEELS

LINN MFG. CO., MORRIS, N.Y.
(1916~1950)
(SEE ALSO "REPUBLIC,"
P. 347)

MISC. = K~L

MISC. M - N

MASON
"ROAD KING"
MODEL 215
MASON   4 CYL.
MOTOR TRK. CO., $1776.25
FLINT, MICH.   (CHASSIS)

('25)

(A DIV. OF DURANT)

(ABOVE)   (C. '48)
MacDONALD   LOW-LOADER

MacDONALD TRUCK and MFG. CO.
SAN FRANCISCO, CALIF. (1920-1952)
(A DIV. OF PETERBILT AFTER W.W. 2)

MASTER TRUCK

ENGINEERED FIBREGLASS CO.,
FOUNTAIN VALLEY, CALIF.
(INTRO. 1972) DETROIT
DIESEL, OTHER DIESELS AVAIL.

160" WB

('72)

MAXWELL

(1905—1925)
ORIGINALLY
MAXWELL-BRISCOE MOTOR
CO., TARRYTOWN, N.Y.,
CARS and TRUCKS to 1912.
(CARS ONLY, 1913-1916.)
1917-1925, MFD. IN DETROIT
BY MAXWELL MOTOR CO.

STAKE
('21)
PANEL

"MICRO-COACH"
(BY GILLIG)

('71)

GILLIG BROS., HAYWARD CALIF. (INTRO. 1971)
ON FORD P-500 DLVRY. CHASSIS (330 CID FORD V8, 190 HP)
(GILLIG ALSO BLT. SCHOOL BUSES)

('25)

4-CYL.
MODEL
"AX"
(3~TON)   ('25)

MORELAND

MORELAND MOTOR TRUCK CO.
BURBANK, CA.
(1911-1941)

NORTHWAY MOTORS CORP.,
NATICK,
MASS.
(1918~
1923)

4 CYL.

('85)

('85)

NATIONAL
COACH CORPORATION

NATIONAL TRANSMARK 30' BUS

Northway

('20)

MISC. ═ M~N

396

MISC. O - R

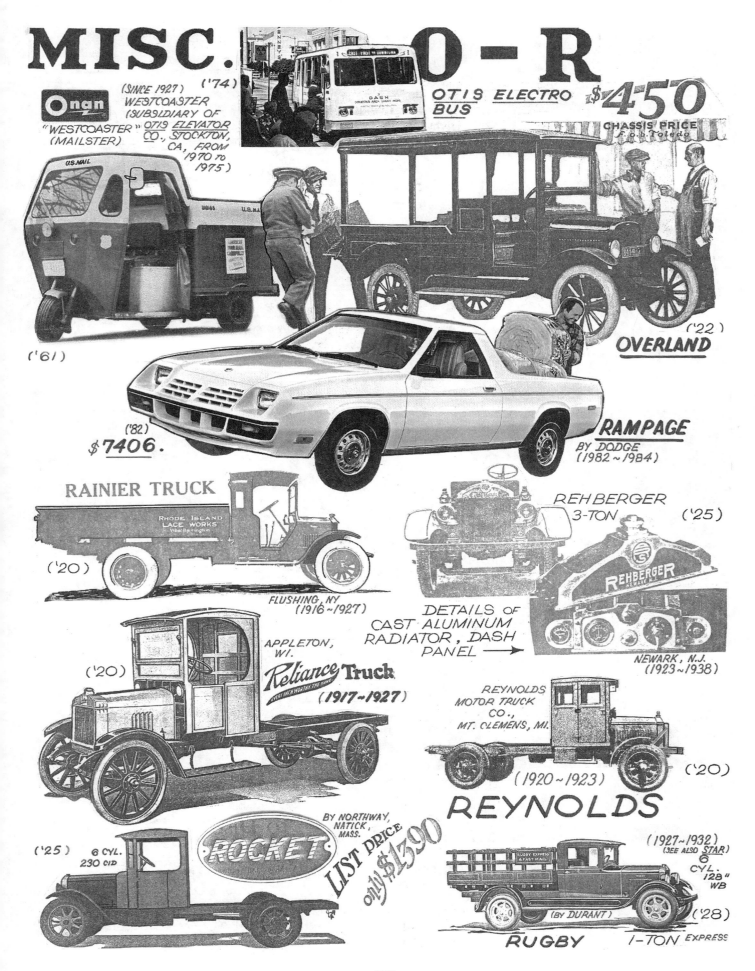

Onan (SINCE 1927)

WESTCOASTER ('74)
(SUBSIDIARY OF
"WESTCOASTER" OTIS ELEVATOR
(MAILSTER) CO., STOCKTON,
CA, FROM
1970 TO
1975)

U.S. MAIL

('61)

OTIS ELECTRO BUS $450 CHASSIS PRICE F.o.b. Toledo

('22) OVERLAND

RAMPAGE BY DODGE (1982~1984)

('82) $7406.

RAINIER TRUCK

RHODE ISLAND LACE WORKS West Barrington

('20)

FLUSHING, NY (1916~1927)

REHBERGER 3-TON ('25)

REHBERGER NEWARK N.J.

DETAILS OF CAST ALUMINUM RADIATOR, DASH PANEL →

NEWARK, N.J. (1923~1938)

APPLETON, WI.

('20) Reliance Truck EVERY INCH WORTHY THE NAME (1917-1927)

REYNOLDS MOTOR TRUCK CO., MT. CLEMENS, MI.

(1920~1923)

('20)

REYNOLDS

BY NORTHWAY, NATICK, MASS.

ROCKET LIST PRICE only $1390

('25) 6 CYL. 230 CID

(1927~1932) (SEE ALSO STAR) 6 CYL. 128" WB

RUGBY EXPRESS & FAST MAIL

(BY DURANT) ('28)

RUGBY 1-TON EXPRESS

397

MISC. S

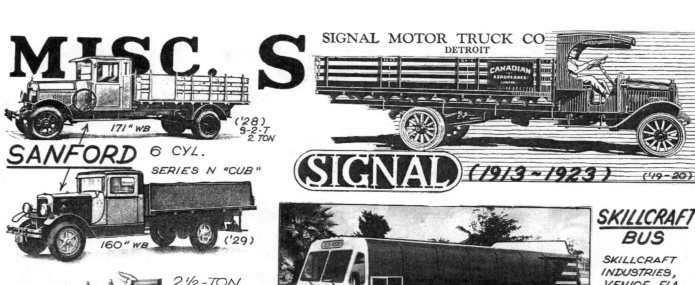

171" WB

('28)
S-2-T
2 TON

SANFORD 6 CYL.

SIGNAL MOTOR TRUCK CO
DETROIT

SIGNAL (1913~1923) ('19-20)

SERIES N "CUB"

160" WB   ('29)

SKILLCRAFT BUS

SKILLCRAFT INDUSTRIES, VENICE, FLA.
('81)

2½-TON MODEL "2½-K"

('25)

STANDARD
(MFD. 1912~1933, DETROIT)

STAR SIX

ONE TON CHASSIS
$975 f.o.b. Lansing
Box and cab not included
40 HP

('27)

Star

DELIVERY WAGON w PANEL TOP and VESTIBULE FRONT 109" WB

('24)

STAR MFD. BY _DURANT_, 1922~1932

COMPOUND FLEETRUCK

The greatest single step forward in a quarter century of Motor Transportation. A new type of transmission with the *economy shift* — a 4th forward gear that increases motor efficiency, gasoline mileage, speed and power range. Easy to operate — a forward push on gear lever instantly changes from 3rd to 4th, reducing fuel cost 20%.

STAR EXPORT TRUCK : RUGBY

('20)

STOUGHTON

STUTZ PAK-AGE-CAR

('36)
DELIVERY VAN

MFD. BY The Stoughton Wagon Co.
Stoughton   Wis.
(1, 1½, 2 - TON EARLY MODELS)
(1920 ~ 1928) WAUKESHA and
HERCULES ENGINES IN EARLY MODELS; AFTER 1923, MIDWEST and CONT'L. ENGS. ALSO USED.

STUTZ
(1926~1941) PAK-AGE-CAR
AFFILIATED WITH:
PACKAGE CAR, CHICAGO (1926~1932)
STUTZ, INDIANAPOLIS (1932~1938)
AUBURN, CONNERSVILLE, IN. (1938~1941)
SALES and SERVICE FROM DIAMOND T, 1939~1941
MISC.——S

MISC. T - U

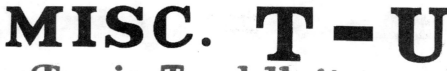

Toppins Truck Unit with **Fordson Power Plant**

('23)

Toppins Tractor Truck

('32) **TRABOLD**
NO FRONT SUPPORTS FOR CANOPY TOP

1¼ TON MODEL B 132" WB

('24)

4 CYL. **TRAYLOR**

5-TON MODEL F 170" WB

FORD FYD

TRANSPORT
INTERNAL GEAR DRIVE TRUCKS

TRANSPORT TRUCK COMPANY, Mount Pleasant, Michigan
Builders of "The Frictionless Truck" (1919~1927)

('21) 1921 MODELS:

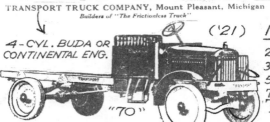

4-CYL. BUDA OR CONTINENTAL ENG.

"70"

20	130"WB	1 TON	
30	140	1½	
50	150	2½	
70	170	3½	

Transport

"Built to Do A Truck's Work"

TRIANGLE (1917~1924)

('19-'20)

1½ and 2-Ton Models

New **TRIVAN**
BY ROUSTABOUT
2 CYL., 32 HP

('63) (3-WHEEL)
1962~1964 FRACKVILLE, PA

United Heavy Duty Express
For full ton-and-half load chassis $1445

United Heavy Haul "35"
For all service up to 3500 lb. chassis $1595

United Heavy Haul "50"
Capacity, 5000 lb. chassis $1795

UNITED MOTORS PRODUCTS CO., Grand Rapids, Mich.

UNITED

$895
Chassis

'28

(1915~1930) (ABSORBED 1927 BY *ACME*)

U.S.A. (A.K.A *LIBERTY*) TRUCKS BLT. FOR THE MILITARY
BY: *SELDEN*; *GRAMM-BERNSTEIN*; *REPUBLIC*; *GARFORD*;
PIERCE-ARROW; *BETHLEHEM*; *DIAMOND T*; *BROCKWAY*;
STERLING; and OTHERS.

U.S.A. (1917~1918)
U.S. (1909~1930)
BY UNITED STATES MOTOR TRUCK CO., CINCINNATI, OH.

MISC. = T~U

MISC. V - Z

('26)

DELIVERY VAN

MFD. BY WARD MOTOR VEHICLE CO.,
MT. VERNON, N.Y. (1915~1934)
(AT BRONX, N.Y., 1910~1914)

Ward Electric
(1910~1934)

(NO "V" TRUCKS)*

('29) MODEL K CHASSIS

(1927-1930)
Whippet

(WHIPPET REPLACES OVERLAND, LATER 1926)

(1911-1931)
WITT -WILL

WITT-WILL CO., INC. WASHINGTON, D.C.

FLEISCHMANN'S

YEAST   SERVICE

EAT YEAST FOR HEALTH

BOTH BY WILLYS-OVERLAND, TOLEDO, OHIO

WILLYS-KNIGHT
('28)   (197)

WATKINS & SMITH COMPANY

1-TON CHASSIS—130" WHEELBASE

$1095

CONTINENTAL ENGINE USED

(c. '21)

*=VELIE TRUCKS 1911~1929, BUT PICTURE PRESENTLY UNAVAILABLE.

YELLOW-KNIGHT
1-TON MODEL **T-2** CHASSIS

4 CYL. 124" WB

('26)

ZELIGSON
6-WHEELER DIESEL TULSA, OKLA.

HVY. TANKER

('79 ON)

MISC. = V~Z